Jungle of Stone

Jungle of Stone

THE TRUE STORY OF TWO MEN,

THEIR EXTRAORDINARY JOURNEY,

AND THE DISCOVERY OF

THE LOST CIVILIZATION OF THE MAYA

WILLIAM CARLSEN

wm

WILLIAM MORROW
An Imprint of HARPERCOLLINS*Publishers*

JUNGLE OF STONE. Copyright © 2016 by William Carlsen. All rights reserved. Printed in the United States of America. No part of this book may be used or reproduced in any manner whatsoever without written permission except in the case of brief quotations embodied in critical articles and reviews. For information address HarperCollins Publishers, 195 Broadway, New York, NY 10007.

HarperCollins books may be purchased for educational, business, or sales promotional use. For information please e-mail the Special Markets Department at SPsales@harpercollins.com.

FIRST EDITION

Designed by Bonni Leon-Berman
Front endpaper: *Monjas, Chichén Itzá*, by Frederick Catherwood. Scan courtesy of the New York Public Library, Digital Collections.
Back endpaper: *Interior of Gateway at Labna*, by Frederick Catherwood. Scan courtesy of the New York Public Library, Digital Collections.
Frontispiece art: Maria Egupova/Shutterstock, Inc.
Map on p. xvi by Nick Springer, copyright © 2015 Springer Cartographics LLC

Library of Congress Cataloging-in-Publication Data has been applied for.

ISBN 978-0-06-240739-9

16 17 18 19 20 OV/RRD 10 9 8 7 6 5 4 3 2 1

For Kathleen O'Shea

Contents

◀◀   The Maya   363   ▶▶

Introduction

As I crossed Guatemala's largest lake and approached the village of Izabal, it was almost impossible to imagine that this loose collection of cinder-block houses and scattered huts was once the chief port of entry to nineteenth-century Central America. The walled army garrison that stood watch on the brow of the hill was now a tumble of stones, the main plaza an exhausted soccer field, and the tombs and markers of the port's cemetery were overgrown and buried.

I had come to the village to see for myself the place where two men came ashore in 1839 and altered the world's understanding of human history. In some ways, John Lloyd Stephens and Frederick Catherwood were a mismatch, an unlikely pair for such a revolutionary journey. One was a red-bearded, gregarious New York lawyer; the other a tight-lipped, clean-shaven English architect and businessman. But their earlier, separate travels through the ancient ruins of Greece, Palestine, and Egypt had prepared them for the unusual archaeological foray they were about to undertake. And their brilliant, perfectly matched skills—Stephens with words and Catherwood with illustrations—made them ideal candidates to record and make sense of their impending discoveries.

I had picked the same week in the year they had landed 170 years earlier. It was near the end of the rainy season, and I wilted under the same kind of oppressive, stifling heat they had described. If time had long passed the town of Izabal by—Guatemala's major Caribbean port was now a hundred miles to the northeast—the surrounding landscape had not changed. The mountain ridge backing the town remained a barrier to the interior, its rain-soaked slopes still coated with dense jungle. As they had for generations, the local people, many occupying palm-thatched huts, still lived close to the earth, nurtured by subsistence tropical agriculture and fish from the lake.

Stephens and Catherwood would lead me on a 2,500-mile chase through the mountains and jungles of Guatemala, Honduras, and Mexico. Where they had traveled on the backs of mules, I would follow in my own primitive beast, a mottled blue 1985 Toyota Corolla sans radio and air-conditioning. Where they complained of problems with muleteers and fretted over the health of their animals, I, driving alone down rutted, bone-cracking gravel and mud jungle roads, envisioned the team of workers on a Japanese assembly line tightening the bolts on my Toyota twenty years earlier and prayed they had done a good job.

For all the rough similarities between our journeys through Central America, I had arrived at Izabal in a world already changed by Stephens and Catherwood's discoveries. The two men fought their way through the thickest of jungles—often only to discover incomprehensible piles of carved stones and mysterious, seemingly inchoate structures. I, on the other hand, would arrive at fully excavated and restored archaeological sites filled with magnificent pyramids, temples, and palaces, sites whose art and hieroglyphics reveal a civilization of extraordinary sophistication and complexity. And while I knew what drove me on my journey—an overpowering desire to learn who these two men were and how they survived against seemingly impossible odds—I did not yet understand the insatiable yearning that drove them to undertake such a crazed and dangerous mission.

Nor did I comprehend the world they had brought with them, carried in their heads. When they arrived, Charles Darwin was still twenty years from publishing *On the Origin of Species*. In the West, the Bible was still the basic template of history, and most Christians believed the world was less than six thousand years old. The natives found populating the "New World" when Columbus and his European successors showed up were considered unrefined savages: sparse and scattered Indian tribes who had never more than scratched out a bare subsistence from the land; idol worshippers who performed bloody human sacrifice atop stone mounds.

After 1839, this worldview, the notion that the Americas had always been a land occupied by primitive, inferior people, would change forever. And so would the assumption that writing, mathematics, astronomy, art, monumental architecture—civilization itself—was only possible through so-called "diffusion" from within one part the "Old World" to another, and from the civilized "Old World" to the uncivilized "New." Stephens and Catherwood's historic journey radically altered our understanding of human evolution. In their wake, it became possible to comprehend civilization as an inherent trait of human cultural progress, perhaps coded into our genes; a characteristic that allows advanced societies to grow out of primitive ones, organically, separately, and without contact, as occurred in Central America and the Western Hemisphere, which were isolated from the rest of the world for more than fifteen thousand years. And, just as with the Old World's ancient civilizations, they can collapse, too, leaving behind only remnants of their previous splendor.

Stephens and Catherwood plunged headlong into a region racked by civil war. They endured relentless bouts of tropical fever, close calls, and physical hardships, and emerged to publish two bestsellers: the first works of American archaeology, so enchantingly written and illustrated that they have become classics and remain in print today. In 1839, they found the remains of what would come to be known as the Maya civilization. More than discovering them, they made sense of them, reaching conclusions that defied the conventional thinking of their time and initiated a century and a half of excavations and investigations, which continue today. After publication of their books, the mysterious stone ruins in Central America, the vast, sophisticated road network of the Inca in South America, and the monuments and temples of the Aztecs could no longer be viewed as vestiges of the Lost Tribes of Israel, the ancient seafaring Phoenicians, or the survivors of lost Atlantis. They were understood to be solely indigenous in origin, the products of the imagination, intelligence, and creativity of Native Americans.

Jungle of Stone tells of the harrowing journey that led to these discoveries and the two extraordinary men who made it. The book weaves their little-known biographies through the narrative of their expeditions and their significant achievements afterward. Stephens would best the British Empire twice, and his successes personified the spirit of America on the rise in the nineteenth century.

The book is the first text to combine the history of prior explorations, the circumstances and context of their discoveries, and their sudden and unexpected race with the British to be the first to show the world the art and architectural wonders of the Maya. Catherwood's illustrations, drawn "on the spot," are the first accurate, strikingly detailed representations of this lost world from a time before photography.

Even in a great age of exploration that would later reveal the source of the Nile in Central Africa and Machu Picchu in Peru, send expeditions to the north and south poles, Stephens and Catherwood stand apart. Known among archaeologists today as the originators of Maya studies, they accomplished much more. Like Darwin to come, they broke through dogmatic constructions of the past and helped lay the foundation for a new science of archaeology. They captured the romance, mystery, and exhilaration of discovery with a vividness and intensity that inspired the explorers of the future. And they opened to the world a realm of artistic and cultural riches of an ancient American Indian civilization whose remains stagger the imagination, draw millions of visitors every year—and still have much to teach us.

When Christopher Columbus and his European successors began arriving in the so-called New World in the late fifteenth century, several advanced societies populated the Western Hemisphere. Hernán Cortés and his Spanish conquistadors marveled especially at the sophistication of the Aztec's capital Tenochtitlan, now buried under present-day Mexico City. But they were less interested in archeological discovery than gold, and more concerned with subjugating the native populations, imposing "civilized" Christianity on their pagan practices, pulling down their temples to construct new cities, and putting the Indians to work for the Spanish overlords. What sophistication and social refinements they had found in Mexico and Peru, they also kept closely to themselves as they jealously closed off Spanish America from the rest of the world for nearly three centuries.

At the time of the Spanish Conquest, the Aztecs dominated central Mexico and the Inca administered a sprawling empire from their home based in the Peruvian Andes. The highly evolved civilization of the Maya, however, had ceased to exist. It was already ancient history. Their civilization was as distant historically from the Aztecs and the Inca as those two empires are from us today. The remains of the Maya's once-dazzling, densely populated cities lay overgrown in the jungle. The lords of the cities, the scribes and astronomers, architects and artists, tradesmen, soldiers, and merchants had mysteriously disappeared. Yet if the Aztecs—geographically separated from the Maya heartland by only hundreds of miles—even knew of the Maya ruins, they had little or no historical understanding of who these ancient Maya were. They were unable to read the thousand-year written history that the Maya left behind, carved in hieroglyphs on their fallen monuments.

At the zenith of their achievements, during a six-hundred-year period lasting through the tenth century A.D., the Maya were in a class of their own in the Americas. Even as archaeologists continue finding traces of long-ago Native American cultures, some predating the Maya, none has compared to the political complexity and artistry, the writing, mathematical and astronomical skills, the architectural acumen, and sheer longevity of the Classic-era Maya. During their civilization's long run, the Maya built more than forty important city-states, and it is estimated that as many as ten million Maya inhabited the Yucatán Peninsula and lowland tropical forests of what is now Guatemala, Mexico, Honduras, and El Salvador. By comparison, today in a region of Guatemala known as El Petén, the Maya's ancient heartland, the population barely exceeds half a million inhabitants.

The Maya civilization was by any measure an exceptionally long and sustainable one. Arriving in the Pacific coast and highlands of Guatemala and spreading north to lowland tropical marshes as early as 1,500 B.C., the Maya developed more and more complex agricultural communities over the next millennium with harvests of manioc, beans, squash, and, most important of all, corn. By the time of the flowering of classical Greece (400 B.C.), the Maya were already constructing pyramids and temples around central plazas. Within a few

Timeline of Early Civilizations

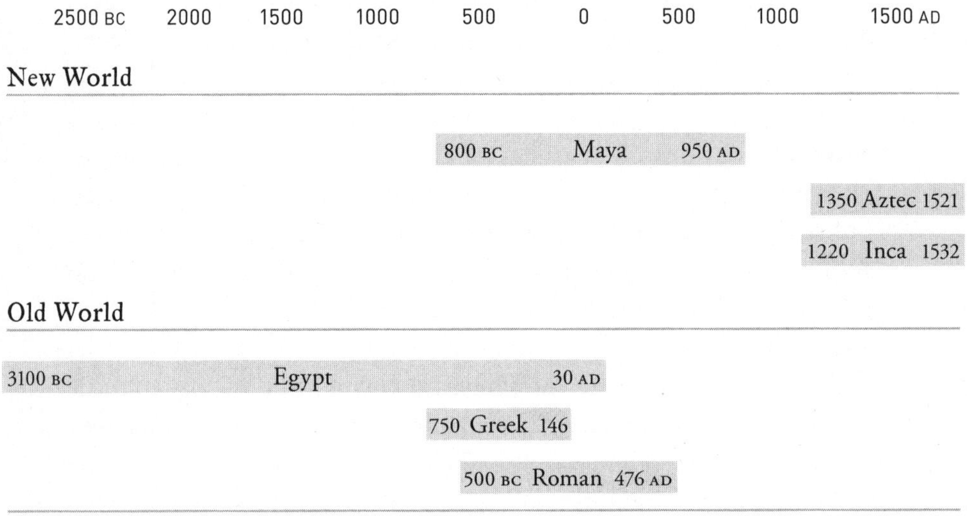

2500 BC	2000	1500	1000	500	0	500	1000	1500 AD

New World

800 BC　　Maya　　950 AD

1350 Aztec 1521

1220　Inca　1532

Old World

3100 BC　　　　Egypt　　　　30 AD

750 Greek 146

500 BC Roman 476 AD

hundred years the structures took on a scale that required millions of man-hours of labor, and technical and organizational expertise. Without the benefit of metal tools or the wheel, they quarried thousand-pound stone blocks and constructed pyramids that rose above the jungle canopy.

Over the next millennium dozens of city-states evolved, each governed by powerful lords, some with populations larger than any city in Europe at the time, and connected by long roadlike causeways of crushed limestone. Though ruled by separate royal dynasties often warring among themselves, the Maya nonetheless developed a cohesive, unified cosmology, an array of common gods, a creation story, and a shared artistic and architectural vision. They created stucco and stone monuments and bas-reliefs, sculpting figures and hieroglyphs with refined artistic skill. They coated their temples in brilliant, showy colors, decorated their palaces with stone mosaics, and painted vivid storytelling murals. They studied the night sky from astronomical observatories, created one of the world's most complicated set of inter-locking calendars, worked out great cycles of time mathematically—in the process inventing the concept of "zero"—and recorded their history with the only true writing system in the Americas, which allowed them to transcribe anything they could say.

Then it all came to an end. The great Maya civilization—one of the most complex and advanced in the ancient world—dissolved and the tropical forests reclaimed their accomplishments, leaving a hidden jungle of stones that one day two explorers would bring to the world's attention, and begin the process of unraveling the Maya's amazing, improbable story.

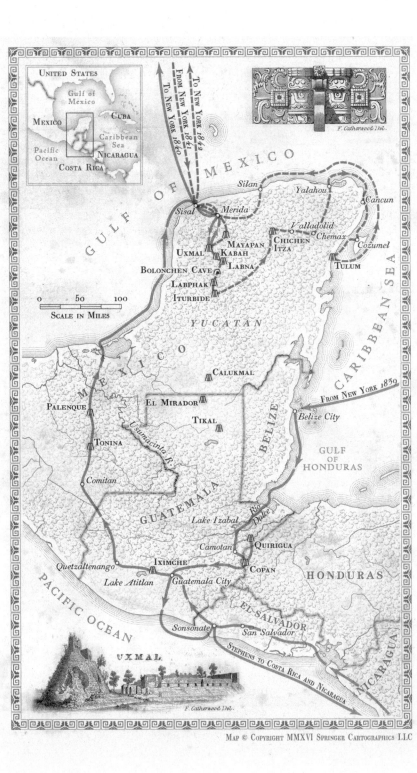

UNITED STATES

Gulf of Mexico

MEXICO

CUBA

Caribbean Sea

Pacific Ocean

NICARAGUA

COSTA RICA

F. Catherwood Del.

GULF OF MEXICO

To New York 1842
From New York 1841
To New York 1840

Silan

Yalahou

Cancun

Sisal

Merida

Valladolid

Chemax

UXMAL

MAYAPAN

KABAH

CHICHEN ITZA

Cozumel

BOLONCHEN CAVE

LABNA

TULUM

LABPHAK

ITURBIDE

0   50   100
SCALE IN MILES

YUCATAN

MEXICO

CALUKMAL

CARIBBEAN SEA

PALENQUE

EL MIRADOR

TIKAL

BELIZE

FROM NEW YORK 1839

Belize City

TONINA

Usumacinta R.

GULF OF HONDURAS

Comitan

GUATEMALA

Lake Izabal

Rio Dulce

Camotan

QUIRIGUA

Quetzaltenango

IXIMCHE

COPAN

HONDURAS

Lake Atitlan

Guatemala City

PACIFIC OCEAN

EL SALVADOR

Sonsonate

San Salvador

STEPHENS TO COSTA RICA AND NICARAGUA

NICARAGUA

UXMAL

F. Catherwood Del.

MAP © COPYRIGHT MMXVI SPRINGER CARTOGRAPHICS LLC

Jungle of Stone

Prologue

John Lloyd Stephens was exhausted. It was April 1852 and he was in his second year as president of one of the most brazen undertakings of the age: construction of a railroad across the narrow, vicious, almost impenetrable Isthmus of Panama. It had been the dream of explorers and traders for centuries to find or build a link connecting the world's two great oceans. Canal propositions had come and gone. They cost too much; the technology was not yet there. But now the timing seemed right. By midcentury, pressure to slice through the Western Hemisphere somewhere in Central America, if not by canal then by rail, had reached a breaking point. There was a stampede for gold in the California Sierras. It was the era of steamships, railroads, and the telegraph, an age compressing time and space. Technologically almost anything seemed possible.

Early in April, weakened by overwork, his liver ravaged by chronic bouts of malaria, Stephens could no longer continue. His iron road was already years behind schedule. Unlike his well-heeled business partners living comfortably in New York, Stephens had spent most of the previous three years in Panama. Though not physically imposing, he possessed a steely constitution that had fought off every corporeal abuse imaginable during travels across the most disease-ridden regions of the planet. And he was intimately familiar with the treachery of Central America's mountains and jungles. But the rain forest of Panama was different. It was dark and sadistic, more opaque and un-forgiving than anything he had known.

From the beginning almost everything had gone wrong. Instead of starting the railroad from the center of the isthmus, as first planned, where the ground was higher, drier, and more favorable, they were forced to start from an island in the mangrove swamps of the Caribbean coast. From there they had to hack their way inch by inch through the jungle toward the Pacific. The men waded up to their chests through waters infested with crocodiles and poisonous snakes. Where the swamps ended, the quicksand and mud began. The swarms of disease-laden mosquitoes were so thick they darkened the sky. And the volume of rain that fell, broken only by intervals of unbearable sun, seemed beyond human comprehension.[1]

Sometimes it seemed like only sickness and death. Malaria and other tropical diseases, lumped together under the dreaded catchall known as Chagres fever, took a devastating toll. At times it was impossible to keep the workforce up. There had been more than one mutiny. Entire work crews perished or the men became so sick they could no longer carry on, their health damaged for the remainder of their lives. Some went mad. Others ran off to the gold fields in California or paid for passage home at their own expense just to get out. Later, in mid-1852, cholera would again sweep the isthmus, and within weeks leave hundreds of new dead in its wake.

The iron tracks stretched twenty miles through filled-in swamps and on good days it seemed like the whole crazy idea might work. But only a few months before, the money began to run out. More and more Stephens felt he was carrying the whole enterprise on his back. In letters to friends, he had predicted that by 1852 the railroad would have breached the continental divide and would be closing in on Panama City and the Pacific Ocean. The entire distance, after all, was less than fifty miles. Then, gradually, he stopped making any more predictions. Three years of hardship and labor, sickness and death, and they had not yet crossed halfway. The Chagres River, the most formidable obstacle, a river that in the rainy season raged like the wrath of God, remained to be crossed, and the summit dividing the Atlantic and Pacific watersheds still loomed miles away.

Stephens rarely complained, but he started hinting darkly that he hoped to live long enough to see the hemisphere's first transcontinental train run sea to sea. At the age of forty-six, his body was breaking down. He had crossed and recrossed the isthmus so many times, he had lost count. The rainy season would soon be upon them and the work would slow to a crawl. It was time to go home.

There is no record of the exact state of his health when he boarded the steamer for New York, but not long before he left, he wrote his father a confession: "I am growing old and wearing out with hard knocks and hard service, but it is not worthwhile to put upon you the labors and anxieties and responsibilities which I must continue to bear."[2] He would see his father soon, he said.

The railroad—a railroad across Panama—would happen, of that he was certain. He had faced incredible hardships and obstacles before and had triumphed. He was a visionary and Central America had never defeated him. He had seen things in its jungles few men had ever seen, made astonishing discoveries, and brought back stories almost impossible to believe, accounts that had changed the world's view of human history—and made him rich and famous.

And—for a time—he had basked in the acclaim.

He believed, now, in a new dream—a very American dream—and that when the rainy season ended, nothing could stop him from returning to Panama to finish the work he had started.

PART ONE

Expedition

View of Manhattan in 1851.

◄ 1 ►

South, 1839

Thirteen years earlier, before dawn, Stephens stepped aboard a British brig to embark on the boldest, most extraordinary journey of his life. In the early morning as the tide began to ebb along the docks on New York's Hudson River, the *Mary Ann*, her sails slack in the dead air, slipped from her moorings. "The streets and wharves were still," wrote Stephens, "the Battery was desolate, and, at the moment of leaving it on a voyage of uncertain duration, seemed more beautiful than I had ever known it before."[1] It was the third day of October 1839.

The ship rode the outgoing tide around Castle Garden, a onetime fortress in the waters just off the Battery, and then swung slowly around Governors Island in the company of a large whaler bound for the Pacific. With Stephens aboard the *Mary Ann* was a single fellow passenger, an English artist and architect named Frederick Catherwood. Stephens was about to turn thirty-four and Catherwood, taller and leaner than his companion, was six years older. They made an odd pair, opposites in many ways, but were friends, and now by written agreement, working colleagues. Stephens, a lawyer, had drafted their unusual contract himself.

Several friends accompanied them as far as the Narrows, at the bottom of Brooklyn, where they said their farewells and disembarked, followed an hour later by the harbor pilot. Now alone with only the *Mary Ann*'s captain and small crew, Stephens and Catherwood waited for the wind. After a time the sails began to fill and slowly pointed the two-masted transport east toward the Atlantic. Finally they rounded Sandy Hook and the two men watched the New Jersey highlands drop with the sun below the western horizon. The next morning they were well at sea.

They were headed south for the Gulf of Honduras. At the time, the Honduran gulf was unknown to most North Americans. U.S. trade routes to the south focused chiefly on the islands of the Caribbean: the West Indies, Cuba, and Jamaica, all well east of the gulf. The sea routes continued south through the Caribbean, skirted the eastern hump of South America, then dropped down around the southern tip of the continent at Cape Horn and into the Pacific.

The Gulf of Honduras, a blunt triangle of water that cut into the side of Central America just south of Mexico, lay removed from U.S. sea-lanes for good reason. More than three hundred years earlier, in 1502, not long after Columbus crossed its water on his final voyage to the New World, a great curtain was drawn from Mexico south around the landmass of Central and South America. The conquistadors who followed Columbus and their rulers in Spain had closed off Spanish America from the rest of the world.[2] It was not until the political up-heavals in Europe at the turn of the nineteenth century that the situation began to change. The French Revolution and rise of Napoleon Bonaparte set in motion the dissolution of the Spanish Empire. One by one, Spain's American colonies broke free from Spain and the curtain began to lift. And the mysterious lands to the south, shut off for so many years to North Americans, finally began to open.

While U.S. traders were slow to exploit the opening, their rivals, the British, always pushing the boundaries of their own empire, had already secured a foothold along one side of the Honduran gulf. They had carved a niche into the edge of the Yucatán Peninsula, where they had established a colony called Belize. The English settlement lay shel-tered behind a long string of coral reefs and small islands that for hundreds of years had protected British buccaneers who preyed on Spanish galleons sailing back and forth between Central America and Spain.

Just to the south of Belize, the triangular gulf narrows to a point at the base of the Yucatán Peninsula where a river named Río Dulce (Sweet River) had funneled most of Spain's trade into and out of Cen-tral America. Stephens and Catherwood were headed to that point, then inland to their ultimate destination: Guatemala City, the former capital of Spain's Central American colonies. Stephens's mission had been set out for him by U.S. secretary of state John Forsyth. As chargé d'affaires and confidential agent appointed by President Martin Van Buren, he was directed to meet the leaders of the recently formed United Provinces of Central America and conclude a trade agreement.[3] There was, however, one problem. The two men were landing in a region lacerated by civil war, and the odds that Stephens would be able to complete his diplomatic assignment were uncertain at best.

But he and Catherwood were on another mission as well, one they had carefully planned months before Stephens unexpectedly and fortuitously landed his presidential appointment. They had read vague reports of intricately sculpted stones buried within the Central American jungle. And the accounts had aroused in them suspicions and hopes that these remains might be more than random scattered stones—something perhaps more sophisticated, signs possibly of a hidden unknown world. So, after Stephens settled his official duties—successfully or not—the two men were determined to cut a path into the jungle and see for themselves what they could find.

It is unclear exactly when or where Stephens and Catherwood first met.

Neither man left an account of the meeting, nor do we have a description of the encounter by any of their contemporaries. It has been long assumed that the meeting took place in London in the summer of 1836, three years before they boarded the *Mary Ann*.[4] Catherwood had been working in London, and Stephens passed through the city on his way home to New York after traveling for two years through Europe, Egypt, and the Near East. While visiting Jerusalem earlier that year, he came across a tourist map of the holy city that had been drawn up and published by Catherwood—his first encounter with the artist, if by name only. In London that summer, adventurers like Stephens and Catherwood made up a small society, and it's logical to conclude they crossed paths. But recently discovered ship manifests show Catherwood had left London to move with his family in New York before Stephens arrived in the English capital.[5] Most likely, they met in New York City later that year or the next. Again, their interests would have made such a meeting almost inevitable given New York's small but growing circle of artists and intellectuals. (New York's population was less than a quarter that of London.) And indeed the two men had had remarkably similar adventures. Each had covered the same rough ground of the Middle East, explored many of the same ancient historical sites—Catherwood preceding Stephens by nearly a decade—and they had both survived the region's often hostile political and natural environment. It was as if both men, following parallel tracks for years, were destined to be drawn together.

As a youth Catherwood apprenticed with an architect-surveyor in London, then continued his studies in Rome and Greece before landing in Cairo in 1824. He arrived in the same year that Jean-François Champollion announced to the world that he had cracked the ancient Egyptian hieroglyphic code with the help of the Rosetta Stone. Europe was in the grip of an Egyptian "craze," and over the next decade Catherwood took part in two expeditions on the Nile surveying and illustrating pyramids and temples. He became conversant in Arabic, wore a turban, and at times risked his life dressing as a native to gain entrance to forbidden Muslim holy sites in order to record them.[6]

Stephens, too, had put on the costume of a Cairo merchant, a disguise that helped him cross the Sinai desert unmolested to one of the most dangerous historical sites in the region, the ancient stone city of Petra, located in a rock canyon in what is now southern Jordan. Petra was sealed off from the outside world and guarded by wild Bedouin tribesmen—a destination as far removed from Stephens's comfortable life as a New York lawyer as he could find.

Whatever the circumstances of their first meeting, something had taken hold of both men in the desert. Neither was exactly reckless. In fact in many ways they were conventional men. Catherwood was a professional architect, married, a father of three, conscientious about supporting his family. Stephens practiced law, owned property, and had dabbled in politics for nearly a decade before leaving for Europe and the Middle East. Yet something viral—an almost pathological compulsion to push to the edge, to test the limits—had infected both men in the desert, and neither man seemed able to shake it. The adrenaline had never quite worn off. The comforts of New York seemed unwarranted; something was missing from their lives. Then after three years in the city, they read the tantalizing references to mysterious carved monuments and ruins of stone buildings found in the jungles of Central America—along with windy speculations about what the discoveries meant. Could these possibly be remains of an old civilization lost and buried under the jungle—unlike the Egyptian ruins they had witnessed lying open on the desert sands? It seemed too much to hope for, but the thought was intoxicating. The old cravings flooded back, the hunger for adventure, the quest, the whiff of danger—insatiable curiosity.

Still, there were mundane matters to be settled first.

In 1836, when Catherwood moved his family to New York, he quickly found work as an architect. But within a year he embarked on construction of a cavernous "panorama" exhibition hall to show his huge canvases of the Middle East. The enterprise took off instantly and drew in healthy profits.

Stephens, meanwhile, was coming off two phenomenal publishing coups. He had never drafted anything more exciting than law briefs and contracts, but on his return from Europe he decided to try his hand at writing up his European and Middle Eastern adventures. He turned out to be a gifted storyteller. His first book, *Incidents of Travel in Egypt, Arabia Petraea, and the Holy Land,* was a runaway bestseller.[7] According to John R. Bartlett, an Astor Place bookseller, "No book awakened a deeper interest in New York." The book was so successful Stephens immediately followed with a second work, an account of his travels through Greece, Turkey, Russia, and Poland.

In the span of two years he managed to turn out two incredibly popular and critically acclaimed works totaling nearly a thousand pages, containing some of most refreshing prose of his time. He had left the law far behind and was primed for another adventure—and another book. He also understood that if he could work Catherwood's artistry into it, the next book might be even more successful. The two men began plotting their escape to Central America, then, unexpectedly, the U.S. attaché to the region died, followed by the sudden death of his replacement, and fate appeared to seal the matter. Drawing on old Democratic Party connections, Stephens won the diplomatic assignment from President Van Buren.

A long journey south was not so easy for Catherwood, who had a family and a new business to look after. So Stephens, flush with book royalties, made him an offer. Under a "memorandum of agreement" signed by both men on September 9, 1839, Catherwood was to accompany Stephens to Central America and remain with him until Stephens finished his official duties for the U.S. government, at which time the two of them would be free to travel to "ruined cities, places, scenes and monuments."[8] Catherwood would make drawings for the "sole use and benefit" of Stephens. In exchange, Stephens agreed to pay all of Catherwood's expenses during their journey and $1,500—a significant sum at the time—deducting $25 a week that would be paid to Mrs. Catherwood during his absence.[9] Catherwood put the operation of his panorama hall into the hands of a business partner.

It is difficult to know how much the agreement, with its spelled-out contractual language, reflected a lack of familiarity and trust between the two men or something else, something more formal, more typically nineteenth century. Certainly, Catherwood had his family to look out for, and Stephens was still a lawyer, with a lawyer's mind and a lawyer's appreciation for the value of contracts. Yet the two men would reveal so little about their personal relationship over the coming years that it remains an enduring mystery despite their famously public travels together. In the more than 1,800 pages of storytelling and illustrations that were to pour forth from their future adventures, Stephens never once described Catherwood. In fact no image of Catherwood, no drawing or daguerreotype of him, has ever been found.[10] And he remained "Mr. Catherwood" or "Mr. C" throughout Stephens's writings, even if the "Mr." was sometimes dropped in Stephens's letters. But this was also the advent of the Victorian era, when two men's restraint and decorum toward one another, at least publicly, would have been expected. In this regard, the outward formality between the two was not much different than that of other famous traveling partners of the time: Meriwether Lewis and William Clark, or Alexis de Tocqueville and Gustave de Beaumont, or Alexander von Humboldt and Aimé Bonpland.

In addition, the Mr. Catherwood indirectly revealed in Stephens's writing is taciturn by nature, droll in his sense of humor, a man of deep reserve, a perfectionist. In part, his training as an architect and especially as an artist—the observer who trafficked in images—may have made him stand back and let the voluble, gregarious Stephens hold the stage. If they were opposites in personality, there was no question about their loyalty and respect for one another, which would surface again and again over the next thirteen years of their partnership and close friendship. They loved history, shared a compulsive interest in antiquities, and possessed a physical courage and doggedness of such staggering scope that it would see them through the greatest hardships that lay ahead.

It was an especially precarious time to sail south. The hurricane season was not yet over. Ship captains and their passengers had none of today's weather forecasting and sailed into Caribbean waters in the late summer and early autumn on courage and blind faith, aware of the great dangers they faced. But within eight days the *Mary Ann* was moving easily between Cuba and Hispaniola. Then they were hit by a tropical storm. The little brig headed straight west into the Gulf of Honduras through a torturous eighteen days of rain, wind, and pounding seas before drawing into the protected harbor at Belize just as the last of the storm abated.

The scruffy frontier town rose from aquamarine waters as a flat mile-long white line against the dark green backdrop of coconut palms and jungle. The night before, a teenager, the son of one of the harbor pilots, came aboard to steer them safely through the jagged coral reefs. The *Mary Ann* came to anchor next to several rafts loaded with mahogany logs, the colony's chief export. A dozen ships, brigs and schooners, lay at anchor, along with one old steamboat. The coastal settlement, clinging to the edge of the great Yucatán Peninsula, was more like an island than a country. It had evolved from its pirate days into the major trading post for disbursal of European goods headed for the Honduran, Guatemalan, and Moskito coasts and then inland to the Central American states. But its warehouses, residences, and six thousand inhabitants were isolated from the interior by dense, virtually impassable jungle. A river bisected the town. Referred to as simply "Old River," it was the only way inland, its source so deep within the rain forests it remained a mystery.

Many of the streets were ankle-deep in mud from the downpours that had just swept in from the sea. Some of the houses were elevated on pilings and surrounded by open verandas to catch any wisp of air that might alleviate the damp, crushing afternoon heat. Wood planks served as sidewalks, crowded round with tropical flowers and palms. A wooden bridge over the river connected the two ends of town. At the southern end was a tidy complex of white clapboard public buildings—the residence of Her Majesty's Superintendent, the courthouse, offices, a hospital, jail, and free school. In the middle sat a stone church complete with tall spire as if transplanted straight from the English countryside.

As Stephens was to record, he was stunned at his reception on landing, unfamiliar with the exalted formalities and perquisites that came with his new diplomatic office. He was immediately invited to Government House to meet with the settlement's superintendent, Colonel Alexander MacDonald. Then, while arranging for passage down the coast to Guatemala on the old steamboat in the harbor, he found the agent willing to delay the steamer's departure for several extra days to allow Stephens more time in Belize. "Used to submitting to the despotic regulations of steamboat agents at home," Stephens wrote, "this seemed a higher honor than the invitation of his Excellency; but, not wishing to push my fortune too far, I asked for a delay of one day only."

In another contrast with home, slavery had been banned in all of Britain's colonies five years before, but it quickly became clear to Stephens that slavery had never really taken hold in Belize, where two-thirds of the population was black and most whites were descendants of shipwrecked or retired English pirates. He marveled at the mixture of the races. "Before I had been an hour in Belize," he wrote, "I learned that the great work of practical amalgamation, the subject of so much controversy at home, had been going on quietly for generations." He described his first meal, breakfast at the table of a merchant and his wife with two British army officers and two men Stephens identified

as well-dressed, well-educated mulattos. "They talked of their mahogany works, of England, hunting, horses, ladies, and wine."

Stephens was a New Yorker, a northerner, but his grandfather on
his mother's side, Judge John Lloyd, had been a slaveholder in New
Jersey until his death in the 1820s.[11] Thus Stephens, growing up in a
close-knit family, was familiar with the institution of slavery firsthand. In his writings, he never commented on his childhood experience, but it is clear where his sympathies lay from his reaction to what
he witnessed in Belize. He barely disguises his delight at shocking
some of his American readers with descriptions of the equality among
the races. During a visit to the colony's law court, for example, he was
invited to take one of the judges' vacant seats. Of the five sitting
judges, one was a mulatto, as were two of the jurors. The judge sitting
next to him said he was aware of the racial feelings in the United
States, but in Belize, he said, "there was, in political life, no distinction whatever, except on the ground of qualification and character,
and hardly any in social life, even in contracting marriage."

Stephens was also clearly amused by another Belize custom he
knew would provoke his later readers, or at least a select group with
whom he was intimately familiar. There was not a single lawyer in the
place, there never had been, and the court got along fine without
them, he wrote. None of the judges had legal backgrounds, either,
even though they heard civil disputes involving large commercial
transactions. One judge was a mahogany cutter, two were merchants,
and the mulatto judge was a doctor.

Stephens and Catherwood were given a full tour of the settlement
by the fifth judge, Patrick Walker, secretary of the colony. He also arranged for a boat excursion up Old River and into the jungle. Stephens felt immediately drawn into the mystery of the dense forest,
which closed over the river and blotted out the sun. "We were in as
perfect a solitude as if removed thousands of miles from human habitation," he wrote. But the river was in full flood and the rowers were
struggling against the current, so the boating party turned back.

When they finally arrived at Government House, the settlement's
superintendent, Colonel MacDonald, made a deep impression on Stephens. He was, according to Stephens, "one of a race fast passing

away." He had entered the British army as a young officer at eighteen, served for years in the Spanish campaign, and later commanded a regiment at Waterloo, receiving battlefield honors from the king of England and the czar of Russia. Conversing with the six-foot-tall MacDonald, a man of rigid military bearing, "was like reading a page of history," Stephens wrote.

The colonel greeted Stephens and Catherwood warmly and had assembled a dinner gathering of local officeholders and military men. While Stephens was clearly taken in by MacDonald's graciousness, he was under orders not to discuss his official diplomatic assignments, in particular the negotiations over a trade pact with the new Central American republic. But he and Catherwood seemed to mesmerize the colonel with talk about their plans to search for traces of an old civilization buried in the forests of Honduras, Guatemala, and Mexico. Catherwood, they explained, would use his surveying and artistic skills to record what, if anything, they found.

The afternoon of their departure, MacDonald arranged another dinner. There were toasts to Queen Victoria and President Van Buren. Then another round, and another. When it was all over, the colonel walked Stephens arm in arm down the sweeping lawn of Government House to the water's edge, where a launch waited to take them out to the steamboat belching black smoke in the harbor. MacDonald turned to Stephens and warned him a second time about the political turmoil and bloody disturbances then under way in Central America. If he should find himself in danger, he said, Stephens was to assemble the Americans and Europeans in Guatemala City, hang out the flag, and send word for him. Stephens well knew of the dangers ahead and found the offer reassuring. "I knew these were not just words of courtesy," he wrote, "and, in the state of the country to which I was going, felt the value of such a friend at hand."

The moment was a magnificent one and quite unlike their quiet, almost surreptitious departure from New York. As Stephens and Catherwood crossed the bay in the launch they were accompanied by the boom of a thirteen-cannon salute. Flags were run up at Government House, the fort, and courthouse. The whole scene was a classic

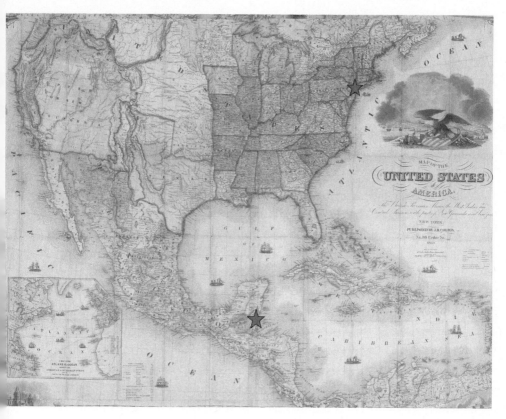

North and Central America: stars mark New York Harbor and Belize City.

display of British imperialism—the perfectly ordered outpost of civilization set against the wild, dark, barely suppressed jungle. It would be a final moment of comfort and security both men could recall in their days ahead.

"I had visited many cities," Stephens wrote, "but it was the first time that flags and cannon announced to the world that I was going away. I was a novice, but I endeavored to behave as if I had been brought up to it; and to tell the truth, my heart beat, and I felt proud; for these were honors paid to my country, and not to me."

Aboard the *Vera Paz*, the baggage was stowed and Stephens settled into his cabin. That evening they took tea on deck. When the captain came to them at ten o'clock asking for his orders, Stephens said he began to understand why men accepted the responsibilities of official appointments. "I have had my aspirations, but never expected to be able to dictate to the captain of a steamboat. Nevertheless, again as coolly as if I had been brought up to it, I designated the places I wished to visit, and retired."

Stephens's and Catherwood's free talk about their plans to hunt down old ruins, meanwhile, had not been lost on Colonel MacDonald. Back at Government House, he set immediately to work. He summoned Patrick Walker and an army lieutenant named John Herbert Caddy, a royal artillery officer stationed at the settlement. They were ordered to assemble an expedition and prepare to go up Old River, deep into the jungle of the Petén and across Yucatán Peninsula to a Mexican town called Santo Domingo de Palenque. There they were to conduct a thorough survey of the remains of old ruins whose existence had undoubtedly come up in the dinner conversation with Stephens and Catherwood. Lieutenant Caddy was a talented artist whose off-hours sketches of local scenes had earlier drawn MacDonald's attention. Employing his artistic gifts and his training as a military engineer, Caddy was to make a visual record and a survey map of whatever they found at Palenque. Walker, whose list of offices and duties now included one more, was to lead the expedition with Caddy and draft the official written report.

MacDonald made clear the mission was an urgent one despite the fact that Stephens and Catherwood were headed off in the opposite direction, south toward Guatemala and Honduras. There was to be no delay even though the rainy season was still upon them and the river was running high, swollen with treacherous logs and other debris. The strong current would work against them for more than a hundred miles but the two men accepted their orders without demurrer.

Within two weeks, provisioned with barrels of flour, rum and pork, medicines, and other essentials, Walker and Caddy stood ready with twenty-seven men and two long dugout canoes called "pitpans." In his haste to get the expedition off, however, MacDonald would make a serious mistake that he would later come to regret.

Upriver

Leaving Belize for Guatemala, the *Vera Paz* steamed south along the Yucatán coast and then cut diagonally across a scalloped bay formed by the long, crooked finger of the Manabique Peninsula. A low wall of dark verdant hills rose slowly before them. In the distance white puffs of surf burst up before the blue-green backdrop, the spray vaporizing and mingling with the mist rising from the jungle. The heavy air pressed in around them. Inside the surf line, patches of sand marked the edge of a region so thick with mountains, rain forest, and swamps that few white men had ever passed through it. One of them was Hernán Cortés, the great conquistador himself, who, after his conquest of Mexico in the early 1500s, and slightly crazed by his success, set out overland with a small army for Honduras, intent on disciplining a rebellious subordinate. He had no idea what lay before him. He and his men left the civilized highlands of central Mexico with a large entourage and anticipated quick passage southeast across the Yucatán Peninsula. Six months later, stunned, exhausted, many of his men emaciated or dead from hunger and disease, most of their horses gone, Cortés emerged from the malignant horror of the Petén wilderness, finally hacking his way through the deep jungle to the same coast where the *Vera Paz* was now headed.

This was an edge of a land where few humans, let alone white men, had planted a foothold against the raw force of nature. As Stephens and Catherwood approached the shore, a mass of tangled vegetation loomed. There seemed no way in. Then an opening finally appeared in what had seemed a solid wall of green, and they could make out the banks of a river. The *Vera Paz* crossed the bar and swung into the

TOP   Catherwood's illustration of Río Dulce.
BELOW   Photo of present-day Río Dulce. (Carlsen)

channel. High along the right bank a group of huts came into view, where Stephens briefly considered stopping. The settlement of Carib Indians and West Indian blacks barely clung to the skirt of the shoreline yet it held a key position as one of the only river entry ports to Central America. The ambitious cluster of houses bore the name of Livingston. Oddly enough, it had been named in honor of a former

New York mayor and U.S. secretary of state, Edward Livingston. Among Livingston's varied accomplishments, he had streamlined the civil, criminal, and penal codes of Louisiana, and these reforms were now being copied and imposed by the Central American government on its peasant population—over its violent protest.

Stephens instructed the captain to move in closer to the embankment. The inhabitants, listless in the afternoon heat, gazed down from their palm-thatched huts set among groves of plantain and coconut trees. But it was already four o'clock, too late to stop if they hoped to reach inland anchorage by sunset. So the steamer swung again into the center of the river.

Ahead, a rampart loomed above them with a vertical cut that drew the *Vera Paz* slowly into a twisting, watery gorge of overwhelming beauty. Sheer walls of foliage rose hundreds of feet above them on each side, tropical plants sprouting from every crevice of the limestone cliffs. From the canopy of trees high above, lianas drooped to the river surface, and a profusion of bromeliads and orchids covered the tree limbs and vines. The air was delicious with fragrance. Another turn through the serpentine passage and they were enclosed again by the jungle walls. In the shadowed darkness they could see no entry and no exit—the passage had closed behind them—and they feared the boat might drive in among the encircling vegetation.

Belize had been mere prologue. Here enveloping them was claustrophobic, delirious jungle they could reach out and touch, a narrow tropical fjord magnificent and enervating in the same moment. They had heard about this river, heard about its overpowering beauty. How was it possible this was the entrance through which much of the commerce of Central America flowed?

Sparkling clear water drawn down from the Guatemalan cloud forests flowed beneath them to the sea. There was a brief choking odor of sulfur from hot springs that boiled up along the river's edge. As they passed on, the late afternoon air became oppressive, saturated with wet, smothering heat, yet the deep shadows gave the illusion of coolness. The only birds they saw at first were pelicans. Monkeys scrambled along the vines, driven ahead by the "unnatural bluster" of the *Vera Paz*'s engine reverberating off the walls. Beneath the engine's racket and the thumping of the paddle wheels lay a timeless, prehistoric stillness. Herons and parrots rousted from their perches on the cliffs and trees flew on before them.

"Could this be the portal to a land of volcanoes and earthquakes, torn and distracted by civil war?" Stephens wrote. It was, he continued, "a fairy scene, combining exquisite beauty with colossal grandeur."

Nine miles up the river, it widened into a small lake dotted with islands and surrounded by a shoreline of reeds and clumps of mangrove trees. Behind swaths of lily pads and patches of reeds lay mirror-surface lagoons. The whole was encircled by ominous, forbidding green mountains. Ahead the lake narrowed again into the upper Río Dulce, and the setting sun floated like gold on the water as the *Vera Paz* plodded into the gathering darkness.

Sometime during the night or early morning they passed Castillo San Felipe de Lara, a small stone fortress so picturesque it could have been designed by boys for their toy soldiers. It stood alone between the water and jungle, ghostly crenellated turrets rising above its ramparts and crumbling, moss-encrusted walls. The isolated garrison straddled a spit of land that nearly closed off the river before it opened again into a broad lake beyond. It was a natural defensive location for a fortress built from a single tower in 1595, a solitary guardian against pirates who came up the river to raid the Spanish storehouses on the lake. But like other failed attempts to domesticate the surrounding countryside, law and order here served only to delay the inevitable. Despite being enlarged several times with extra fortifications, more cannons, and finally a moat and drawbridge, the Castillo was overrun and sacked time and again by the English raiders.

In the morning Stephens and Catherwood found themselves anchored off the town of Izabal, the main port of entry for Guatemala and much of Central America. They were surrounded by the waters of the Golfo Dulce, the largest body of water in Guatemala, known today as Lago de Izabal (Lake Isabel). Like the settlement at Belize, the town of Izabal was at once a major trading station and isolated outpost pressed between water and jungle. Izabal was smaller and more primitive by comparison, and the jungle rose dramatically on a

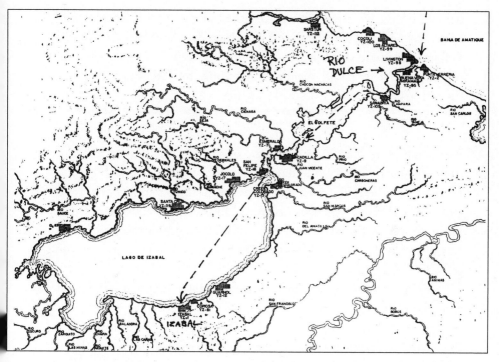

Map showing Stephen's and Catherwood's route to Lago de Izbal via Rió Dulce.

wall of mountains around it. From here the trade route went inland, up through the thick growth and over the top of the mountains.

Stephens and Catherwood went ashore in search of an authority to approve their passports. Traveling with them now was an attendant and cook named Augustin, whose services they had engaged in Belize. The town contained a single wood-frame house. The rest were adobe or cane huts, thatched over with palm leaves, housing a population of about 1,500. They finally found the town's commandant, Juan Penol, who had recently taken command of a barefoot troop of thirty men and boys dressed in white cotton shirts and trousers and armed with rusty muskets and old swords. Only three weeks earlier, Penol's predecessor had been driven from the post when the balance of power in the current civil war tipped in favor of the party Penol represented.

The new commandant expressed some trepidation over how long

he could hold his command before the balance tipped again. Here there was nothing like the grand treatment Stephens had received in Belize. Penol barely acknowledged Stephens's official capacity and he explained that he could authorize visas only for Guatemala because the rest of the Central American provinces were in a state of upheaval.

◎ ◎ ◎

As the day wore on, the heat became overwhelming. During most of the nineteenth century, the damp heat of the tropics, and the rising mists or so-called miasma exhaled by the swamps and lagoons, were still believed to be the cause of fever and death in northern white races, almost as a matter of course. Stephens had been warned Izabal was a particularly sickly place—that to pass through it was to "run the gauntlet" of death.

More than one U.S. envoy to Central America did not make it. In fact, the whole enterprise of mounting a diplomatic mission to Central America was an act of nerve bordering on the presumptuous; it took ever-increasing amounts of courage. Since the Central American provinces declared their independence from Spain and the first U.S. diplomat was named to the region in 1824, only two out of eight appointees made it to Guatemala City. They included a former U.S. senator and a congressman, who were perhaps more fit for the job than the others because they had survived the rough-and-tumble of early U.S. politics. Four of the envoys died either en route, soon after they arrived, or before they had even left the United States. Two other appointees turned back shortly after landing at Izabal. It was as if some impermeable barrier of illness, death, or fear blocked entrance to the country.

One of the two who succeeded in reaching Guatemala City was Charles G. De Witt, a former congressman from New York. He accepted the post in 1833 but dallied and did not book passage to Central America until five months had elapsed. At one point, he was so deterred by Izabal's reputation for sickliness and the long, hard ride inland necessary to reach Guatemala City that he decided to sail all the way around Cape Horn to approach Guatemala from the Pacific side. This did not go down well with President Andrew Jackson, who had appointed him. Jackson, the stern war hero who defeated the British army at the Battle of New Orleans, had not earned the nickname "Old Hickory" from abundance of caution or a weak will. He made clear to De Witt, through Secretary of State Livingston, that De Witt's planned route to the Pacific was unacceptable. "[The president] cannot by any means," Livingston wrote De Witt, "approve the project of making the voyage to the South Seas, round Cape Horn, in order to get to Central America, a place almost at our doors. Add to this, that when you arrive at Valparaiso [Chile] you will be twice as far from your destination as you are now." Chastened, De Witt quickly booked more direct passage to Guatemala, then promptly fell ill and was delayed an additional five months before finally departing.[1]

Despite his slow start, De Witt endured at his post in Guatemala a remarkable five years. At the end he repeatedly pleaded for permission to come home, if only on temporary leave to take care of his ailing wife in New York. His relations with the State Department, however, never fully recovered from his inauspicious start, and he was ordered not to leave Guatemala until he renewed the trade treaty that was about to expire between the United States and the republic. De Witt's dispatches became more and more desperate. At one point he described being hidden in the home of two widows when Indian guerrillas briefly overran Guatemala City, murdering its citizens and executing the republic's vice president. He said he had been warned to leave the city. But, he wrote—with considerable bravura—"I invariably answered that if I must perish, let me perish in the house known as the North-American Legation beneath the flag of the United States."[2]

Finally, a year later, with the political situation disintegrating around him and conditions growing more dangerous by the day, he left for home without completing the treaty renewal. When he arrived in the States, he was ordered by the State Department to return to Guatemala at once to complete his duties and finalize the treaty. Instead, on April 12, 1839, while aboard a Hudson River steamboat opposite Newburgh, New York, De Witt killed himself. He was forty-nine years old.[3]

These accounts of death and failure circled like a flock of vultures over the diplomatic mission and ought to have dissuaded any sensible person from considering such an assignment. Yet somehow the position carried enough prestige to attract a man of the caliber of William Leggett, who was named to replace De Witt. Leggett's appointment turned out to be the shortest. He was a well-known writer, a radical Democrat and anti-monopolist who along with William Cullen Bryant edited the *New York Evening Post*. Leggett's incendiary editorials were greatly influential during the 1830s (and helped form the basis of later libertarian doctrines). But the popular thirty-eight-year-old editor was plagued by ill health, the result of yellow fever contracted while serving in the navy. All the more reason he should have avoided a post in Guatemala. Yet when President Van Buren, a moderate Democrat who often felt the sting of Leggett's pen, appointed him to replace De Witt, it was at the behest of a number of Leggett's friends, who thought, bizarrely, that the change in climate would do him some good. Leggett died a month later, in May 1839, while preparing for his departure to Guatemala. The post of chargé d'affaires to Central America was nothing short of cursed.

Van Buren next appointed an eager Stephens. No firebrand like Leggett, Stephens was a staunch Jacksonian Democrat like the president, and both men had deep roots in New York's Democratic Party. Van Buren had been a powerful state legislator and the state's governor before he joined President Jackson's administration and succeeded him as the nation's eighth president. Before traveling to Europe and beyond, Stephens had been particularly active in Democratic Party politics in New York City. But he owed his appointment as much to his success as a writer as to his party affiliations. His travel books were not only extraordinarily popular but had won high critical acclaim. And the president had a weakness for literary connections. The "Little Magician," as Van Buren was called because of his small size and his brilliance as a political tactician, had never gone to college. He suffered from a lifelong sense of intellectual inferiority, which he sought to assuage through association with literary men.[4] Washington Irving and William Cullen Bryant were close friends, and he appointed Nathaniel Hawthorne and historian George Bancroft to government posts. Whatever the motivations, Van Buren seemed to recognize in

Stephens that he had the right man for the job. Clearly Stephens was intellectually up to the challenge and, if his extensive travels were any indication, he was physically hardy enough as well. As important, Stephens seemed crazy enough to actually want the assignment. But then he and Catherwood had already been eagerly charting their course south.

◉◉◉

In the early evening, as the exhausting heat of Izabal began to ebb ever so slightly, Stephens set out to find the grave of James Shannon, a Kentuckian who had been the sixth U.S. envoy sent to Central America. With a local guide, he crossed Izabal's primitive plaza and followed a path out of town that led after a few minutes to a deep gully recently flushed with the latest downpour. He crossed it on a plank and turned up a hill into a dark forest that overlooked the lake. There, among the rudimentary markers, Shannon's grave was pointed out to him. It had no raised stone and was barely distinguishable from the earth around it. Stephens's spirits sank at the sight.

Shannon had come to Izabal in the summer of 1832, more than a year before De Witt finally arrived as his replacement. Optimistically or naïvely, he had brought with him his wife, his son Charles, and a niece, Miss Shelby. Soon after they had landed, both Shannon and his niece were struck down with yellow fever. They died a short time later.

"I was melancholy that one who had died abroad in the service of his country was thus left on a wild mountain without any stone to mark his grave," wrote Stephens. Returning to the town, he arranged for a marker and a fence to be built around the grave. The local priest promised to plant a coconut tree at its head.

Catherwood, in the meantime, had been visiting the engineer of the *Vera Paz,* a fellow Englishman named Rush. He had taken ill aboard the steamer and was laid up in a hammock surrounded by townspeople. At a stout six feet, four inches, he was man of huge proportions, Stephens noted, but he lay in the hut "helpless as a child." It was not a good omen.

◁ 3 ▷

Mico Mountain

At seven the next morning Stephens and Catherwood carried their baggage out to a large gathering of men and animals lining up for the trip over Mico Mountain. The scene deflated any romantic notions of swashbuckling their way across the Guatemalan countryside on a couple of stallions. The journey would be made on mules, the sure-footed beast of burden that dominated the rugged trails of Central America. Before them was a scene of great commotion as goods were being hauled from the storehouses and loaded onto nearly a hundred mules lining up in an endless caravan attended by twenty to thirty muleteers. Stephens and Catherwood's separate party consisted of five mules, one for each of them and their new traveling companion, the cook Augustin, and two for their baggage. Four natives had been hired to carry additional supplies on foot and attend to the mules.

In the weeks before their departure, Stephens had sought out as many scientific instruments as he could muster. In a letter to Secretary of State Forsyth, with a copy to the president, he asked if it would not be too "impertinent" to obtain from the government a sextant, telescope, pocket chronometer, artificial horizon, and two mountain barometers.[1] His request apparently was denied because he was only able to secure—at his own expense—one glass barometer, which he now slung over his shoulder, fearing to entrust it to one of the Indian carriers. This made the expedition a small-time scientific operation at best. Given the advancement of measuring instruments by early-nineteenth-century standards, their two-man team was bringing along the technological minimum. For example, Stephens's hero, the

Port of Izabal in 1860.

great naturalist Baron Alexander Von Humboldt, in his much-celebrated trek through South America forty years earlier, carried a cyanometer, rain gauge, pendulum, magnetometer, eudiometer, and galvanic batteries, as well as the usual run of sextants, thermometers, compasses, artificial horizons, chronometers, and barometers. And on the same day Stephens and Catherwood were mounting up in Izabal, a tiny fleet of U.S. naval ships was weighing anchor in Apia Bay, Samoa, and sailing toward Australia in preparations for an assault on Antarctica, if such a place existed. The Americans were in a race with the French to claim first landfall on the still-undiscovered continent. The operation, called the U.S. Exploring Expedition, though small, was still outfitted with the best scientific instrumentation available.[2] Stephens's marching orders from the state department, however, were solely about trade, not science. He and Catherwood would have to accept their postdiplomacy explorations as no more than a private adventure by freelance antiquarians. The term *archaeologist* had not yet been created.

Catherwood, however, was an accomplished professional artist with a great deal of field experience. He knew what he needed and it wasn't much—a variety of sketchbooks, paper, and drawing and painting instruments. His most technologically advanced tool was a "camera lucida," an optical device invented in 1807 and used by artists in the pre-photography era to draw true proportions of objects. It consisted of a reflective prism mounted on a small stand that attached to a drawing board. By directing the prism at an object at just the right angle, a tricky process requiring some patience, an artist would be able to look through the glass and see an outline of the object as if it were cast onto the surface of the paper. The object could then be traced. Catherwood also carried an old chronometer to help with longitudinal calculations and the expedition's only pieces of surveying equipment: a compass and a long stretch of calibrated tape that he had used to measure the temples and monuments of Egypt.

For Stephens, the writer, it couldn't be simpler. He brought pencils, pens, and blank notebooks to jot down daily notes. It was a story, after all, and Stephens knew a good story when he saw one. But he was also the U.S. chargé d'affaires. So he brought, carefully packed in one of his bags, a custom-made diplomatic coat tailored from the finest blue cloth to be found in New York, and decorated with a profusion of gold buttons. If rarely worn, it was, still, the requisite costume for his position as a minister of state. There was also the obligatory medicine chest. And though they were men of artistic temperament and sensibilities, both were nonetheless practical about traveling through unknown lands in troubled times. They were, Stephens wrote, "armed to the teeth." Each had a double brace of pistols, ammunition, and large hunting knives strapped in belts across their bodies. Augustin was given a pistol, as well as a sword.

They mounted at eight o'clock, an hour behind the mule train, and set off straight for Mico Mountain and the old Spanish highway, the Camino Real, which wound 120 miles inland to Guatemala City. It was over this road that most of the trade of Central America passed. It was, however, like no road or highway back home, and consisted of little more than a steep mountain track, which at this time of year— the rainy season runs from June through November—was filled with treacherous mud holes, narrow, slippery gullies, and deep ravines, with exposed tree roots stretching across the path three or more feet high. Rain poured down as they rode. Soon they were overwhelmed by blue muck and sweltering heat, and were barely able to squeeze through the ravines.

The first hours proved a hard test of the two men's friendship. Up to this point, their journey had been smooth going, even through the rough seas to Belize. Stephens's mule fell first. "I lifted myself from off her back, and flung clear of roots and trees, but not of mud," he wrote. "I had escaped from a worse danger: my dagger fell from its sheath and stood upright, with the handle in the mud, a foot of naked blade." Mr. Catherwood—Stephens's usual moniker for his friend—was thrown next and with such violence that he momentarily lost his reserve and at full volume cursed Stephens for dragging him into this godforsaken country.

Soon all discourse ended entirely as the two men, coated in mud, struggled just to stay mounted. The jungle became thicker and the climb more precipitous. The trees and forest growth closed in around them so completely that little daylight came through. They peered ahead through the gauzy light. Eventually they caught up with the mule caravan as it ascended in a meandering line up a stony streambed. Loads slipped off the mules, some of the animals fell, and the curses and shouts of the mule drivers sounded through the forest. Stephens and Catherwood dismounted and tried to walk but the stones and tree roots were too slippery to gain a foothold. They had struggled upward for hours when Augustin's mule fell backward in a mud hole and they thought for a moment they had lost him. He tried to kick free as the mule tumbled, but his leg was caught and he disappeared as the animal rolled over him. Stephens was certain their cook had broken every bone in his body, then Augustin and the mule rose together, plastered with mud but miraculously without serious injury.

Finally, at one o'clock the rains stopped and they reached the summit of Mico Mountain. After a few minutes' rest in the clammy heat, they pushed on and were soon surrounded again by the caravan. The descent from the top was as slippery and treacherous as the climb, and the muleteers seemed bent on covering ground as fast as possible as they drove the mules down. At one point Stephens and Catherwood were nearly crushed in a narrow ravine when a fallen mule blocked the passage in front of them and mules piled in on them from behind.

But the worst was still to come, according to Stephens. After eight hours of grueling, steaming labor, most of it just to stay atop their mounts, they finally reached a wild mountain stream called, appropriately enough, El Arroyo del Muerto, or Stream of the Dead. They stopped next to the cool, clear water, their stomachs growling ravenously for their first meal of the day. As they rested under the shade of a large tree, dipping their cups into the water, their spirits lifted and, as Stephens recalled: "We spoke with contempt of railroads, cities and hotels."

Then Augustin unrolled their provisions: three days' supply of bread, roasted fowl, and hard-boiled eggs. "The scene that presented itself was too shocking, even for the strongest nerves," wrote Stephens. Augustin had mistakenly put in with the food a large paper roll of gunpowder that had broken, leaving the food "thoroughly seasoned with this new condiment."

"All the beauty of the scene, all our equanimity, everything but our tremendous appetites, left us in a moment."

There were other setbacks. The expedition's sole barometer did not survive the trail. After struggling to stay mounted, Stephens became convinced the glass instrument would be safer on the back of one of the local men traveling on foot. The carrier toted it on his back with extreme care, along with a red-rimmed ceramic pitcher that hung from his belt. This he had held up proudly after every stumble, a sign he was up to the task. And in fact, he succeeded in carrying the barometer intact over the mountain, but they found the mercury had not been secured tightly enough and had drained off, rendering the instrument useless.

After ten hours of riding—the hardest he had ever experienced, Stephens wrote—they had covered only twelve miles. With dusk approaching, they descended to an open patch of grassland, then through an arching grove of palms to a small rancho, no more than a hut, where they would spend the night. They were furious to find that their baggage mules had been taken ahead with the rest of the caravan, and they would have no change of clothes.

They were now more than a dozen miles into Guatemala, looking out over a magnificent valley cut through by the Motagua River, an important drainage connecting the interior central highlands with the Gulf of Honduras. When they finally reached the river, they were down nearly to sea level again, having survived Mico Mountain. To the northeast the valley broadened into a wide alluvial plain running to the sea. At its far western end, it narrowed like a rapier thrust toward the heart of the shattered republic, Guatemala City. The city sat on a plateau five thousand feet above sea level; it still lay more than one hundred miles distant.

The valley they were entering was tamer and more civilized than the wild mountain they had just crossed. There were ranches and small swales of agricultural land scattered on both sides of the river. But as in almost all of Central America, few comforts existed for travelers along the Camino Real. There were no inns or hotels or eating establishments. Much of Central America remained a primitive place, not unlike the western United States at the time, and traveling through it was a hit-or-miss proposition. If one had the proper introductions or a little luck, accommodation in someone's house was possible. Town halls, called *cabildoes,* and church buildings also provided shelter to travelers. Occasionally there were thatched huts made with cane or mud walls, where one could sleep at a cost of a few pennies.

Food was another matter. When they agreed to hire Augustin in Belize, neither Stephens nor Catherwood believed he was very quick-witted. But despite their fury over the gunpowder incident, it did not take long for them to change their minds. Augustin was born on the Caribbean island of Hispaniola to Spanish and French parents, and he grew up in the port town of Omoa, on the north coast of Honduras. He turned out to be resourceful, ambitious, and fiercely proud. He would always maneuver in the background along the trail, then as if by magic, he would emerge with chickens and eggs, chocolate, beans, and tortillas at just the right moment, and cook it all up to provide the fuel that kept the expedition moving. He was young, though Stephens never gives his exact age or a physical description. And he spoke no English. But his French-Spanish upbringing proved crucial. Stephens's and Catherwood's grasp of Spanish was weak to nonexistent when the journey began. Therefore Augustin would speak with the two men in French, which both spoke, and he served as their interpreter in Spanish, which most of the locals spoke.

In the afternoon heat of the second day, they reached the Motagua. There, in a scene Stephens describes almost as a dream sequence, he and Catherwood finally freed themselves for the first time from their mud-caked, sweat-stained clothes. As the sun set, they plunged into the river, a luxury he said that could only be appreciated by those who had survived Mico Mountain. They stood up to their necks in the cool, crystal water, surrounded by distant mountains and lush tropical foliage lining the riverbanks as flocks of parrots and other brilliantly plumed birds chattered and flitted through the air above them. Their enchantment was broken only by Augustin, who came down the opposite bank to call them to supper.

They emerged from the river and realized in agony they still had not caught up with their baggage. They looked at their "hideous" clothing. "We had but one alternative, and that was to go without them," wrote Stephens. "But, as this seemed to be trenching upon the proprieties of life, we picked them up and put them on reluctant."

That night they stayed with a family in a modest hut. They were invited to hang their hammocks in the central room, which contained the beds of their host, his wife, and their seventeen-year-old daughter. Stephens was already impressed by the various states of undress of the host and his wife. He woke several times during the night at the sound of steel clicking against flint and saw one of his neighbors lighting a cigar. During one such awakening, he found the teenage girl sitting sideways on her cot at the foot of his hammock. She was smoking a cigar and wearing nothing but a piece of cloth tied around her waist and a string of beads. "At first I thought it was something I had conjured up in a dream," he recalled. "I had slept pell-mell with Greeks, Turks and Arabs. I was beginning a journey in a new country; it was my duty to conform to the customs of the people: to be prepared for the worst, and submit with resignation to whatever might befall me."

The Motagua Valley is one of the hottest and most arid regions in Central America during the dry season. Only twenty inches of rainfall reach the valley floor each year during the rainy season, compared to six times that amount in the surrounding mountains. Spiny cacti and thorny shrubs are among the few plants that thrive on the parched earth. But like the Nile, lush vegetation covers the banks of the river year-round, and now, near the end of the rainy season, the whole valley was green. Stephens and Catherwood followed the road southwest along the river through long galleries of trees, then along an open ridge with commanding views of the valley. They met stray cattle beside the road and a few Indians carrying machetes on the way to work in the fields. They finally crossed an open plain to enter the town of Gualán, the largest municipality they had so far encountered in the country. Without a whisper of a breeze, the sun hovered over them with blistering power. "I was confused," Stephens said, "my head swam and I felt in danger of a stroke of the sun." Then they felt the rumble of a slight earthquake, their first.

Three days later, with a new guide and mules, they approached the next town, Zacapa, traveling in the shadow of the Sierra de las Minas, a soaring range of cloud-capped mountains prized for its deposits of jade. Along the road, the surrounding trees and bushes were covered with red and purple flowers. Waterfalls cascaded down the distant mountainsides, reminding Stephens of Switzerland. Entering Zacapa, a sizable municipality with an impressive Moorish-style church, whitewashed houses, and regular streets, they rode directly to the house of Don Mariano Durante, one of the town's leading citizens, to present a letter of introduction. The Don was out but a servant took their mules and invited them into a huge reception room.

"We had candles lighted and made ourselves at home," Stephens wrote. "A gentleman entered, took off his sword and spurs, and laid his pistols upon the table. Supposing him to be a traveler like ourselves, we asked him to take a seat; and when supper was served, invited him to join us. It was not until bedtime that we found we were doing the honors to one of the masters of the house."

Over the next two days, Stephens learned much about the political state of the countryside and the conditions of the road ahead. He was given conflicting accounts by different party factions, but all the informants agreed on one fact: the road to the capital was so treacherous at the moment with bandits and Indian guerrillas that to take it would be to face serious dangers. The risks they faced coming to Central America were no longer abstract but now real and immediate. There would be no more pleasant jaunts through the countryside. The single road to the capital was beset by the worst kind of violence—fueled, they were told, by the natives' hatred for all foreigners.

It was a sobering moment and the two men quickly drew up an alternate plan. They would delay the journey to Guatemala City. And instead of waiting in Zacapa until the latest political upheavals cooled and the road to the capital was more secure, they would veer off east into the state of Honduras. Although Stephens was under official orders to go to Guatemala City, he clearly had some discretion over how to proceed—protecting his life certainly fell within that discretion. But there was another motive for the detour: a village named Copán lay just across the border in Honduras. He and Catherwood had read that carved stones had been found scattered through the jungle near Copán, along with many structures of uncertain age. In large part, it was this report that had drawn Stephens and Catherwood to Central America. They were so close—a three-day journey, they were told, though few people even in Zacapa had heard of Copán. Stephens had talked himself into it.

On the morning of November 12, they rode east out of Zacapa, heading for Copán—whether it was any safer going in that direction, no one could tell them.

⊲⊲ 4 ⊳⊳

Passport

The way to Copán was south over a ridge to the town of Chiquimula, then east through a gap in the mountains into Honduras.
Here the land changed radically from the rich, abundant foliage of the
Motagua Valley to parched hills, dotted with prickly pear and cactus.
As they descended to Chiquimula, the landscape turned to dense vegetation again. From a distance they could see a white church outlined
sharply against surrounding green mountains spotted with rose-
colored mimosa trees. It was a substantial edifice, Chiquimula's original Spanish church, now abandoned, its roof caved in by earthquakes.
The church was the first of many such desolated structures they would
see over the next few days, victims of heaving earth and war.

The church ruins were located on the edge of town. Huge blocks
of stone and mortar, some as tall as a man, lay inside exactly where
they had fallen from a quake years earlier. Part of the site was now a
graveyard, and Stephens had a keen eye for picking out incongruities.
He noted that the tidy graves of the town's better-heeled residents
were located inside the nave and the bones of the town's succession of
priests were lodged in crypts in the massive cracked walls. Outside
were the common people. Parts of their moldering bodies were visible
in hastily dug, shallow graves, surrounded by flowers growing wild
along the ground and drooping from the branches of trees. The air
was thick with gaudy parrots whose "senseless chattering" irreverently
cut though the stillness of the sacred ground.

During a short walk around Chiquimula's main plaza, the two
men met a pretty young woman who lived in a corner house and invited them to stay for the night. It was an unusual welcome for two

Church at Chiquimula. (Catherwood)

conspicuous foreigners considering the place and the times. And Stephens, always ready to fall under the charms of women, found their hostess especially appealing. In this rough place she seemed a proper lady. She wore a frock, shoes, and stockings and her eyebrows were finely penciled. His hope that she was unmarried, however, was dashed when he discovered that the man of the house, whom he initially took to be her father, was actually her husband.

Palms and jacaranda trees shaded the plaza, scattering sunlight on a group of women who drew water from a fountain in the center. A sense of peace settled over the late afternoon scene, and it seemed unimaginable that the country was torn by violent conflict. Then hundreds of soldiers began assembling in a large formation for evening parade, and the war, of which they had heard so much, began for the first time to take on a tangible presence. Stephens found them banditlike and ferocious looking but took solace at the sight of criminals peering out through the bars of the nearby jail, "as it gave an idea that sometimes crimes were punished."

Though the town was far enough north to be out of the direct line of fighting that now seesawed between Guatemala City and the current federal capital of San Salvador, the area surrounding Chiquimula had been savaged in the recent civil war. Party loyalties in the region were deeply divided between federal authorities and the insurgents. At times lawlessness and anarchy had been worse than the pitched battles. For the moment, a kind of uneasy calm had crept across the area. The insurgents were led by a twenty-four-year-old former pig herder named Rafael Carrera, who had overrun Guatemala City with his Indian partisans several times and was now in full possession of the capital city. Earlier in the year he had also seized control of the Chiquimula district, and he had appointed a professional mercenary named Francisco Cáscara to pacify the area. Cáscara was a former Sardinian general who had learned his trade as an officer in the French army under Napoleon.[1]

As Stephens and Catherwood watched the straggling contingent of soldiers form up on the plaza, the sixty-two-year-old Cáscara rode up the line with an aide at his side. Stephens noticed that the general appeared ghostly pale and ill. After the inspection, they followed the old commander back to his house, where Stephens presented his credentials. Cáscara was immediately suspicious. And he was not pleased with the route the two men were taking. Who in their right mind would be rambling through the countryside to the tiny village of Copán in the midst of civil war? He seemed apprehensive that they were, instead, on their way to San Salvador to meet with the federal authorities. But he accepted that Stephens was a credentialed minister of the United States, and besides, Copán was outside of his department. He signed the visa allowing safe passage through the department, but not before cautioning them of the risks they were taking. His signature was no guarantee of safety, he warned.

The next morning Stephens and Catherwood were off. Not far from Chiquimula, they passed a village that had been destroyed a year earlier by federal soldiers, its church roofless and abandoned. Leaving the road, they turned onto a little-used trail and crossed a mountain, riding for some distance in cloud forest and rain. Then they descended into a deep, snakelike river valley that wound for more than ten miles.

After a while they came to a village along the river called San Juan Ermita, where their mule driver declared they had covered enough ground for the day. But it was only two o'clock, and a band of unruly, threatening soldiers occupied the town's only mud hut, which was enough to convince Stephens they should push on. The cursing muleteer followed. Their path now paralleled a stony riverbed that cut through cottonwood trees along the valley floor. The countryside was rugged, extravagant. Steep mountains on each side towered above them, some pyramidal in form, blunt peaks in the clouds. As they continued up the valley, they slowly gained altitude and pine forests could be seen along the upper slopes. The soil was a rich rust color. Rain poured down fitfully, soaking them as they rode, reminding them of Mico Mountain. Huts, enough to count as hamlets, cropped up here and there on the far mountainsides, every one with a church or chapel crisply whitewashed against the dark green slopes. Late in the day they arrived at a village called Camotán. As they approached, they saw their seventh church of the day. "Coming upon them in a region of desolation, and by mountain paths which human hands had never attempted to improve, their colossal grandeur and costliness were startling," Stephens wrote.

The small plaza in front of Camotán's church consisted of little more than dirt and a patch of weeds. No one was around. In fact, the entire village appeared deserted. Stephens and Catherwood rode over to the municipal *cabildo* across from the church, forced open the door, and started unloading the mules. Augustin was sent to forage for dinner. He returned with a single egg, though apparently he had roused the town in the process. A group of village officials, including the alcalde carrying the silver-headed cane of his mayoral office, came down to survey the scene. Stephens showed them their passport and visa and explained where they were going, and the officials left, but not before explaining that there was no extra food in the village to give them.

The expedition quickly settled in and dined on the lone egg, along with their own bread and chocolate. The alcalde sent a jar of water. The village hall was of good size, forty by twenty feet, and equipped with wall pins for travelers' hammocks. Still hungry and exhausted from the day's long journey, they hung their hammocks and prepared for sleep. Catherwood had already climbed into his hammock and Stephens was half-undressed when the door burst open. More than two dozen men rushed in. As Stephens later described them, they included the mayor and his assistants, as well as "soldiers, Indians, and Mestizoes, ragged and ferocious-looking fellows, and armed with staves of office, swords, clubs, muskets, and machetes, and carrying blazing pine sticks."

For a moment everyone froze. Stephens and Catherwood were taken totally by surprise. There was no chance for the two men to grab their pistols—such a move would have been suicidal anyway.

Then stepped forward a young officer, who they learned later was a captain of one of Cáscara's army units. He wore a glazed hat, a large sword, and a smirk. As he glared at the two foreigners, the mayor, who was clearly intoxicated, asked again to see Stephens's papers. The passport was handed over and the mayor quickly passed it on to the officer. He examined it closely and then stated flatly that it was not valid.

With the help of Augustin, Stephens, by now dressed, explained the purpose of their visit and pointed in particular to the visa endorsements of Commandant Penol of Izabal and General Francisco Cáscara. The captain was unimpressed and ignored the explanations. He said he had seen a passport once before and it was much smaller than the one Stephens possessed. More important, it should bear the seal of the state of Guatemala, not the department of Chiquimula. There was nothing more to do, he said, but they must remain at Camotán until a dispatch was sent to Chiquimula and orders received directly from the general.

This, Stephens was not disposed to do. He had slogged through muck and rain, endured blistering rides on the backs of mules, and had played by the rules getting visa endorsements attached to his passport—twice. Besides, he felt guilt for veering off, for personal purposes, from the most direct route to his diplomatic assignment in Guatemala City. Now, to be delayed further at the arbitrary whim of a smirking martinet—that was not going to happen. Stephens threatened them with the consequences of holding up a representative of the United States government. When that had no effect, out of frustration he said that he would return immediately to Chiquimula himself. But both captain and the alcalde said that he was not going anywhere.

The captain demanded that Stephens give him his passport again. Stephens refused. It was issued by his government, he asserted, and was the property of the United States. Then the usually reserved Catherwood weighed in, launching into a learned discourse on the "law of nations" and the legal rights of ambassadors, and added that the captain was in great danger of bringing down on his head the wrath of the government of "El Norte," the United States. The captain was unmoved. When Stephens offered again to go to Chiquimula, under armed guard if necessary, the officer said that he wasn't going anywhere, not forward or backward, and that he must immediately hand over the passport.

At that Stephens placed the document inside his vest and buttoned his coat tightly across his chest. The captain sneered that they would take it by force. As Stephens later recounted, during the escalating confrontation, two "assassin-looking scoundrels" sat on a nearby bench and carefully leveled their muskets at his heart, the muzzles a mere three feet away. The other men stood with their hands at ready on their machetes and swords. As the burning pine sticks cast flickering shadows against the walls, the long, tense silence was broken by a familiar voice from a dark corner of the room. It was Augustin, who had secured his pistol and begged Stephens in French to give the order to fire. He could scatter them with a single shot, he said. Stephens later recalled their naïveté at that moment: "If we had been longer in the country, we should have been more alarmed; but as yet we did not know the sanguinary character of the people and the whole proceeding was so outrageous and insulting that it roused our indignation more than our fears."

Just then, a man wearing a glazed hat and short roundabout jacket stepped forward, having entered after the others. He asked to see the passport. Judging the man to be of a better class than the rest of the rabble, Stephens carefully removed the passport from his vest, and clutched it firmly in his fingers as he held it up to the blazing torchlight. At Catherwood's request, the man read it aloud. When the official language was finally communicated to those in the room, a murmur broke out and the tension seemed to wheeze out of the building. It occurred to Stephens later that it was probable that neither the captain nor the mayor was able to read. The demand for the passport was dropped. But they were ordered to remain in custody.

Now Stephens insisted that a courier be sent at once with a note to Cáscara, and the captain and mayor agreed only after Stephens said he would bear the expense of the trip. Catherwood and Stephens then went to work drafting the note in Italian, describing their imprisonment.

> Not to mince matters, Mr. Catherwood signed the note as Secretary; and, having no official seal with me, we sealed it, unobserved by anybody, with a new American half dollar, and gave it to the alcalde. The eagle spread his wings, and the stars glittered in the torchlight. All gathered round to examine it, and retired, locking us up in the cabildo, stationing twelve men at the door with swords, muskets, and machetes; and, at parting, the officer told the alcalde that, if we escaped during the night, his head should answer for it.

Finally they were gone, but now what should they do? They looked out. The guards sat around a fire directly in front of the door, smoking cigars, their firearms immediately within reach. Stephens was sure any attempt to escape would be fatal. The prospects did not look pleasant. They fastened the door as well as they could, and to steady their nerves, they broke out the bottle of wine that Colonel McDonald had sent along with them from Belize and drank a toast to his generosity. Exhausted, they fell into their hammocks.

In the middle of the night, the door was forced open again and the same crowd rushed in. This time, however, the young captain was not among them. As quickly as the whole affair had started, it was over. The mayor handed Stephens back his letter with the big seal—the silver half dollar pressed in wax—unbroken. And without explanation, he told them they were free to go when they pleased. Later, Stephens, mulling over the episode, was not sure why they had so suddenly changed their minds. He speculated that their aggressiveness in defending themselves no doubt helped. But he guessed that it was the seal, the American eagle on the half dollar, that had decided it.

When the alcalde and his men withdrew, Stephens and Catherwood were in a quandary. If they continued on into the interior, they might well run into similar situations or possibly much worse. Again they fell into their hammocks, and again they were jolted awake in the early morning by the alcalde and his assistants. They had come to pay their respects, they said. It was the soldiers and their captain, they explained, who created the disturbance the night before, and they had now passed through the village and were gone.

Their spirits bolstered, Stephens and Catherwood agreed to press on. After their morning chocolate, they loaded the mules. Copán, after all, the mystery at the center of their quest, the remote possibility that they might find evidence of something ancient and lost, beckoned less than ten miles away. But mountains still separated them. When they finally saddled up and left Camotán, it appeared as deserted as it had been when they arrived. It was as though nothing had changed; not even a mote of dust had altered course. The two men, however, more wary than ever, strapped on their weapons and took a deep breath. As they rode out, the great, empty quiet of Camotán was unnerving, broken only by the warble and caw of the morning birds.

Lieutenant John Herbert Caddy of the Royal Artillery lit a "genuine Havana" as they pushed off the embankment into Old River the afternoon of November 14. They were surrounded by plantain and fig trees along an airy stretch of the river. Puffing casually on his cigar, Caddy ordered the boats upstream. The boatmen struggled, going no more than four miles an hour against the stiff current. Twenty-four hours had lapsed since the British expedition left Belize City for Palenque under orders to investigate large ruins reportedly found there—and to outflank Stephens and Catherwood by publishing a detailed, illustrated report of their findings. At a farewell lunch with Colonel MacDonald at Government House, a last-minute glitch threatened to delay the expedition's start: the disappearance of the Spanish interpreter, Mr. Nod. By the end of lunch, however, two policemen had rounded him up in an advanced state of drunkenness, and put him aboard the main canoe.

Besides Caddy and the expedition's co-leader, John Walker, the party included fifteen soldiers of the Second West India Regiment, the interpreter, an artillery gunner who served as Caddy's personal aide, and nine specially hired boatmen—a total of twenty-eight individuals in all. The men were spread between two pitpans, one for the luggage and the other carrying Walker and Caddy. The main canoe was forty feet long and five feet across, one of the largest pitpans on the river, and was carved from a single mahogany tree. A canvas canopy at the back shielded Caddy and Walker from the broiling sun.

Just before they left, MacDonald wrote to Lord John Russell in London, the secretary of state for the colonies: "It has been my intention for some considerable time past to bring the subject before the Secretary of State and to suggest that an attempt should be made to explore Polenki with the view of deciding satisfactorily whether those ruins from their huge and extraordinary nature are such to justify the reports concerning them, or whether these reports are exaggeration and the place unworthy of the notice of the modern traveler." Months would pass before his correspondence reached Lord Russell and months before he received a response.

The settlement's weekly newspaper, the *Belize Advertiser*, was a bit more candid about what led to the hastily thrown-together expedition. "We are happy to find the design of Mr. Catherwood has aroused the jealousy of our Settlement, and induced a visit with like object to the same place by a different route." The article went on to note the danger involved. "We fear the two gentlemen from this, who have taken the direction of the Old River, and on by way of Petén, have chosen an unseasonable period, and will be greatly retarded both by water and by land." Then, with typical British cheer, the writer added: "'a stout heart . . .' gets over many difficulties, and may add to their personal experiences."[2]

Walker and Caddy spent their first night—the evening Stephens and Catherwood were toasting MacDonald in Camotán—quartered comfortably in a government cottage at a pretty bend in the river. The clearing was planted with fruit trees. It would be one of their last nights in such comfort. The next camp was set at Bakers Bank, where the men hung their hammocks under canvas and net pavilions.

Though Caddy was trained in military engineering and artillery and possessed considerable artistic talent, his skills extended to language as well. "The mosquitoes were insufferable and had it not been for our Pavilions we should have been well-phlebotomized," he wrote in a journal entry dated November 14. "As it was, their constant humming almost deprived me of sleep. Shakespeare could never have experienced the nuisance of these nocturnal musicians when he says 'and hush'd with buzzing night flies to thy slumber.' "

The next day brought unpleasant encounters with even more vicious, blood-drawing "bottle rump" and "doctor" flies; deadly snakes and alligators the size of logs watched from the mud banks while the pitpans fought their way up the river. It was hard going for the boatmen. They strained mightily to maneuver the giant, heavy canoes against the fast current of the river, now at flood stage. At one point they approached a waterfall marked on their map, but never found it because the river ran so high that the two pitpans passed over its location without seeing it. The boatmen switched from paddles to poles at the shallower turns in the river. "The steersman has a rather difficult task," wrote Caddy, "as from the great length of the Pitpan if he does not keep her directly against the stream, the current takes effect and turns her broadside on, to the great loss of time and labour, and to the risk of being upset—which is not at all an infrequent occurrence."

Yet for all its treachery and power, the river possessed a haunting beauty that grew the farther up they went. Gold- and crimson-breasted toucans snapped their enormous bills like "the sounds of castanets," wrote Caddy. Orange and black orioles appeared to catch fire in the blazing sun; bright green, almost fluorescent iguanas (which made for tasty meals) waddled along splintered mahogany logs embedded in the banks. And over the river towered the largest, wildest trees Caddy had ever seen, their gnarled roots sometimes projecting dangerously out into the river, their branches draped with bromeliads, orchids, and vines as thick and twisted as the braids of a ship's rigging.

The morning of November 16, they passed under an old pitpan suspended in the lianas twenty feet above their heads. The river was capable of such extreme surges during the rainy season—rising and

falling by as much as forty feet in a single day—that the rushing tor-
rents had apparently swept the canoe downriver until it lodged upside
down in the tangle of vines. There was no trace of what had become
of its crew. It was an ominous sign for the men in the pitpans. They
knew that no one in their right mind should be attempting a journey
up river during this season, after weeks of continuous rain, with more
sure to come. At this time of year, survival on the river was pure
chance.

But the order had been given: get to Palenque as quickly as possible, before Catherwood and Stephens. The route mapped out for
them, even under ideal weather conditions, was brutal and unforgiving. Going by sea would have been much easier. But Palenque was still
a mysterious, little-known place, whose exact proximity to the coast
was not clearly understood. Their path, straight west across the wild
Petén, the demon heart of Yucatán Peninsula, would lead them over
much the same ground Cortés had covered so grievously three hundred years earlier, going in the opposite direction. After three centuries, not much had changed. The jungle terrain was just as relentlessly
difficult, equally as murderous.

Caddy was born to follow orders. The son of an English artillery
captain, he was expected from his birth in Quebec in 1801 to follow in
his father's footsteps. Growing up in Canada, he understood the violence of armed conflict when England and the United States went to
war in 1812. Three years later he was sent to England, where he entered
the Royal Military Academy at the age of fifteen. By the time he and
Walker set out for Palenque, Caddy was an army veteran with nearly
twenty-five years of service as a cadet and officer in the Royal Artillery, and yet there was nothing of the hardened soldier about him. A
rare, surviving portrait shows a man with large, doe-like eyes set in a
soft, round boyish face.[3] He had never served in combat. At one point
he was a general's secretary. And somewhere along the line he developed into a fine watercolorist.

On the river, he showed all of the entitlements of a British officer.
He brought along a personal aide-de-camp and he drank fine Ma-
deira. He hunted for sport (and food) with his double-barrel shotgun

during stops along the embankments, and he saw all the men around him, with the exception of Walker, as inferiors. He also had a sharp eye, like Stephens, for details.

As they continued upriver past Labouring Creek to put in for the night at Beaver Dam, Caddy took another puff of his Havana. "We smoke nearly all day to keep away the flies," he wrote, "but they seemed to care little about smoke, except those which had the temerity to attack our faces, and which were now and then brought down by a well-directed puff."

Monkeys Like the Wind

Southeast of the Motagua River valley, the mountains run parallel, piled high, riven by deep fertile valleys, a landscape formed by two massive slabs of the earth's crust gnashing against one another—the great North American and Caribbean tectonic plates. When Stephens and Catherwood crossed the river valley days earlier, they traveled over the fault zone where the two plates meet. From above, the mountains to the north and south look like dark green sheets shoved up and crumpled against the long, flat valley. Here along the fault, more than 100 million years ago, North America was isolated from South America by the Caribbean Sea. Millions of years later, the land bridge of Central America began to rise from the sea, and the north and south continents were reconnected along the long, narrow Isthmus of Panama. The reunion melded the flora and fauna of both continents and set the stage for one of the richest biological shows on the planet.[1]

To the west, under the Pacific, lies the third geologic behemoth, the Cocos Plate, which thrusts eastward and northward under the lip of the Central American coastline. The collision of these three floating slabs makes Central America one of the most geologically violent regions on earth, battered by frequent earthquakes and perforated by a string of fiery volcanoes that run the length of the west coast.[2] So brutal are these forces of nature that Central America sometimes seems like a step back into the elemental beginnings of time.

Stephens and Catherwood continued east over this steep, corrugated terrain. Within a day of their departure from Camotán, they caught their first glimpse of the Copán River coursing through the mountain valleys. They forded it several times and rode up a stony path along the mountainside, looking straight down on the rushing waters from a narrow, slippery trail high above. A damp rain forest surrounded them, dense and impenetrable.

Eventually, the party halted at a rustic wood-slatted hacienda. Unlike the disruptions of the evening before, this stop brought them a measure of rest. They spent the night in the hacienda's single room, surrounded by nine men, women, and children. "All around were little balls of fire shining and disappearing with the puffs of the cigars," wrote Stephens. "One by one these went out, and we fell asleep."

The next morning, they crossed into Honduras—though no sign marked the border. A short time later, they stood looking down on the Copán Valley. They were no more than forty miles due south of where they had landed at Izabal, but they had traveled two weeks and more than a hundred hard miles. From the opposite end of the valley, the Copán River flowed down from the Sierra del Gallinero, cutting through a floodplain that formed the valley floor nearly two thousand feet above sea level. The river flowed westward, the direction from which they had come, and emptied eventually into the Motagua, joining its run to the sea.

In spite of the fertile earth, the exuberant foliage on either side of the river, and the mix of pine and subtropical forests along the slopes, the valley was surprisingly unpopulated. It had been all but empty of people for hundreds of years. There had been a time, however, more than a thousand years earlier, when its pockets of rich alluvial soil supported a dense population, and the Copán River formed the lifeblood of a stunning civilization.

Stephens had no way of knowing this in 1839. Nothing was known of the valley's extraordinary history. Not only did Stephens and Catherwood lack the archaeological concepts and tools to unravel the mystery they were about to encounter, they shared their era's near total ignorance of Native American societies as they existed before Christopher Columbus arrived in the New World. As Charles Darwin was to show two decades later with the 1859 publication of *On the Origin of Species,* the earth was only gradually giving up its secrets.

In the first half of the nineteenth century, much of the world's physical and human history was still unknown. The U.S. Navy's Exploring Expedition was racing at that moment toward Antarctica, a continent many believed did not exist. This around-the-world expedition would yield valuable scientific findings, gathering thousands of biological specimens, South Sea island artifacts, charts, and maps, all of which would form the initial collection of the Smithsonian Institution.[3] The history of Central and South America, opening finally to the outside world, was next. But it, too, would take time. And Stephens and Catherwood would be among the first to bring it to the world's attention.

As they looked east into the Copán Valley, they stood on the brink. There would be no turning back—and what they were about to discover would change the understanding of human history in the Western Hemisphere.

◎◎◎

Well into the twentieth century, the belief persisted even among prominent ethnographers and historians that there existed a kind of natural Eden in the Western Hemisphere before the Europeans arrived, two virgin continents filled with endless empty forests, deserts, jungles, and grasslands. The area was thought to be sparsely populated by small primitive tribes isolated from one another by great distances, with only a few scattered pockets of semicivilized life. These suppositions could not have been more wrong.

The first reports of encounters between the Europeans and American natives in the fifteenth and sixteenth centuries were scarce and often inaccurate. In what would later become known as Mexico, Central America, and Peru, some cities were found. But the Spaniards who landed in those areas were preoccupied with conquest and gold, not discovery. Few extensive histories or ethnological observations were recorded. Very little of the advanced native Indian culture survived the European onslaught.

The Spanish Conquest was particularly brutal. Idols, monuments, and entire cities were destroyed; Indian books and other written texts, some recording histories that spanned centuries, were systematically gathered into piles and burned. The pyramids, palaces, and temples the conquistadors found—evidence of the native societies' advanced level of social organization and technological skill—were quickly torn down, in part to provide material for the Spanish churches and residences that rose on their ruins, but also to subjugate the natives. The Spanish saw the Indians as pagan savages who indulged in human sacrifice and idolatry. Their culture and all vestiges of their religion were to be obliterated and the people converted to Christianity. Total submission was essential, according to the Spanish priests who accompanied the conquistadors, to save the Indians' souls.

The problem was there were fewer and fewer souls to save. Diseases brought from the Old World and the inhumane, homicidal treatment often doled out by the Spanish quickly decimated the Indian populations. A debate continues today among scholars over how many Native Americans lived in the Western Hemisphere in 1491 and what percentage lost their lives because of Europe's discovery of America. In Hispaniola, Cuba, and the islands of the West Indies, the first part of the New World settled by the Spaniards, the massacres, disease, and starvation were so horrendous that the Indian natives virtually disappeared within the first twenty years of Spanish occupation. The conquerors' demand for workers on the plantations they established eventually led to a new network of human exploitation, the transatlantic African slave trade, created to supply the islands with replacement labor.[4]

Until the middle of the last century, ethnographers and historians believed that in 1491 no more than 20 million Indians inhabited the entire hemisphere, from the Arctic Circle to Tierra del Fuego. Much lower estimates were widely accepted, as low as one million inhabitants for all of North America. Most demographers today dismiss these figures as wild underestimates. They now calculate that up to 100 million "Amerindian" peoples lived throughout the Western Hemisphere, though an accurate count will never be known. If true, this upper range means that the population of the Americas equaled or exceeded Europe's at the time of Columbus's first voyage.[5]

Yet by 1650, only 160 years later, the Indian population had plummeted to no more than six million, a decline of as much as 95 percent. Although the initial population figures and the amount of the decline are still debated, most scholars now agree that Europe's discovery of

America almost certainly resulted in the greatest demographic calamity in human history.

"The population losses were undisputedly considerable and swift," writes University of Texas historian Alfred W. Crosby, an expert on the biological consequences that followed Europe's discovery of the Americas, or what has come to be known as the "Columbian Exchange." Crosby adds, "The conclusion must be that the major initial effect of the Columbian voyages was the transformation of America into a charnel house. The European invasion of the New World reduced the genetic and cultural pools of the human species."[6]

The primary cause of this annihilation was disease.

According to scientific studies, all Native American Indians are descended from a small number of hunters who crossed the Bering Strait from Asia—from today's Siberia to Alaska—over a land bridge that appeared during the last ice age, and they began populating the Americas approximately 17,000–13,000 years ago. As the ice age ended, the glaciers melted, the seas rose, and the land bridge was covered over by the ocean waters once again. Cut off from Asia, the hunters and their succeeding generations were now trapped in North America. They moved southward, and finding limitless fertile land, they multiplied rapidly, many settling within the hospitable climate zone of Mexico and Central America and traveling as far as the tip of South America.

Isolated from the rest of the world for thousands of years, the American Indians never developed antibodies and immunities to the diseases that later emerged in Asia, Africa, and Europe. Thus a form of biological genocide struck when the conquistadors and other European colonists arrived, bringing with them smallpox, measles, influenza, bubonic plague, diphtheria, whooping cough, chicken pox, and tuberculosis. Wave after wave of disease swept through native populations, with catastrophic results.[7]

As a consequence, Europeans arriving in America greatly underestimated the size of the original Indian population. They concluded that they had stumbled into empty, largely uninhabited lands when in fact their diseases were racing ahead with such speed that by the time the settlers reached inland native areas, they were already greatly depopulated. This made conquest and settlement easier, especially for the Spaniards, who seemed to accomplish so much with so few men. For example, Western historians have celebrated Hernán Cortés and his band of 550 fellow conquistadors as ingenious, tenacious warriors who overcame unbelievable odds in vanquishing central Mexico's Aztec Empire. While there is some brutal truth to that assessment, a smallpox epidemic in 1521 cut down so many Aztec leaders and warriors that the disease played a significant role in the Spaniards' final military victories. Without smallpox, history may well have turned against Cortés.

Smallpox and the other European diseases continued southward with such speed that, by the time the conquistadors marched into Peru a decade later, the damage was done.[8] Francisco Pizarro arrived in the South American region in 1532 with only 168 men, a pitiful number with which to take on the sprawling Inca Empire of five million, which stretched from present-day Ecuador through Peru to Bolivia and Chile. Smallpox, however, had arrived well ahead of Pizarro and killed the great Inca leader Huayna Capac, along with his designated heir and many captains of his army. The deaths set in motion a civil war between Capac's two surviving sons, further weakening the empire militarily. Pizarro was able to seize on this opportunity and conquer most of the Inca holdings in less than three years.[9]

The Indians of Central America suffered the same huge losses. Experts now calculate that the region's indigenous population plunged from nearly six million people in the year 1500, soon after Columbus's voyages, to fewer than 300,000 by 1680.[10] The population was finally beginning to recover by the time Stephens and Catherwood arrived, and was approaching one million, but this was still one-sixth of what it might have been when the Spanish first landed.

The Copán Valley did not escape the wave of devastation. According to early Spanish historians, the area was heavily populated and the center of some of the fiercest native resistance to the invading conquistadors. Thousands of Indians, led by a powerful leader named Copán Calel, fought battle after battle with the Spaniards and their allied Indian troops from Mexico. After incredible bloodshed on both sides, the Spaniards finally succeeded in subduing Calel and his warriors.[11]

Ultimately the defeated Indians succumbed to "a pestilence"—most likely smallpox—that soon wiped out most of the local population.

For centuries afterward, the Copán Valley remained a hidden rural backwater, all but empty of people despite its mild climate and ideal growing conditions. But there was something different about this valley. It had been depopulated and left a ghost town once before. It had suffered a demographic calamity that long predated the arrival of the conquistadors when, centuries earlier, a powerful dynastic kingdom, the southern and easternmost outpost of an astonishing civilization, collapsed and disappeared.

The few remaining inhabitants in the valley, those whom Stephens and Catherwood were about to meet, had no idea what lay beneath their feet. In other parts of Mesoamerica, the bludgeoning force of the Conquest had all but erased Indian memory. Here time and nature had done so. There were the odd, mysteriously carved stones. The inhabitants were aware of those, had seen them half-buried in the jungle along the valley floor. But biological forces, fecund and regenerative, were so hard at work that nature itself had obliterated their history—their grand story of Indian genius and glory, failure and desolation—and had seemingly wiped the slate clean.

At two o'clock on the afternoon of November 15, 1839, Stephens and Catherwood rode into the small village of Copán. It consisted of no more than half a dozen dirt-floor thatched huts. Of the few inhabitants who quickly gathered around them—"our appearance created a great sensation," Stephens noted—none could direct them to the ruins. They were sent instead to the largest hacienda in the area, a sprawling ranch owned by a local man of influence and importance, Don Gregorio.

After a friendly welcome by the women of the ranch and a quickly prepared meal, the two men congratulated themselves on their good fortune. The country's reputation for hospitality at last seemed deserved, they told each other, and this was an ideal place from which to launch an investigation of any old stone ruins they might find.

But the welcome lasted only until late afternoon and the arrival of the Don himself, a surly man of about fifty, thick with whiskers and wearing the scowl of a tyrant. He did not like their looks, and he let it be known that they were not welcome.

Stephens and Catherwood were in a bind. Don Gregorio was purposely ignoring them; the women, his sons, and the laborers coming in from the fields quickly followed his cue. Despite this rudeness, however, the two men could not afford a falling-out with "the great man of Copán" if they were to have any chance of finding and exploring the ruins. They were suspect foreigners, a delicate status.

The two men smothered their pride. They had nowhere else to go, and nightfall was fast approaching. Eventually an unspoken truce prevailed. The Don was willing to tolerate their presence, apparently to prevent a "stain on his name," but only if they slept in a cramped, sheltered area outside the house with the ranch hands. Stephens described the scene: "There were three hammocks besides ours and I had so little room for mine that my body described an inverted parabola, with my heels as high as my head." The uneasy standoff continued the next morning when the Don appeared, still in the same bad mood. "We took no notice of him, but made our toilet under the shed with as much respect as possible to the presence of the female members of the family, who were constantly passing and repassing."

Finally, a guide was brought from the village to lead them to the ruins. The small caravan moved slowly down the southeastern slope, traversing the center of the seven-mile-long valley toward what is now called the "Copán pocket." At this point, the valley is relatively narrow, no more than a few miles from ridge to ridge. At an altitude of two thousand feet, they were in a more temperate zone, finally free of the suffocating heat and humidity of the lowlands around Lake Izabal and the Motagua.

The valley floor was nonetheless thickly overgrown with tropical and broadleaf forest, punctuated by colorful flashes of bougainvillea, hibiscus, and other exotic displays. The few huts scattered across the valley were surrounded by gardens and clearings cut from the jungle and planted with small plots of tobacco and corn. Cattle ranged through some of the fields, which were hedged with cacao plants, papaya, and mango. The fragrance of jasmine and frangipani, mixed with lemon, wafted through the air, and traces of cinnamon and nutmeg drifted from clusters of allspice trees.

But the backdrop remained dense and gloomy, the forest ominous. In this rich bottomland, composed of silt and volcanic ash, almost anything seemed to grow, watered by the river and sixty to seventy inches of rain each year. Now, at the end of the rainy season, the earth was so saturated it gave off a heavy, cloying smell of loam, mixed with fresh, wet chlorophyll from the undergrowth. They stopped briefly to rest, and between the birdsong and screeches of scarlet macaws, they could feel the vegetation around them pulsating and swelling with life.

José, their guide, took them along a narrow path some distance from the ranch, across a large field planted with corn. They tied their mules at the edge of the jungle. Using his machete, José methodically worked his way into the forest through the tangled underbrush. After a time, they emerged on the eastern bank of the Copán River. As they approached, Stephens and Catherwood looked through the trees—

And were stunned by what they saw.

They had been expecting scattered stone ruins, at best. But what appeared on the other side of the river was a massive stone wall that rose to a height of nearly one hundred feet. A large section had fallen, eroded and undermined by the river at its base. Stephens and Catherwood had read one eyewitness account and one vague historical reference to the ruins at Copán. Yet the enormity of the wall in front of them took their breath away. They had been to Italy, Greece, the Middle East. They had seen the pyramids and the remnants of ancient cities. But this place was assumed to have been occupied by savages. This was aboriginal America. No one expected its vanished peoples to engineer a solid face of stone rising far into the air and spanning hundreds of feet along the riverbank.

After they crossed a shallow stretch of the river and arrived at the base of the wall, the two men realized that sections of it were faced with what appeared to be well-cut, finished stone. They climbed a set of stone steps, many jumbled and forced apart by tree roots growing through the crevices, and emerged high above the river on a small terrace pressed in and covered by so many trees that it was difficult to gauge its dimensions. José went to work again, hacking a pathway across the level

LEFT AND RIGHT Catherwood's illustrations of a stela at Copán,
from *Incidents of Travel in Central America, Chiapas, and Yucatán.*
MIDDLE Stela today. (Carlsen)

ground through the underlying foliage, and soon they made out what
looked like the side of a pyramid.

A short time later, stumbling through the trees and underbrush,
they came upon something they had never imagined possible and
stopped in their tracks, struck with wonder. It was a tall monument of
such size and artistic mastery, wrote Stephens, that it equaled the
finest sculptures they had seen in Egypt.

The two men had ventured two thousand miles, risked disease and
injury, traveled in great danger through a land torn by civil war, all in
the hopes of what they might find. This monolith alone exceeded anything they had dared to imagine. The massive twelve-foot stone idol
loomed over them, sculpted from top to bottom on all four sides in
bold relief.

"The front was the figure of a man," Stephens wrote, "curiously
and richly dressed, and the face, evidently a portrait, solemn, stern,

Buried Stela at Copán. (Catherwood)

Fallen Monument in Copán. (Catherwood)

and well-fitted to excite terror. The back was of a different design unlike anything we had ever seen before and the sides were covered with hieroglyphics. The sight of this unexpected monument put to rest at once and forever, in our minds, all uncertainty in regards to the character of American Antiquities."

Ahead, José continued slicing through the dimly lit jungle, making a path through the tangle of vines and undergrowth. The forest was so thick with trees—immense ceibas and grasping strangler figs—that it was difficult at times to see very far; the tops of the trees formed a solid canopy that blocked the midday sun. The men tripped and climbed over roots and vines that snaked along the forest floor. Mosses, lianas, and epiphytes wrapped themselves around every available tree and limb. Even José lost his way, leading them down several dead ends to walls of impenetrable green foliage.

Before long, however, he guided them to fourteen more carved stone monuments, similar in appearance to the first. Some had toppled to the ground; some were half-buried, covered in creepers and roots. One was "locked in the close embrace of branches of trees and almost lifted out of the earth," Stephens recalled. "One, standing, with its altar before it, in a grove of trees which grew around it, seemingly to shade and shroud it as a sacred thing; in the solemn stillness of the woods, it seemed a divinity mourning over a fallen people."

As they went on in the defused light, they began to make out half-buried walls, huge, round sculpted altars, and other carved stone fragments. Fat roots of the strangler figs wrapped themselves like pythons around broken cornices and rows of sculpted death heads. All around them, trees grew out of great shattered structures; enormous mounds of stone towered far above their heads. Trunks and roots had torn apart and dislodged ochre-colored building stones, mottled with green-gray patches of lichen, and had sent the precisely cut blocks tumbling down into huge piles at the foot of the pyramids.

Yet for all its jumbled desolation, the remains left by the natural force of the jungle still displayed delicate tracings and intricate sculptured heads and figures, artistry carved into stone and frozen in time. Set in the overpowering forest, it was bewildering devastation and mystery, too much to grasp in a single take. The two men stumbled through the jungle after José in a state of disbelief. Yet Stephens realized almost immediately that they were in the presence of something extraordinary, something with the potential to change the understanding of history. These were not the remains of a raw and unrefined people, he wrote, but works of art that proved "the people who once occupied the continent of America were not savages."

Stephens was alive as never before, his every sense and nerve stretched to its limit. Even the stillness of the jungle caught his attention—and the whispers he detected in it:

> The only sounds that disturbed the quiet of this buried city were the noise of monkeys moving among the tops of the trees, and cracking of dry branches broken by their weight. They moved over our heads in long and swift processions, forty and fifty at a time, some with little ones wound in their long arms, walking out to the end of boughs, and holding on with their hind feet or a curl of their tail, sprang to a branch of the next

tree, and with a noise like a current of wind, passed on into the depths of the forest. It was the first time we had seen these mockeries of humanity, and, with the strange monuments around us, they seemed like wandering spirits of the departed race guarding the ruins of their former inhabitants.

Climbing over the mounds, the men finally found the level ground and terrace where they had entered. Their eyes had grown accustomed to the filtered light, and they could now distinguish what appeared to be a large, rectangular plaza surrounded by steps on each side, which gave it the appearance of a Roman amphitheater. A huge sculpted head, embedded in the steps, stared at them from across the plaza. They crossed toward it, climbed the steps to a long, narrow terrace, and found themselves looking down at the river more than a hundred feet below.

They had come to the crest of the wall they had viewed hours before from across the river. Above them, looming over the amphitheater, were two giant ceiba trees, their smooth gray trunks as much as twenty feet in circumference, their buttressed roots stretching out for hundreds of feet like the tentacles of an octopus holding down mounds of stones in its tight grip.

The two men, emotionally and physically exhausted, sat down on the edge of the plaza and tried to comprehend what they had just found. Who were the people, they wondered, who had built these monuments and pyramids? And how long ago? The inhabitants of the valley had no idea. There were no written records, and apparently no oral accounts passed down from generation to generation. "All was mystery, dark, impenetrable mystery," Stephens wrote. In Egypt, the temples stood out on the desert sands in open, unguarded nakedness. Here the temples and pyramids lay buried under thick jungle, lost to time and history. Stephens sought to capture the wonder of it:

Architecture, sculpture, and painting, all the arts which embellish life, had flourished in this overgrown forest; orators, warriors, and statesmen, beauty, ambition, and glory had lived and passed away, and none know that such things had been, or could tell of their past existence. It lay before us like a shattered bark in the midst of the ocean, her mast gone, her name effaced, her crew perished, and none to tell whence she came, to whom she belonged, how long on her voyage, or what caused her destruction.

It was a mystery of staggering implications—but there seemed no immediate answers. Not only had Stephens and Catherwood found in Copán evidence of an advanced, seemingly ancient civilization, but the ruins lay in the jungle heart of Central America, a place where no one believed such a civilization could have existed.

They knew immediately the challenge they faced—that this could not be the only proof of civilization in the region, that there must be other signs of ancient settlements in the jungle, other ruins for them to find, and when their existence was made known to the world, human curiosity would not be satisfied until the answers to all their mysteries, their untold stories, were unearthed as well.

◅◅ Stephens ▻▻

I.

At dusk Friedrich Wilhelm Heinrich Alexander, Baron von Humboldt, appeared at the door of President's House late in the spring of 1804. The famous Prussian naturalist had just arrived in Washington to visit with Thomas Jefferson after five years of exploration in Spanish America. Humboldt was always rushing somewhere, hyperactive, restless. He told his American host, the painter Charles Willson Peale, that he had been traveling since he was eleven years old and never lived in any one place for more than six months.[1] After he had landed in Philadelphia, he eagerly accepted the invitation from President Jefferson to come to Washington to talk about his South American discoveries. The District of Columbia was only recently carved out of the Maryland wilderness, still sparsely populated and filled with empty, mud-rutted streets. The stately presidential mansion, which would be named the White House a century later by Theodore Roosevelt, stood out on a naked hill overlooking the Potomac River in the distance.

When Humboldt was shown into the drawing room unannounced, he found the president on the floor surrounded by his grandchildren. An awkward moment passed as Jefferson continued playing with the children before he realized Humboldt was standing in the doorway. Jefferson rose immediately to shake Humboldt's hand. The president loomed tall and slender over the short, sturdy Humboldt. "You have found me playing the fool, Baron," Jefferson said.[2]

During the following two weeks of Humboldt's visit the two men became close friends. They could easily have been father and son, Jefferson still vigorous at sixty-one and Humboldt bursting with energy at thirty-four. They had much in common. They were cultured, well-read offspring of the Enlightenment and Age of Reason, both of them scientists, philosophers, botanists. And each man was coming off a diplomatic and geographic coup of enormous magnitude. They had become, in their different ways, the masters of immense parcels of real estate, covering broad swaths of the Western Hemisphere. Jefferson had accomplished the feat just a year earlier with the purchase of the Louisiana Territory from Napoleon Bonaparte for a paltry $15 million, thereby doubling the size of the United States in a single, brilliant stroke. And Humboldt through the good luck of aristocratic connections had convinced the Spanish crown five years earlier to let him mount a grand, far-reaching exploration of South America in the name of science. Impressed with Humboldt's credentials as a onetime mining expert, the royal court in Madrid was particularly eager to have him survey its colonies' gold and silver resources, even if it meant opening South America to a foreigner.[3]

The Prussian and his assistant, a French doctor and botanist named Aimé Bonpland, sailed for Venezuela in June 1799 carrying with them crates of instruments, every advanced turn-of-the-century tool for scientific measurement. Humboldt underwrote the expedition with a substantial inheritance that had come to him following his mother's death. For the next several years, enduring hardships and danger, the two men roamed through interior regions of the southern continent in parts never before explored or recorded. At one point in 1802, the indefatigable Humboldt set a world altitude record—at least for a Westerner—climbing 19,700-foot Chimborazo, a dormant Ecuadoran volcano thought at the time to be the highest mountain in the world. During their five-year journey the two men collected thousands of specimens in the equatorial jungles and recorded an untold number of measurements.[4] They added Mexico and Cuba to their itinerary before stopping in the United States on their way back to Europe.[5]

Humboldt was an early-nineteenth-century prototype. Explorers arrived first, then the scientists. But few had fashioned a public image of the dashing explorer-scientist plunging into the unknown better than Humboldt, who in his time was nearly as famous as Napoleon. Vast regions of the globe still remained uncharted. Armed with the instruments of science, seemingly inexhaustible energy and daring, Humboldt became an awe-inspiring figure for the giants of natural science to come. "You might truly call him the parent of a grand progeny of scientific travelers," wrote Charles Darwin, who took Humboldt's account of his journey along with him thirty years later when he traveled to South America on HMS *Beagle* and uncovered the biological underpinnings of evolution.[6]

With Jefferson, Humboldt could barely contain himself as he explained the details of his explorations.[7] Jefferson soaked up every tidbit. Even before the Louisiana Purchase had passed Congress, the American president was already scheming to send an exploring expedition up the Missouri River and across unknown regions of the West to the Pacific Ocean. And just three weeks before Humboldt arrived in Philadelphia, two men left St. Louis under orders from Jefferson with a group of hardened frontier soldiers assembled under the name "Corps of Discovery." Their commanders: U.S. Army captain Meriwether Lewis and William Clark.

More than a year after Humboldt returned to Europe, Lewis and Clark reached the Pacific at the mouth of the Columbia River. On November 28, 1805, the date the two men searched for a spot for their winter quarters, John Lloyd Stephens was born in Shrewsbury, a New Jersey farm town located a few dozen miles south of New York City. He was born into a new century whose advent was marked by two of the greatest explorations of the Americas, North and South. For Stephens and the rest of his generation, however, full knowledge of what Lewis, Clark, and Humboldt had accomplished would be slow in coming. Stephens was a one-year-old when the two American explorers arrived back in St. Louis but would be nine before their official narrative was finally published. On the expedition's return, Lewis was assigned to prepare the account but he had not even started when he committed suicide in October 1809. It fell to Clark to take up the project but it was not until 1814 that the *History of the Expedition under the Command of Captains Lewis and Clark* was published.

In Paris, Humboldt had also been struggling with his own long-delayed publications. In the same year that Lewis and Clark's *History* appeared, Humboldt's narrative account of his expedition was published for the first time in English.[8] He was painstakingly putting together volume after volume of the expedition's scientific findings. There would be thirty volumes, the last published in 1834, by which time the great Prussian had exhausted his entire fortune on the project.[9]

Stephens, from his early school days to his practice as a lawyer, like so many of his contemporaries grew up with these two epic tales of discovery. They infused the ethos of his generation. They were thrilling and inspiring, and young John Stephens grew up in a place in America that readily lent itself to boyhood dreams of exploration. His family had left Shrewsbury for New York in 1806, which meant that by the age of one, young John was living in a city with ships sailing in and out of its harbor from every part of globe, offering as wide a view of the world as any place on earth.[10] Though the world was shrinking, large regions of the planet still remained unexplored—and beckoning.

New York was a small city in 1806, the equivalent of a good-size American town by today's standards. It occupied a fraction of the long, narrow island of Manhattan, its seventy-five thousand citizens crowded into a few square miles on the island's southern tip. Most of Manhattan was made up of farms and forest and one could still hunt in the meadows and hills above what is now Houston Street, then the city's northern boundary. Philadelphia was more populous but New York's population was doubling every twenty years. The early Dutch gabled houses along the narrow streets of the old town were giving way to more fashionable two- and three-story brick buildings in the Federal style. Nearby swamps were being filled and streets were being paved with cobblestones even as pigs still ran freely through some districts.

The city held the distinction of serving as the United States' first capital. But the government soon moved on to Philadelphia while the new federal city of Washington was being laid out in Maryland along the Potomac. Twenty years after George Washington's inauguration in 1789, New Yorkers added another touch of grandeur. During John Stephens's preschool years, a grand City Hall was under construction, a flamboyant and shimmering confection faced with white Massachusetts marble, and set in a park in the city's northernmost section, known as the Commons. It would take nine years to complete, and by the time it was finished in 1812 it cost an astounding $500,000 (twice the amount originally budgeted).[11]

A second and even greater sign of civic ambition was the appointment of a special commission in 1807 to lay out plans for the orderly development of the city as it marched northward up the island of Manhattan. It was a visionary act. When the city surveyors finally submitted their plan in 1811, the physical layout of a future New York was fixed, set in stone, literally (stone markers delineated every single corner).[12] The map showed a rigid eight-mile grid of long parallel and short perpendicular streets over the mostly unoccupied island, a street system that remains in place today.[13] The plan set off a frenzy of land speculation that did not cease until the city spread north so fast the entire island was built out in less than a hundred years.

The first few years of Stephens's life were boom times for New York, drawing hundreds of new merchants like his father, Benjamin Stephens. The Napoleonic Wars in Europe had created enormous demand for United States' exports, mainly meat, grain, leather, and timber. From 1790 to 1806 the value of exports flowing out through the city's docks increased tenfold.[14] Equally large quantities of imported European manufactured goods poured in.

Benjamin Stephens entered business as early as 1796, operating between Shrewsbury and New York.[15] By 1806 he was working out of a building on lower Greenwich Street in a live-work arrangement common at the time. His growing family—there would eventually be five children—lived upstairs. Greenwich Street was paved several years earlier and was lined with upscale residences. Its south end terminated at the Battery, which served as John's and his siblings' playground. It was a large open space of mostly landfill, originally set aside by the Dutch and the British for defensive fortifications, overlooking the harbor. By the time the Stephens family arrived, it had evolved into a popular promenade lined with elm trees.

Tensions were mounting, however, over Britain's policy of impressing American sailors into the Royal Navy during its war with France, and the U.S. government wanted new defenses put in place in case of a conflict with England. But instead of lining the promenade with guns, the military began construction in 1808 of a circular sandstone fortress just offshore on a rock outcropping. The fort was fitted out with twenty-eight cannons and connected to the Battery by a two-hundred-foot wooden bridge. As a child, John Stephens watched wide-eyed from the Battery as the fort took shape and its cannons were periodically tested.

From his earliest years, his world was almost entirely circumscribed by water. The masts and spars of sailing ships, thick as forests, filled the end of almost every street. His front yard was not only the parklike Battery but the red-brick sidewalks around Bowling Green at the foot of Broadway. He and his boyhood friends played ball near the green and climbed its iron railings to retrieve the ones that got away.[16] They swam in the clear waters off the Battery in the summer and fished from the wooden bridge to the fort.

The economic boom did not last. No sooner had Benjamin Stephens moved his family to New York than the trade on which he pinned his economic future came to an abrupt halt. In late 1807 President Jefferson ordered a total trade embargo to force England and France to respect American neutrality and the rights of U.S. sailors at sea. The embargo proved a blunder of monumental proportions.[17] It plunged the country, and especially New York, into depression, throwing thousands out of work and bankrupting businesses.

No records remain to indicate how the Stephens family survived, but with one foot still in nearby rural New Jersey, there were family connections to fall back on. Documents and promissory notes, however, show that the firm of "Stephens and Lippincott" survived to handle substantial business transactions in the years right after the embargo was finally lifted.[18] Then war broke out in June 1812 and a British blockade brought New York to its knees again.

Stephens was seven when the conflict started and for his elementary schooling he was under the charge of a teacher known only as Mr. Boyle. As the threat of a British invasion loomed, Stephens and his schoolwork were undoubtedly tested by the distraction. The danger became so palpable, by 1814 it drove New Yorkers into a frenzy of defensive preparations. Anticipating a British attack down the Hudson River from Canada, volunteers dug trenches and built breastworks across upper Manhattan and through Brooklyn. Thousands of militiamen swarmed into the city. Artillery units constantly tested their cannon from the surrounding forts.[19] For a nine-year-old it must have been an anxious yet thrilling time. But the attack never came. The British burned Washington and landed at New Orleans instead. A peace treaty was signed in 1815, and the city's economic fortunes rebounded.

Benjamin Stephens's business began to thrive. Shipments of tea, silks, and lacquered boxes came in from China. In 1816 an expensive china table service arrived from Liverpool for Mrs. Stephens, along with an even more expensive camel-hair shawl.[20] Then, just as the good times returned, the family suffered a series of staggering personal losses. In early 1817, John's grandfather, Judge John Lloyd, died, followed five months later by the death of Clemence, John's mother, who was thirty-three years old. The loss of his mother must have been a devastating blow to eleven-year-old John, and it appears to have drawn him extremely close to his father, to whom he would remain deeply attached for the rest of his life.

By the time of Clemence Stephens's death, Benjamin Stephens had already settled on ambitious plans for his son. John was entering his final year in the school of Joseph Nelson, a blind scholar and expert in classics who later became a distinguished professor of languages at Rutgers College. Nelson appears to have been a calculated choice because entrance to nearby Columbia College, where Stephens was headed, required more than passing familiarity with Latin and Greek. To be admitted, candidates had to demonstrate mastery of Caesar's *Commentaries,* the orations of Cicero, the books of Virgil, Livy, and Homer, the Gospel of St. Luke and St. John and Acts of the Apostles, as well as command of the rules of arithmetic, algebra, and modern geography. School under Nelson was a grueling six-day-a-week assignment with only a few weeks off each year. Stephens must have been a particularly bright and diligent student despite the distractions of war and the trauma of his mother's death. He was able to pass the entrance exams and enter Columbia in 1818 at the age of thirteen, one of the youngest enrollees in school history.

Columbia was housed at the time in a brick and stucco building on Park Place, a short walk from the Stephens home. It was founded by royal charter sixty-five years earlier as King's College. Former students included Alexander Hamilton, later the nation's first secretary of the Treasury; John Jay, the first Supreme Court chief justice; and Robert R. Livingston, who helped draft the Declaration of Independence. The school was closed during the Revolutionary War and reopened after the war as Columbia College.

Columbia was known for producing practical men, mostly homegrown New Yorkers who went on to careers in business, law, and politics. Although the faculty included some excellent teachers, the college was no Harvard or Yale. One professor, however, proved a towering exception: Charles Anthon. A graduate himself of the school, Anthon was twenty-three when he was hired in 1820 to teach Greek and Latin. He was young and brilliant, and a serious influence on Stephens. During his time at Columbia, he published works on the classics that became standard textbooks as far away as Cambridge and Oxford. "This gentleman has done more for sound scholarship at home, and for our classical reputation abroad, than any other individual in America," Edgar Allan Poe wrote in 1837.[21] Stephens would come to deeply appreciate his time with Anthon when he traveled later through Greece and Turkey and wrote so confidently about their history and literature.

During his time in college, Stephens's gregarious nature emerged in full force. Sociable almost to a fault all his life, he became a favorite among his Columbia classmates.[22] He joined both of the school's literary societies, which was unusual since they were rivals. The societies were devoted to oratory and debate, and Stephens was often singled out as a prime speaker.[23] He was a brilliant but generally lax student who nevertheless ably worked his way through the college's tough four-year program of classics, rhetoric, literature, mathematics, geography, ancient antiquities, English grammar, composition and criticism, history, the science of fluxions, chemistry and astronomy, philosophy and political economy.

When his college career was over, Stephens joined New York City's educated elite.[24] The school produced only twenty-three graduates in 1822, and Stephens ranked fourth in his class, a significant achievement given his unusually young age of sixteen. His senior class oration, "On the Oriental and Classical Superstitions as Affecting the Imagination and Feelings," provided a clue to his future.[25] It had cost his father eighty dollars a year in tuition, a handsome sum but readily within the budget of his father's expanding business interests, which increasingly included New York real estate.

Charles Anthon or no, these were practical times in hard-headed New York, and his father decided John would enter the law. Thus, shortly after graduation, John began an apprenticeship at the law offices of Daniel Lord, a twenty-six-year-old Yale graduate just establishing his practice. Lord's former studies at a law school in Litchfield, Connecticut, inspired Stephens's next move. After less than a year as a clerk, he was on his way in June 1823 to enroll at Litchfield Law School.

Set in the green hills of western Connecticut, Litchfield was a primly countrified town with white picket fences and tidy houses, and was nothing at all like New York. Arriving by stagecoach, seventeen-year-old Stephens was enthralled. Litchfield was the nation's first full-time law school. Legal education at the time was mostly conducted through apprenticeships in lawyers' offices. But Litchfield Law School was founded in 1784 as a systematic course of lectures on the principles and practice of the law. Aaron Burr, the U.S. vice president infamous for killing Alexander Hamilton in a duel, was the school's first pupil, instructed personally by Tapping Reeve, his brother-in-law and founder of the school. More than 1,100 young men from every state found their way on horseback or stagecoach to isolated, picturesque Litchfield. In Stephens's class alone, seven of his forty-four classmates became congressmen and more than a third became state supreme court judges or legislators, including one Georgian who drafted the bill of secession for the southern states at the start of the Civil War.

They were taught in a one-room wooden building located in the garden next to Tapping Reeve's home, where daily lectures required detailed note taking and cases were presented weekly by the students in a moot court. It proved a wrenching experience for Stephens. Away from home for the first time and again the youngest member in his class, he was immediately and deeply homesick. He begged his father, brother, and sisters to write and visit him. He missed his family desperately and the New York newspapers—"bring the paper up with you"—but he was also so smitten with the open pastoral countryside around Litchfield that he wondered if he could ever again tolerate the grime, dirty air, and chaos of New York City. He wrote his father: "I would wish no handsomer legacy than that some unknown friend should bequeath to me some little spot within the vicinity of

New York where I could place about a hundred and fifty acres of land with a good house on it."[26]

Over the course of the next year, Stephens would rise at four thirty in the morning six days a week to start his studies. He noted that at Columbia "we would take a sort of pride in showing a neglect of our studies. Here it is considered the best character to be considered a 'hard student.'" Ever affable and outgoing, he enjoyed socializing with schoolmates in their rooms and attending local balls. Even New Year's Day was spent at lectures, but that night he went to a ball, and wrote his father that while he did not know a single lady when he entered, "in a short time I was acquainted with all the belles in the room."

He wrote home every Sunday after attending Episcopal Church services, signing each letter to his father as he would throughout his life with his full name: "Your affectionate son, John L. Stephens." Yet his letters were intimate and personal, and in all the volumes of his later writings and correspondence, nothing captured him so directly and left such a clear and unassuming self-portrait. His affection for his sisters is obvious as he discusses their schooling, their health, and the recent departure of Mrs. Madden, the family's housekeeper, who apparently had become a mother figure after the death of Clemence six years earlier. It saddened him deeply when he learned his father was not coming to visit and he said he felt terrible when his brother Benjamin paid an unexpected visit. "I had to keep up notes and lessons and he felt I was not paying enough attention to him." And he struggled mightily with his handwriting, which everyone had complained was virtually illegible. He tried out a variety of writing styles on the family, including a nearly horizontal script that was as bad if not worse than the one he was trying to replace. "A person can hardly imagine the difficulty of such an apparently trifling an operation as that of altering his writing," he explained. "I have said to my fingers make it so and they make it not so."

The most telling aspect of the letters is his mastery of language at seventeen, an indication of what was to come, and his already strong ambivalence about becoming a lawyer, a feeling that would continue to plague him through his relatively short legal career. The law was not only supposed to provide him with a respectable profession, he said, but provide for him financially as well. But he was skeptical when his father mentioned a sum that Daniel Lord said he would pay him on his return to Lord's law office in New York. "If I am not mistaken his own business after a practice of six or seven years yields him very little if more than the sum he named," he wrote. He added that he heard there were now many more entering law practice than there were clients. In the end, however, he admitted that he could probably make a living at it, if in the profession "many dull, stupid ignoramuses do thrive and soon are able to live upon the fat of the land . . . though [it's] a mortifying idea to hope to succeed because other blockheads do. . . ."

Homesickness, his young age, and the hard labor of his studies undoubtedly contributed to his doubts about continuing at the school. But there was also a lingering sense of youthful literary dreams he felt he was giving up. "This profession is no fairyland in which a person can indulge his heart, content to build castles in the air," he told his father. "Fact, stubborn fact, stares him too broadly in the face to suffer that he should long rove in this world of his own creation, including himself with hopes which can never be realized . . . and show him the slender foundations on which his visionary fabric is erected."

But the matter was out of his hands. While he was several months at the law school, long enough, he thought, to make a case for his misgivings, the final decision about whether he should continue was up to his father. "I have promised to abide by your opinion," he wrote. And when the decision came back that his father wanted him to finish and resume his apprenticeship with Lord, Stephens dutifully accepted it. Doubts and restlessness now banished, he concluded in a letter dated November 30, 1823, "I am now two days past eighteen. Three years yet before the law will allow me to think of living by it."

Never again does Stephens reveal himself so personally. There are flashes of such a Stephens in his scattered future letters, but his books reveal little of his inner life. In all the thousand pages of his writings and letters, for example, there is not a single hint of a significant romantic relationship. Mysterious, unknown Shakespeare with all his cryptic poetry revealed more. And while a reader of Stephens's books would come away with a full and distinct impression of him, often disarming and formal in the same moment, it is the batch of Connecticut letters that most captures his essential character and heart. His father kept most of the letters together; he too must have felt their poignancy.

The correspondence also reveals Stephens struggling in his prose between the charming easygoing style for which he would become famous and the unwieldy constructions of too much learned Latin and Greek. Already he senses it. Responding to a letter from his youngest sister, Clemence, he compliments her on her writing, her use of the words "supremely" "roaring fire," and "bombazet frock," and her pure, unpretentious style. "It all seems so natural," he wrote. "She has put on paper just what she would have said in person."

Stephens's legal career would be one of fits and starts. He concluded his studies in Litchfield at the end of the summer of 1824 and eventually would spend only seven years earning his living at the law, although his training sharpened his mind and served him well in his later work. Yet even before he resumed his clerkship in New York, he fled—a sign of what was to come. Homesickness now abated, he and a cousin, Charles Hendrickson, with their families' reluctant blessing, went on a long "jaunt" out to the Illinois territory. Officially it was a visit to Aunt Helena Ridgway, one of Judge Lloyd's five daughters. Like so many Americans at the time, she had migrated west, with her husband, Caleb Ridgway, to make a new life, and landed in the tiny Illinois prairie town of Carmi. For the two young men in their late teens, driven by wanderlust, it was an adventure too enticing to pass up.

The trip took them first to Pittsburgh and then by keelboat down the Ohio River to Cincinnati, where they visited a Lloyd cousin living in a one-room log cabin. From there they traveled on to Carmi, a place on the very brink of the "wild west." They passed primitive farms and Conestoga wagons, and encountered Indians along the way. The Ridgways were living a hard frontier existence, according to Hendrickson, who described the trip in a series of letters to his mother. Correspondence from Stephens, if there was any, has vanished. Uncle Caleb was reduced to making the family's shoes, Hendrickson reported after their arrival, and for the coming winter he planned to start up a school with twenty pupils. "You know it must be pretty hard times to drive Uncle Caleb to that," Hendrickson wrote.[27]

After more than two months of travel, Hendrickson admitted that they had had enough and couldn't wait to get home. The easiest way was down the Mississippi River by flatboat, then by ship around to New York. His mother wrote and begged them to avoid New Orleans, where yellow fever was then rampant. But Hendrickson assured her it would abate with the cooler weather. Leaving Carmi, the cousins traveled though sparsely populated Shawnee Indian country, one night camping in the woods with pistols drawn and ready. They journeyed down the Mississippi in early December and reached New York sometime in early 1825.

Stephens next took up a clerkship in the law office of George W. Strong. After two years' apprenticeship with Strong, he traveled to Albany, where in 1827 he was finally admitted to the bar. There is little in the record about the next seven years of Stephens's life, during which he practiced in New York. He mentions that he served briefly in the local militia, as was common for young men at that time. And he became seriously involved in local party politics. But his law career remains a mystery, as there are no documents to indicate even what kind of law he practiced—criminal or civil, or both. The only account of this period of his life comes from the Reverend Francis Lister Hawks, who published Stephens's obituary in a New York magazine shortly after his death. According to Hawks, Stephens "never felt or exhibited much ardor or zeal in the pursuit of his profession." His primary interests were political and he was a frequent speaker at Tammany Hall, Hawks wrote. There he undoubtedly displayed the debating skills he had carefully honed at Columbia and Litchfield.

Tammany was a powerful political organization that had used its muscle to help put Andrew Jackson into the presidency. What part Stephens played is not known but he was a committed Jacksonian Democrat and must have spoken in his support. Hawks noted that Stephens delivered impassioned speeches opposing monopolies and in support of free trade. "He spoke from the heart," wrote Hawks. "His manner was earnest and everyone who heard him could see that he felt what he spoke."[28]

Then, in 1834, Stephens's life took an abrupt turn. In an odd twist, the very instrument on which he depended for his political and professional life failed him. He had contracted a serious throat infection that was to change the course of his life.

II.

Stephens was twenty-nine years old when he arrived later that year in Le Havre, France, on the packet ship *Charlemagne*. He had left behind his law practice and a particularly brutal political year in New York. President Andrew Jackson had made good the year before on his promise to, in effect, shut down the Second Bank of the United States, which touched off a vicious mayoral campaign in the spring of 1834. During the election, riots broke out between pro-Jackson and pro-bank partisans. Then riots against abolitionists followed during the summer with ugly attacks on New York's recently emancipated African-Americans. There are no records of Stephens's role in these events but he likely had been drawn into the frays through his connection with Tammany Hall.

By late summer, his throat infection had become so serious

he was forced to consult a doctor. He was told to leave New York, where the city's notoriously bad air would worsen with the fires and smoke of winter. The doctor apparently suggested the balmy air of the Mediterranean, a typical antidote prescribed for throat and lung problems—for those who could afford it—and Stephens readily complied.

From Le Havre he went to Paris, then traveled to Rome, and by February 1835 he had crossed the Adriatic Sea to Greece. There he soaked up site after site of the classical world. What had been mere words and images at Columbia under the tutelage of Charles Anthon now lay in stone before him. Far from nursing himself with the prescribed rest and recuperation, Stephens climbed the acropolis above Corinth to view snowy Mount Parnassus, visited the Lion's Gate and Agamemnon's tomb at Mycenae, and with a copy of Herodotus clambered up the burial mound covering the Greeks who had fallen on the Plain of Marathon. There, sitting alone, he read the account of the epic battle in 490 B.C. between the Persians and the greatly outnumbered Athenians.[29]

In Athens, a city still in ruins from the Greek revolt against the Turks a decade earlier, Stephens made several trips up to its famous Acropolis. "Solitude, silence, and sunset, are the nursery of sentiment," he wrote of his final visit. "I sat down on a broken capital of the Parthenon: the owl was already flitting among the ruins." Looking down on the shattered city, however, sentiment gave way to the pure New Yorker within him:

I said to myself, "Lots must rise in Athens!" The country is beautiful, climate fine, government fixed, steam boats are running, all the world is coming, and lots must rise. I bought (in imagination) a tract of good tillable land, laid it out in streets, had my Plato, and Homer, and Washington Places, and Jackson Avenue, built a row of houses to improve the neighborhood where nobody lived, got maps lithographed, and sold off at auctions. I was in the right condition to "go in," for I had nothing to lose; but, unfortunately, the Greeks were very far behind in

Acropolis at Athens. Illustration from Stephens's book *Incident of Travel in Greece, Turkey, Russia, and Poland,* 1838.

the spirit of the age, know nothing of the beauties of the credit system, and could not be brought to dispose of their conse-crated soil "on the usual terms," ten percent down, balance on bond and mortgage; so giving up the idea, at dark I bade fare-well to the ruins of the Acropolis, and went to my hotel to dinner.[30]

However serious his throat ailment, Stephens was reenergized by his travels. Italy and Greece had been his goal but now the Aegean Sea beckoned, and he found an old brig headed for the Turkish coast. On a whim he took it. He traveled first to Smyrna, today named Izmir, and then on horseback rode south to the ancient ruins of Ephesus. Everything he saw went into his note-book and his description of his journeys ended up in a long letter sent home to friends. Without his knowledge, this correspon-dence came to the attention of Charles Fenno Hoffman, editor of *American Monthly Magazine* in New York, who published the letter serially in four separate issues of his periodical. Later Ste-phens acknowledged the impact those publications had on his life. "Favorable notice taken of it," he wrote, "had some influence in inducing me to write a book."[31] The letter would create an author but, in consequence, also end Stephens's career in the law.

He would gradually gain better control of his writing, but the style in the letter shows the flamboyance of his school days and probably his speeches at Tammany Hall, which were no doubt filled with the rhetorical flourishes common in orations of the time. Earlier, for example, as he prepared to leave Greece, he visited the tomb of Themistocles, one of Athens's greatest heroes. "For more than 2000 years," Stephens wrote, "the waves have almost washed over his grave—the sun has shone and the winds have howled over him; while, perhaps, his spirit has mingled with the sighing of the winds and murmur of the waters, in mourning over the long captivity of his countrymen; perhaps, too, his spirit has been with them in their late struggle for liberty—had hovered over them in battle and breeze, and is now standing sentinel over his beloved and liberated country."[32] This was the writing style of the time, which Stephens was about to transform. The poetics would melt away, not overnight, but Stephens's language would become spare, stripped down, and eventually acquire the fresh, conversational tone for which he would become well known.

He traveled by steamboat to Constantinople, today's Istanbul. "Join me, now in this race," he told his unknown eventual readers, "and if your heart does not break at going at the rate of eight or ten miles an hour, I will whip you over a piece of the most classic ground. . . ."[33] Although the ruins of Troy had yet to be unearthed, Stephens knew they lay somewhere on the plain along the Turkish coast south of ancient Hellespont and the Dardanelles. As his ship steamed along the coast, the poetry of Homer rang through his head with the tales of Helen and Paris, Ajax and Achilles. In the distance he was thrilled to see the island of Tenedos, behind which the Greeks had withdrawn their fleet pretending they had given up the siege of Troy while leaving behind a giant wooden horse as a gift.

Approaching Constantinople from the Sea of Marmara, Ste-

Mosque of Sultan Suleyman in Istanbul.

phens was dazzled by the "glittering crescents and golden points" on the mosques and minarets. His ship swung around the Seven Towers and walls of the seraglio into the Golden Horn, whose banks were covered with tiered gardens and Oriental palaces. His writing captures much of the city's mystery, its filth and pestilence, the beauty of the dome of St. Sophia and mosque of Sultan Achmet, the walls and gates of ancient Byzantium. He visited a slave market and witnessed the launch of a huge ship commissioned by Sultan Mahmud II, the supreme potentate of the Ottoman Empire, who attended the ceremony. "I could not divest myself of the lingering idea of the power and splendor of the sultan," he wrote, "the shadow of God upon the earth. I had wished to see him as a wholesale murderer, who had more blood on his hands than any man living." Instead, Stephens said he found "the plainest, mildest, kindest" man dressed in a "military frock-coat and red tarbouch, with his long black beard the only mark of a Turk about him."[34]

Stephens fell ill in the city, probably from a return of his throat infection which continued to plague him in the months to come. Throughout his journey, however, he managed to escape the horror of a far more serious illness, the plague, which was infecting several of the ports he visited, including Constantinople. His trip to regain his health was, in fact, putting him in even greater peril. Yet he showed some prudence. He desperately wanted to sail to Egypt, but on learning the plague had been ravaging that country for months, he held back. Indeed, at that moment more than a thousand people a day were dying in Alexandria and Cairo. By the time the epidemic burned itself out late that summer, it would claim the lives of up to two hundred thousand Egyptians.[35] There was no way to ignore the disease. Yellow flags at many ports around the Mediterranean indicated they were disease-free but also warned arriving travelers they would be detained for weeks in quarantine stations called lazarettos. A red flag, as was then flying in Alexandria, signaled that the plague had gotten there first.

Stephens's ailment did not keep him down for long. Within days he was on his feet arranging to travel by horseback through the Balkans and by boat up the Danube River to Paris. On impulse he instead took a steamer leaving from Constantinople up through the narrow Bosphorus Strait and across the Black Sea for Russia. Three days later he was anchored off Odessa. Yellow flags flew in the harbor and a Russian health officer came alongside. Stephens and his fellow passengers got their first clue of what was to come when the officer climbed aboard and offered to take letters to the town, then purify and deliver them. "According to his directions," wrote Stephens, "we laid them down on the deck, where he took them up with a pair of long iron tongs, and putting them into an iron box, shut it up and rowed off."

Stephens and the other passengers were soon quarantined together in the lazaretto, a complex of cottages, offices, and inspection and purification buildings—for fourteen days. He was physically examined, his clothes and personal effects fumigated with sulfuric gas, and he and the other passengers were assigned guards who stationed themselves outside their quarters. It was not as unpleasant as he expected. Friendly as ever, he took tea daily with the other passengers, ate at the single restaurant on the grounds ("not first-rate perhaps, but good enough"), and enjoyed an unobstructed view of the sea. But he was ill again and was inundated with advice and prescriptions from the others. They were all apprehensive that his sickness might delay their

Kremlin in Moscow.

release, but on June 7, 1835, they were freed from their confinement on schedule.

What followed for Stephens was an arduous, sometimes exhilarating four-month journey. He had turned his back on the easy route to Paris for a long, roundabout passage through Russia and Poland. At the start, he was so impressed with the sophistication and quality of Odessa—a city built, he wrote, seemingly overnight on command of the czar—that he couldn't help comparing Russia with the United States. Both were young nations bursting with energy, he said, with cities like Odessa emerging out of nowhere—not unlike Rochester, Buffalo, and Cincinnati.

The next part of his journey—the longest and hardest—was over the steppes of Russia, the unending grasslands north of the Black Sea. Stephens was accompanied by an Englishman he had met in Odessa, and a quarrelsome Frenchman they hired as a servant-interpreter. They went by carriage at breakneck pace through the unbroken grasslands, traveling night and day with only post stops for new horses and food, and covered the nearly nine hundred miles to Moscow in fifteen days, with a four-day stopover in the city of Kiev. It was a journey of sweeping vistas and astonishing monotony, and Stephens was one of the first Americans to undertake it, or at least write about it in detail.

In Moscow, he returned several times to the holy ground of the Kremlin. He was struck by the grandeur and beauty of the palaces and domed churches, and haunted by a vision of Moscow only twenty-three years earlier, eerily quiet, empty, abandoned by the Russians as Napoleon's army marched in on September 14, 1812. Within a day of their occupation, fires erupted in different quarters and soon the mostly wooden city began to burn.

> I knew that the magnificent city at my feet had been a sheet of fire. Napoleon, driven from his quarters in the suburbs, hurried to the Kremlin, ascended the steps, and entered the door at which I sat. At midnight again the whole city was in a blaze; and while the roof of the Kremlin was on fire . . . the panes of the window against which he leaned were burning to the touch. Napoleon watched the course of the flames, and exclaimed, "What a tremendous spectacle! These are Scythians indeed!" Amid the volume of smoke and fire, his eyes blinded by the intense heat and his hands burned in shielding his face from its fury, traversing the streets arched with fire, he escaped from the burning city.

Napoleon's glorious victory over the Russians, won just days earlier not far from Moscow in the Battle of Borodino, was irrevocably lost in the flames.

Later, far to the west near the Polish border, Stephens came to a crossroads where Napoleon's demoralized army suffered its final crushing blow. He had been a young boy in New York at the time. But he knew his history. Now it was late summer when he arrived with a traveling companion at the small town of Borosoff, along the Berezina River. While awaiting fresh horses for their carriage, they dined at the post house near a wooden church on the town's square. Then they strolled to the bridge that crossed the river.

"It was a beautiful afternoon, and we lingered on the bridge," Stephens wrote. "Crossing it, we walked up the bank on the opposite side toward the place where Napoleon erected his bridges for the passage of his army." It was here in the freezing days of late November 1812 that the Russians slaughtered thousands of retreating French soldiers. The Russians had burned the only bridge spanning the river, momentarily trapping Napoleon in Borosoff. As a Russian army was approaching on the opposite side, French engineers worked night and day in the icy waters to construct two bridges to carry their beaten army across. Constantly harassed and attacked in its retreat from Moscow, Napoleon's Grande Armée, which that summer had crossed into Russia 400,000 strong, was already reduced to ragged packs of exhausted, starving men fighting for mere survival as an early and particularly brutal Russian winter closed in on them. Napoleon, his Imperial Guard, and two-thirds of the little that remained of his army got across the river before the two Russian armies attacked and trapped the French on both sides. As the French rear guard tried to cross the temporary bridges they were mowed down by Russian artillery and musket fire. By the time it was over Napoleon lost well over half the thirty thousand men he still had who were capable of fighting. But it was the army's thousands of stragglers and camp followers who fared the worst. Most drowned in panic trying to cross the river or were massacred by Russian Cossacks along its banks. It was a scene of horror that had etched itself into Stephens's imagination as a young boy while the Napoleonic epic was still unfolding. And now, as he walked along the peaceful river on a summer afternoon, he visualized the carnage, the blood-soaked ground, fresh details of which had been imparted to him just days earlier by several retired Russian officers he met in St. Petersburg who had lived through the battle.

When Stephens reached Warsaw he once again fell ill. He dutifully took his medicine, rebounded with his usual irrepressible energy, and took in a number of historic Polish sites. As with Russia and Greece, a page of history had been turned recently in Poland. Only four years earlier the Poles had risen against their Russian occupiers, but their revolution was short-lived and violently suppressed. Stephens was taken to the battlefield outside the city where thousands of the Polish resisters had fallen repulsing waves of Russians attacks. And he visited the celebrated site of Vola, five miles outside Warsaw, where the country's nobles traditionally camped and elected each new Polish king. Now, Stephens noted, most of Poland's leaders were dead or in exile. And the country's population, still fiercely proud, was deeply demoralized by the continuing Russian occupation.

"I felt all the time I was in Warsaw, that though the shops and coffee-houses were open and crowds thronged the streets, a somber air hung over the whole city; and if for a moment this impression left me, a company of Cossacks, with their wild music, moving to another station, or a single Russian officer riding by in a drosky, wrapped in his military cloak, reminded me that the foot of the conqueror was on the necks of the inhabitants of Warsaw."

Stephens's next stop was Krakow, and there he abruptly ends his travel account. The full story of his journey takes up more than five hundred pages in *Incidents of Travel in Greece, Turkey, Russia and Poland,* a book he published three years later.[36]

He left no account of his next months in central Europe. We know only that he arrived at Paris sometime in the fall of 1835 with the apparent intention of returning home to New York but something changed his mind. He decided instead to risk a trip to Egypt. Stephens's biographer Victor Wolfgang von Hagen speculates that his new plan may have been prompted by a book he found in Paris by two Frenchmen describing their exploration of the mysterious ancient city of Petra, located today in southern Jordan. Also in Paris, Stephens undoubtedly learned that the plague in Egypt had abated. And he was about to turn thirty. For many men of that era, thirty was no longer young. Most of Stephens's friends had already settled into careers and marriage. Stephens for the moment was free of such encumbrances but a life of conventional respectability like his father's was looming before him. As was his unsatisfying mistress: the law. Egypt and Petra must have represented one last escape.

Whatever the reason, his change of plans would prove momentous, another turning point in his life, and would have more to do with his becoming an explorer and author than anything that had come before. "It was also to change the course of American archaeological history," wrote Von Hagen.[37] Stephens boarded a steamer in Marseilles for the island of Malta. There he was again quarantined in a lazaretto, this time for a month. He finally landed in Alexandria in December 1835.

Like his ramblings through Greece, Russia, and Poland, Stephens's adventures in the Near East—his journey up the Nile and trek across the Sinai desert—would provide rich, entertaining material for a book. Like many other "gentleman travelers" of the nineteenth century, he was, in effect, a tourist, traveling to see the sights. Yet he was also a preternaturally keen observer and compulsive note taker. And when he later sat down and worked his notes into books, he understood the value of being selective. He was conscious that readers were interested in novelty, in being taken to places they had never been, or at least had not already read about. So he left out all detail of his travels through England, France, Italy, and Germany, which must have filled more than a few notebooks. He wrote about countries few had visited and, like a true journalist, timely places—Greece soon after its war with the Turks, Poland after its revolt against the Russians—and novel, historic figures: he describes in sharp detail a personal interview in Cairo with Muhammad Ali, Egypt's all-powerful pasha who had gained world renown at the time for bloodthirsty ruthlessness. Stephens also found in these places that he himself was a novelty, one of the first Americans on the scene. And he would be the first American, with an American perspective, to report back to his young country what he found.

Yet in deciding to travel to the stone city of Petra—and he would be the first American to do so—Stephens understood that the stakes were especially high. Only a handful of Europeans had visited the isolated ruins and lived to tell of it. The sprawling site filled with classical architecture lay hidden in a deep canyon for nearly two thousand years, occupied and guarded by the possessive Bedouin tribes of the surrounding desert. It was finally "rediscovered" by the Swiss explorer Johann Burckhardt in 1812, and

Boat on the Nile in Cairo. Illustration from *Incidents of Travel in Egypt, Arabia Petraea, and the Holy Land*, 1837.

afterward only six other Europeans had dared to venture there.

On his journey up the Nile, in contrast, Stephens was the classic sightseer, albeit a pioneering one whose writings would open a path for the thousands who would follow. Few Western-ers in the seventeenth and eighteenth centuries had penetrated Egypt and Arabia while those areas were under the control of the Turkish Ottoman Empire—until Napoleon landed his army in Alexandria in 1798. Bonaparte insisted that a large group from the French academy—eminent scientists, linguists, geographers, and artists—accompany him on his conquest of Egypt. In the decades afterward, the French were followed by a hardy band of proto-archaeologists, treasure hunters, and artists like Rifaud, Belzoni, Wilkinson, Hay, and Stephens's eventual traveling part-ner, Catherwood, all of whose visual and textual works began to reveal in great detail the wonders along the Nile.

Stephens knew he was traveling over well-covered ground. And he understood, when he later sat down to write, that any contribution he could make would not be scholarly or artistic, but rather to make Egypt accessible, readable. For most Ameri-cans and Europeans, Egypt was still intriguingly exotic. Thus the ancient temples would provide a first-rate backdrop to his personal story—the hiring of a boat and its ten-man crew, his loneliness (homesickness again?) and struggle to communicate, his frustration over surprisingly cold nights and the maddening headwinds on the river, his eager encounters with other English-speaking travelers, his attempt to mount a caravan to the "great oasis" in the Sahara thwarted by yet another attack of his old sickness. He rambled through Luxor, Karnak, Philae, Edfu, and other well-documented sites, crawled deep into a shaft inside the Great Pyramid at Giza, and visited the catacombs of the sacred birds near Memphis. And, like any good chatty tourist, he talked about ease and comfort—and prices:

> For myself, being alone, and not in very good health, I had some heavy moments; but I have no hesitation in saying that, with a friend, a good boat well fitted up, books, guns, plenty of time . . . a voyage on the Nile would exceed any traveling within my experience. The perfect freedom from all restraint, and from the conventional trammels of civilized society, form an episode in a man's life that is vastly agreeable and exciting. Think of not shaving for two months, of washing your shirts in the Nile, and wearing them without being ironed. You may go ashore whenever you like, and stroll through the little villages, and be stared at by the Arabs, or walk along the banks of the river till darkness covers the earth; . . . and then it is so ridiculously cheap an amusement. You get your boat with ten men for thirty or forty dollars a month, fowls for three piasters (about a shilling) a pair, a sheep for half or three-quarters of a dollar and eggs almost for the asking. You sail under your own country's banner; and when you walk along the river, if the Arabs look particularly black and truculent, you proudly feel that there is safety in its folds. From time to time you hear that a French or English flag has passed so many days before you, and you meet your fellow-voyagers with a freedom and cordiality which exists nowhere but on the Nile.

◦◦◦

Stephens did not invent this type of personal storytelling. By the middle of the nineteenth century such travel writing had become a well-worn genre, the writing pedestrian and formal. In Stephens's hands it was much more—natural and refreshing.

Visiting Petra, however, was no tourist stroll around pyramids. It was dangerous exploration, thrilling and infectious—a true adventure that would reorient Stephens's life and help explain why, a few years later, he would be standing in the heart of the Central American jungle, in Copán, in the middle of a civil war.

To get to Petra, Stephens would have to cross the harsh desert east of Cairo and risk his life among the nomads of Arabia Petraea, fierce Bedouin tribesmen whose reputation for robbery and murder were hard earned. He planned to stop first at Aqaba, travel north to Petra, and then cross through a region known as Idumea to Palestine, his final destination. Travel through Idumea presented another danger, and one he did not take lightly. To do so, he had been told, would mean defying an old biblical curse at the risk of death. According to the Hebrew prophets, the ancient inhabitants of Idumea, the Edomites, had provoked God's wrath and were destroyed, and a curse was laid upon their land "that none shall pass through it forever and ever."[38] Stephens was determined to risk it. He had no intention of following the usual safe route through Gaza to Jerusalem, which he learned would force him to endure another lengthy quarantine.

Everyone he consulted in Cairo tried to dissuade him from going. Their warnings in particular about Idumea only spurred him on. He had learned that none of the earlier Petra explorers had risked traveling all the way through desolate Idumea. This fact alone was the most salient for Stephens. Unlike his earlier travels, here was the chance to accomplish a real first. Yet he knew the odds of success did not look good. He still had not fully recovered his health. There were ruthless Bedouin to contend with. He could not speak Arabic. The desert itself could be treacherous and unforgiving. And he would be alone except for his interpreter, Paolo Nuozzo, from Malta, "who, instead of leading me on and sustaining me when I faltered, was constantly torturing himself with idle fears, and was very reluctant to accompany me at all."

None of it mattered. The temptation to set a precedent, to face down the dangers, even the wrath of God, was simply too great. It was a pivotal moment for Stephens. He could return home a tourist, or go forward, overcome all obstacles, and carve out at least a footnote in history.

There was one stop, however, Stephens felt compelled to make before reaching Petra. It would lead him miles out of his way, but as a lawyer it was a detour he had to take. And after ten days of traveling across the Sinai Peninsula by camel, surviving a blinding sandstorm, going without water for days, and camping along the shore of the Red Sea where Moses led his people through the parted waters, Stephens finally arrived at the mountain where God had handed down his laws—the Ten Commandments. "Can it be, or is it a mere dream?" he asked in wonder, standing on the summit of Mount Sinai. "Can this naked rock have been the witness of that great interview between man and his maker? Where, amid thunder and lightning, and fearful quaking of the mountains, the Almighty gave to his chosen people the precious tables of his law . . . ?"

Stephens arrived next at the fortress at Aqaba, exhausted and sick again with his old ailment. This time, however, he felt bad enough to self-medicate with everything he could find in his medicine case, doubling the dosage. He was so ill that he half-fell from his dromedary before the fort's gate and was carried to an open room in the fortress where the Bedouin crowded in day and night to see the curiosity—the white man with the red beard. Approaching Aqaba, which is located at the tip of northeastern branch of the Red Sea, Stephens had been warned by his Arab guides that they were entering a district of dangerous tribes and must "look to our weapons." Stephens broke out the disguise he had been carrying with him: a Turkish outfit designed to make him look like a merchant from Cairo. It consisted of a red silk gown over baggy white pants, a green and yellow striped cloth twisted like a turban around the red felt tarboosh on his

"Merchant of Cairo with pistols and sabre." Stephens adopted the look
—including the weapons.

head, and yellow slippers covered by red shoes. He wore around
his waist a wide sash, which held his sword and two large Turkish pistols. He was immediately complimented by his guides for
his "improved" appearance. But the Bedouin of Aqaba were not
fooled. By this time news that he was coming had reached the
fort. They pushed and shoved their way to view him lying on his
sickbed like some exotic, wounded animal.

He already had misgivings about staying the course to Petra,
and now, with his health failing, he was utterly despondent. Earlier he saw a Turk in a caravan of pilgrims on their way to Mecca
die in the desert, and he wondered if he, too, would meet a stranger's death in a foreign land. It was the lowest point in his travels.
"I was sick body and soul," he wrote. "I was ten days from Cairo;
to go there in person was impossible: and if I should send, I could
not obtain the aid of a physician in less that twenty-five or thirty
days, if at all; and before that I might be past his help."

He passed a wretched night and felt even worse in the morning. He was laboring under the effects of a double emetic, "an-
noyed to death by seeing twenty or thirty pairs of fiery black eyes

Fortress at Aqaba.

constantly fixed upon me," and then, seemingly out of nowhere Sheik El Alouin appeared. Stephens had met the sheik weeks earlier in Cairo, where the tribal leader agreed that if Stephens made it to Aqaba he would provide him with an escort to Petra. "He looked surprised and startled when he saw me," Stephens wrote. "But, with a glimmering of good sense, though, as I thought, with unnecessary harshness, told me I would die if I stayed there . . ." Stephens agreed, thinking it would be better to die in a tent in the desert than spend another night in the fortress. His spirits rose when the sheik told him that he had brought Stephens an Arabian horse of the very best blood. "He could not have given me more grateful intelligence for the bare idea of again mounting my dromedary deprived me of all energy and strength."

Stephens had taken the precaution of carrying only the amount of money that he calculated would be needed for his journey, including generous payments to the sheik and his entourage for their services and the hire of their camels. But on his departure from Aqaba, Stephens sensed for the first time that he may have miscalculated. Because of the largesse of the two

Frenchmen who traveled to Petra nine years earlier and generously "showered" the Bedouin of Aqaba with gold, Stephens received only scowls when he had Paolo sprinkle small amounts of
goodwill cash among the inhabitants. His bigger concern, however, was the sheik, who had brought provisions for ten days'
journey for ten men, six camels, and two horses. The cost of the
camels had been settled in Cairo but the sheik had put off how
much "baksheesh," or payment for services, he expected personally, and they never arrived at an amount. It proved a constant
irritant during the expedition as the sheik repeatedly attempted
to pry from Paolo just how much money Stephens was carrying
and what he planned to pay.

The desert air the first night helped revive Stephens. The next
day they traveled north through an immense valley, forbidding
and empty with barren mountains on each side. But the weather
was perfect and Stephens was rapturous about his horse. "If anything connected with my journey in the East could throw me
into ecstasies, it would be the recollection of that horse," he
wrote. "Mounted on the back of my Arabian, I felt a lightness of
frame and an elasticity of spirit that I could not have believed
possible in my actual state of health." Each day Stephens grew
stronger.

Every report Stephens had received about the Bedouin in the
area, including the sheik's own tribe, had been harrowing.
Burckhardt, who journeyed as an Arab and spoke Arabic flaw-
lessly, said the route was "the most dangerous he had ever traveled." He described how those who guarded Petra had even
robbed him of the rags that covered his wounded ankles. Four
Englishmen who explored Petra in 1818 reported that in the year
before their visit thirty Muslim pilgrims had been murdered at
the ruins. Stephens's own escort was reputed to be one of the
"most lawless tribes of a lawless race." He described them as "by
far the wildest and fiercest-looking of all I had yet seen; dark
eyes, glowing with a fire approaching to ferocity; figures thin
and shrunken, though sinewy; chests standing out, and ribs projecting from the skin, like those of a skeleton." The sheik was

Bedouin near Petra.

dressed in a red silk gown like Stephens with a scarlet cloak, and he carried pistols, a curved sword, and a twelve-foot spear with steel points at both ends.

Stephens did not have to wait long to discover the risk he had taken. The second night out, as they camped around a fire, his party was attacked by two men. "Hardly had they reached my men, before all drew their swords, and began cutting away at each other with all their might." He could not, he wrote, but "admire the boldness of the fellows, two men walking up deliberately and drawing upon ten. The sheik, who had been absent at the moment, sprang in among them, and knocking up their swords with his long spear, while his scarlet cloak fell from his shoulders, his dark face reddened, and his black eyes glowed in the firelight, with a voice that drowned the clatter of their weapons, roared out a volley of Arabic gutturals which made them drop their points and apparently silenced them with shame." Stephens was stunned when only a short time later one of the attackers was helping to bind the wounds of the sheik's brother. Then they all sat down together to share pipes and coffee.

It took several more days through empty desert before they entered the mountain approaches to Petra. Throughout, the sheik constantly harped on the dangers of the route, his friendship and loyalty to Stephens "from the first moment he saw me," and his willingness to sacrifice his life for him. "I suspected him of exaggerating the dangers of the road to enhance the value of his services," Stephens said. As they veered off the main route toward Petra, the sheik explained to Stephens that he would need plenty of money to buy off the hostile Bedouin tribe living near the ruins' entrance. It could cost Stephens thirty to forty dollars if there were only thirty to forty of them, the sheik said. But there might be two or three hundred and Stephens should give him his purse so that the sheik could go ahead and pacify them with baksheesh. Stephens, already disgusted with the sheik's constant harassment about money, refused. That night there was a showdown in Stephens's tent. He explained that he had brought a specific sum and all of it was intended for the sheik and his men at the end of the journey, and that if the sheik scattered money along the way it would have to come out of his pay. "He was evidently startled," Stephens wrote, "and expressed his surprise that a howaga, or gentleman, should have a bottom to his pocket, but promised to economize in the future."

The next morning the sheik left half his men to guard their baggage and tents, while he took Stephens, Paolo, and the rest around the base of Mount Hor, the mountain that held the tomb of Moses's brother, Aaron, on its summit. The sheik's plan, though he did not disclose it to Stephens, was to enter Petra through the back door. After Stephens's warning the night before, the sheik had no intention of sharing his baksheesh with the Bedouin guarding the main, and far more dramatic, entrance into Petra. Instead, Stephens and the sheik, riding in advance on their horses, ascended for some time a steep stony path and eventually came to a series of tombs cut into the sides of the rock walls. They stood finally at the alternate, unguarded entrance to Petra, a stunning city carved out of rock in the second century B.C. by the Nabateans. For hundreds of years it had served as the principal crossroad for trading caravans coming up from the Red Sea, a stronghold protected by stone cliffs forming a natural mountain fortress. And for centuries, Petra's wealth and magnificence had made it an attractive target. In A.D. 106 it fell to the Romans. Hadrian later made it a provincial capital. Christian sects flourished for a time, but eventually it fell into ruins following the Arabian conquests in the seventh century. It lay abandoned and desolate, slowly collapsing under the effects of earthquakes and erosion.

Descending into the main valley that formed the central part of the city, Stephens stared in wonder at the temples, the elaborate façades of dwellings and public buildings, the burial grounds, stairways, and perfectly columned porticos, all cut directly into surrounding rock walls. He was disappointed, however, that he had not entered through the narrow gorge that had been described by earlier explorers as the main pathway into Petra. He asked if this was the only way in and the sheik insisted it was. After riding through the length of the city, however, Stephens spied the entrance he had read about, and he set out on foot through what appeared no more than a long vertical crack in a rock wall located across from a fabulous temple. The narrow defile, hardly wide enough for two horses, wound in serpentine fashion through the spectacular gorge, its vertical sides nearly touching above and casting the passage in deep shadows. On each side were the doorways of tombs. "Wild fig-trees, oleanders and ivy were growing out of the rocky sides of the cliffs hundreds of feet above our heads; the eagle was screaming above us," he wrote. After he had gone almost a mile through the twisting corridor, the sheik and his men came running up the deep ravine after him, shouting "El Arab, el Arab!" Stephens finally realized what the sheik had done, and that up ahead, if he had gone much farther, he would have come out upon the dreaded Wadi Musa tribe, which lived just outside the entrance and considered Petra their private property.

When he turned and hurried back to reenter Petra, he saw through the crack in the narrow canyon walls the dramatic scene

Al Khazneh ("The Treasury") in Petra. Illustration by Léon de Laborde, reproduced in Stephens's *Incidents of Travel in Egypt, Arabia Petraea, and the Holy Land.*

others had described so vividly: the astonishing façade of the temple opposite, cut deeply into the rose-colored rock. As he emerged from the passageway, across the small open space stood Al Khazneh, as it was called by the Arabs, or the Treasury, its portico framed by Corinthian columns and richly ornamented with classical figures. Rising more than one hundred and thirty feet, the façade was decorated with eagles, equestrian groups, and winged statues, all chiseled out of the rose rock with such precision it looked brand-new. The sight took Stephens's breath away. "Entering by this narrow defile," he wrote, "with the feelings roused by its extraordinary and romantic wildness and beauty, the first view of that superb façade must produce an effect which could never pass away."

Stephens knew he had a single day at most to take it all in.

Tomb at Petra.

The sheik warned they could not spend the night in the ruins without great risk to their lives. "I hurried from place to place, utterly insensible to physical fatigue," Stephens wrote. "I clambered up broken staircases and among the ruins of streets; and, looking into one excavation, passed on to another and another, and made the whole circuit of the desolate city." He and Paolo finally came to rest at a huge amphitheater carved into the mountainside and capable of holding an audience of thousands. "I could have lingered for days on the steps of that theater, for I never was at a place where such a crowd of associations pressed upon my mind." But the warm light of the sinking sun was already bathing the canyon's wall, and the cliffs above glowed with "veins of white, blue, red, purple, and sometimes scarlet and light orange, running through it like rainbows . . . a peculiarity and beauty that I never saw elsewhere." The sheik hovered impatiently in the background, insisting they leave "while there was still time." Stephens mounted his Arabian and they galloped through the ruins, rising up to the high pass where they had entered. It was already dark when they found themselves just outside the valley, facing the initial range of tombs they had encountered. They selected an empty one to make their bed for the night and Stephens threw himself on the floor exhausted. "I had just completed one of the most interesting days in my life," he wrote, "for the singular character of the city, and the uncommon beauty of its ruins."

Days later they entered Hebron, the southern outpost of Palestine and one of the world's oldest cities. Stephens had clambered over the ruins of Petra, then climbed Mount Hor to Aaron's tomb, endured more encounters with the Bedouin of the desert, and, most important, had survived the curse of the prophets, convinced he was the first non-Arab to completely traverse the full length of Idumea since God laid waste to its once-fertile valleys.

Now he had only to survive the sheik and his men. Hebron, a whitewashed town located on a hillside in the heart of Judea, was the place where the sheik's contract with Stephens ended. The city was under the rigid control of the Turks and because of it, its population was largely disarmed. Stephens agreed to secure the protection of the governor for the sheik and his men, who as outlaw Bedouin of the desert were reluctant to enter. They proceeded nonetheless, and in dramatic fashion, with the sheik leading the way. "Leaving the baggage camels at the gate," wrote Stephens, "with our horses and dromedaries on full gallop, we dashed through the narrow street up to the door of the citadel, and in no very modest tones demanded an audience with the governor." Although Turks and Arabs, Stephens noted, are "proverbial for their indifference," their entrance had created such a sensation that "men stopped in the midst of their business; the lazy groups in the cafes sprang up, and the workmen threw down their tools to run out and stare at us. It was a strange and startling occurrence to see a party of lawless Bedouins coming in from the desert, armed to the teeth, and riding boldly up to the gates of the citadel."

Although outraged by their intrusion, the governor fortunately was ill and, seeing a Westerner, asked if Stephens could supply him with some medicine. "I was quite equal to the governor's case, for I saw that he had merely half-killed himself with eating, and wanted clearing out," Stephens recalled. "I had with me emetics and cathartics that I well knew were capable of clearing out a whole regiment." Stephens and his wild entourage were then taken to the Jewish quarter, where he was warmly welcomed by the rabbi of Hebron. "I shall never forget the kindness with which, as a stranger and Christian, I was received by the Jews in the capital of their ancient kingdom."

The final showdown with the sheik, however, could no longer be put off. All along the route from Aqaba to Hebron, the sheik had hounded him about money, and now Stephens offered him all that he had, holding back only enough to get to Beirut, where a letter of credit awaited him. "The sheik and his whole suite had been following close at my heels, through the narrow lanes and streets, up to the very doors of the synagogue," Stephens wrote. "And their swarthy figures, their clattering swords, and grim visages prevented my seeing the face of many a Hebrew maiden. I expected a scene with them at parting, and I was not disappointed." When he laid out on a table the agreed price for the camels and separately the baksheesh for each of them, they appeared so stunned that "not one of them touched it, but all looked at the money and at me alternately, without speaking a word (it was about ten times as much as I would have had to pay for the same service anywhere else)."

They were furious. Stephens argued that he had paid them extravagantly and had also given them all of his tent and camp equipment, his arms and ammunition. He took some comfort knowing that he now had the protection of the Turkish governor, whereas in the desert he would have been totally at their mercy. "As I rose the sheik fell," Stephens wrote, "and when I began working myself into a passion at his exorbitant demand, he fell to begging a dollar, or two, in such moving terms that I could not resist." Finally the sheik was reduced to begging for the clothes off Stephens's back. Stephens refused. The sheik became so outraged he took the money Stephens had offered and threw in it onto the floor, raving that no foreigner would ever traverse his country again, and rushed out of the room.

Of course, it was not over. A short time later the sheik and his brother were back. Both sides were remorseful. Stephens conceded he would part with his merchant costume, and the sheik said all he wanted was to be Stephens's friend and protector— and a letter of recommendation to any other Westerners who might want to visit Petra. The next day they settled up. Stephens gave him the money, the clothing, the letter, and "pretty much everything I had except my European clothes, completing my present with a double barreled gun, rather given to bursting, which I gave to the sheik's brother." The sheik kissed Stephens on both sides of his face, declared he loved him as much as his own brother, said that if Stephens returned and converted to Islam he would give him four of the most beautiful girls from his tribe for wives, and then he was gone. "I looked after them as long as they continued in sight," Stephens recalled, "listened till I heard the last clattering of their armor, and I never saw nor do I wish to see them again."

Stephens suffered several more bouts of illness as he crisscrossed the Holy Land. He visited the River Jordan and took a boat out onto the Dead Sea. In Jerusalem he got around the city using the map published a year earlier by an artist named "F. Catherwood," whose name he recognized had been carved, along with others, on monuments along the Nile. Sometime in late April Stephens reached Beirut. "My travels in the East were abruptly terminated," he wrote. "After lying ten days under the attendance of an old Italian quack, with a blue frock-coat and great frog button, who frightened me to death every time he approached my bedside, I got on board the first vessel bound for sea, and sailed for Alexandria." From there he went to Genoa, traveled up to London, and finally, later that summer, crossed the Atlantic.

In New York, when his first book came out it created an immediate sensation. The two-volume work, *Incidents of Travel in Egypt, Arabia Petraea, and the Holy Land*, was released in September 1837, only a year after Stephens's return. The work met with uniformly gushing reviews and was so popular that within a year it went through ten editions, including two in England. "These volumes are amongst the most agreeable of travels that we have ever read," wrote the *Monthly Review* in London. "Nor is it possible to arrive at their conclusion without desiring that another such pair by the same hand were within reach for instant consultation. He has eminently distinguished his narrative by impressing upon every such object the feelings which they excited in him, conferring upon them the vividness and freshness which enable the reader to accompany him with an ardour, if not equal, at least akin, to that which the writer partook of in his own person. We do not perceive any striving after effect, or any sort of exaggeration."[39]

The success of the publication was an unprecedented achievement for an American author, a feat all the more astounding because the book came out at the start of one of the worst economic depressions since America's founding.[40] In other ways, the New York City that Stephens left in 1834 was not the city he returned to two years later. On a freezing December night in 1835, about the time he was stepping ashore in Egypt, a fire raged through lower Manhattan that was so fierce its glow could be seen as far away as New Haven, Connecticut, and Philadelphia. It roared across the city's commercial district, only blocks from where Stephens had grown up, consuming fifty-two acres of buildings from Broad Street to the East River and from Coenties Slip in the south to Wall Street in the north, destroying almost everything in its path. It burned for two days, and it took two weeks before its last embers were put out. It was the greatest urban fire since the conflagration that burned London in 1666 and Moscow in 1812. When the blaze ended, 674 buildings had been destroyed. Twenty-three of New York's twenty-five fire insurance companies went bankrupt.

We have no account of whether Stephens's father's business had been directly affected. But by the time Stephens arrived home in late summer of 1836, less than a year following the fire, a new city was rising from the ashes. Five hundred buildings were under construction or already built. The old seventeenth-century Dutch lanes, narrow and crooked, that had once meandered through the district were being straighten and widened into modern gas-lit streets. And a new inferno was raging: a real estate boom fueled by easy, inflated paper money. A speculative surge in Manhattan land values had already been under way when Stephens left for Europe, but now it flared out of control. So feverish had the reconstruction boom become, some of the burned and cleared properties now commanded prices that far exceeded their values with their previous structures intact.

And then it was over. Stephens was back barely nine months and the nation's economy collapsed in the infamous "Panic of 1837." In May of that year New York banks could no longer pay their depositors in hard currency, or gold and silver "species," as it was known. The crisis spread as bank after bank failed across the country, businesses shut down, and unemployment soared to record levels.[41]

When the panic began, Stephens was nearing completion of his book. He started it not long after his return, putting off any full-time return to the law. Encouraged by favorable comments from friends regarding his published travel letter, he dropped in at 82 Cliff Street, a plain brick building seven blocks north of Wall Street in an area untouched by the fire. There he met James Harper, the oldest of four brothers whose firm, Harper & Brothers, was one of the country's foremost publishing houses. The brothers had begun years before as printers but quickly branched out into publishing. They were making a small fortune reprinting mostly English authors, a lucrative business since America had no international copyright laws, and thus they were not obligated to pay out any royalties to the foreign authors. By the time Stephens showed up, however, the house was beginning to nurture homegrown American writers.

Stephens asked Harper, according to one account, what kind of books sold the best. "Travel sells about the best of anything we get hold of," Harper said. "They don't always go with a rush, like a novel by a celebrated author, but they sell longer and in the end, pay better." Aware that Stephens had just returned from two years of travel, Harper suggested he write a book about his journeys.

"Never thought of such a thing," Stephens replied. "I traveled in out-of-the-way places and went very fast."

"That's no matter. You went through and saw the signs. We've got plenty of books about those countries. You just pick out as many as you want, and I will send them home for you. You can dish up something."[42]

By the next summer, the first plates for Stephens's book were being readied for the printer. But Harper & Brothers, like nearly every firm in New York, was in serious financial straits. With the boom over, the brothers had cut back severely on the number of books they published, going from an average of two a week in 1834 to one a month in the summer of 1837.[43] Stephens's manuscript, however, had generated so much enthusiasm among the brothers that they decided to go ahead with it. It helped that Stephens was also able to put up four hundred dollars of his own—or his father's—money, a substantial sum at the time, toward the cost of getting the first edition into print. It would turn out to be one of the best investments he ever made. Not only did Stephens get the usual royalty arrangement with the house—an even split of all net profit—but his agreement stipulated that after seven years he would be allowed to purchase the copyright and the stereotype printing plates at no more than the cost of the plates.[44] The book would ultimately make a fortune, selling straight through the end of nineteenth century, and it continues in print today.

Stephens poured himself into the work, and incredibly, finished the 522-page, two-volume book in less than eight months. He then employed the often-used convention of the day by publishing it anonymously, yielding to the notion that writing books was not a respectable pursuit for gentlemen and professionals. As a result, the author of the first edition is identified only as "An American."

There was another reason for the anonymity. Stephens had doubts about whether the book was any good. In fact, as the publication date approached, he decided to leave town and traveled up the Hudson River to Albany to pay a visit to the family of Stephen Van Rensselaer III, one of the state's wealthiest landowners. While upstate, Stephens found he had not escaped the publication of his book after all. He was seated at the family's dinner table one night when a servant brought in the latest edition of the *Albany Evening Journal*. One of the young ladies opened the newspaper and started reading when her father asked "if there was any news."[45] She replied there was a new book that the *Journal* thought was extremely charming "and I suppose must be, for ma believes everything the *Journal* says." She was asked to read the article, which delighted everyone so much they sent a servant to "Little's," the local bookstore, for a copy. Unknown to the family, the guest sitting at their table was the book's "American" author. Stephens, however, said nothing and soon excused himself.

He tracked down the paper's editor, Thurlow Weed, and in a short time showed up at his house. Weed, who would later become a major force in American politics, had once worked alongside the Harpers as a journeyman printer and usually received advanced copies of their books to review. Later, in his autobiography, he explained: "I wrote an elaborate and glowing review, predicting an extended sale of [Stephens's] book, and bestowing high praise upon its unknown author." Stephens arrived at his house, he wrote, "with emotions that cannot be described." He introduced himself, related what had just taken place at the Rensselaer residence, and thanked Weed for his review. Weed continued: "He left New York, he said, nervously anxious and doubtful about the reception of his book, the publication of which had been urged by those whose affection he feared had misled their judgments." Stephens's successful style, Weed went on to say, had come about from writing long letters he thought would be read by only family and friends, and "this circumstance imparted a freshness and freedom to his letters which constitutes the peculiar charm of his books. Stephens was not less interesting in conversation than as a writer. We became close friends."[46]

Stephens's anonymity did not last long, as it was obvious to many in New York City that only Stephens could have written *Incidents*. In the October issue of the *New York Review*, he received one of his most glowing reviews yet, from a writer who himself was trying hard to get his first novel published by Harper & Brothers. Edgar Allan Poe, who was at the time an influential critic, devoted seventeen pages to a detailed analysis of the book, in which he identified Stephens in the first paragraph. "Mr. Stephens has here given us two volumes of more than ordinary interest—written with a freshness of manner, and evincing a manliness of feeling, both worthy of high consideration," wrote Poe, who, as a reviewer, could be savagely caustic at times. He devoted a large part of the review to discussing Stephens's journey through Idumea; he was fascinated with the prophets' biblical curse and Stephens's ability to survive it. But in the end, he was taken by the sheer appeal of Stephens's writing and the persona he had created on the page. "The volumes are written in general with a freedom, a frankness, and an utter absence of pretension, which will secure them the respect and good-will of all parties. We take leave of Stephens with sentiments of hearty respect. We hope it will not be the last time we shall hear from him. He is a traveler with whom we shall like to take other journeys."[47]

Stephens had hit a vein of gold. Everyone, it seemed, wanted the journey to continue, so he quickly "dished" up his second two-volume work: *Incidents of Travel in Greece, Turkey, Russia and Poland*, which was published by the Harpers the next year. It, too, brought favorable reviews—and considerable money. "Before Mr. Stephens shall have attained his 'middle age,'" wrote the *Southern Literary Messenger* in August 1839, "he will accumulate a competent fortune from his writings—an extraordinary fact in the history of American authorship, and the more remarkable when it is considered that he was not educated to literature."[48]

The reviewer was obviously referring to Stephens's education at law and was unaware of how much Stephens had learned from his classical education, from Charles Anthon, and how much—stylistically—he had had to unlearn.

Stephens now had little interest or need to return to the law. But what now could take its place, given that he had exhausted all his travel material? The answer came in a petition from the New-York Historical Society to the state legislature to finance an investigation into the early colonial history of the state and New York City. In response, in May 1839 Albany lawmakers passed a bill providing four thousand dollars for the retrieval of early colonial documents from the Netherlands, France, and England. Stephens, along with several other local literary figures, lobbied for the prestigious appointment. Governor William Seward was a Whig, however, and Stephens's well-known affiliation with the Democratic Party clearly hurt his chances. Seward instead appointed a member of the powerful Bleecker family, descendants from New York's original Dutch settlers.[49]

The setback for Stephens was fleeting. He had already met Catherwood. The ruins of Central America beckoned. The death in quick succession of the United States' chargé d'affaires, Charles De Witt, and his appointed replacement, William Leggett, then created the opening. Democratic president Martin Van Buren closed the deal with his appointment of Stephens as special agent to the disintegrating republic. Stephens was thrilled. Despite its uncertain and dangerous prospects, the journey into the dark heart of Central America loomed before him like another Petra. Returning from Washington on June 20, 1839, with his new appointment in hand, he wrote his friend Daniel S. Dickinson, a future U.S. senator and New York State attorney general:

It seems ordained that I shall quit the country. The Whigs prevented my going to England and Holland; or, as the *Herald,* my stanch friend on the occasion, expressed it: "going to bob for Dutch records." Virtue is its own reward; and I have been ap-

pointed Diplomatic Agent to Central America. You will doubtless believe me when I say this hits my humor infinitely better
than the Albany project; indeed, now I consider that it would
have been very unfortunate if I had succeeded in that.

My friends are full of badinage; they call me the "extraordinary Envoy," and persist that there is no such country on the
map; but fortunately an arrival from that region bringing accounts of a revolutionary army overrunning the country and a
revolutionary general entering the capital, brought it to notice.
The mission promises some incident; for the "government"
seems to be playing "hide and seek" about the country, and at
this moment, the "extraordinary Envoy" does not know exactly
where to find it. Is it not almost enough to make a man commit
himself blindly to fortune and fate? The course of my life is
changed by an accident. . . .[50]

With that, Stephens went off to his tailor to be fitted for a
dark blue diplomat's coat, complete with gold buttons, as befits
an envoy extraordinaire sent off in search of a republic few in the
United States were aware existed.

◁ PART TWO ▷

Politics

◅ 6 ▻

Ruins

Across Honduras, to the east of Stephens and Catherwood's tenu-
ous Copán encampment, Colonel Juan Galindo was preparing,
he was certain, for the final battles to save the republic. Galindo was
an Irishman turned Central American patriot who had been struggling for some time to rebuild his reputation after an ill-fated diplomatic mission to England. He had gone to London on behalf of the
republic to push back Belize's border but had returned in failure and
near disgrace.[1] Now, with the central government under siege and his
adopted world crumbling around him, he understood that his future
and only chance at redemption lay in picking up arms once again to
defend the federation.

He was born John Galindo in Dublin in 1802 and had zealously
taken up the republican cause after traveling to Guatemala as a young
man in 1827.[2] Wounded in battle during the country's first civil war
in 1829, he was awarded Central American citizenship by the new
liberal federal congress. Over the next ten years, he took on a series of
military and government assignments, at one point serving as governor of El Petén, Guatemala's northernmost department and the area
directly bordering on Belize and Mexico. He was intimately familiar
with the ground over which Stephens and Catherwood and Walker
and Caddy were now treading. In 1831, he explored the stone ruins at
Palenque on the Mexican–Guatemalan border. Three years later, he
was commissioned by Guatemalan government to investigate a mysterious grouping of stones rumored to lie near the Guatemalan–Honduran border. He arrived at Copán in April 1834, more than five years
before Stephens and Catherwood.

His years before arriving in Central America remain a mystery. His mother was an Irish actress and his father an English actor and fencing master of Spanish descent. The extent of Galindo's schooling is unknown but he undoubtedly advanced through grammar school and probably had some higher education. He was darkly handsome, with swirls of black hair ringing his forehead, thick lashes, and oversize eyes dominating a Roman nose and small, almost feminine mouth.[3] Ambitious and intelligent, he possessed kaleidoscopic curiosity and a scientific mind. While deeply involved in military and diplomatic matters for his adopted country, he still found time to become a member of the Royal Geographical and Horticultural Societies in London, the American Antiquarian Society in the United States, and the Société de Géographie in Paris, contributing papers and reports to each of them.

In June 1834, Galindo drafted a report to the Guatemalan government from Copán describing the stone ruins he had found there, an account filled with the chauvinistic pride of an adopted son.[4] The report stated the ruins supplied clear evidence of an advanced civilization in America that not only predated the arrival of Columbus but indicated American Indians were the oldest race on earth. In fact, he claimed America may well have been the cradle of human civilization, a statement daringly out of step with prevailing intellectual thought at the time.

Though he gave little scientific evidence to back up his statements, Galindo's ambitious assertions go some way to evidence the dizzying impact an encounter with Copán and Palenque could have on the European imagination. Buried in his sweeping, if erroneous, pronouncements are clear, concise, and valuable descriptions of the Copán ruins. He describes the fallen statues, carved obelisks, and crumbling stone steps, plazas, and temples at the site. He correctly pointed out that the architects of the temples and the artisans of the elaborately carved monuments accomplished their work without the benefit of iron tools. Most presciently, he guessed that the hieroglyphs he found were at least partially a form of phonetic writing, representing sounds and not merely ideograms. It was a remarkable guess.[5] His assessment would turn out to be right, though it would take another hundred years of investigation to support that conclusion."[6]

Galindo also claimed to be the first explorer to investigate Copán—
but he was not. Lying in the Royal Archives in Spain, unknown to
Galindo, was another Copán report. It would not surface until 1858,
long after Galindo and, for that matter, Stephens and Catherwood,
were dead.[7] It was written in the late sixteenth century, only thirty
years after the conquistadors had subdued the Indian warriors of Guatemala and Honduras.

Diego García de Palacio, a magistrate in the governing council
known as the Royal Audiencia of Guatemala, set out in 1576 from the
colonial capital at Santiago, known today as Antigua, to inspect the
conquered provinces on orders from King Philip II of Spain. Palacio
was an intelligent, educated government man born in Asturias, Spain,
in 1530 who had quickly grasped the importance of Central America in
the grand scheme of Spain's expanding empire. He saw the region, in
particular Honduras, as a good crossing point to connect the crown's
small but growing Pacific fleet with its powerful Atlantic armada. He
appears also to have had personal reasons for exploring the hinterlands
of what are now Honduras and El Salvador. He wanted to become
governor of the Philippines, a region he thought more worthy of his
ambitions, and he no doubt thought that finding a quick and easy way
across Central America would aid him in reaching that goal. It appears
he never made it to the Philippines but ended up some years later in
Mexico writing naval manuals and leading a coastal armada that went
after English marauders, such as Francis Drake, who were playing
havoc with Spain's shipping along the Pacific coast. At that point Palacio's name disappears from the record books.

His small place in history, however, was already secure. Palacio
was the first non-Indian to investigate the stone monuments of the
"Classic" Maya civilization, having visited Copán in 1576. Amazed by
what he found, he was also the first to set down what he observed in
writing.

In a letter addressed to his king, dated March 8, 1576, Palacio
writes: "Here was formerly the seat of a great power, and a great population, civilized, and considerably advanced in the arts, as is shown in
various figures and buildings." He gave a generalized description of
the ruins, noting that he found six large statues of men, two of women,

altars, terraces, and a large plaza resembling the Colosseum at Rome. Much of the stone work was of such skill, he told the king, it could not possibly have been created by people "as rude as the natives of that province." He added that the local inhabitants had little knowledge of the site's history.

It was a section of only about 850 words, coming at the end of his lengthy account of his entire journey through the provinces, and it is not known if the Spanish king ever personally read it. It was added to the mound of intelligence piling up from the colonies and eventually filed away in one of the royal court's swelling archives. There it lay for nearly three centuries, until it was discovered by an American diplomat, translated, and published in English for the first time—two decades after Stephens and Catherwood arrived in Copán.[8]

Galindo, like Stephens and Catherwood, had no way of knowing the existence of Palacio's unpublished letter, and, believing he was the first to investigate Copán, Galindo worked to make certain the world heard about his discovery.[9] On June 19, 1834, the same day he completed his full report to the Guatemalan government, he also drafted two brief "remarks," as he called them. The first he sent to the *London Literary Gazette and Journal of Belle Lettres, Arts, Sciences, etc.*, which published it in July 1835. The second account showed up in the 1836 edition of a journal published in Cambridge, Massachusetts, by the American Antiquarian Society. A third, longer version, this one complete with his drawings and maps, was sent to the Société de Géographie in Paris. It was never published, though a summary without the drawings appeared in the society's bulletin.

Galindo anticipated that his long report to the state of Guatemala, with all his maps and drawings, would be published by his government as well. But for unknown reasons it was filed away in the bureaucratic archives at Guatemala City and not discovered until decades later. The report was published by the Carnegie Institution in Washington, D.C., in 1920. The maps and drawings have never been found.[10]

By November 1839, however, publication of his scientific explorations was the last thing on Galindo's mind. Following his diplomatic failure in England, he had fallen out of favor with the federal administration.[11] Now, with the Liberal cause in grave danger and seeing a chance to redeem himself, Colonel Galindo cleaned his pistols and sharpened his sword in preparation for the final battles to save the Central American Republic.[12]

Although the abbreviated "remarks" Galindo published on Copán had all but faded into obscurity, they nevertheless caught the attention of a few antiquarians in New York and eventually reached Stephens. They were the reason Stephens and Catherwood now found themselves in the Honduran jungle. "He is the only man in that country who has given any attention at all to the subject of antiquities," wrote Stephens. "These accounts, however vague and unsatisfactory, had roused our curiosity. Though I ought perhaps to say that both Mr. C. and I were somewhat skeptical, and when we arrived at Copán, it was with the hope, rather than the expectation, of finding wonders."

Galindo's accounts, flat and plodding in style, were just enough to fire the imagination of adventurers like Stephens and Catherwood. But it would take Stephens's energetic, sometimes romantic prose, along with the stark beauty of Catherwood's detailed and accurate drawings, to finally put Copán on the world map.

Stephens and Catherwood spent their second night at Copán swinging in hammocks outside the house of the ill-tempered Don Gregorio. "In the morning," Stephens wrote, "we continued to astonish the people with our strange ways, particularly by brushing our teeth." Don Gregorio was as unimpressed and unfriendly as ever, and the two men were determined to find another place to stay.

Meanwhile, Stephens and especially Catherwood had achieved a reputation as "medicos," having used their traveling medicine chest to treat several people attached to Don Gregorio's household. Word spread and soon nearly a dozen people showed up for treatment. Then, as they prepared to leave for the ruins, a tall, cleanly dressed man stepped forward, announced he was José Maria Asebedo, and handed Stephens a bundle of papers. He declared the ruins were located on his land—and he produced the documents to prove it. Stephens reviewed the papers, and then, drawing on his charm, assured Asebedo that

Hut occupied by Stephens and Catherwood near Copán ruins. (Catherwood)

none of the ruins would be disturbed. He added that he would be happy to compensate him for their time there before they departed.

"Fortunately," Stephens wrote, "he had a favor to ask. Our fame as physicians had reached the village, and he wished remedios for his sick wife." Seizing on the opportunity to win Don Asebedo's favor, Stephens set out at once for the village to treat the landowner's spouse while Catherwood left for the ruins with some hired workmen.

That afternoon the rain began again and it soon reached such a torrent it halted all further exploration. Catherwood and Stephens, who had rejoined him, sought refuge just outside the ruins in a modest hut whose inhabitants, a family of three, kindly offered to take them in for the remainder of their stay in Copán. The structure consisted of a single room, half of it open to the air on one side. The family slept on a rawhide bed in one corner; there was room for only a single hammock, so Stephens agreed to sleep on a stack of corn husks. There, too, they treated the woman of the house, who was suffering from severe intermittent fevers, and her son, who had an infected liver.

That evening, wrapped in a blanket and smoking a cigar made from Copán tobacco—"the most famed in Central America"—grown and hand-rolled by the hut's owners, Stephens had a vision. He would buy Copán. Ever the merchant's son, he outlined for Catherwood his grandiose scheme. They would remove some of the monuments from the ruins and set them up in New York in a "great commercial emporium." After all, he said, Copán was on "the banks of a river that emptied into the same ocean by which the docks of New-York are washed." Stephens's idea was not entirely far-fetched. Although public nonprofit museums had not yet come into existence in America—the founding of the Smithsonian Institution was still six years off—profit-making museums existed in New York and Philadelphia. They were filled with taxidermied animals, all kinds of scientific curiosities, and Indian artifacts. It would be only another two years before one of those establishments, John Scudder's American Museum in New York, would be purchased and transformed into a world-famous emporium to scientific enlightenment and "freak" entertainment under the genius of Phineas Taylor (P.T.) Barnum.[13]

Stephens's idea was not entirely profit driven. The commercial venture he envisioned would become, he wrote, "the nucleus of a great national museum of American Antiquities." Even the comment from his host across the room, Don Miguel, who explained that downriver rapids made the Copán River impassable, did not dampen Stephens's enthusiasm—or cultural chauvinism. Some of the large monuments could be cut up and transported in pieces, and portable plaster casts could be made of the others, he said. If casts of the Parthenon in Athens could be exhibited in the British Museum, those from Copán could be displayed in New York. And other ruins they hoped to discover on their journey might prove even more accessible. "Very soon their existence would become known and their value appreciated, and the friends of science and the arts in Europe would get possession of them," he explained. "They belonged of right to us, and though we did not know how soon we might be kicked out ourselves, I resolved that ours they should be."

Several days later, Stephens bought Copán.

It wasn't easy. Don Gregorio took every opportunity to defame the two men in the village. His campaign was successful enough that the village alcalde came out to the hut to ask them to leave, out of concern their presence would bring the army. However, the mayor retreated as soon as he saw them. "When we returned to the hut to receive his visit," Stephens wrote, "as usual, each of us had a brace of pistols in his belt and a gun in hand."

Stephens still had to win over Don Asebedo, who held title to six thousand acres through a contract due to expire in three years. Fortunately, Stephens had a letter of introduction from a politician on the correct side of the civil war, and the next day an Indian courier trotted up with a letter from General Cáscara apologizing for their arrest in Camotán. Though these impressed Don Asebedo, he still balked. He was afraid, he said, he might get in trouble with the government for handing over the land to a foreigner. Finally, Stephens opened his trunk and put on his blue diplomatic coat with its large gold eagle buttons.

"I had on a Panama hat, soaked with rain and spotted with mud, a check shirt, white pantaloons, yellow up to the knees with mud," Stephens recalled, "but Don Jose Maria could not withstand the buttons on my coat. The only question was who should find the paper on which to draw up the contract. The reader is perhaps curious to know how old cities sell in Central America. I paid fifty dollars for Copán. There was never any difficulty about price. I offered that sum, for which Don Jose Maria thought me only a fool; if I had offered more, he would probably have considered me worse."

With the ruins now under their control, the expedition went to work in earnest. While Catherwood set up to draw the monuments, Stephens and the workmen began methodically clearing away sections of the jungle. Right away Catherwood ran into trouble. The sculpting of the monuments appeared so enigmatic and complex as to be incomprehensible.

First, there was the problem of light. Although the monoliths were carved in deep relief, the gloomy light filtering through the forest canopy flattened everything, leaving the human forms and their fantastic headdresses and skirts hard to differentiate. And this was when Catherwood could even get a good look through vines, branches, and tree roots that smothered many of the "idols." This problem proved fixable. Stephens and his workers were able to hack away the brush and bring down enough of the surrounding trees to open a hole in the canopy to allow the light in. When the cloudy skies cleared periodi-

Side-by-side comparisons of a Copán stela: present day (LEFT)
and Catherwood's rendering (RIGHT).

cally, the sun's rays intensified the deeply etched shadows and brought
out the monuments' bizarre and eccentric features.[14]

The second problem was more mental than visual and not so easily
remedied. How was a Westerner, a European as Catherwood was, to
reproduce sculptures that were so profoundly different, otherworldly,
decorated so inscrutably, and covered in hieroglyphs from a mysterious but obviously advanced civilization? The two veteran travelers,
who each had visited the singular wonders of Egypt and the Near
East, now stood, wrote Stephens, on entirely "new ground."

As he squinted through the steam and heat of the jungle, Catherwood, in particular, had arrived at an existential moment. Through all
his work leading up to his arrival in Copán, he had been thoroughly
schooled and practiced in a Western tradition of art that led from
Greece and Rome through the European Renaissance to the present.
When he journeyed through Tunisia, Egypt, and the Levant what he

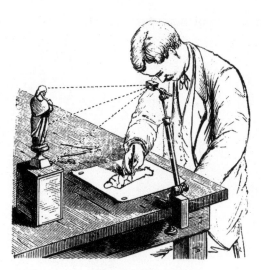

Camera Lucida.

saw and what he drew were also intelligible, informed by centuries of cultural exchange. In Copán, he was lost. The monuments he stared at in the midst of the forest were so alien from anything he had ever seen that at first they didn't register sensibly in his brain. During his first full day of work, the stone idols defeated him. Even his camera lucida, which helped project on his familiar drawing paper the outlines of the monoliths through its half-silvered mirror, was of no help. He was disgusted with the sketches he attempted. His skills seemed no match for the indecipherable complexities of the statues' designs.

Stephens, returning from a scouting survey in which he easily had located fifty new objects for his partner to draw, found Catherwood utterly dejected. "He was standing with his feet in the mud and was drawing with his gloves on to protect his hands from the mosquitoes," wrote Stephens. "Two monkeys on a tree on one side appeared to be laughing at him and I felt discouraged and despondent. In fact, I made up my mind, with a pang of regret, that we must abandon the idea of carrying away any materials for antiquarian speculation, and must be content with having seen them ourselves. Of that satisfaction nothing could deprive us."

The next morning, the discovery of lost waterproof boots, a good night's sleep, and a brilliant sun seemed to clear Catherwood's head.

Standing on a piece of oiled canvas, his feet finally dry in his boots, he set down the first in a series of rough sketches that, while not yet satisfactory, helped restore some of his confidence. As the day wore on, with each new series he seemed to reach another level of perception that allowed him to draw the monolith before him with greater and greater precision. It may have been only a subtle shift in perspective caused by the sharp edge of the shadows cast by the sun, but it seemed he had broken down some cognitive barrier and had begun finally to grasp if not comprehend what he was seeing. His mastery and skills returned, driven by his perfectionism. He was resolved to catch every complicated detail of the stones before him, leaving nothing out, adding nothing. There would be no distortions. Such had always been Stephens's intention: "from the beginning our great object and effort was to procure true copies of the originals, adding nothing for effect as pictures. Mr. Catherwood made the outlines of all the drawings with the camera lucida, and divided his paper into sections, so as to preserve the utmost accuracy of proportion."

After capturing the larger-than-life figures with their preposterous costumes from the front, some with patches of original red paint still visible on the surfaces, Catherwood would move to the side and then to the back of the monuments, filling his drawing paper with the rich details of their unfathomable hieroglyphics. His drawings would prove so accurate that archaeologists long in the future would be able to read them when they finally broke the Maya Code, grateful to have his copied glyphs when some of the originals were lost to erosion and defacement.

The two men continued on for days, Stephens clearing the jungle, measuring the temples, the pyramids, other stone structures, endlessly jotting down notes. He would capture and bring home the context, the broad strokes, the sentiments:

> We could not see ten yards before us, and never knew what we should stumble upon next. At one time we stopped to cut away the branches and vines which concealed the face of a monument, and then to dig around and bring to light a fragment, a sculpted corner of which protruded from the earth. I leaned

Reverse view of stela at Copán. (Catherwood)

over with breathless anxiety while the Indians worked and an eye, an ear, a foot, or a hand was disentombed. The beauty of the sculpture, the solemn stillness of the woods, disturbed only by the scrambling of monkeys and the chattering of parrots, the desolation of the city, and the mystery that hung over it, all created an interest higher, if possible, than I had ever felt among the ruins of the Old World.

Catherwood, the man of few words, would bring out the first true renderings for the larger world to see of this hidden civilization, and his work would win him celebrity and a permanent place in the annals of archaeology. Day after day he stood working stoically through the mosquitoes, the ticks, heat, rain, and mud. Like the jungle surrounding him, it was one of the most luxuriant, fertile moments in his artistic life, and he would not fail in making the most of it.

For his part, Stephens had to go about his tasks with hardly any surveying instruments, just a good compass, the reel of tape Catherwood had used to measure the temples of Jerusalem and Thebes, and an "artificial horizon" to help determine their longitude. But when Catherwood attempted to use the device with their sextant, they discovered it was bent, and like their broken barometer, useless.

They dodged scorpions and snakes, wore their pants tightly tied around their boots, buttoned their collars to the chin to ward off the mosquitoes, and sewed up their sheets to make sleeping sacks to protect them at night from the fleas in Don Miguel's infested hut. One day they took a break from the work and crossed two miles over broken terrain and jungle to the top of the ridge paralleling the river. There they were shown the quarries that produced the stone used for the giant idols and other structures in the city. Large blocks of stone still lay about, covered in brush and vines, apparently rejected centuries earlier for some defect or another. Some distance away, one huge block lay across a ravine, as if the work of transporting it to the city below had been only momentarily suspended with the intention of it soon being taken up again. The two men couldn't resist: on one of the blank quarried blocks they carved their names into the stone.

When they returned to the ruins and finally cleared away enough of the jungle to complete their survey, they concluded they were in the middle of what must have been a much larger city, and were standing within its ceremonial center, complete with pyramid-like temples, plazas dotted with monolithic statues and altars, and courts surrounded by steps that gave the appearance of amphitheaters. Farther out, many large, suggestive earth-covered mounds topped with trees and thick foliage spread from the exposed ruins in every direction. The two men could only guess what other treasures lay beneath and what future generations might find.

In fact, Stephens and Catherwood had stumbled onto a city that twelve hundred years earlier had sprawled up and down the valley and climbed toward the ridges on each side of the river. In a space of a quarter square mile as many as nine thousand inhabitants lived in the city's center, another ten thousand in immediate outlying districts, and thousands more in the surrounding countryside.

Future archaeologists would discover ceramic evidence that villages began forming in the valley as early as 1100 B.C. Later research would show that hieroglyphic monuments began to appear by the fifth century A.D.; carved upon them would be the story of a dynastic line of kings who ruled Copán for the next four hundred years. This history emerged in the later half of the twentieth century as scholars slowly began to unlock the meaning of Copán's glyphs. One key was a solid block of sculpted stone, six feet square by four feet high, that Stephens and Catherwood discovered and Catherwood illustrated in perfect detail. The top of the block was covered with hieroglyphs, and carved deeply into each side were four seated figures. When the glyphs were finally deciphered, it turned out the figures depicted sixteen of Copán's seventeen kings—starting with the dynasty's founder, dating from A.D. 426, and ending with Copán's penultimate king, whose death in A.D. 822 is now believed to have coincided with the beginning of the city's collapse and eventual abandonment.

The kings told their stories on the towering statues, or stelae, in the plazas, on the façades of their palaces, altars, and temples, on the ball court, and on the great hieroglyphic stairway, which displays the longest Maya text ever found. Each ruler employed a succession of architects and sculptors who built Copán into a city now considered one of

Ruins at Copán. (Catherwood)

the most beautiful of the Classic Maya period. Copán grew into a small mountain as each king built on top of his predecessors' palaces and temples, layer by layer, adding ever more brilliant refinement and artistry.

Stephens and Catherwood knew they were in the presence of art and architecture of astonishing sophistication. But they did not realize what they were seeing was the final veneer of the fallen city, covered not only by jungle but the last layers of Copán's long, dramatic history. Neither did they have a clear understanding of who could have built and occupied such a city, how such an advanced society could have sprung up and then disappeared, or how old it might be. They grasped, however, that no matter how many descriptive passages Stephens wrote, the only way they could convince the outside world of what they had found—of not only its existence but its uniqueness and exceptional elegance—would be through Catherwood's careful, painstaking art. There was more than enough work for another month at his current pace.

Before they arrived in Copán, they had expected to stay no more than a few days, not knowing the extent of the ruins and the difficulties they would face. Now they had spent nearly two weeks at the site, and Stephens worried he was shirking his diplomatic duties. "I did not consider myself at liberty to stay longer," he wrote. "I apprehended a desperate chase after the government; and fearing that among these ruins I might wreck my own political fortunes, and bring reproach upon my political friends, I thought it safer to set out in pursuit." Several "councils" were held, and as reluctant as they were to split up, it was finally concluded that Stephens and Augustin should go on to Guatemala City while Catherwood stayed in Copán to finish his drawings.

Once the decision was made, Stephens wasted little time preparing the mules and supplies. Catherwood accompanied him partway to Don Gregorio's. Stephens was tempted to heap indignation upon the Don for his discourtesies, but aware that Catherwood was stuck behind and still within the Don's influence, he took satisfaction instead in demanding that the Don tally up the bill for the milk, meat, and eggs they had consumed, and paid the full sum, which totaled two dollars. He wrote: "I afterward learned that I had elevated myself very much in his estimation and that of the neighborhood generally, by my handsome conduct in not going off without paying."

◁ 7 ▷

Carrera

Most of the way over the mountains it rained. At several points along their route Stephens and Augustin learned the road ahead was blocked by insurgent troops known for committing atrocities, especially against foreigners. The two men took detours. Some weeks later, when Catherwood followed Stephens's route, he learned from a town's padre that there had been a plot to murder and rob Stephens. He escaped only because he left earlier in the morning than the conspirators had expected.

In another town, Guastatoya, a second alleged robbery plot was foiled by the alcalde and a posse of townspeople who in the middle of the night rounded up Stephens—and his highly regarded firearms—to help them chase the suspected robbers through the countryside. Several shots were fired into the darkness. No robbers were found.

Wild, foreigner-hating insurgents roaming the countryside was bad enough. But as he and Catherwood quickly learned, the country was infested with brigands and cutthroats of every type. And as their experience in Camotán had demonstrated, even encounters with simple townspeople carried the risk of violence.

It was becoming increasingly clear to both men that they faced more hurdles than heat, jungle, mountains, and mosquitoes. The exploration they had undertaken in the disturbed arena of Central America would not be simply a venture of man versus nature like the polar explorations early in the next century or the assaults on Mount Everest that followed decades later. Stephens and Catherwood had plunged into an ugly man-made tempest. Daunting enough were the physical obstacles if they focused only on looking for ruins, but Stephens was forced now to hurtle himself into the eye of a political maelstrom to fulfill his diplomatic obligations.

◎◎◎

Ten days after leaving Copán, Stephens and Augustin entered Guatemala City. It was exactly two months since Stephens had left New York, although, he wrote, it seemed like a year. The night was moonless and black when they reach the outskirts of the capital, where they found groups of drunken soldiers sitting around fires, sporadically firing their muskets into the air. Within the city walls there was hardly a soul on the eerie, lightless streets to welcome the exhausted travelers, nor did the city offer any hotels.

Finally, after fruitlessly stumbling around in the darkness in search of accommodations, Stephens resorted to imposing upon the British vice consul, William Hall, to whom he had several letters of introduction. Greeting him and quickly closing the door, Hall was stunned Stephens had been able to cross the city without being assaulted. The soldiers, furious at not being paid that day, had threatened to sack the city, the vice consul said; the citizens were in a state of terror. Stephens and Augustin were welcome to spend the night.

"For the first time since I entered the country," Stephens wrote, "I had a good bed and a pair of clean sheets."

The next morning he took a walk around the city and was impressed by its spaciousness and grandeur, comparing it favorably to the "best class of Italian cities." The capital sat in a valley on a large plateau five thousand feet above sea level surrounded by barrancas, or deeply etched ravines. Although the city was well established, it was still relatively new by Spanish colonial standards. Sixty-six years earlier, it had been no more than a ranching village, its most impressive feature a convent called El Carmen. All of that changed in 1773 when a swarm of devastating earthquakes demolished the former capital of Central America, Santiago de los Caballeros, located only twenty-four miles to the west. Santiago, today known as La Antigua Guatemala, or "The Old Guatemala," had been founded by the conquistadors who invaded Mexico with Cortés in the 1500s. It had served as the Spanish capital of all Central America and parts of southern Mexico for more than two hundred years. Throughout its history, it had been regularly rocked by major earthquakes, but the quake of July 1773 and its aftershocks were of such a magnitude the Spanish colonial authorities decided they'd had enough. The royal court in Spain ordered Santiago evacuated and its surviving inhabitants moved to the next valley to the east.

Nuevo Guatemala de Asunción rose from the valley plateau in the usual Spanish north–south, east–west grid, surrounding a great plaza. The new city's plaza was much grander than Santiago's and the streets wider. Whole convents, monasteries, and churches were transferred from Santiago to the new capital, their names intact. Residents were given plots similar to those they had owned in the old city, with the richest and most prominent families located closest to the main square. Everything of value—the artwork, religious sculpture, gold, silver, even the wood beams and columns—were stripped from the buildings in Santiago and carried off to the new capital. Nuevo Guatemala was constructed in the traditional Spanish colonial style: the whitewashed stucco walls of the houses flowing contiguously along the streets, broken only by iron window grilles and huge portals, some decorated in the Mudéjar style, with heavy wooden double doors tall enough for horsemen to enter without dismounting. The structures stood one story high with walls thick enough to resist the force of most earthquakes. By the time Stephens arrived, the relocated capital, commonly called Guatemala City or simply Guatemala, was a thriving center, with an imposing cathedral on one side of the great plaza, the seat of government (Palacio Real) on another, and the municipal building on the north side of the square.

"I have seldom been more favorably impressed with the first appearance of any city," Stephens wrote, "and the only thing that pained me in a two hours' stroll through the streets was the sight of Carrera's ragged and insolent-looking soldiers."

◉ ◉ ◉

Stephens finally located the residence of Charles De Witt, the recently deceased U.S. chargé d'affaires. The house was closed up but remained

the diplomatic mission of the United States and contained the legation's archives. As Stephens made himself at home, he was delighted
by the home's large size and characteristic Spanish layout, which often
surprises first-time visitors fooled by the unassuming exterior walls
fronting the streets. The house was constructed around an inside
courtyard paved with stones and surrounded by flowers. This space
was ringed by covered corridors and doors leading to interior rooms,
including kitchen, bedrooms, and the house's main room, or reception *sala,* with its barred windows opening onto the street. In this reception room two imposing bookcases filled with bound diplomatic
papers flanked De Witt's writing desk, above which hung a copy of
the U.S. Declaration of Independence. For a moment, Stephens was
brought back home, to his college and law school libraries; then as the
room's small details came into focus, the poignancy of the scene gave
him a momentary shudder as he recalled De Witt's tragic end.

Diplomatic protocol required Stephens to present his credentials to
the central authorities as soon as possible. Normally, this would have
been a routine matter, but there was nothing settled about Central
America at the moment. As special agent of the U.S. president, he was
given specific orders and a list of instructions that were at the same
time optimistic and realistic—and thus contradictory. His principal
assignment was to arrange re-ratification of the recently expired treaty
of "commerce, navigation and friendship" between the United States
and the United Provinces of Central America. But because of the cha-
otic state of the republic, he also was ordered to close the U.S. mission
upon achieving the treaty's ratification; he was to secure the legation's
archives, ship the records back to the United States, and take formal
leave of the Central American government.

It was a delicate mission, to say the least. Surrounded by political
and military turmoil, Stephens effectively had to advance with the
aim of withdrawing. In addition to settling the trade treaty, he was
directed by Secretary of State Forsyth to deliver a letter to the republic's foreign minister explaining why the U.S. mission was being withdrawn, while expressing the United States' full support for the fragile

federation. "You may, in conversation with the minister," Stephens's instructions said, "afford such additional explanations as may tend to remove any unfavorable impression, and to persuade him that in adopting this step the President has been actuated solely by views of the expediency unmixed with any feeling of unkindness toward Central America."[1] He was to add that as soon as the republic's internal difficulties were resolved, the United States would reopen diplomatic relations.

At the time of Stephens's mission, the United States was not yet a serious player on the international stage, nor did U.S. secretaries of state enjoy the power to influence world events they do today. In 1825, the United States had been the first non-Latin country to formally recognize the United Provinces of Central America. Then followed the string of tragicomic attempts to establish a presence in the country, as one U.S. diplomat after another failed even to reach the new republic's capital in Guatemala. Now, as the intrepid John L. Stephens finally settled into De Witt's former residence, his British counterpart, Frederick Chatfield of her majesty's foreign service, was racing on horseback through El Salvador doing everything within his considerable power to tear the young republic apart—backed, of course, by Britain's all-powerful Royal Navy.[2]

Great Britain was the power player of nineteenth-century geopolitics. And though it was not interested in annexing the whole of Central America to its empire, its imperial impulses were hard to contain. Along with its attractive natural resources, the region offered a ready market for British manufactured goods. From its foothold in Belize, Britain sought to expand its influence west and south into Guatemala, and east and south along the so-called Moskito Coast into Nicaragua and Costa Rica. And while Central America was a small affair to the foreign and colonial offices, it was not a backwater to Britain's two aggressive representatives in the region—Colonel MacDonald and Chatfield, who held the formal title of minister plenipotentiary to Central America.

Chatfield had been dispatched to the region in 1834 after serving several years on assignment in Europe. At thirty-three, he was ambitious, abrasive, and shrewd. Because of the distance between London and Central America—round-trip correspondence sometimes took four to five months—Chatfield often felt free to set British policy toward the new republic. Like Stephens, his primary assignment had been to negotiate a commercial treaty, but he could not resist meddling in the new republic's internal affairs.[3]

One nettle in his side turned out to be Colonel Juan Galindo. Because Chatfield considered him still a British subject, Galindo's zeal on behalf of the federation grated on him, particularly when Galindo mounted a diplomatic mission to the United States and England to push back the borders of Belize. Given his Irish background, Galindo, for his part, had little love for Britain and he detested its representative's interference in his newly adopted country.[4] The animosity between them finally broke into the open in 1838, when a fourteen-year-old English servant employed by Galindo sought the protection of the British consulate in San Salvador claiming that he had been severely beaten by Galindo. Chatfield took the teenager in, enraging Galindo. The next day Galindo challenged Chatfield to a duel, which the consul ignored, but the scandal made the newspapers. Finally, the central government stepped in to resolve the quarrel.[5]

Chatfield initially supported the republic, believing it easier to deal with a single federation than five feuding provinces. Then territorial disputes over Belize and the Moskito Coast—at one point Colonel MacDonald personally led a charge onto islands off the Honduran coast after they were occupied by the republic—turned Chatfield against the central government. When General Francisco Morazán, the republic's president, levied forced loans on British and other foreign businesses to finance his army, Chatfield informed his superiors in London that the time had come to support the opposition. And while Stephens was playing archaeologist in Copán, Chatfield scrambled round Central America to cut a deal with the separatist factions, promising them the support of the British navy even though Britain's secretary of state, Lord Palmerston, had rejected an earlier proposal of armed intervention.

By the time Chatfield rode into Guatemala City in mid-December, Stephens had already met with members of the Conservative faction now controlling the state of Guatemala under the absolute authority of the mestizo rebel general, Rafael Carrera. He found no trace of Liberal republicans or the federal government left in the city. He made special note of the heavy hand priests played in the new Guatemalan government. Visiting the state assembly, he saw that half of the thirty deputies gathered in the old, dimly lit Hall of Congress were priests dressed in black gowns and caps. It reminded him, he said, of a "meeting of inquisitors." The deputies were busy restoring the privileges of the church that had been so rudely torn away earlier by the Liberals.

Stephens was advised by those close to the government to present his credentials formally to the Guatemalan chief of state, Mariano Rivera Paz, recently installed by Carrera, and to the chiefs of the other Central American provinces individually, so as to preclude him doing so officially to the federal government, now based in El Salvador. But he considered the suggestion "preposterous" because he had been accredited only to meet with the central government. He recognized, however, that the suggestion meant he must act with great care in Guatemala. As the future of the republic still hung in the balance, he must at least appear neutral, even though his political views, and those of the U.S. government, clearly favored the Liberals over the Conservatives.

Having paid and sent Augustin on his way back home, Stephens arranged for an escort to retrieve Catherwood from Copán. Carrera was out of town but his soldiers were everywhere. Stephens had a tense encounter with them one night after dining across the street at the home of the woman who rented out the legation's building. As he left to cross over to his house in the darkness, one of the sentries at the end of the street called out for the required password, which Stephens had not yet learned. The tone of the sentry's voice was so fierce it "went through me like a musket-ball and probably in a moment more the ball itself would have followed, but an old lady rushed out of the house I had left, and, with a lantern in her hand, screamed 'Patria Libra.'" Stephens scurried to the safety of his doorway. He later learned that a sentry had fired and struck a woman not long before for failing to give the password promptly enough.

Carrera returned to the city and Stephens went to introduce himself the next day, fascinated to meet the former pig driver who was

Rafael Carrera, as portrayed some years after his meeting with Stephens.

now master of all Guatemala. He was advised to wear his diplomatic coat because Carrera was taken with such external displays, even though the guerrilla leader lived modestly in a small house down a side street. Arriving, Stephens met Carrera's guard of eight or ten soldiers outside the door. Unlike the rest of the ragtag army, each was well dressed in a red jacket and plaid cap. Stephens was led down a corridor along a row of well-maintained muskets and then shown into a small room off the parlor where he found Carrera seated at a table counting money.

"He rose as we entered," Stephens wrote, "pushed the money to the side of the table, and, probably out of respect for my coat, received me with courtesy, and gave me a chair at his side." He wore a short black jacket of thin wool and close-fitting trousers. He was no more than five feet, six inches tall with a light Indian complexion and no trace of a beard. Stephens was shocked by how young he looked, estimating that he could be no older than twenty-one. Stephens remarked on his youth and Carrera replied that he was twenty-three (he was actually twenty-five), and knowing how extraordinary that might seem, he went on to explain how he had started with no more than thirteen men who lit and fired their ancient black-powder muskets with cigars. He pointed to eight places where he had been wounded, adding that three musket balls still remained in his body.

He wanted to correct lies that were told about him, he said. He was not a robber or a murderer, and he had changed his opinions about foreigners over the last two years. He had come to know several of them, he said, and one, an English doctor, had removed a musket ball from his side. They were the only people who never deceived him, he explained.

Stephens responded that he had seen newspaper accounts of his last entry into Guatemala City, including one article in the United States, which had praised his moderation and his attempts to stop pillaging and massacres by his troops. Given his young age, Carrera appeared to have a long career ahead, Stephens told him, and there was much good he could do for his country. Hearing this, Carrera put his hand on his heart and in a burst of passion that surprised Stephens, said he would sacrifice his life for his country.

Stephens was impressed. "With all his faults and crimes," he wrote, "none ever accused him of duplicity, or of saying what he did not mean. My interview with him was much more interesting than I had expected; so young, so humble in his origin, so destitute of early advantages, with honest impulses, perhaps, but ignorant, fanatic, sanguinary, and a slave to violent passions." Stephens saw something else, too, a quick natural intelligence. And as boyish as he appeared, Stephens wrote, Carrera never smiled, was deadly serious and highly conscious of his power, even though he did not flaunt it. He said he was teaching himself how to write and could now throw away his stamp and write his name. Stephens suggested he would benefit from travel to other countries. "He had a very indefinite notion as to where my country was; he knew it only as El Norte, or the North; inquired about the distance and facility for getting there, and said that after the wars were over, he would endeavor to make El Norte a visit."

Stephens came away with a prescient sense of Carrera's potential. "I considered that he was destined to exercise an important, if not controlling influence on the affairs of Central America," he wrote.[6] Carrera was nevertheless a hard man to read. He cared little for wealth. He required no salary, but asked only for money for himself and his troops as he needed it, totaling a fraction of what it had cost the Guatemalan aristocracy and merchants to keep up the federal army. Carrera was both flattered and righteous about the title the Guatemalan government had given him—brigadier general—and he considered himself at the orders of the state. But in reality he remained capricious and unbound by law, Stephens noted. As Stephens returned home that morning, he witnessed a detachment of soldiers drawn up before the house of a member of the Constituent Assembly who had made the mistake of crossing Carrera. The soldiers were searching the house for him. "This was done by Carrera's order, without any knowledge on the part of the government," Stephens added.

◦◉◦

Despite his successful meeting with Carrera, day-to-day life for Stephens did not change as he anxiously awaited Catherwood's arrival. As one who thrived on human company and social intercourse, he found it unbearable to be locked up in the residence every night while the city remained under virtual siege. Lying in bed, he could hear the *pop, pop* of the soldiers' muskets, the volleys of gunfire echoing down the streets from the plaza.

When he could no longer bear it, he set out on a whirlwind tour of the nearby countryside, which for the moment seemed relatively pacified under Carrera. His first stop was a nearby hacienda where he witnessed cattle being rounded up and branded, a stunning sight for the New Yorker and east coast merchant's son. In the company of a group of young aristocratic women he followed a religious procession through the city and traveled north to an Indian village where an annual festival was under way.

With no word from Catherwood and a week until Christmas, he decided on one more trip. In all his travels, he had never seen the Pacific Ocean, now less than a hundred miles to the south. Passing through the historic city of La Antigua, he was impressed with the number of churches and other buildings still in ruins from the 1773 earthquake, many with their untouched remains laying exactly where they had fallen.

Just south of Antigua rose a massive cone capped by a jagged crater, Volcan de Agua, its slopes covered with cornfields and dark verdant forest. Clouds ringed the top. It was too great a temptation for Stephens. After a good night's rest, he set out on the steep, miserable climb. Reaching the top, he was 12,300 feet above sea level. In the bitter cold, clouds and vapors swirled in the dormant crater. At its bottom he found several inscriptions written on the rocks. Blowing on his fingers to keep them limber, he copied a message left by three travelers from Russia, England, and Philadelphia. They described drinking champagne together, no doubt in celebration at reaching the top.

Several days later he reached the Pacific Ocean. "I had crossed the continent of America," he wrote. Covered in mosquitoes and sandflies, he left his mule at the edge of the jungle and forded a river by canoe to the volcanic black sand beach beyond. The port was an open roadstead; a ship from Bordeaux bobbed at anchor a mile out.

Stephens meticulously recorded his mini-expeditions in his notebooks. He was compulsively curious, a prototypical journalist determined to paint in words the fullest possible picture of life in Central America for his countrymen to the north. Along the way, he visited cochineal plantations, priests in their churches, and sugar mills, and met a fellow New Yorker living on a farm. He would describe it all in his book, lacing the eight-day journey with a history of La Antigua, and notes about the conquistadors, who in their endless lust for gold fitted out their fleet to sail to Peru from the shore on which he stood.

On his return to the capital Stephens found a disturbing letter from Catherwood. It explained he had been robbed, had fallen ill, and was forced to leave the ruins for the shelter of the disagreeable Don Gregorio. Despite his ordeals, he was on his way to the capital. It was Christmas Eve. "I was in great distress," Stephens wrote, "and resolved, after a day's rest, to set off in search of him."

That night he attended a Christmas party at the house of Central America's former minister to England, and there for the first time met Frederick Chatfield. He had arrived in Guatemala during Stephens's absence. Since his arrival, Chatfield, unknown to Stephens, had been plotting the final demise of the republic. Hearing that Stephens was sent to meet with the central government, Chatfield explained that his assignment was futile since the republic, as an effective entity, had already ceased to exist.

Stephens did not get home until three in the morning and, waking late, heard a knock on the door. Into the courtyard rode Catherwood "armed to the teeth, pale and thin, most happy at reaching Guatemala, but not half so happy as I was to see him."

◉ ◉ ◉

With intense sun beating down on his broad-brimmed Panama hat, Lieutenant John Caddy of the Royal Artillery held his double-barrel shotgun at ready. Since leaving the Belize River at Duck Run, he had taken the lead as chief huntsmen for their expedition, ready to shoot down anything that might prove the least edible. Sitting astride his old gray cob and outfitted in a green hunting jacket and blue serge trousers, he headed a column of horses, mules, and riders as they struck out from the village of Santa Ana on the last leg to Lake Petén Itzá, in the middle of the Petén. Caddy and his party were now nearly halfway through their difficult march across the Yucatán Peninsula.

Weeks before, Caddy sent back to Belize City the pitpan canoes, their crews, and most of the soldiers from the Second West Indian Regiment who had accompanied them on their seven-day journey upriver. Now the remaining overland party consisted of Caddy; the expedition's co-leader, Patrick Walker; their interpreter, Mr. Nod; and five soldiers. As they departed Duck Run, they also picked up a guide, several muleteers, and Indian carriers for the baggage. The next two weeks of travel westward into the depth of the Petén were as grueling as anything Caddy and Walker had ever experienced. The trail led through jungle so thick it blotted out the sun, and they struggled crossing swollen streams and nearly impassible swamps and marshland. At times they were forced to camp in the swamps, inches deep in mud, plagued by mosquitoes, and even worse, microscopic ticks called *garrapata*s that buried themselves in their skin and caused intolerable itching.

"The swamps again were so much inundated," wrote Walker in his official report to Colonel MacDonald, "that for five consecutive days we hardly advanced a step without the horses being up to their girths in mud or water. Besides the path in some places was absolutely shut up and reduced us to the necessity of cutting away with our machetes thro' the bush."[7] Food ran desperately low for days, with little or no game to feed the men. Caddy killed what he could find—a few birds, an occasional wild hog, a small fox, and an emaciated cow left for dead on the trail. At one point, he noted in his diary that the natives had a particular way of cooking and smoking the game, which they called "barbecue."

Eight days into the journey, an artillery gunner identified only as Private I. Carnick, Caddy's personal attendant, came down with a severe fever and was unable to proceed. After a day's delay, during which Caddy administered various pills, salts, and a hot gruel to induce sweating, Carnick revived sufficiently to travel on. Two days later, however, Carnick was so weak he could barely stay on his horse. "I was obliged to have his horse led," Caddy wrote, "and a man to walk along side of him to prevent his falling."

On December 12, after two punishing weeks, they emerged from the forest and entered "a magnificent undulating plain—as far as the eye could reach over uninterrupted open pasture with here and there a clump of trees," Caddy wrote. "I shall never forget the joyous sensation I experienced, and indeed it was felt by all." They came upon a cattle ranch and took possession of the main hacienda building, which though deserted and filthy nevertheless felt like a luxury hotel. Carnick's deteriorating condition tempered their mood, however. Now dysentery added to his fever, leaving him with intense craving for water. Caddy attributed his illness to the foul water they were forced to drink along the way, describing its appearance as tarlike.

They were visited the next day by a mestizo named Torribio, who offered to take Carnick into his nearby house, where his wife and daughter, who spoke English, would care for him and nurse him back to health. Walker and Caddy agreed, realizing the gunner was too ill to carry on. A cautionary letter was sent ahead to notify the Guatemalan authorities at Lake Petén Itzá that their party was approaching with the intention of traveling onward to Mexico. Six days later, when they arrived at the lake, Caddy was astonished by its beauty—"a magnificent sheet of water which sparkled in glorious sunshine, bearing the island town of Flores, with some smaller fairy looking Islets." Walker estimated that Flores was separated from the lake's shore by a half mile of water. In his diary he recounted what he had learned of the history of the lake as the last stronghold of the Maya Indians against the Spanish. It wasn't until 1697, more than 150 years after the conquest of Guatemala, that the Indians of Itzá were finally subdued in battle. The Spanish had constructed a road through the savanna and jungle to the lake and then built a small fleet of boats on the shore for a direct assault on the island. In the end, Spanish technological superiority—cannons, muskets, and gunpowder—prevailed. As was their custom. the Spaniards then set to work destroying every temple, idol, and monument they could find, and a large church was erected over the ruins.

When Caddy and Walker arrived, only about five hundred people were living on the island. The houses and streets were in disrepair and the thatched roof over the town's church had fallen in. A large dilapidated barracks and a monastery in ruins ran along one side of the main plaza.

The remaining seven-man expedition had been traveling for more than a month but had covered a distance of less than one hundred and fifty miles as the crow flies from Belize City. The men were exhausted. It was almost Christmas, and they fell easily into the local festivities. Dances were gotten up for them, hosted by the district commandant and a parade of the local ladies. Then they got news that drew a dark cloud over their entertainment. Private Carnick was dead.

Oddly, given Carnick's close contact with Caddy as his personal attendant, Caddy makes no mention of Carnick's death in his journal. Perhaps it was too painful. We are informed of it only in Walker's official report. "From what I saw of this man on our journey," Walker wrote, "he appeared a most respectable person." Walker sent a letter to the local priest enclosing a fee so that prayers could be said for Carnick's soul.

◁◁ 8 ▷▷

War

I n regard to my official business," wrote Stephens, "I was perfectly at a loss what to do."

He had not found the government he was looking for in Guatemala City. The talk there was entirely one-sided: the federal republic no longer existed. But by Stephens's count, the states were evenly divided on the question. Three provinces still clung to the republic—El Salvador, Honduras (by force), and the new breakaway state of Quetzaltenango (until recently a western department of Guatemala that had seceded and was now controlled by the Liberals). On the other side were the recently declared independent states of Costa Rica, far removed to the east, Nicaragua, and, of course, Guatemala, the most populous and powerful state in Central America. Stephens was convinced, however, that the entire equation could change quickly. The leader of the republic, General Francisco Morazán, had never been defeated on the battlefield, and even Carrera had always run before him. Now the two men were gathering forces for a final showdown. Like two lions pacing back and forth, they eyed one another across the border, waiting for an opening. Yet the contest would be decided not simply by the military acumen of Carrera and Morazán but by the still-beating heart of Mesoamerica itself, the peasant survivors of the lost civilization Stephens and Catherwood had come to find. Aroused from centuries of conquest, abuse, and servitude, the Maya Indians were rising up to take back control of their history.

◎ ◎ ◎

The war had begun two and a half years earlier, during an outbreak of cholera in the countryside outside Guatemala City. The state government, then firmly under the control of the progressive Liberal party, ordered quarantines of the infected areas and sent doctors to treat the stricken. At the time, unfortunately, treatments were misguided and as ill-understood as the mysterious source of cholera itself. The remedies included bloodletting and water restriction (cholera victims die in the throes of extreme dehydration), the administration of brandy and the opiate laudanum. Many of the cholera victims, therefore, continued to die, sometimes at an even greater rate at the hands of the well-meaning doctors.

Finally, on May 6, 1837, Rafael Carrera led an enraged mob of nearly two thousand people to confront the health officials in Mataquescuintla, a town in the mountains forty miles east of the capital. Many in the crowd believed that cholera was poison put in their wells and streams by the Guatemalan ruling class in order to exterminate them so foreign companies could be brought in to develop their land. The medical officials, they claimed, were then sent to finish them off by dispensing poisonous medicines. By the end of the day the mob forced one or two doctors—the record is not clear—to consume all of the medicines they were dispensing. Laudanum taken in that quantity is fatal and the doctors' deaths left little doubt in the people's mind that the medicine was, in fact, poison. Armed revolts followed throughout the countryside, culminating in a list of grievances against the government.

The Mataquescuintla incident was Carrera's first recorded appearance on the public stage. Within a short time, the pig herder who several years earlier had served as a drummer boy in the federal army was leading small bands of insurgents out of the mountains on lightning strikes against government troops—and his reputation began to take on almost mythological dimensions. Though he suffered a number of bullet wounds, his Indian followers came to believe he could not be killed and had been divinely appointed to save them. And by February 1838—only nine months after the insurgency began—Carrera headed an army of Indians and mixed-blood mestizos. At the age of twenty-three, he was on his way to becoming the most powerful man in Central America.[1]

Only one person stood in his path: Francisco Morazán, the powerful leader of the Central American Republic.

Morazán's story began fifteen years earlier, soon after Central America's independence from Spain, when the five original Spanish colonies joined into a federal republic that quickly weakened into a sharp contest for power. Underlying the conflict was a split between the conservative old guard—the powerful Catholic Church and wealthy aristocratic families—and a growing class of liberal thinkers, mostly aspiring creoles educated in science and the Enlightenment who were motivated by the revolutions in the United States and France and wanted to curtail the power of the church, forge a union, and develop the region economically.

Morazán was born in 1792, the son of a minor businessman of Italian descent and a mother of Spanish ancestry. Growing up in provincial Honduras, he had little chance for formal education. But he was a quick study and intelligent enough that by his late teens he was reading law in a notary's office in the Honduran city of Tegucigalpa.[2] After independence from Spain, he rose quickly through the new political order from clerk to secretary general of the Honduran state in 1824, and two years later became the Liberal president of the state legislature. He was dashing, handsome, politically astute. That same year, he married Maria Josefa Lastiri, who reportedly brought money into the marriage.

Then, in 1827, the Conservatives in Guatemala City seized control of the federal government, deposed the Liberal leaders of Guatemala's state government, and marched the federal army in an attack on El Salvador and Honduras, both dominated by the Liberal party. Morazán fled to neighboring Nicaragua, where he assembled a small army of Liberals for a counterattack. In an amazing series of battles that followed, the former provincial clerk, an untested commander with no military background, led one surprisingly successful assault after another against the large, well-trained federal army. He inspired his men with daring charges across the battlefields on horseback. As a

TOP   Battle at Trinidad, in which Morazán won his first victory
(as depicted on a present-day bank note).

BELOW   Francisco Morazán, whose birthday is celebrated as a
national holiday in Honduras (as depicted on the reverse side of the note).

military leader, he was bold and charismatic and possessed extraordinary coolness under fire. He used his organizing skills to weld together an effective army of Hondurans, Salvadorans, and Nicaraguans, and in 1829 he swept through Guatemala and took its capital.

He reinstalled the Liberal Guatemalan state government. He exiled sixteen of the top Conservative leaders.[3] Then on his orders, the archbishop and hundreds of Franciscan, Dominican, and Recollect friars were rounded up, transported to the coast, and also expelled from the country. New legislation was enacted abolishing the monastic orders and confiscating their properties, some of which were converted to schools and government buildings.

Through battlefield machismo and sheer force of personality, Morazán had in two years blazed from relative obscurity to become supreme master of Central America. Quickly elected president of the republic, he and others in the governing Liberal party over the next decade established programs to modernize the united provinces. But they moved too far too fast, particularly in Guatemala. "The Guatemalan liberals were essentially calling for a capitalist revolution in a country that was in large part still feudal," explained historian Ralph Lee Woodward, who wrote a brilliant study of the period.[4] And a new economic boom did not find its way down to the people. Ruling-class whites—Liberals and Conservatives—made up only a fraction of Guatemala's population. The great majority of the population consisted of an illiterate underclass of Maya Indians and mixed races, few of whom took any part in the political and economic life of the country—except when pressed into service as soldiers or laborers.

These peasants had achieved a measure of stability, however, under the old Spanish colonial system. They lived hard lives in the same poor rural villages their ancestors had farmed for centuries. They had survived the shock of the Spanish Conquest. And after more than three hundred years of colonial rule, they had taken the Catholicism imposed on them and had woven it through the fabric of their own social and spiritual life. They might be willing to embrace any measure that actually improved their lives, but to them, independence from Spain meant little more than a change in masters. Except now they were being forced to stop tilling their land to build jails for a new penal system, and to serve on juries and road gangs. The native weaving industry suffered as imported textiles entered the country under new trade policies. Their sense of injustice grew when the government levied a head tax on them to finance its Liberal programs, and opened unused Indian lands for foreigners to invest in. They were devoutly religious and infuriated by the repression of their church leaders.

The Conservatives, meanwhile, had not disappeared. Many had gone into hiding. Others secretly returned from exile determined to regain control. And a large number of parish priests, who as a group had not been exiled, now became their chief collaborators. As the Liberals systematically removed the church from its traditional roles in politics and education, limiting it solely to the religious realm, the priests moved among the villages stirring up hatred against the government. Every earthquake or poor crop, they told the Indians, was a sign of punishment from God against the devils who had taken power. Foreigners were being invited, they said, to take over communal Indian land.

Finally, in 1837, the Liberals in Guatemala City ruled that divorce could be granted by the state and marriages performed under civil contract, a direct assault on the church's most holy and sacred authority. The decrees drove the Conservatives and church leaders into a frenzy. For the priests and most of their flock, it was the last straw.[5]

Then cholera came to Guatemala.

Many of Carrera's contemporaries believed him to be an Indian, in part for his role as leader of the Indian uprising, but also because of his dark skin and ink-black hair. He was born, however, in an impoverished section of Guatemala City in 1814, the son of mestizo parents. His father was a mule driver and his mother a domestic servant.[6] Little is known about his childhood except that he received no schooling and never learned to read or write. He emerged from the barrio at the age of twelve to join the Conservative-led federal army as a drummer boy, reportedly rising to the rank of corporal or sergeant during the 1827–29 civil war.

When the conflict ended, the teenage Carrera drifted restlessly through the Guatemalan countryside, finding work as a servant, taking on menial jobs until he finally settled in Mataquescuintla in 1832 and began buying hogs in the countryside and driving them to market. By 1836 he had accumulated enough substance to marry Petrona Garcia Morales, the daughter of a local rancher. It is not clear how much political influence she exerted over her young husband, but in the months to come the haughty, fiery Garcia would become one of Carrera's closest confidantes. She was skilled in the use of the lance and pistol and often accompanied him into battle. She later became legendary for her violent fits of jealousy, bragging about how she mutilated and disfigured her husband's mistresses.

Physically, Carrera was not imposing. Though not tall, he was solidly built, and his frame and square shoulders were packed with energy. A doctor who attended him marveled at his preposterously tough constitution.[7] He was famous for his ability to survive one battle wound after another and recover with amazing speed. His followers were certain he could not be killed, and it was said that Carrera came to believe it himself. But there was another quality that set Carrera apart, an overpowering vitality and charisma that enabled him to dominate men and armies. He possessed an explosive mix of violence, cunning, and courage.

After Mataquescuintla, the Guatemalan government responded with swift, brutal military force. Carrera and his small army of insurgents took to the mountains and waged a classic guerrilla war. The troops sacked villages. Carrera and the rebels countered by going town to town assassinating government officials and judges. The struggle took on aspects of a religious crusade and grew inexorably into a class and race war as the Indians, mestizos, and mulattos united against the white ruling class and foreigners. The battle cries soon became "Death to all foreigners!" and "Viva religion!"

President Morazán, who years before had moved the federal government to El Salvador, tried to negotiate a peace from his headquarters in San Salvador. But it was too late. Carrera had molded his ragtag rebels into a sizable army, and in 1838 they marched on Guatemala City and its Liberal defenders. After five days of street fighting, Carrera entered the city's center victorious. Terror-stricken residents barricaded themselves in their homes and braced for the worst.

De Witt, still the U.S. diplomat in residence, described the assault in a dispatch to U.S. secretary of state Forsyth: "On Monday the 29th [of January] at 1 o'clock in the night, the battle commenced. The firing of musketry was kept up briskly for an hour near the western gate. . . . From this time till Friday morning the warfare continued day and night, chiefly from the street corners and barricades, with various intervals of intermission. On Wednesday, the 31st, Carrera with three thousand Indians entered the city by the eastern gate. They perpetuated many excesses and on Thursday afternoon barbarously murdered the Vice President [José Gregorio Salazar had been sent by Morazán to negotiate a peace] in the presence of his family, as he was walking in the parlor with an infant in his arms."[8]

Within a week, Carrera and his peasant army were gone. With the Liberals deposed, Carrera's main objective had been achieved, and he seemed not to know what else to do in the capital. Terrified Conservatives and municipal officials had quickly transferred new rifles to his men and commissioned Carrera a lieutenant colonel with command of his home district in Mataquescuintla.[9] Though Carrera and his mob army withdrew, the demons had already been let out of the bag, according to De Witt, who wrote to Forsyth: "What wise men do now most fear, is that the Indians, having for the first time since the conquest of the country discovered that they can by a use of their power force the whites and [mestizos] into terms, will hereafter return to repeat their atrocities upon the slightest provocation. They outnumber the other classes in the proportion of ten to one."[10]

Morazán soon arrived from San Salvador with fifteen hundred federal troops, restored the Liberals, and over the next eighteen months pursued a counterinsurgency campaign to capture or kill Carrera and wipe out his partisans. The federal troops won virtually every battle, but most of the rebels escaped and Morazán could not catch Carrera. "Morazán is master of no more ground than he can cover with his troops," wrote De Witt.[11] The insurgents continued bloody hit-and-run strikes from strongholds in the mountains east of the capital. Acts of butchery escalated on both sides.

In the middle of Morazán's campaign against Carrera in Guatemala, Conservatives in Nicaragua, Honduras, and Costa Rica seized power, formed an alliance to dissolve the federation, and by early 1839 were marching on El Salvador. De Witt summed up the situation in one of his final dispatches. The republic's constitution was, he said, "a mere rope of sand, and the people are wholly unfit for a republican government. The machinery will not work."[12] As the federation began to crumble around him, Morazán now alone represented the republic.

War broke out across Central America and Morazán was forced to return to El Salvador with the core of his army to contain it. Carrera had won a war of attrition. On April 13, 1839, he marched into Guatemala City unopposed. By fiat, he reinstated the Conservatives and some political moderates to power. They, in turn, commissioned the former drummer boy a brigadier general and named him commander in chief of the Guatemalan army. This time Carrera, or one of his surrogates, was in the city to stay.

Hundreds of miles to the east, in El Salvador, Morazán succeeded once again in doing what he knew how to do best—win military engagements. In early May, outnumbered two to one, he defeated a combined Honduran-Nicaraguan army, but he suffered a serious bullet wound to his right arm during the battle. The victory was not decisive; his small army of Liberal loyalists was unable to follow up. He was now isolated. Even his native state of Honduras had turned against him. The federal congress disbanded. Morazán's dream of a united Central America was disintegrating around him.

In rapid succession, Guatemala seceded from the federation, the archbishop was invited back to Guatemala, the Roman Catholic Church was reestablished as the state religion, the civil marriage act was revoked, and the monastic orders were restored. Under Carrera's watchful eye, the state government was reverting to the old colonial system. In September, around the same time Stephens and Catherwood were preparing to sail from New York, Carrera heard rumors that Morazán was about to attack and he rode to the El Salvador border to survey the situation. While there he was fired on by a small group of Salvadoran troops and hit in the chest with a musket ball.

In San Salvador, Morazán, recovering from his wound, isolated and surrounded, continued to fend off invaders from Honduras. Then a serious earthquake rocked San Salvador, causing heavy damage. The Honduran general, Francisco Ferrera, gave Morazán twenty-four hours to surrender. Instead Morazán rode north with the remainder of the Salvadoran army to face the Hondurans at San Pedro Perulapán. The battle appeared lost until Morazán, greatly outnumbered again, personally led one of the final attacks, appearing up and down the line of his troops urging his men on. It was the decisive moment and swung the tide of the battle. Ferrera and another senior Honduran officer were wounded, and large quantities of munitions were captured, including

Ferrera's sword, the ultimate humiliation. The Honduran general was forced to flee on foot with his soldiers. Morazán stood victorious on the battlefield once again, seemingly never to taste defeat.

◉ ◉ ◉

Stephens had not wasted his time in Guatemala City. A sharp-eyed observer, he had taken careful measure of the overall political situation and arrived at a very low opinion of the public men he met in social and official gatherings. He had no sympathy for their politics. They were the wealthy and privileged who after years of exile had taken back their properties and political power. He noted how they humored Carrera and the Indian castes for their own ends, manipulating them through the priests, playing on their ignorance and stoking their religious fanaticism. He wrote that in "their hatred of the Liberals they were courting a third power that might destroy them both, consorting with a wild animal which might at any moment turn and rend them to pieces. And in the general heaving of the elements there was not a man of nerve enough among them, with the influence of name and station, to rally around him the strong and honest men of the country, reorganize the shattered republic, and save them from the disgrace and danger of truckling with an ignorant uneducated Indian boy."

He concluded that the only responsible thing for him to do was to go to El Salvador, where he could decide for himself if any legitimate form of central government had a chance of succeeding. But traveling overland was out of the question. Chatfield had taken a circuitous route by sea on his return to Guatemala City. The master of a French ship anchored off El Salvador, Captain De Nouvelle, had come up to Guatemala City riding hard to reach the capital. He reported a number of atrocities, including the discovery of three men found dead with their faces disfigured beyond recognition. Rather than return overland, the captain sent a courier with orders to bring his ship up to the Guatemalan port of Iztapa. He offered to take Stephens aboard when he returned to El Salvador.

Meanwhile, 1840 and a new decade clanged to life with the bells of the city's thirty-eight churches, convents, and monasteries. Shops were closed, the sky was clear, flowers bloomed in the courtyards, green mountaintops and volcanoes circled a city bathed in sunny warmth so unlike the snow and cold of New York on the first day of January. Visiting the cathedral as "Mozart's music swelled through the aisles," Stephens observed Carrera taking his seat directly in front of the pulpit with the chief of state, Mariano Rivera Paz, at his side. When the service ended, the way was cleared as Carrera, "awkward in his movements, with his eyes fixed on the ground, or with furtive glances, as if ill at ease in being an object of so much attention, walked down the aisle." When he emerged on the church steps overlooking the main plaza, Stephens saw a thousand "ferocious-looking soldiers were drawn up before the door. A wild burst of music greeted him, and the faces of the men glowed with devotion to their chief."

◁◁ 9 ▷▷

Malaria

Stephens left for Iztapa on January 5 accompanied by Catherwood, who planned to go only as far as the coast and return to the city. His contract, after all, said nothing about chasing after governments. They left in the afternoon, stopping for the night on the edge of a lake.

Sometime during the night Stephens fell violently ill. Plasmodia parasites were swarming through his body. A week or two before, probably during his visit to the coast, he had been bitten by a female anopheles mosquito. In her saliva were microscopic protozoa that slipped into his bloodstream and lodged in his liver. After days of consuming cells and reproducing up to forty thousand times, they burst out and entered his red blood cells. There they continued replicating in such vast quantities the blood cells had now swelled past the breaking point. Unknowingly, Stephens had contracted malaria.

"I woke the next morning," he recalled, "with a violent headache and pain in all my bones." Though very sick, he was still able to travel. He suffered from high fever the next several nights as he struggled to reach the coast. One morning in great pain he could not move for hours. The last night on the trail, his condition took a turn for the worse. "Mr. Catherwood," he wrote, "who, from not killing anyone in Copán had conceived a great opinion of his medical skills, gave me a powerful dose of medicine and toward morning I fell asleep."

The next day they reached the port of Iztapa, where Stephens left Catherwood and boarded De Nouvelle's ship. The cool sea air revived him. That night, as the ship caught an evening breeze for El Salvador, his cabin filled with mosquitoes, but he had no way of knowing that some of them almost certainly carried the same protozoa that caused his sickness. The next day his fever returned and remained all day. When they arrived off the coast of El Salvador, Stephens was too sick to go ashore. De Nouvelle, with pressing business, went on ahead, saying that he would arrange to have horses waiting for Stephens once he was able to land. To catch the air that afternoon, Stephens went on deck, where he counted six volcanoes along the coast. That night he sat in wonder watching the incandescent top of Volcan Izalco, whose fiery golden lava served as a navigational guide for sailors far out at sea.

In the morning he felt well enough to go ashore. El Salvador's chief port was a bleak place, no more than a sandy beach, a few soldiers, some dilapidated Spanish warehouses, several huts, including one for the port captain, and a small rancho. Weak and wobbly, Stephens sought shelter from the heat in one of the rancho's huts. "It was close and hot," he wrote, "but very soon I required all the covering I could get." He was shivering violently with chills, suffering the classic paroxysms of malaria. The fever returned. He craved water. "I became lightheaded, wild with pain, and wandered among the miserable huts with only the consciousness that my brain was scorching. I have an indistinct recollection of speaking English to some Indian women, begging them to get me a horse to ride to Sonsonate; of some laughing, others looking at me in pity, and others leading me out of the sun, and making me lie down under the shade of a tree. At three o'clock in the afternoon the ship's mate came ashore. I had changed my position, and he found me lying on my face asleep, and almost withered by the sun."

The sailor wanted to take Stephens back to the ship, but Stephens insisted on riding on to the town of Sonsonate, where he could get medical attention. Somehow he recovered sufficiently to mount a horse and ride three hours through the heat, reaching the town just before dark.

Just outside Sonsonate he unwittingly encountered the federal republic he had been looking for. He wrote: "I met a gentleman well mounted, having a scarlet Peruvian pellon over his saddle, with whose appearance I was struck, and we exchanged low bows." The gentleman, as Stephens later discovered, was Diego Vigil Cocaña, the vice president of the republic and the last remaining constitutional officer of the central government. "When I left Guatemala in search of a government, I did not expect to meet it on the road."

Even if he had recognized the rider, Stephens was in no condition to conduct official business. His first stop was the house of Captain De Nouvelle's brother, where he was given a room and spent a number of days recovering. As soon as he was well enough, he sought out the government and to his surprise was introduced to Vigil. At the age of forty-five and suffering partial paralysis in both legs, the tall, thin, well-educated Honduran was a longtime confidant of Morazán. He had been serving as the acting president of what was left of the fractured republic ever since Morazán resigned from his second term as president a year earlier to become El Salvador's chief of state and lead the army. In the discussions that followed, Stephens explained that he was on his way to present his diplomatic credentials in Cojutepeque, the republic's temporary capital pending reconstruction of earthquake-damaged San Salvador. However, he told Vigil candidly that he did not want to make a "false step" if the federation no longer existed. Stephens understood that presenting his U.S. credentials would give valuable legitimacy to the government, while to withhold them would appear "disrespectful" and show favor to the rebellious states. "I was in a rather awkward position," he wrote. Vigil assured him that the legitimate government did indeed exist in his own person, but sensing Stephens's predicament, he did not ask him for his diplomatic documents.

A compromise was settled on after Vigil explained that at that very moment delegates from the individual states were assembling in Honduras to resolve the constitutional crisis. He was confident, Vigil said, that they would reinstitute the republic, and if Stephens wished, he could wait for the official pronouncement before acting. In a dispatch to Secretary of State Forsyth a short time later, however, Stephens was pessimistic based on his experience in Guatemala. "My own opinion," he wrote, "is that the convention will not do anything."[1] He felt, however, that his instructions required him to make every effort to complete his mission and that he was obligated to await the outcome. The impasse was frustrating. He was anxious to settle the matter and return with Catherwood to the search for more ancient regimes, which had been their primary motive for their coming to Central

America. But he also saw an opportunity in the delay and seized on it. Within days he was sailing down the coast to the distant province of Costa Rica.

Although not explicitly instructed by the State Department to examine the matter, Stephens was well aware of his government's interest in the creation of a ship channel from the Caribbean to the Pacific by way of the San Juan River, a waterway along the border of Nicaragua and Costa Rica. The river connected the Caribbean to Lake Nicaragua, and from there, if a short canal were to be built, ships could make their way to the Pacific.[2] The route had been studied before; the biggest obstacle was the narrow ridge of land separating the lake from the Pacific. Stephens wanted to inspect it firsthand. To abandon his diplomatic post with the outcome of the treaty still pending was risky. But now recovered from his bout of malaria, he did not have the patience to sit around while Central America sorted itself out.

The vision of a water route through Central America had captivated just about every ship master, adventurer, and entrepreneur since a surprised Columbus ran into the Western Hemisphere on his way to the East Indies. From the sixteenth century on, a number of routes were proposed but it was Humboldt who gave the possibility of a canal some scientific credibility. The great naturalist and geographer undoubtedly mentioned the San Juan route to President Jefferson during their visit in 1804.[3] Years later, President Andrew Jackson dispatched a special agent to investigate both Nicaraguan and Panamanian routes.[4,5] Eventually the ubiquitous Juan Galindo became involved. When he arrived in Washington on his way to England in June 1835, he carried with him surveys, historical accounts, and other documents bearing on the feasibility of the channel through Nicaragua, copies of which he left with the State Department.[6] Stephens was aware of this history.

His first stop, however, was San José, the capital of Costa Rica, where he met briefly with the chief of state, Braulio Carrillo. In Carrillo, a short, stout man of fifty who had been installed as head politico in a coup, Stephens encountered one of the reasons the federal republic was disintegrating. "He was uncompromising in his hostility to General Morazán and the Federal Government," wrote Stephens, "and strongly impressed with the idea that Costa Rica could stand alone. Indeed, this was the rock on which all the politicians of Central America split: there is no such thing as national feeling."

Stephens arrived in Costa Rica with the intention of examining the San Juan River between Costa Rica and Nicaragua. But soon after he arrived in early February, his lips turned blue and his teeth started to chatter. Malaria struck him down again. As he lay bedridden in a convent for days, the plan to investigate the river faded. He was six hundred miles from Guatemala, lonely, depressed, and sick.

When he recovered, he considered returning immediately to El Salvador by ship, but two things changed his mind. His health returning, he felt a surge of his usual nervous energy. And he had an opportunity to purchase one of the best mules in San José: "a macho, not more than half broke, but the finest animal I ever mounted," an obvious overstatement since he said the same about the Arabian horse given him by the sheik of Aqaba. This "macho," however, did prove special. A deep bond formed between the two as the animal carried him on its back for the rest of his journey through Central America and Mexico.

Determined at minimum to explore the likely canal terminus on the Pacific side, Stephens and his macho headed up the coast, traveling through wilderness and staying at rough frontier haciendas along the way. Crossing into Nicaragua, he arrived finally at a stream that led down to the Pacific and the "port" of San Juan del Sur. The horseshoe bay was lined with bluffs tall enough to shelter ships and would thus provide an excellent outlet for any canal. The harbor and the surrounding area, however, were uninhabited. No ship had entered for years. "It seemed preposterous to consider it the focus of a great commercial enterprise," wrote Stephens, "to imagine that a city was to rise up out of the forest, the desolate harbour to be filled with ships, and become a great portal for the thoroughfare of nations."

Stephens spent the afternoon walking along the shore, set up camp, and bathed in the ocean. "The scene was magnificent," he wrote. "It was perhaps the last time in my life that I should see the Pacific." It was an odd moment. Even as he was drawn to San Juan del

Sur, convinced of an eventual connection between the two great oceans, he had no way of foreseeing the role he would play years later in just such a project, and one that would bring him back to the Pacific again and again.

The next day he left the bay and explored the most probable path of the canal up through the jungle, over a ridge of hills and across an open plain to Lake Nicaragua, the largest inland body of water in Central America. The distance between the coast and the lake was slightly over fifteen miles, but they were rugged, difficult miles. Still, the distance was nothing compared to the stretch covered by the Erie Canal, which spanned nearly the entire width of New York. Yet this place bore no resemblance to Stephens's home state. Before him, rising majestically from an island in the lake, were two towering, perfectly conical volcanoes. By the time he arrived in the old Spanish colonial town of Grenada, situated at the northern end of the lake, he was satisfied that the ship canal to the Pacific was feasible. When he entered the town he had been riding nearly two weeks, was still weak from malaria, and was nearing total exhaustion.

Then fortune took another turn. Stephens found in Grenada a British engineer who had completed the most thorough survey of the canal route to date. John Bailey, hired by the Central American Republic to make the examination, had completed all but a small part of it when civil war broke out. With the collapse of the federal government, Bailey was never paid and was surviving in Nicaragua on half pay as a British naval officer. He happily put before Stephens all his maps and measurements, allowing Stephens to copy as much as he wanted for his book. Later, with the help of an engineer from New York, Stephens calculated that construction of the canal and the dredging of the San Juan River would cost $25 million, a gross underestimate by later accounts.

Still, as he would prove later in Panama, Stephens was one of his era's great evangelists for progress and trade. He was the son of a merchant, born in a city that substituted sailing masts for trees. "As yet," he wrote, the idea of a canal "has not taken any strong hold upon the public mind. It will be discussed, frowned upon, sneered at, and condemned as visionary and impracticable." He wrote of the undeniable trade and travel advantages of such a canal but he had in mind more than economic or mercantile benefits:

> It will compose the distracted country of Central America; turn the sword, which is now drenching it with blood, into a pruning hook; remove the prejudices of the inhabitants by bringing them into close connexion with people of every nation; furnish them with a motive and a reward for industry, and inspire them with the taste for making money, which, after all, opprobrious as it is sometimes considered, does more to civilize and keep the world at peace than any other influence whatever. The commerce of the world will be changed. . . . Steamboats will go smoking along the rich coasts of Chili, Peru, Ecuador, Grenada, Guatimala, California, our own Oregon Territory, and the Russian possessions on the borders of Behring's Straits. New markets will be opened for products of agriculture and manufactures, and the intercourse and communion of numerous and immense bodies of the human race will assimilate and improve the character of nations. The whole world is interested in this work.

Though focused on probing deeply into the past, Stephens could not keep his eyes from the future. In a book whose business was the discovery of an ancient civilization, he proffered an unabashed, utopian vision of the possibilities ahead. And because of the enormous success of his books, Stephens did more than anyone in his day to plant in the public consciousness the idea of such an oceanic connection. His readership included capitalists and investors—New York entrepreneurs in particular—who had the commercial instincts and means to do something about it. In the future they would become both his associates and competitors. Ironically, as he later struggled to build a railroad across Panama, his competitors sought to undermine the project by insisting Nicaragua was the better route and sending steamboats up the San Juan River to prove it.

In 1840, however, as Stephens rambled over the ridgeline and saw the wild and fanciful volcanoes rising from the waters of Lake Nicaragua, no commercial self-interest drove his zeal. It was his belief—driven by his era's raw American optimism—that the world could be improved, that progress was not only inevitable but inevitably good.

Patrick Walker was the first member of the British expedition to reach the ruins at Palenque. Lieutenant John Caddy remained five miles behind in the village of Santo Domingo de Palenque, where he lay "indisposed" from tick bites on his legs so painful he could barely walk, much less ride horseback. Walker, accompanied by a local guide and two Indians, approached the ruins from the northeast over a rolling grassy plain covered with wildflowers, clumps of woods, and a latticework of streams. Thickly forested hills and mountains rose before them to the south. The remains of the ancient city were located on a flat escarpment that jutted out from the foothills into the plain. It was a steep ride up and onto the shelf of land, made even more difficult by dense jungle growing over piles of stones and the uneven fragments of fallen structures. Walker noticed a fast-moving stream that flowed out of the rocks from what appeared to be a subterranean aqueduct. Following the stream along a man-made stone channel, he was surprised to see the water emerge from the underground through the sculpted head of an alligator.

He left his horse and, fighting to keep his footing, gingerly scrambled sixty feet up a large mound of loose stones. At the top he found the solid wall of a building flanked, he wrote, by well-constructed corridors, "the sight of which at once repaid me for all the toils of my travels past." After two and a half months of often brutal transit, they had finally reached the ruins of Palenque. "The peculiar structure of the edifice and its splendid exterior ornature stamped it at once with the impress of great antiquity," he continued. Rarely given to poetics in his official report, Walker could not resist an attempt here: "On further examination, the 'cloud capped towers, the gorgeous palaces and the solemn temples,' though shorn of their pristine proportions, were yet spared enough of time's defacing hand to indicate that here had once existed a people, great and powerful, and perfected in art, the grand test of advancement in civilization."[7] After a quick look around, with shadows lengthening in the late afternoon, he hurried back to Santo Domingo and arrived just before nightfall to tell Caddy what he had found.

The expedition had been on the move for more than three weeks since leaving the island town of Flores on Lake Petén Itzá. Half the time was spent on horseback through the empty, trackless savanna and forests of the Petén. The final leg was by canoe down the Usumacinta River, then on horseback to Santo Domingo de Palenque. Somewhere they had crossed an unmarked border leaving Guatemala and had entered the Mexican state of Chiapas. Caddy was already in agony. "I had been suffering much from the torments caused by the bites of mosquitoes and warri ticks," he wrote, "and my legs from the knees downwards were in a state of rawness anything but agreeable." But, riding from the river to Santo Domingo, he was ever the huntsman and still able to blast away with his shotgun to bring down a number of yellow-headed parrots that he noted made for an excellent stew.

In Santo Domingo they easily gained permission from the local authorities to visit the ruins, which was a relief because they had heard reports along the way that no foreigners were allowed at the site. The only condition was that they must take a guide from the town who would watch that nothing was damaged or removed.

Caddy's excitement grew as he listened to Walker's description of what he had found. Caddy had spent the day in his hammock rubbing his legs with a concoction made from a local plant called *malbi*. The cure worked well enough that within a few days he, Walker, and the rest of the expedition saddled up and headed out to the ruins with enough provisions to set up camp on the site. They were accompanied by the part-time Mexican army captain, identified only as Don Juan, who had acted as official guide for Walker on his first visit to the ruins.[8]

For the next two weeks they probed the jungle, cleared away some of the growth, and took measurements of the principal buildings. Caddy spent most of his time making careful, accurate drawings of the structures and the bas-relief figures that decorated the walls, sketching an overall map of the central site and a floor plan of the main building, called the "palace." In his drawings he was also able to capture details of some of the hieroglyphs that accompanied the human figures. Besides the main palace complex, which was the largest structure they encountered and which sheltered them at night, they explored several other temple-like structures perched on the summits of nearby mounds of crumbling stone. Most of the buildings they found were overgrown with trees and dense foliage, and many were defaced, cracked and thrown down by the forces of time and nature. The structures butted up against a steeply rising jungle hillside that all but engulfed them. Searching the surrounding areas, they found the broken walls and rubble of what they assumed had been numerous other buildings and temples of a city that possibly extended for miles.

Lieutenant Caddy's final report on the ruins was fairly short and straightforward, consisting chiefly of dry factual descriptions and measurements. For some reason, perhaps the seriousness with which he approached the work, his account carried little of the lively personal details and amusing asides that characterized his diary entries of their journey. Most of his drawings, too, were honest, uncomplicated representations, limited in scope, concentrating only on key features. Some were truly remarkable—the first illustrations to give a viewer a true idea of what the ruins of Palenque actually looked like. Yet even in his most sweeping statement, he came to no conclusion about the origins of Palenque, and only carefully and conservatively summed up what they had found: "From the extent of these remains, whose fallen structures cover a space of some miles—the massiveness of the buildings which are still standing, the elegance of the Basso relievos—both sculptured on stone and moulded in stucco—and the beauty of the internal, and external ornature, stamp it as one of the most extraordinary and interesting monuments of the arts of the ancient people of this country—and proves that, at some far distant period it must have been inhabited by a race both populous and civilized." His five-thousand-word report, however, which he kept separate from his daily journal, comes across as bureaucratic and lifeless, expressing none of the enthusiasm or emotion of discovery. Perhaps he was looking ahead to its intended audience—colonial officials, scholars and antiquarians.[9] Caddy seemed more interested in getting back to his hunting, which accounted for the happiest and most exciting parts of his journal. Time would prove, however, that what he found at Palenque left a deep impression on him, and he would come to view it as one of the more important events in his life.

Walker, on the other hand, devoted only a few pages of his official report to the ruins, something he—and especially Colonel MacDonald—would come to regret. He acknowledged in the report, however, that he was disappointed they had spent so little time and had not gathered more information. A year at least was needed to do it justice, he said. But they had taken too long to get to Palenque through the Petén, and he was worried about what they were thinking back in Belize. He "judged it prudent" to cut their investigation short and start for home.

In the end, their rush to leave would only add to their eventual undoing. In a journey that had already lasted more than three months, they ended up devoting only two weeks to the object of their mission. Even in his official report, Walker sometimes seemed confused as to the expedition's real purpose. He devoted far more space to the agriculture, geography, and politics of the Petén than to the ruins. As a result, they left with too few descriptive passages and illustrations. But more important, their reports conveyed little of the wonder the ruins inspired in other explorers—or any sense of urgency to tell the world. This may have reflected the fact that, unlike Stephens and Catherwood, neither man had initiated the expedition. They had been drafted for the project by Colonel MacDonald, and no matter how dutifully they tried to carry out their assignment, they were still only following orders.

They came out of the ruins, however, with one clear goal. They were determined not to return home to Belize the way they had come. It had been too grueling. They planned, instead, to take the Usumacinta River down to the Gulf of Mexico and return to Belize around the peninsula, by the sea. For a now-unknown reason, even that plan failed.

◁◁ 10 ▷▷

Crisis at Hand

Colonel Juan Galindo was dead, cut to pieces. Stephens heard the news shortly after he arrived in Grenada. According to the report, the colonel fell to machete-wielding Indians after a battle near the Honduran city of Tegucigalpa. In his desire to save the republic, the Irishman had joined General José Trinidad Cabañas of the Liberal party and at the end of January their small army was routed at Hacienda del Potrero by Conservative Honduran forces and an army from Nicaragua. "The records of civil wars among Christian people nowhere present a bloodier page," wrote Stephens of the battle. "No quarter was given or asked. After the battle, fourteen officers were shot in cold blood, and not a single prisoner lived as a monument of mercy." Cabañas managed to escape. But Galindo, accompanied by two dragoons and a servant boy, was recognized in a nearby Indian village and cut down.[1]

Stephens was deeply affected by the news. He had hoped to meet Galindo, in whom he saw something of himself. Both were adventurers, political idealists, modern men possessed with great curiosity about antiquities. Stephens was carrying a letter of introduction to the colonel from Forsyth, who had met with Galindo in Washington. Galindo no doubt would have been interested in Stephens's experiences in Egypt and the East. And Stephens, in turn, would have credited him for inspiring him to visit Copán, as he would later do in his book. Now, at the age of thirty-eight, the colonel was dead, his plans and dreams annihilated by war. And Stephens lost his chance to talk with the only person to have explored both Palenque and Copán.[2]

Meanwhile the war clouds were darkening. El Potrero was only a first skirmish. Stephens learned in Grenada that Morazán had quit his post as El Salvador's chief of state to take full command of his forces and had sent his family by sea to Chile for their safety. Armies were on the march in Honduras and Nicaragua. "The crisis was at hand," Stephens concluded, adding that he had to get to Guatemala "while yet the road was open."

He mounted his macho for El Salvador, stopping on the way at León, then the capital of Nicaragua. He found the town smoldering in ruins, half of it razed to the ground in a furious struggle between the local Liberals and Conservatives. It was now occupied by the same Nicaraguan army that had defeated Galindo and Cabañas in Honduras. Stephens watched as six hundred of the soldiers marched out of town, headed not for El Salvador to battle their archenemy Morazán, but for their sister city Grenada, which had refused to contribute to the expenses of the last campaign in Honduras. "War between the states was bad enough," wrote Stephens, "but here the flame which had before laid the capital in ruins was lighted again within its own borders."

Stephens crossed the Gulf of Fonseca by boat and entered El Salvador. When he landed at La Unión with his two mules and baggage, he learned that Morazán had left the port only days earlier after sending his family aboard a ship to safety. He was told that the general was planning an immediate attack on Guatemala. Stephens set out at once to catch up with him, hoping he could cross into Guatemala under his protection.

Five days later, after dodging Hondurans forces invading El Salvador from the north, Stephens reached the earthquake-ravaged capital of San Salvador. But Morazán was gone. He had already left with his army for Guatemala. That evening Stephens met again with Vigil, the republic's vice president, and his aides, and was stunned by their optimism given the chaos of the situation. "It was a higher tone than I was accustomed to," wrote Stephens, "when the chief men of a single state, with an invading army at their door, and their own soldiers away, expressed the stern resolution to sustain the Federation, or die under the ruins of the capital. All depended upon the success of Morazán's expedition. If he failed, my occupation was gone; in this darkest hour of the Republic I did not despair. In ten years of war Morazán had never been beaten; Carrera would not dare fight him . . . and out of the chaos the government I was in search of would appear."

Stephens thought it necessary to get to Guatemala City as quickly as possible. Despite repeated warnings not to proceed, he set off for the Guatemalan border. The way was treacherous; bandits roamed freely. Mounted, heavily armed soldiers were commandeering every mule and horse they could lay hands on, and pressing boys and old men into service. After several days Stephens arrived at Ahuachapán, a Salvadoran border town with close ties to Morazán. He entered just before dark and found shelter with a widow whose late husband had been a personal friend of Morazán and whose son had joined the general's army for the invasion. A second son was imprisoned by Carrera in Guatemala City.

Stephens, weary from the journey, settled in for the night—but there would be little sleep. First, he was awakened by a report that Carrera had crushed Morazán in Guatemala City. The news created immediate panic in the town. Morazán apparently had escaped and was headed back to Salvador with Carrera's army in pursuit. A few hours of sleep later, a second report came that armed men on horseback were approaching Ahuachapán. The church bells began tolling and the townspeople began to flee the city. It was a pathetic sight, Stephens recalled: sick and disabled old men and women huddled on the steps of the church. Stephens was warned to escape while he still could. "We did not know whether the whole army of Carrera was approaching, or merely a roving detachment," he wrote. "If the former, my hope was that Carrera was with them and that he had not forgotten my diplomatic coat." Stephens returned to the house with one of his companions and waited anxiously. He smoked, went out, and looked around but there was nothing to see. The bells had stopped ringing and a ghostlike quiet fell over the town, now nearly empty. "We became positively tired of waiting; there were still two hours to daylight; we lay down, and, strange to say, again fell asleep."

○◎○

General Francisco Morazán's much-acclaimed invincibility disintegrated in the early morning hours of March 20, 1840. He barely escaped Guatemala City's blood-soaked central plaza with his life. Much had transpired since Stephens left Guatemala more than two months earlier. In January Carrera rode out of the city with some one thousand men and invaded the liberal stronghold of Quetzaltenango, the breakaway district in western Guatemala allied with Morazán. With two quick strikes, Carrera and his small army routed the Liberals. Carrera returned to Guatemala City in triumph, riding into the capital on February 17 under flower-decked arches, with bands playing, flags flying, and cannons firing. With the Quetzaltenango Liberals vanquished and the military threat from the rear removed, all that remained was the long-awaited showdown with Morazán from the east. Carrera then turned to face his most dangerous foe with virtually all his forces intact and battle hardened.

Morazán finally obliged. He crossed the border into Guatemala on March 12 at the head of a column of only 1,500 men, with the expectation that Guatemalan liberals would quickly rise up and join him and the republican cause. Carrera, meanwhile, rode out of the capital with nearly a thousand of his most loyal Indian and Mestizo fighters and took up a position about five miles away on a nearby plantation. He left eight hundred men digging in and fortifying the city under the leadership of one of his chief officers.[3] Carrera's plan was to catch Morazán and his army just as they approached the city, and like a hammer and anvil, crush them between his men and those waiting inside the city walls.[4] But Morazán struck more quickly than expected, attacking at 3 A.M. on March 18 through the Buena Vista gate and taking the Conservative forces in the capital by surprise. After a series of vicious battles, the defenders fell back and Morazán captured much of the city by noon. He immediately opened the city's jails and freed more than forty Liberals who had been imprisoned by Carrera. They included the humiliated commander of the Quetzaltenango army, who had been so badly abused as a prisoner that he was unable to take up arms when his chains were removed. Then Morazán ordered his men to take up defensive positions as Carrera, reinforced by Indians from the countryside, circled the city.

The next day Carrera launched an all-out attack. According to accounts Stephens later compiled from eyewitnesses, the battle raged all

morning in savage, bloody street fighting.[5] Carrera and his men fell
first upon Morazán's reserves on the edge of the city. Morazán left the
main plaza with a small force to join the fight. The two sides clashed
in hand-to-hand combat and a large number of Morazán's best officers were killed or badly wounded. Carrera later boasted that he had
personally encountered Morazán during the battle and nearly split the
general's saddle in two with his saber. Morazán and his men retreated
through the streets to the plaza, leaving behind nearly four hundred
dead and wounded, three hundred much-needed muskets, and all of
his army's baggage and equipment. By ten o'clock in the morning
they were penned up in the plaza, surrounded by the enormous mass
of Carrera's Indians. Morazán stationed men on the rooftops of the
surrounding houses and buildings but his men in the square were
under fire from all corners. By noon, the firing slackened as Carrera
and his men gradually ran out of ammunition, or began hoarding it
for a final assault. Carrera himself, it was reported, sat down to roll
cartridges. A sinister quiet descended over the plaza as the firing
stopped. "Pent up in this fearful position," Stephens wrote, "Morazán
had time to reflect."

> But a year before he was received [by the city's residents] with
> ringing of bells, firing of cannon, joyful acclamations, and dep-
> utations of grateful citizens, as the only man who could save
> them from Carrera and destruction. [Now] among the few
> white citizens in the plaza at the time of the entry of Morazán's
> soldiers was a young man, who was taken prisoner and brought
> before General Morazán. The latter knew him personally, and
> inquired for several of his old partisans by name, asking whether
> they were not coming to join him. The young man answered
> that they were not, and Morazán and his officers seemed disap-
> pointed. No doubt he had expected a rising of citizens in his
> favour, and again to be hailed as a deliverer from Carrera.

Dead bodies clogged the streets and lay scattered across the floor
of the plaza. It was already a scene of great slaughter. The silence was
broken only by Carrera's Indians shouting jeers and catcalls from the

Main plaza of Guatemala City in 1860, with market stalls filling the square.

corners where they massed along the approaches to the square. At sunset, the Indians fell to their knees and took up the prayer "Ave Maria." The chant swelled to such a volume it sent chills through Morazán and his trapped men, who now fully realized the odds they were facing. The hymn was followed by the thunderous roar of "Viva la religión! Muera el General Morazán (Death to General Morazán)! Viva Carrera!" and the bullets poured into the plaza once again with more ferocity than ever. The fighting went on for hours; finally, at two o'clock in the morning, Morazán's men made a desperate attempt to cut their way out but were driven back. The plaza was now littered with piles of the dead, including Morazán's eldest son and forty of his most loyal veteran officers.

What happened next is the subject of debate. According to the official record of the battle—meaning the victors'—Morazán stationed a hundred men at each of the plaza's three corners and ordered them to open fire at 3 A.M. Then, while attention was diverted, the general and five hundred men shouting "Viva Carrera!" made their escape in the darkness via the fourth corner, leaving the other men to fend for themselves. The French consul, Auguste Mahelin, however, noted that there was a bright moon that night, which lent little credibility to the report of Morazán sneaking off in the darkness.

Whether Morazán fought his way out or escaped by ruse, the official "victor's" record is largely silent about the horror that followed. While Morazán fled the city, many of those in the plaza who were taken prisoners were summarily shot by Carrera's men. Wounded men were bayoneted as they lay on the ground. "Carrera stood pointing with his finger at this man and that," wrote Stephens, "and every one that he indicated was removed a few paces from him and shot."[6] A dozen survivors dropped down from their rooftop perch and took refuge in the courtyard of the British vice consul's house, located near the plaza. Somehow Carrera found out—possibly alerted by British consul general Chatfield, according to one account. Carrera demanded the men be turned over. Chatfield agreed but only on condition that they be tried legally. The men were taken and several minutes later executed around the corner.[7]

As the massacre in the plaza continued, Morazán made his way over the mountains to the town of Antigua. A faction of the townspeople still loyal to the Liberal cause implored him to declare martial law and launch a new attack on the capital. He refused, noting that "enough blood had been shed." He stayed long enough to write a letter to Carrera asking him to treat the prisoners with mercy. Then he retreated along the coast to El Salvador.

◎◎◎

When Stephens woke in Ahuachapán, a boy came running with the news that Carrera's men were coming toward the town. A short time later a cavalry detachment appeared at the end of the street. Stephens went out to face them. More than a hundred lancers filed by, two abreast, red pennants on the tips of their spears, shouting "Viva Carrera!" They were led by a general named Figueroa. The lancers were followed by the infantry, mostly Indians, many in rags, carrying machetes and old flintlocks. They too cried "Viva Carrera!" with a ferocity that demanded equal reply. "There was no escape," Stephens wrote, "and I believe they would have shot us down on the spot if we had refused to echo the cry."

Stephens, ever the diplomat, invited the general to breakfast. But before long, Figueroa and his men were mounting up and dashing off to investigate a report that allies of Morazán were lurking not far outside the town. In the afternoon, they returned apparently unsuccessful in finding anyone. With General Figueroa billeted in the plaza once again, Stephens prevailed on him to draw up a passport that he hoped would give him safe passage on the road to Guatemala City. Then word came that Morazán himself was approaching the city. Figueroa and the lancers immediately took to their horses and headed out of the plaza to face him. Straggling behind ran the long line of Indian infantrymen. Next came a volley of gunshots, followed by a riderless horse galloping through the plaza. Several more followed, and soon bullets were flying in every direction. Figueroa and thirty or forty of his lancers came dashing down the street. They rallied, turned, and attacked up the street again. Stephens and several traveling companions, along with an old servant woman, scurried back into the house they had been occupying, and as the battle raged in the street outside, they sought refuge in a small inside room closed off by a door three inches thick. "In utter darkness," he wrote, "we listened valiantly."

Finally, the firing died down, and they heard a blast of a bugle and the hooves of the cavalry. They went to the front door and carefully peered out as they heard the cry "Viva la Federación!" Night had fallen. A passing lancer asked for water, which they provided. Within no time, a group of Morazán's men trooped into the house, which was well known to them because of the family's connection to Morazán. They had been on horseback for six days zigzagging through enemy country to avoid pursuit. "Entering under the excitement of a successful skirmish," Stephens recalled, "they struck me as the finest set of men I had seen in the country." Wiping blood from their swords, they explained that they were taken by surprise by Figueroa. Morazán, who had been riding in the lead, dodged two bullets before he could even draw his pistol. Had their horses not been so tired they would have killed every one of Figueroa's men, they claimed.

LEFT   A portrait of John Lloyd Stephens from an 1854 London reprint of *Incidents of Travel in Central America, Chiapas, and Yucatán*. Frederick Catherwood put together an abridged version of Stephens's account of their travels and added this portrait as a frontispiece, stating that it was from a daguerreotype of Stephens. The image was possibly taken by Catherwood himself during their 1842 expedition to Yucatán. As Stephens's longtime traveling companion, Catherwood knew well what he looked like, so the portrait is likely one of the most accurate of those few that still exist. It captures an expression of fierce determination that Catherwood must have thought characterized his old friend, who had died two years earlier.

RIGHT   This indistinct image is the only known "portrait" of Frederick Catherwood in existence. Oddly, although he was well known to many artists during his lifetime, no other depictions of him have been found. Nor was he apparently given to self-portraiture, which has only added to an aura of mystery that has come to surround him. This image is enlarged from an illustration he made of the Maya ruins at Tulum in Yucatán. He is shown holding a tape as he and Stephens are measuring the length of the stone structure, their figures used merely to give the viewer a sense of perspective to indicate the size of the building.

The illustrations on the following fourteen pages are taken from Frederick Catherwood's *View of Ancient Monuments in Central America, Chiapas, and Yucatán*, which he published in oversize folio in London and New York in 1844. Catherwood created only 300 such folios, each with 25 lithographed plates, of which 250 were tinted light blue or brown. The 50 remaining folios, illustrations from which are displayed here and are today extremely rare, were hand colored. (Pages 2–15, courtesy of the Museum Library at the University of Pennsylvania Museum of Archaeology and Anthropology)

○ ◉ ○

Stela at Copan.

TOP Pyramid and pieces of sculpture, Copan.

BOTTOM Broken stela at Copan.

Stela and altar, Copan.

TOP General view of Palenque.

BOTTOM Palace courtyard, Palenque.

TOP General view at Uxmal with Stephens directing workmen.

BOTTOM General view of the Governor's House and House of Pigeons, at Uxmal.

Elaborate ornamentation and archway at the Governor's House, Uxmal.

Section of decorative façade of the Nunnery at Uxmal.

LEFT TOP General view of Kabah, with Stephens directing workmen
carrying lintel for shipment to New York.

LEFT BOTTOM Archway at Labná.

Interior of main building at Kabah with decorative step.

LEFT A part of the Nunnery structure, Uxmal.

Cave at Bolonchen.

TOP Main pyramid, Chichen Itzá.
BOTTOM Elaborately decorated building at Chichen Itzá.

Stairway to the "Castillo," or citadel, at Tulum.

RIGHT TOP Temple at Tulum with image of Catherwood on the right
and Stephens or Cabot on the left with measuring tape.

RIGHT BOTTOM Giant stucco head at Izamal in Yucatán.

A view of a temple in Palenque today. (Carlsen)

Morazán put out word that he and his soldiers would be resting in the plaza. Stephens seized the opportunity to finally meet the famous general. He stood conferring with some of his officers when Stephens entered the *cabildo*.

> A large fire was burning before the door, and a table stood against the wall with a candle and chocolate-cups upon it. He was about forty-five years old, five feet ten inches high, thin, with a black mustache and week's beard, and wore a military frock-coat, buttoned up to the throat, and sword. His hat was off, and the expression of his face mild and intelligent. Though still young, for ten years he had been the first man in the country. He had risen and sustained himself by military skill and personal bravery; always led his forces himself; had been in innumerable battles, and often wounded, but never beaten. From the best information I could acquire, and from the enthusiasm with which I had heard him spoken of by his officers, and, in fact, by everyone else in his own state, I had conceived almost a feeling of admiration for General Morazán, and my interest in him was increased by his misfortunes. I was really at a loss how to address him; and while my mind was full of his ill-fated expedition, his first question was if his family had arrived in Costa Rica, or if I had heard anything of them. It spoke volumes that, at such a moment, with the wreck of his followers before him, and the memory of his murdered companions fresh in his mind, in the overthrow of all his hopes and fortunes, his heart turned to his domestic relations.

Introducing himself in his official capacity, Stephens spoke briefly about the treaty he was sent to Central America to negotiate, though it must have seemed awkward if not absurd at the moment. Morazán said he regretted deeply that it had not been accomplished. "He expressed his sorrow for the condition in which I saw his unhappy country," Stephens recalled. "Feeling that he must have more important business, I remained but a short time, and returned to the house."

That night Stephens tried in vain to arrange for a guide to help

him reach the inaptly named Río Paz, or River of Peace, which separated El Salvador from Guatemala. The prospects were not good.
Every man capable of guiding him was in deadly fear of encountering
Carrera's men. Stephens was filled with trepidation as well, but he
relished even less the bloody battle in Ahuachapán that would occur
if Carrera arrived while Morazán was still in residence.

The next morning Morazán came to the house. Their conversation
this time was "longer and more general." Stephens did not ask him his
plans and the general alluded only to vague designs to confront the
northern commander, General Cáscara, who now occupied the Salvadoran town of Santa Ana. "He spoke without malice or bitterness of
the leader of the [Conservative] party, and of Carrera as an ignorant
and lawless Indian, from whom the party that was now using him
would one day be glad to be protected." The general warned Stephens
not to travel to Guatemala, as it was extremely unsafe. But if he insisted, Morazán said that he would send for the mayor and find him
a guide.

> I bade him farewell with an interest greater than I had felt for
> any man in the country. Little did we then know the calamities
> that were still in store for him; that very night most of his sol-
> diers deserted, having been kept together only by the danger to
> which they were exposed while in an enemy's country. With the
> rest he marched to Zonzonate, seized a vessel at the port, man-
> ning it with his own men, and sent her to Libertad, the port of
> San Salvador. He then marched to the capital, where the people,
> who had for years idolized him in power, turned their backs on
> him in misfortune, received him with open insults in the
> streets. With many of his officers, who were too deeply compro-
> mised to remain, he embarked for Chili. His worst enemies
> admit he was exemplary in his private relations, and, what they
> consider no small praise, that he was not sanguinary. He is now
> fallen and in exile, probably forever, under sentence of death if
> he returns. I verily believe they have driven from their shores
> the best man in Central America.[8]

Not long after Morazán left, an old man loyal to the general appeared before Stephens with his twenty-two-year-old son, whom he offered as a guide. But when the young man learned they would be going toward the Guatemalan border he excused himself saying he was going to get a horse; he never came back. A ten-year-old boy, dressed in a straw hat and riding bareback, was substituted instead. It was thought the little boy would run less risk from the soldiers prowling the countryside. Better a ten-year-old than no one, Stephens thought, and a short time later they set out on the road to Guatemala.

◁ 11 ▷

Reunion

I had finished a journey of twelve hundred miles," wrote Stephens, "and the gold of Peru could not have tempted me to undertake it again." The buildings and cobblestone streets were dark with blood as Stephens rode on his macho into the Guatemalan capital. In a passageway near the plaza, twenty-seven of Carrera's Indians had set up a barricade outside the door of the city's mint. When Morazán's men finished their assault, twenty-six of the defenders lay dead or wounded, and ten days later their blood still blackened the steps. The whitewashed walls of the houses along the side streets were pockmarked with bullet holes and ruddy with splattered blood. All the structures fronting the central square were "fearfully scarified." And at the U.S. consul's house near the plaza, Stephens's official residence, he was shown three musket balls that had been plucked from the woodwork for his inspection.

The city remained in shock. Morazán's impossible defeat and the consequences of Carrera's victory were all that people talked about. Meanwhile, Carrera and the main force of his army had left the capital. He had set out after Morazán but was diverted to Quetzaltenango to put down another uprising there. The soldiers who had been left behind as guards confronted Stephens as he took his first walk through the streets; they demonstrated how they had dispatched their enemies by pointing their muskets at his head. He hurried back to the safety of the consul's residence.

In spite of the dangers still lurking in the streets, Stephens felt after months of hard travel that he had returned "home" to a place he could finally rest secure. "I still felt anxieties; I had no letters from home, and Mr. Catherwood had not yet arrived."

The next afternoon, unexpectedly, Catherwood was at the door. He had just returned from a second visit to Copán, to which he had retreated while Morazán and Carrera battled for the city. "In our joy at meeting," Stephens wrote, "we tumbled into each other's arms." They resolved for the remainder of their journey never to part again.

Over the next few days, the two men excitedly exchanged notes. During Stephens's absence, Catherwood kept occupied with work. In addition to returning to Copán to make more drawings, he made an extraordinary discovery that again roused Stephens's archaeological yearnings. Earlier, when traveling to the capital from their first visit to Copán, Catherwood had heard rumors of stone ruins buried in the jungle along the Motagua River not too far from Copán. Stephens had heard similar stories in Guatemala City from three brothers who had inherited a vast tract of land along the river. The Payes brothers said they were once told by their father that the land contained mysterious stone objects at a site the locals called Quiriguá, but they had never visited the land or seen the objects for themselves. It had been decided that while Stephens traveled to El Salvador, Catherwood would try to determine if there was any truth to the rumors.

Catherwood hit gold—but only after a complicated, arduous journey. After reaching the Motagua and enduring several dugout canoe rides through nearly unbearable heat and humidity, he and the Payes brothers hiked through spongy fields and forests of tall cedar and mahogany trees until they finally came upon a pyramid structure overgrown with vegetation. In quick order, they found a "colossal" carved head six feet in diameter and covered in moss, several stone altars sculpted with unusual animal-like features, and a large group of sculpted vertical stone blocks resembling the monoliths that Catherwood and Stephens had found in Copán. These bore carvings of human figures and were covered with hieroglyphics, executed in the same style as Copán but with one astounding difference—these monuments were gigantic. They soared two and three times the height of those they had found at Copán and were proportionally more immense in girth.

Based on notes and drawings Catherwood made, Stephens calculated that one "obelisk or carved stone" stood twenty-six feet out of

Gigantic stela at Quiriguá. (Catherwood)

the ground. "It is leaning twelve feet two inches out of the perpendicular, and seems ready to fall. . . . The side toward the ground represents the figure of a man, very perfect and finely sculptured. The upper side seemed the same, but was so hidden by vegetation as to make it somewhat uncertain. The two [sides] contain hieroglyphics in low relief." Catherwood explained to Stephens they had discovered five other similarly enormous monuments that were still erect and two others that had toppled to the ground. There were fragments of stone and carvings scattered over a larger area, which indicated much more remained to be discovered. He worked as quickly as he could to make several rough drawings over the next day, but they had failed to bring along provisions and the Payeses had already gone on to another part of their estate. Catherwood soon followed.

Going over his notes and sketches, Stephens and Catherwood

speculated that Quiriguá must have had some affiliation with the larger site of Copán, some twenty-five miles to the south. "Of one thing there is no doubt," Stephens wrote, "a large city once stood there; its name is lost, its history unknown; and, except for a notice taken from Mr. C's notes, and inserted by the Senores Payes in a Guatimala paper after the visit, which found its way to [the United States] and Europe, no account of its existence has ever before been published. For centuries it has lain as completely buried as if covered in the lava of Vesuvius."

Stephens relished the thought of seeing the site for himself. But there was not enough time to go to Quiriguá and get to Palenque before the start of the rainy season. Each site was located in a different direction.

There also were other official matters Stephens had to complete before they could leave. While his chief assignment ended with Morazán's defeat and the final collapse of the republic, he also had orders to close up the mission, pack up the delegation's archives, and ship them back to Washington. These affairs were settled quickly. And he sent a final detailed dispatch to Forsyth, which concluded with "After diligent search, no government was found."

With the completion of his duties, Stephens wrote: "I was once more my own master, at liberty to go where I please, at my own expense, and immediately we commenced making arrangements for our journey to Palenque."

In order to withdraw from the capital as diplomatically as possible, Stephens made the rounds of the Conservative Guatemala government, including its political chief of state, Mariano Rivera Paz. The leader provided him with a passport for his journey. To smooth his path, a favorable notice concerning his travel plans was placed in the government newspaper, *El Tiempo*. "But these were not enough," Stephens wrote. "Carrera's name was worth more than them all, and we waited two days for his return from Quetzaltenango."

Meanwhile, he paid a visit to Narciso Payes, one of the three brothers on whose land Quiriguá was located. Although the discovery of the site was stunning, what excited Stephens most was its proximity to the Motagua River. Based on Catherwood's calculations, the depth of the water indicated that one or more of the giant monu-

ments could be transported by boat to the Gulf of Honduras and
then by ship to New York City. He arrived at Payes's doorstep to
make a deal. After all, with minimum effort and his diplomat's coat
he had acquired the rights to the Copán ruins for fifty dollars. This
time, however, his diplomatic cover worked against him. No matter
how hard he tried to persuade Payes that he was acting as a private
individual and thus did not have the monetary resources of the
United States government behind him, Payes remained unconvinced.
At any event, Payes continued, he would have to consult his brothers
when they returned to Guatemala City in the next few days.

Stephens departed in frustration; the two brothers did not arrive
before Stephens and Catherwood left for Palenque. But the odds of
negotiating a deal were fading fast anyway. During the interval, Narciso Payes consulted with the French consul general, who informed
him that his government had paid several hundred thousand dollars
to acquire just one of the Egyptian obelisks of Luxor for transport to
Paris.[1] Before they had sought out the consul, Stephens wrote, "the
owners would have been glad to sell the whole tract, consisting of
more than fifty thousand acres, with everything on it, known and
unknown, for a few thousand dollars." Stephens remained optimistic,
however, that a deal could still be worked out, and he left an undis-
closed offer with a friend to be presented when the two Payes brothers
returned.[2]

Palenque beckoned. After only a week in Guatemala City, Stephens and Catherwood had gathered supplies, mules, and horses and
were prepared to start. But people arriving from outside the city still
warned of dangerous roads. And nearly everyone they met urged them
to reconsider. An aide-de-camp of Colonel MacDonald arrived from
Belize and ran into Stephens at an official gathering. He informed
him for the first time of the Walker-Caddy expedition to Palenque.
The news was not good, he added. The two men had been killed by
the Indians, speared to death, according to the latest accounts received
at Belize. This, as Stephens was to learn later, was untrue. The greatest
apprehensions, however, came from rumors filtering back from Carrera's campaign in Quetzaltenango, through which Stephens and
Catherwood were to pass on their way to Palenque. Carrera, it was

whispered, had committed yet more atrocities, the Indians had risen up, and they were massacring whites.

Waiting to meet Carrera for a personally signed passport, Stephens decided to take a last stroll through the suburbs of the city. He was entranced once again by the natural beauty of the place and especially the volcanoes Agua, Fuego, and Acatenango, not far in the distance, standing like guardians over a troubled Garden of Eden. Then he was drawn, as he so often was, to a nearby cemetery. It had been established in the time of the cholera outbreak but now served also as a final resting place for more than four hundred men killed in the recent contest for the city. Their bodies lay tumbled together under a large square of newly turned earth. "It was a gloomy leave-taking of Guatimala," he wrote.

The next day the rumors about Quetzaltenango were confirmed. The violence had been set in motion two weeks earlier when a message reached Quetzaltenango that Morazán had attacked and successfully occupied Guatemala City. In response to the news, the townspeople of Quetzaltenango rose up and drove Carrera's garrison from their city. Then city officials made the mistake of sending a letter of congratulations by courier to Morazán. Carrera learned of the uprising during his march in pursuit of Morazán. He altered his course instantly and marched off for Quetzaltenango. With great trepidation, the city's leaders gathered in the plaza to meet him. Just as he arrived, the Indian courier, who had never traveled to the capital as he was instructed, gave Carrera the city's letter of congratulations meant for Morazán. For the municipal leaders, it was monumental bad timing. Carrera flew into such a fury listening to his secretary read the words that he drew his sword and wounded the mayor and two others before he somehow got hold of himself and stopped. He ordered his soldiers to seize the leaders and march them off to jail. The next day, he had the mayor and seventeen of the city's leading men brought to the plaza. Then, Stephens wrote, "without the slightest form of trial, not even a drum-head court-martial," one by one they were seated on a stone in front of the wall and executed.

Word then reached Guatemala City that upon Carrera's return, he intended to march the hundreds of surviving Morazán prisoners into the plaza and have them all shot down as well. The fear in the city was palpable. "Again the sword seemed suspended by a single hair," Stephens wrote.

> Even among the adherents of the Carrera party there was a fearful apprehension of a war of castes, and a strong desire, on the part of those who could get away, to leave the country. I was consulted by men having houses and large estates, but who could only command two or three thousand dollars in money, as to their ability to live on that sum in the United States. Heretofore, in all the wars and revolutions the whites had the controlling influence, but this time the Indians were the dominant power. Roused from the sloth of ages, and with muskets in their hands, their gentleness was changed into ferocity. Carrera was the pivot on which this turned.

The day after Carrera returned, Stephens went to see him. Carrera was now living in a much larger house and his guards were more numerous and well appointed. When Stephens entered his chambers, the general was standing behind a table holding a gold chain in his hand. His military coat lay on the table and he had on the same "roundabout" jacket Stephens had last seen him in. His wife, the fiery, infamous Petrona, stood nearby examining a pile of gold necklaces with President Rivera Paz and one or two others. Stephens was immediately struck by how pretty, young, and delicate she looked. She was, Stephens noted, "not more than twenty, and seemed to have a woman's fondness for chains and gold. Carrera himself looked at them with indifference."

The general recognized him immediately. Despite all the trials Carrera had gone through over the last months, Stephens noted, he had lost none of his youthfulness: "His face had the same . . . quickness and intelligence, his voice and manners the same gentleness and seriousness, and he had again been wounded." Stephens explained the purpose of his visit: his need of Carrera's personal endorsement in his passport. Carrera took the passport out of Stephens's hand and threw it on the table stating that he would draft a new one and sign it himself. He turned to his secretary and instructed him to make it out to the "Consul of the North."

The secretary left and Carrera motioned for Stephens to join him at the table. The general revealed he had heard Stephens met Morazán during his retreat and asked about the encounter. Carrera then explained he was planning an assault on San Salvador in a week, with three thousand men. He noted that Morazán would have been driven from the plaza in Guatemala City much sooner if he had cannons. Stephens asked if the report was accurate that early in the battle he and Morazán had met. Carrera said it was true, that Morazán's dismounted troopers had torn off Carrera's holsters, that Morazán himself had gotten off one shot at him, and that he had gotten close enough to take a good slice at Morazán with his sword, but missed and cut his saddle.

Stephens wrote that he found the whole meeting bizarre: "I could not but think of the strange position into which I was thrown: shaking hands and sitting side by side with men who were thirsting for each other's blood, well received by all, hearing what they had to say about each other, and in many cases their plans and purposes, as unreservedly as if I was a traveling member of both cabinets."

The secretary called Carrera from the other room and after a few minutes the general returned with Stephens's passport in hand, the ink still drying with Carrera's signature. "It had taken him longer than it would have done to cut off a head, and he seemed more proud of it," wrote Stephens. "I made a comment upon the excellence of the handwriting, and with his good wishes for my safe arrival in the North . . . I took my leave."

That evening Stephens packed up his diplomatic coat, its large gold buttons glowing rich and warm in the lamplight, and bundled it with the other items he was sending home. He and Catherwood wrote out the last of their letters, and the next morning, April 7, 1840, they set out for Chiapas, Mexico—and Palenque.

⊙ⓒ⊙

Two days earlier, on April 5, Caddy and Walker sailed into Belize harbor. It was nearly five months since they had launched their expedition up the Belize River and a month and a half since they left Palenque. Their return took them down the Usumacinta River— Caddy blasting away with his shotgun at twenty-foot-long alligators on the river banks—to the large estuary on the Gulf of Mexico called Laguna de Términos. From there they made their way north by boat along the Yucatán coast to the port of Sisal, and traveled inland to Mérida, Yucatán's capital. They then journeyed overland across the dry upper reaches of Yucatán to the peninsula's east coast, where they boarded a ship and sailed south to Belize. Compared to their agonizing journey through Petén to Palenque, their path home crossed the much more forgiving scrubland of the north and they must have wondered why they hadn't taken that route to Palenque in the first place. Sailing into the Belize harbor they were greeted by an anxious Colonel MacDonald, who with the rest of colony breathed a sigh of relief. The report of their demise was unfounded and their expedition an obvious triumph.

There was only one problem. Shortly after their return, MacDonald received a troubling dispatch from the Colonial Office. MacDonald's November letter to the office outlining the expedition had not been well received in England. There were concerns deep within the bowels of the bureaucracy that the colonel had acted out of place by advancing government money for the expedition without prior approval.

The dispatch from Lord John Russell, secretary of state for the colonies and soon-to-be prime minister, noted that he had not received MacDonald's November communication until February, which, as it turned out, was about the time Caddy and Walker were leaving Palenque to return to Belize. Lord Russell's letter, dated February 19, said that he had learned that MacDonald had appropriated two hundred pounds sterling from the "Military Chest" for the expedition.

> The deputy Asst. Commissary Genl. in Honduras has advised the Lords of the Treasury of this advance having been made & their Lordships have communicated to me their opinion, in which I concur, that you were not in any respect warranted in directing an issue from the Military Chest for objects of the

description to which your dispatch refers without the previous authority of Her Majesty's Government.

Their Lordships further state that they would not be justified in giving their sanction for relieving you of the responsibility on account of this advance, until the manner in which the money may have been disbursed has been distinctly specified, & such report of the Expedition has been made as may shew that the result of it has proved beneficial to the Public.

So much for "English scientific prestige" when fiscal accountability was in question, wrote David Pendergast in his 1967 book, *Palenque: The Walker-Caddy Expedition to the Ancient Maya City, 1839–1840*.[3] Instead of praise for his initiative to advance science in the queen's name—and of course to beat out an American rival—the colonel now faced the possibility of having to personally reimburse the "Military Chest" two hundred pounds simply because he failed to observe bureaucratic protocols. The pressure was now on MacDonald and he put his two explorers to work immediately.

The interchange of dispatches was one more example of the paralyzing slowness of communications in the early nineteenth century, unimaginable today. Just a few months earlier, a worried MacDonald wrote Chatfield in Guatemala asking if he had heard anything there about Walker and Caddy. In his March reply, weeks after the two men were already on their way back to Belize, Chatfield said he had heard nothing. He wrote again on April 8, three days after Walker and Caddy were safely home in Belize, that he still had no news. But he filled MacDonald in with some other intelligence: "Mr. Stephens & the Yankified English artist who accompanies him are gone to Quesaltenango, intending to get to Palenque across the Mexican frontier."

Within six weeks of Walker and Caddy's return, MacDonald had in hand Walker's official ten-thousand-word report. He seemed pleased enough with it that on May 13 he wrote Lord Russell: "I am quite sensible that previous to authorizing any expedition of the kind I ought to have had the authority of H M Government but I trust that when I have submitted to Your Lordship my explanation on the subject that Your Lordship will free me from the imputation of having acted prematurely or without consideration in the matter." He added that he was now only waiting for completion of Caddy's drawings "illustrative of the expedition" before forwarding Walker's report on to London.

With one casualty, the two Englishmen had beaten Stephens and Catherwood to Palenque, a point of national pride for them, Mac-Donald, and the rest of the colony. Others, however, including Juan Galindo, had visited the ruins before them. And it would soon become evident that it wasn't so important who got there first but who made the most of the visit. Walker's businesslike report would prove no match for the written account Stephens would make of Palenque. The contrast would be clear enough in the prose—Stephens unquestionably the more talented writer—but the greater problem was the lack of attention Walker gave to the ruins. Although it was the primary goal of their expedition, Palenque received no more than four paragraphs of description in his thirty-page report (Stephens would write more than forty pages on Palenque). Walker devoted the bulk of his report to describing the local populations, their customs, agricultural production, the geography and terrain, as well as the politics of Guatemala and Mexico, mixed with blatantly chauvinistic comments. So many of Walker's remarks touched on delicate political issues that the Colonial Office later ordered them deleted.

Though short on descriptions of Palenque, Walker was perfectly willing to speculate on theories concerning the ruins' origins: "The one I am most prone to indulge in is that a large fleet had ploughed the Atlantic in search of undiscovered country." Once they sailed up the Usumacinta River, he wrote, they found this fertile site nestled against the mountains and they decided to stay. "Each building rigidly constructed according to one undeviating model marks the despotic character of Egyptian architecture." He added that Asians from the Far East or India might also have built Palenque. The one hypothesis Walker rejected out of hand was that the aboriginal natives of the Americas could have created such an advanced city. He called the Indians who inhabited the land prior to the arrival of the Spanish "an unskillful and feeble race, incapable of great designs or the ability to execute any work of magnitude and art." Curiously, he failed to notice that the human figures carved so artfully throughout the ruins—also drawn by Caddy—and who clearly represented the ancient city's lords and nobles, bore a distinct resemblance to the contemporary Indians of the district.

In fairness to Walker, he may have believed Caddy's drawings were intended to tell the real story of the ruins, and that his report was to be no more than a travelogue of interesting observations "beneficial to the public." After all, MacDonald appeared satisfied with it.

Everything now depended on Caddy, who labored for months on his illustrations. Some of his drawings would prove exceptional, the best to date—that is until Catherwood started his work at Palenque. Yet in the end, the molasses of colonial communications would prove a maddening obstacle. Lord Russell would not receive Walker's report and Caddy's drawings until the following February. And by then it was too late.

◅ Catherwood ▻

In Stephens's books, which are filled with vividly delineated characters met along the road, "Mr. Catherwood" is never once described. He remains forever the faithful companion—but elusive, enigmatic, almost invisible. And even though he associated with artists and writers all his life, there exists no known description or portrait of him, except for one indistinct image that he sketched of himself in Yucatán—a simply drawn figure, beardless, with a slightly sagging chin, tall and slim, wearing a broad-brimmed hat, spectacles, and long brown coat. Viewed at a distance, standing before the remains of a temple with a measuring tape in hand, he appears no more than a faint accessory used to show the scale of the crumbling structure. His innate modesty and reserve seemed a deterrent to any more fully formed, tangible self-portrait.[1] And yet certainly as much as Stephens, Catherwood had lived an outsized life.

He was born forty-one years earlier, on February 27, 1799, in Hoxton, a district then on the northern fringe of London, and he grew up in a three-story townhouse similar to most of the adjoining brick residences surrounding Charles Square. The pragmatic, faceless buildings were marked by level rows of windows and façades protected by spiked wrought-iron grillwork separating the buildings and their below-grade basement wells from the sidewalks. The square's central garden had a feeling of the country, "set with greens, plants, fruit and other trees," and the neighborhood—some buildings on the square dated from the 1600s—was known for its genteel residents.[2]

The Catherwoods, while not patrician, were solidly upper

middle class. Catherwood's grandfather, William Catherwood, had come to London in 1745 from the central English town of Coventry. He was originally listed on his children's christening records as an apothecary but later took the job of landwaiter, a civil service position collecting duties at London's custom house. Of his many sons, two became watchmakers, one a teacher and later a brass founder, and another a type founder. His middle son, John James, who would become Frederick Catherwood's father, followed his father's path into the civil service and eventually rose to become "receiver general of corn returns and accountant general of excise," positions of significant fiscal responsibility in the government service. He also became a partner in one of England's most important letter type foundries, a firm established half a century earlier by William Caslon that produced popular typefaces for printing presses.

Prosperous and well established, John James Catherwood married late, at age forty-one, to Anne Rowe in 1793. Little is known about Anne other than that she descended from a prominent aristocratic family whose lineage included Sir Thomas Rowe, an ambassador to Queen Elizabeth I, and Sir Henry Rowe, lord mayor of London. Over the next nine years, she and John had six children, three sons and three daughters, one of whom died young. Frederick was their fifth child, followed by Alfred, the youngest, who was born in 1802.

Nothing is known about Frederick's childhood other than that it appeared to be a comfortable one. Charles Square at the time was on the edge of London, where nurseries for decades occupied much of the surrounding open space. The countryside was close by, so it would have been easy for young Frederick to ramble through the northern fields much as Stephens had done as a boy in the rolling rural meadows of Manhattan, not far from New York City's then-northern boundary. And during the first decades of the 1800s, like Stephens, Catherwood witnessed the open areas surrounding his neighborhood fill in rapidly as London's population expanded northward.

For years the Hoxton district had been known for its almshouses and mental asylums, some transformed from old country manor houses constructed centuries earlier by rich Londoners escaping the smoke and disease of the central city. Yet Charles Square was insulated, looked in on itself, and must have seemed an oasis of intimacy and security as young Catherwood grew up alongside his many siblings and cousins. Frederick's family lived at 21 Charles Square, while his father's brother, Nathaniel Catherwood, with his wife and children occupied No. 20, and his aunt Elizabeth, his mother's sister, lived close by with her family.[3] The Reverend John Newton, the famous abolitionist and author of the hymn "Amazing Grace," once lived just down the street at No. 13. Newton wrote that he often gazed out his back window at nearby fields filled with cows, birds, and trees.[4]

There was no public school system in London at the time and nothing is known about Frederick's early education. He likely attended one of the many private schools established for middle- and upper-class children. Whatever schools the Catherwood children attended, they received a solid education. Alfred, Frederick's younger brother, went on to Glasgow University and became a prominent London physician, authoring a major treatise on pulmonary diseases.[5] Frederick, whose literary skills are evident in his writings, also mastered mathematics and science well enough to become a surveyor, architect, and railroad engineer.

His initial career path, like Stephens's, was undoubtedly decided by his father. At sixteen he entered into a five-year apprenticeship with architect-surveyor Michael Meredith on Great Winchester Street.[6] Around that time he also appeared to take an interest in art. On January 17, 1817, in the middle of his apprenticeship, he registered at the prestigious Royal Academy of Arts as a "probationer." This allowed a three-month period within the academy to produce work sufficient to gain him full admission. But no records exist showing that he became a full-time student.[7] He achieved a measure of recognition, however, when a work of his, described only as "Buckingham Gate, Adelphi" (now lost), was shown in an exhibition at the Royal Academy in 1820, the year he left Meredith's office.[8]

England was at war in both Europe and the United States during Catherwood's childhood and teenage years, and though he was not directly affected, he would eventually feel the consequences of Napoleon Bonaparte's relentless military campaigns. On July 1, 1798, eight months before he was born, Napoleon landed with a large expeditionary force at Alexandria, Egypt. The British would eventually defeat the French army in Egypt but only after Napoleon opened the country's ancient temples and pyramids for the first time to scientific examination, an act that would influence the course of Catherwood's life.

Before Egypt, Napoleon had conquered much of Italy. The subsequent French occupation over the next two decades effectively sealed off what had been an essential component in the education of English artists and architects: firsthand study of Roman ruins, and Italian art and architecture. That ended with Napoleon's abdication in 1814 and his defeat at Waterloo in 1815. The doors to Italy were once again thrown open and waves of British artists and architects poured in to make up for lost time, especially eager to study French excavations of the Roman Forum and other classical sites. The artists were followed in quick turn by English aristocrats and a generation of writers and Romantic poets, including Lord Byron, Percy Bysshe Shelley, and John Keats.

Indirectly, it was Keats's decision to travel to Rome that drew Catherwood there as well. While there is no documentary evidence the two men knew each other, it is very probable they did. They most likely met through a mutual friend, Joseph Severn, an artist who grew up in Hoxton and whose family of musicians were friends of the Catherwoods. In late 1820, Keats, who was seriously ill with tuberculosis and sensed he would not survive another English winter, decided to go to Italy. Severn was devoted to the gifted five-foot, one-inch poet and volunteered to drop everything in London to care for Keats during his journey. They arrived in November and took rooms in the center of Rome at 26 Piazza di Spagna, overlooking a broad white marble staircase that would later come to be known as "the Spanish Steps." The splendid views

LEFT   Portrait of Joseph Severn in 1822.
RIGHT   Poet John Keats on his deathbed in Rome, drawn by Joseph Severn.

from their windows, however, provided little solace as Severn nursed his friend through the Roman winter, rarely leaving his side. On February 23, 1821, Keats died in Severn's arms at the age of twenty-five, painfully aware that his slender volumes of poetry had drawn little but disdain from the critics. As he lay dying, he insisted his gravestone be inscribed: "Here lies one whose name was writ on water." The Italian authorities ordered everything in the room where he died burned and even the walls scraped clean. They were afraid, Severn wrote his father, of "the English Consumption."

The grieving Severn sent word of Keats's death to their friends in England and buried Keats in Rome's small Protestant cemetery. Then he decided to stay on in Italy to complete his artistic studies. He wrote his family of his plan and included a letter to his longtime friend Frederick Catherwood. In September, seven months after Keats's death, Catherwood showed up in Rome.

"Mr. Catherwood arrived here last night in perfect health and safety," Severn wrote his sister Maria. "I found him sitting in my study with the same look and manner that I recollect from London."[9] It was a joyous reunion. Though Severn was five years older, the two had become close in Hoxton and during Cather-

wood's brief time at the Royal Academy. They shared similar up-
bringings. While Catherwood apprenticed to an architect, Severn
spent eight unhappy years as an engraver's apprentice before finally breaking away to pursue his art. Catherwood passed on
family gossip from home. The next day they could barely contain
themselves as they rushed out the door. "We have this morning
seen St. Peters—and the Vatican—with which he is quite delighted or should I say astonished," Severn wrote Maria. "I have
introduced him to many brother Artists here—Englishmen—
there are three Architects among them—whom he will begin to
study with."

Severn explained he had found rooms they could share "at a
most reasonable rate—and with every possible convenience for
us two—there are two studys two sitting rooms two bedrooms
and a view all over Rome." But even before they could settle in,
their plans were disrupted by a domineering British noblewoman
named Jane Huck-Saunders, the countess of Westmorland. Since
Keats's death, the mercurial countess had taken up Severn and
his art. She had found him portrait commissions with other British aristocrats living in Rome and invited him to dinner parties
at her home, Villa Negroni. Then in September, the month
Catherwood arrived, she had fallen under the spell of Egypt and
was preparing a grand tour of its ancient ruins. She insisted
Severn accompany her. Though flattered, Severn declined, noting
that his friend Catherwood had just arrived from England. She
said both of them must then come to Egypt. Writing his sister,
Severn explained:

I said perhaps he would like to go alone—She seem'd very
much to approve of the account I gave of him—of his abilities
and of his family—and said she would take any one of my rec-
ommending because I understood her views—Last night I had
to make another visit to her—and thought it best to make a
Duetta with Mr C—The proposition was made to him by Lady
Westmorland & he was much pleased with the idea—I have
persuaded him not (to) for these reasons—that it will be infi-

nitely better to remain in Rome and study Architecture such as he has prepared for—on the other hand he thinks this a most favorable opportunity and perhaps the only one of going to Egypt. . . .

But the next day the countess showed up at Severn's studio to say she had postponed the trip until the following season for a "lack of servants" and that both men must accompany her then. Severn agreed. In his letter to Maria, he added:

Mr Catherwood begs you to show my letter at Charles Square— and prays them to excuse him writing this Post—his head is so full of Rome and Sleep and he is so tired—that he humbly hopes to be permitted to go to bed—He desires me to present his love and remembrance to all that is dear to him—his Home—He says he can never stay here more than a year without seeing them.

Three months later Severn reported that Catherwood was living with Lady Westmorland in her "palace."

The countess was the second wife of John Fane, the tenth earl of Westmorland, who had been a member of King George's Privy Council and was an immensely wealthy and powerful man. She had borne the earl three children, but by the time she was living in Rome, she and Fane had separated. When Catherwood arrived she was forty-one, imperious, witty, an engaging conversationalist, and nearly twenty years his senior. One account of this episode in Catherwood's life claimed the countess had taken the young, impressionable Catherwood—who in going from Charles Square to Villa Negroni must have been in a state of shock—as her lover.[10] But that is not at all clear from Severn's account. In fact, as he explained to his sister:

She is a little fearful of her servants and wanted me to take up my residence there to keep these Italians in order. I was to live with her on my own terms—but I did not like it—I am so

deeply fixed in my Studies that I think of nothing else—Nor
will I—So I asked Catherwood—he liked it much—and I proposed him with success—so now he has packed up his all and
is Lord and Master.

How long Catherwood spent as "lord and master" of Villa
Negroni is not clear. He and Severn never went to Egypt with
Lady Westmorland. In February 1822 Catherwood and architect
John Davies won permission from Italian authorities to erect
scaffolding to more closely study four temples in recently excavated areas of Rome.[11] And while the date of his departure from
the countess's household is not known, he spent considerable
time during the next two years traveling through Italy and Sicily
in pursuit of his architectural studies.[12]

Some of the mystery surrounding Catherwood derives from
the extremely thin record left of his early travels as well as his time
in England before he landed in New York more than a decade
later. Little of his correspondence has been found, but a few pieces
of his art from this period have survived, including a painting he
made in Sicily in the early 1820s of Greek ruins near the town of
Taormina—with snowcapped Mount Etna looming in the background.[13]

He may have traveled next to Athens, where a propensity for
landing in the middle of revolutions, inadvertent or otherwise,
first began to show itself. The Greeks were embroiled in a war of
independence from the Ottoman Empire, and Catherwood
found himself trapped in the city. He described the situation
later to Stephens. As Stephens recounted it: "Mr. Catherwood,
who had been shut up in Athens during the Greek Revolution,
when it was besieged by the Turks, and in pursuing his artistical
studies, had perforce made castings [of monuments] with his
own hands. . . ." There is no record, however, of exactly when he
visited Greece. The Greek revolution started in 1821 and went on
for seven years, which means Catherwood could have visited
Athens before or after he traveled to Egypt.

Catherwood needed no prompting from Lady Westmorland

to make the trip across the Mediterranean to Egypt. In the 1820s a kind of Egyptomania had seized England, in part inspired by the publication of *Description de l'Égypte*, the massive work put together by the French scholars who accompanied Napoleon to Egypt in 1798. And in May 1821, while Catherwood was still in London preparing to go to Rome, a major exhibition of Egyptian artifacts opened in Piccadilly. Giovanni Battista Belzoni, a one-time circus strongman turned treasure hunter, mounted the exhibit in the Egyptian Hall shortly after publication of his popular book about his adventures on the Nile. More than nineteen hundred people crowded into the hall the first day of the showing.[14]

As important, Egypt had achieved a degree of political stability under the rule of Pasha Muhammad Ali, an Albanian put in power by the Ottoman Turks in 1809. Ali was a ruthless but sophisticated leader who was intent on modernizing Egypt and welcomed any Europeans and Westerners he thought might help. British technicians arrived, followed by aristocrats and artists, many of whom wanted to sail up the Nile to see for themselves the temples and pyramids they had heard so much about.

Catherwood reached Egypt in late autumn of 1823. It was to be a major turning point in his life. Until his arrival at Alexandria, the twenty-four-year-old had focused on Roman, Greek, and Italian architecture, intent on using what he absorbed to begin an architectural practice when he returned to England. Egypt instead opened in him a new path, a parallel life, as if he had tripped into a dimension where history, much more than what he had learned in school, was wider, deeper, and extended much further into the past. And it was as though he had landed on another planet: bone-dry, trackless deserts as far as the eye could see, nothing like the cool green of England. Monuments, pyramids, temples on an unimaginable scale. Art and architecture utterly new and exotic. Built by whom, for what reason, and how many thousands of years ago? Along with other Englishmen drawn to the country, he immersed himself in the Greek and Roman historians who had pieced together ancient Egypt's 2,500-year history—the "Old Kingdom," "Middle Kingdom," and Ptolemaic Dynasty left by Alexander the Great. Egypt was the start of an odyssey that would take Catherwood in the end to Copán and Palenque.

It began routinely. He disembarked in Alexandria with two friends he had known from Rome and possibly as far back as London—architects Henry Parke and Joseph John Scoles. The three architects, as they had done in Italy, began their survey of Egypt with a series of sketches, starting with the catacombs of Alexandria. Some of their drawings were later published in the *Dictionary of Architecture*.[15] Then they made their way to Cairo and sailed up the Nile "delineating every object worthy of attention from the delta to the second cataract."[16] They arrived finally in Nubia in southern Egypt, at the temple of Abu Simbel, in mid-January 1824. Several of Catherwood's drawings of the temples from this period have survived.

Then they fell victim to bad timing. As in Greece and later in Central America and Mexico, for Catherwood—and other adventurers of his era—humans offered as much an obstacle to exploration as the dangers of deserts, jungles, and disease. Behind them as they sailed up the Nile, local farmers and peasants had staged a rebellion against the harsh rule of the pasha. The travelers were trapped on the upper Nile. For more than a month bloody fighting raged along the shores of the river between *fellahin* insurgents and the pasha's soldiers. Villages around ancient Thebes and Luxor were burned to the ground and thousands were killed.[17] The battles posed a mortal threat to anyone on the river and rumors soon spread that a group of Englishmen— Catherwood and his companions—had been slaughtered in the uprising. They had managed, however, to stay just beyond the conflict zone. By mid-April, they finally risked sailing back down the Nile, its banks piled with the dead, and sought refuge at the town of Ghenny, today known as Qena. Another Englishman, John Madox, also caught up in the revolt, arrived on April 26 at Qena, where he found Catherwood.[18] "We were all delighted at meeting," he wrote, "and congratulated each other at our fortunate escape."[19]

The Nile River and pyramids. (Catherwood)

The pasha's soldiers—1,500 Turkish cavalry from the south and four thousand "troops of the line" from the north led by French mercenary officers—moved in and crushed the rebellion. The travelers finally came under the protection of the pasha's men. A short time later, they were free to continue down the Nile to Cairo. Then a major outbreak of plague delayed their journey for another several weeks. They took the opportunity to explore the ruins around Qena, including nearby tombs filled with mummies, and by midsummer were grateful to be in Cairo again despite mounting deaths in the city from the plague.[20] They quickly set to work exploring and drawing the nearby pyramids of Giza.

Months later Catherwood arrived at the tiny island of Malta, in the middle of the Mediterranean off the coast of Sicily. There in early October he met a wealthy Scotsman named Robert Hay.[21] The same age as Catherwood, at twenty-five, Hay was a former naval officer and the heir to an immense estate in Scotland following the death of his two older brothers—one of them killed at Waterloo. He was on his way to Egypt. Catherwood's extensive portfolio of paintings and sketches of the ruins along the Nile impressed Hay, who was himself an accomplished draftsman and artist.[22] The young aristocrat would eventually hire Catherwood, and they would reunite later in Egypt. But for the moment Catherwood was winding his way back to England. There is no record of the next year of his life and he may have traveled to Greece, if he had not already done so. The following year, however, he was apparently once again in Rome. In a December 1825 letter to his sister in London, Joseph Severn asked: "Mr. Catherwood arrived? He will tell you all the particulars about me, that you can want."[23]

Then, for the next six years, Catherwood all but disappeared. As his biographer Victor Wolfgang von Hagen wrote: "It was as if some spiteful poltergeist had followed in Catherwood's wake, destroying every page of his life's testimony."[24] The difficulty in tracing him during these years is due certainly to a lack of correspondence or other written documents. Stephens, who at the time was hard at work at the law in New York (with a similarly barren paper trail), clearly leaves the impression of Catherwood as a man of few words. Perhaps he chose art as his prime means of expression, though he left scant evidence of that behind as well. Regardless of the reason, records of his life between 1825 and 1831 have all but vanished. Presumably he moved back into the family home at 21 Charles Square, where he would continue to live on and off for the rest of his life. His aunt Elizabeth, who lived next door, died in 1827, and two years later, in what must have been a greater blow, his father died at the age of seventy-seven.

We know from a brief profile of Catherwood written by one of his Egyptian traveling partners, Joseph J. Scoles, that he was a practicing architect in London during this time, though apparently without much distinction or success. "Designed a glass house building near Westminster Bridge and some house at Pentonville" was all that Scoles could recall, writing years after Catherwood's death.[25] In fact, in 1826 Catherwood had sent a note of caution to Scoles, who was then passing through Rome on his way back to England. Dated May 2, it is his earliest surviving letter, and it indicates the difficult time he must have had

practicing architecture in England. For along with many contemporaries such as Scoles, Catherwood had apparently miscalculated by pursuing classical studies in Rome and Athens.
"Poynter is building a St. Catherine's hospital in Regent's Park,"
he wrote, referring to a mutual friend. "It is in the Gothic style,
which is indeed the prevailing taste of the time. Our Grecian
and Egyptian lore is worse than useless and Gothic must be
studied *malgre soi* [in spite of oneself]. The very best advice I can
give you, and I do it seriously and sincerely, is to devote the rest
of the time you have to remain abroad to the study of Gothic
architecture. Had I known what I know now my time would
have been differently spent, and I should advise you by all means
to return through Germany."[26]

Meanwhile, Catherwood never gave up on his art. He exhibited once again at the Royal Academy in 1828 and 1831, this time
from his Egyptian portfolio.[27] And after his working experience
in England, the practice of architecture would never be more
than an interruption in his life, a way to make money before
leaving on the next adventure. This interlude in England would
be his longest. He was unable to shake his fascination with antiquity, and in late 1831 he left England, landing several months
later in Tunisia. There he sought out the remains of ancient Carthage, which had been founded between 800 and 700 B.C. by the
Phoenicians on a site close to the modern-day city of Tunis.

In May 1832, traveling two days southwest of Tunis he discovered an extraordinary edifice in a place called Dugga.[28] For
him it was an important enough discovery that he wrote an article about it a decade later for the *Transactions of the American
Ethnological Society.*[29] "It presents a type of architecture totally
different from all the others in the country," he explained, "and
is of much greater simplicity and elegance of form." He described
it in detail. "That which most forcibly struck me as an architect
was the beauty and harmony of proportion . . . and the singular
architectural anomaly, namely a blending of Greek and Egyptian art." He included drawings, a floor plan, and a copy of two
inscriptions carved onto the façade.[30] It is clear from his article

that, like Stephens, who would make his journey to Petra three years later, Catherwood in Dugga felt an intoxicating rush of discovery, the addictive sensation both men would come to know repeatedly in Central America and Mexico.[31]

He surfaced next in Egypt—probably his destination all along—where he joined up with Robert Hay. Since their meeting in Malta in 1824, Hay had continued on to Egypt, where he launched an ambitious project to map and record all of the major temples and monuments up and down the Nile. He intended to pick up where Napoleon's savants had left off, and since the departure of the French, further discoveries had been made and more ruins excavated. Over the next seven years, with only a break in 1828 to manage his affairs in Scotland, Hay expended a good part of his fortune funding a team of artists and experts on the project. Arriving in Cairo, Catherwood lost little time fitting in. Hay put him to work mapping the pyramids of Giza, then the west bank of Thebes, Tell el-Amarna, and other sites. He was employed also in creating 360-degree panoramic views of Cairo and Thebes, and drawings of the so-called colossi of Memmon at Thebes, several of which are among the few Catherwood Egyptian drawings to have survived.[32] Then when Hay proposed a risky journey from the Nile River valley out to the great oases in Egypt's western desert, Catherwood did not hesitate.

Only Hay, Catherwood, and a third artist-traveler, George Alexander Hoskins, were to make the long trek. Hay, whose wife now lived with him in Egypt, made his home and headquarters within a large tomb at Thebes, and on Thursday nights he routinely invited Catherwood, Hoskins, and other artists and foreign travelers who might be in the neighborhood to join him in food, drink, and conversation. Hoskins caught the mood of this band of Egyptian travelers:

Never was the habitation of death witness to gayer scenes. Though we wore the costume, we did not always preserve the gravity of Turks; and the saloon, although formerly a sepulchre, threw no gloom over our mirth. The still remaining beautiful

Temple of Thebes. (Catherwood)

fragments of the painted roof were illuminated by the blaze of wax-lights; and the odour of the mummies had long before been dispelled by the more congenial perfume of savoury viands. Notwithstanding the great civilisation of the ancient Egyptians, I question whether their divans were more comfortable, their tobacco (or their substitute for it, for of tobacco they could have had none) better, or their fare more relished, than that of my friend Mr. Hay. We were all fond of the arts, and had proved our devotion to antiquarian pursuits by sacrificing for a time Europe and its enjoyments, to prosecute our researches in this distant land. Our conversation therefore never flagged; and assuredly I reckon, not among the least happy hours of my life, the evenings I spent in the tomb at Thebes.[33]

They left Thebes on October 13, 1832, riding camels, and heavily armed. There were eighteen in the expedition, including a guide, a dragoman or translator, servants, and an escort of armed camel drivers. Hoskins carried pistols and a saber. Catherwood had already achieved some celebrity because of a seven-barrel pistol he carried. It was, Hoskins wrote, "considered by

the Arabs that saw it, as a most formidable weapon; and the fame
of it was widely spread in the Valley of the Nile." They traveled
west for days through a vast expanse of desert that Hoskins described as "waterless, barren, trackless, dreary, waste." As the
caravan passed over immense drifts of sand they found innumerable bleached bones of dead camels that seemed the only mark of
a trail. Under a burning sun, water supplies began to run dangerously low, then finally on the fourth day they crossed a ridge and
saw the date palms of the Great Oasis in the distance.

> Every countenance was animated with joy, in which even our
> camels seemed to participate, by quickening their pace. We
> were all glad that our present fatigues were over; but the delight
> of the camel-men and of our servants was especially great, as
> they had been on short allowance of bad water for nearly five
> days.

The caravan was welcomed by the local sheiks. It had been
seven years since the last Europeans had visited. Catherwood
and his companions spent the next weeks drawing and measuring the ancient temples scattered among the date palms. They
recorded hieroglyphic and Greek inscriptions, a necropolis and a
Roman fortress, as well as a number of ruins running through a
long string of oases connecting the villages of El-Khargeh,
Boulak, Bryese, and Doosh. The expedition then mounted up
for the long journey back. Catherwood never found the need to
use his big gun, its reputation apparently successful in forestall-
ing any difficulties. They arrived on the ridge overlooking the
Nile more than a month after their departure. "On arriving at
the summit of the hill forming the western boundary of the
valley of the Nile," Hoskins wrote, "our servants fired their guns,
to testify their joy at again seeing the river."[34]
    During his months in Egypt, Catherwood picked up enough
Arabic as well as local costumes to wander the bazaars, towns,
and ancient sites without drawing undue attention. He also
formed the kind of deep bonds that often occur among compa-

triots in remote lands, becoming especially close with fellow
English artists Joseph Bonomi and Francis Arundale. Bonomi, a
small man with a refined, almost delicate countenance, was the
son of a well-known architect. He studied architecture at the
Royal Academy, and like Catherwood and Scoles, continued his
studies in Rome in 1822, where he and Catherwood likely first
met. Arundale joined Hay's project in 1831. He was an architectural draftsman who had worked throughout Europe.

Catherwood eventually left Hay to work in Cairo as an engineer in the pasha's court. By the middle of 1833 he was ready to
leave Egypt altogether. He decided to travel with Bonomi and
Arundale through the Sinai desert, then north through Gaza to
Jerusalem, a path Stephens rejected three years later when he
detoured through Petra. Arundale published a journal of their
journey.[35] They spent weeks preparing in Cairo, buying food,
tents, carpets, and Arab and Turkish costumes; they hired a
sheik as a guide and several camel drivers. Riding through the
bazaars of Cairo in a caravan of nine camels, they finally left the
city through the Baab el-Naar gate as the sun set behind them
on August 29, 1833.

Their passage from Cairo to Jerusalem over desolate rock and
desert—with a long side trip to Mount Sinai—took nearly six
weeks. Catherwood fell ill along the way, and the caravan slowed
to a stop for several days. Once in Jerusalem, the three men went
to work immediately, measuring, surveying, and drawing the
churches, mosques, and other points of interest. Catherwood decided to produce a plan of the city. Eighteen months later in
London, he published a highly accurate map that would become
the standard tourist plan of Jerusalem for the next two decades.
Stephens acquired a copy during his 1836 visit.

Out from Hay's shadow, Catherwood now worked in full
possession of his talents, deciding for himself what to capture on
paper. He carried with him also a "strong firman" or passport,
which named him "an engineer in the service of his highness,"
Pasha Ali. This opened doors in Jerusalem, which was under the
pasha's rule. He took advantage of it to become acquainted with

the governor of the city, who gave him free access to the roof of his palace. From there he was able to make sketches of the surrounding skyline and buildings, drawings that later would prove invaluable. He was attracted by one nearby structure of particular importance—the so-called Dome of the Rock. This golden-domed shrine, one of the holiest in Islam, is believed by many Jews to occupy the ancient site of King Solomon's temple.

In an account he wrote a decade later, Catherwood said he felt "irresistibly urged" to investigate the structure.[36] Non-Muslims, however, were forbidden to enter even the precinct of the shrine. "I had heard," he wrote, "that for merely entering the outer court, without venturing within the mosque, several unfortunate Franks have been put to death" ("Franks" being a common name for Europeans).

For Catherwood, however, it seemed the greater the danger, the greater the attraction. He also may have convinced himself that his cool, unflappable nature, the special "firman" he carried, plus his "usual" dress as an Egyptian official, would provide him all the protection he needed.

He described what happened next: "Notwithstanding the remonstrances of my friends, I entered the area one morning, with an indifferent air, and proceeded to survey, but not too curiously, the many objects of interest it presents." He was about to enter the shrine itself but lost his nerve when a religious official approached from across the courtyard. Catherwood turned and as nonchalantly as possible walked away.

Undeterred, he returned the next day, this time determined to make some drawings. He brought with him his camera lucida, knowing, he wrote, the awkward contraption would probably draw a crowd. At first with his "quiet indifference" in setting it up, he drew little attention. As he began sketching the shrine, however, more devotees gathered at some distance, talking among themselves and becoming more and more agitated. "A storm was evidently gathering." Soon they descended on him cursing and gesturing menacingly. "Escape was hopeless. I was completely surrounded by a mob of two hundred people, who seemed screwing up their courage for a sudden rush upon me—I need not tell you what would have been my fate."

Miraculously, in that moment, the governor, accompanied by his usual entourage, appeared on the steps of the platform. When the crowd ran to him to demand punishment of the "infidel," the governor turned and recognized Catherwood.

> As we had often smoked together, and were well-acquainted, he saluted me politely, and supposing it to be beyond the reach of possibility that I could venture to do what I was about without warrant from the pasha, he at once applied himself to cool the rage of the mob. "You see, my friends," he said, "that our holy mosque is in a dilapidated state, and no doubt our lord and master Mehemet Ali has sent this Effendi to survey it, in order to complete its repair. If we are unable to do these things for ourselves, it is right to employ those who can; and such being the will of our lord, the Pasha, I require you to disperse, and not incur my displeasure by any further interruption." And turning to me, he said, in the hearing of all of them, that if anyone had the hardihood to disturb me in future, he would deal in a summary way with him.

Catherwood spent the next six weeks exploring, measuring, and drawing every aspect of the shrine's exterior and interior, "introducing my astonished companions [Bonomi and Arundale] as necessary assistants in the work." The mosque's name, "Dome of the Rock," describes its prime function of sheltering one of Islam's holiest objects—a limestone rock from which the prophet Muhammad is believed by many Muslims to have stepped in his ascent to heaven with the angel Gabriel. "The St. Peter's of Mohammedanism," Arundale called it.[37]

At the time of Catherwood's visit the octagonal building was more than eleven hundred years old, erected in wood, brick, and stone between A.D. 689 and 691 and later covered in exquisite porcelain mosaics and marble inlaid with Koranic scriptures.[38] Catherwood was struck by its magnificence inside and out. Be-

Interior of the Dome of the Rock in Jerusalem. (Catherwood)

cause of the forbidden character of the shrine, he knew his survey
and drawings would be the first ever to be produced by a European. Arundale described how they systematically moved
through all the surrounding structures, drawing everything, and
used a sextant to determine the golden dome's height.

Then several Englishmen arrived for a visit, and Catherwood

and his companions made an excursion with them to Jericho and the Dead Sea. The travelers included a wealthy British aristocrat, the Marquis of Waterford, who was touring the Mediterranean in his private yacht with two friends. Later, the marquis would gain an infamous reputation and come to play a small but painful role in Catherwood's life. At the time of their encounter in Jerusalem, however, the marquis and his friends were much welcomed. By November 23 Catherwood was back at work again at the shrine.

Catherwood felt certain their efforts would be celebrated in England when they published their unprecedented survey. At the age of thirty-four, he had come into his own, displaying leadership and an enormous capacity for work. Over nearly two months, he had created a detailed map of Jerusalem, drawn most of the city's key monuments and its skyline, and spent more than a month dissecting the architecture of one of its most famous landmarks.

But when he and his companions learned that Muhammad Ali's son, Ibrahim Pasha, was arriving shortly in Jerusalem, they decided, wisely it turned out, to get out of town. They later heard that several English travelers arrived about the same time as Ibrahim and asked him for permission to see the Dome of the Rock. He said they were welcome to visit but he would not provide them any protection. When told of Catherwood's recent survey, Ibrahim exclaimed it was not possible. The governor and the officials of the mosque were summoned, wrote Catherwood, "which must have been a scene of no small amusement."

After a month of winding their way through northern Palestine, the three men arrived in Beirut at the end of December—and Catherwood's life took an unexpected and momentous turn.[39] Over the next three months he fell under the spell of Gertrude Pasquala Abbott y Suarez, the bright, captivating daughter of the resident British consul, Peter Abbott.[40]

Abbott had been born in the Middle East into a prominent English merchant family and later served as agent to the Levant and East India Company. While a young man, he had led a life of daring and adventure. At one point, while sailing to the United States to encourage trade with the Ottoman Empire, he was captured by the French and imprisoned during the Napoleonic Wars. Later, in 1820, after his appointment as consul in Beirut, he somehow incurred the wrath of the Turkish governor in Acre. Under the threat of death he barely escaped during the night with his wife and two young daughters, to Cyprus aboard a small sailboat.[41] Now, nearing sixty—he was to die not long after Catherwood's visit—he had become a fixture in Beirut, serving as a protectorate for Western travelers and a nexus for foreigners' social gatherings.[42]

Gertrude's birth mother was Spanish. What happened to her is not known, but Abbott remarried and his second wife, from Florence, Italy, became Gertrude's stepmother while the young girl grew up in Beirut. When she and Catherwood met, Gertrude was twenty, nearly fifteen years his junior, and was described as "a most beautiful, fascinating and accomplished lady." Bonomi called her "spirited."[43]

No accounts of the courtship have survived, but on March 11, 1834, in the Abbotts' house, Catherwood and Gertrude were married in a ceremony performed by an American Baptist missionary. Shortly after their wedding, they set off for Damascus and stopped at the Roman ruins of Baalbek, overlooking the Beqaa Valley. There Catherwood must have dazzled his young bride with his drawings of the spectacular Temple of Jupiter and other noteworthy remains. As a honeymoon, however, it must have been somewhat awkward. Bonomi accompanied them, sometimes sleeping in the same tent, an arrangement that would later draw unwanted scrutiny and be used to discredit Catherwood's marriage.

When the couple eventually returned to Beirut, Gertrude was pregnant, and they decided to sail for England. In London, they moved in with Catherwood's mother at Charles Square, and in December, Frederick Jr. was born.[44] Marriage, his return to England, and the birth of their son in rapid order must have been a jarring adjustment for Catherwood. No longer the wandering

Dome of the Rock on Temple Mount in Jerusalem. (Catherwood)

artist, he now had a family to feed. Living in the family home in Hoxton relieved some financial pressure, but he quickly found that the prospects for publishing his huge portfolio were not good. His study of the Dome of the Rock, illustrations of the ruins of Baalbek and Dugga, and his scenes of Jerusalem drew academic but little commercial interest. The few illustrated antiquarian books that made any profit were accompanied by travelogues. Arundale published his journal, but Catherwood apparently had no interest in writing, especially about himself.

Money was a serious concern, and Catherwood's extensive travels had put him well behind his contemporaries in building an architectural practice. At thirty-six, his greatest capital remained his portfolio and his accumulated knowledge of the Middle East. He quickly went to work creating his detailed plan of Jerusalem and evidently earned some cash with its publication. But funds remained scarce, as became clear in his correspondence with Robert Hay, his old benefactor from Egypt.

Hay had returned to Scotland not long after Catherwood's arrival in London. Almost immediately the two men began to plot a way to publish some of the enormous amount of material collected during the years of Hay's Egyptian project. Catherwood spent months lining up engravers and preparing views of the tombs and monuments of Thebes, including a pullout panorama of the site. Hay's responses to his letters became less frequent, however, and he realized Hay was losing interest.

Catherwood's tone became urgent when he wrote Hay in April 1835: "I had been expecting an answer for some time and am sorry to hear that your Egyptian energy is giving way. This I imagine arises from your living altogether in the country and being far removed from the excitement of London. . . ." Hay finally sent Catherwood twenty pounds for his work. Catherwood objected and asked for more. Then Hay, seemingly preoccupied with matters on his Scottish estate, closed down the project altogether.[45]

Whether this proved an object lesson for Catherwood in his later contract dealings with Stephens, it is hard to say. He certainly was not alone in lamenting Hay's behavior. Bonomi and others complained that Hay was squandering years of work. After so much effort, often at risk to their lives, there was almost nothing to show for it.

But Catherwood had already moved on. He had decided to use his personal portfolio and some of his work from the Hay expedition in a different way, one with significant financial potential. Even before the project with Hay collapsed, he had agreed to allow his drawings of Jerusalem and Thebes to be converted into two enormous canvas panoramas similar to others that were then mesmerizing audiences in London and beyond. And he was already plotting his next move. Within a year he would gather up his growing family—Gertrude was pregnant again—and they would make a new start, this time in America. Catherwood had a plan, and he had an ingenious entrepreneur named Robert Burford to thank for it.

Panoramas had been around, starting in England, since the late 1700s. In the time before photography, people had as great a craving to visually experience events and places as they have today, and the "panorama" had been created to fill that hunger. They transported people to far off places, dropping them in the middle of Paris, Rio de Janeiro, Cairo, and Versailles. They also played off current events. Spectators could stand on the raised platform in the middle of the 360-degree rotunda, turn around slowly, and take in the full sweep of the battlefield at Waterloo, or the guns blazing from the British and French ships at Trafalgar, or the latest coronation on the Continent, all for the price of a quarter.

Robert Burford was not the only panorama owner in England, but his main rotunda at Leicester Square in London was the most successful. He instantly bought up the rights to drawings from returning artist/travelers like Catherwood, who were the equivalent of later National Geographic Society photographers, and he cultivated admirals and generals to work out the details in the giant battle canvases he commissioned to hang in his exhibit halls.

The first notice announcing the "Jerusalem Panorama" at Burford's Leicester rotunda appeared in the March 31, 1835, London *Times*. It explained that the canvases had been painted from drawings made the year before by Mr. Catherwood "on the spot"—a phrase routinely used to give authenticity to the panoramas. The perspective from the spectators' platform was from the roof of the governor's palace, the vantage point where Catherwood had sketched so many of his drawings and where he had sometimes shared a water pipe with the governor. Catherwood was even reported to have drawn himself and Bonomi into the foreground as two figures in Arab clothing. The *Times'* reviewer, however, appeared most captivated by the Dome of the Rock. "It is a magnificent building, and though at variance with all ideas of taste derived from specimens of Gothic or Grecian excellence, has an imposing grandeur of appearance, which arrests the eye and excites the admiration of the beholder." Catherwood's study had not gone entirely to waste after all.

Jerusalem was so successful that within three months Burford mounted a second Catherwood-inspired panorama in an adjoining room in the rotunda, this one straight from his work at Thebes. "The talents of the artist are eminently displayed in this painting," wrote the *Literary Gazette* in June. "And it affords the most perfect idea of the magnitude and character of this extraordinary place. . . ."[46] Catherwood had found his new métier.

There is no record of how much Burford paid Catherwood for his drawings. It was enough, it appears, to get his family across the Atlantic and settled in New York, where they arrived in the spring of 1836. From later accounts it seems probable that Catherwood took with him the huge canvases of the Jerusalem panorama, as well as plans to set up his own rotunda in New York. But first he needed work. In October Gertrude gave birth to Ann, their second child. So he threw himself again into the practice of architecture, opening an office at 94 Greenwich Street in partnership with another English architect, Frederic Diaper.

The two men had little trouble finding projects in the aftermath of the fire that destroyed a large part of the city the year before. New York was undergoing a major building boom. Diaper's name soon became associated with the design of many Wall Street banks and he would go on later to design country manors for the rich and famous, as well as some of the city's finest hotels.[47]

Catherwood would leave much less of an architectural footprint. By 1839, however, he had gained enough of a reputation to win a commission from the heirs of Edward Livingston, the late New York mayor who also served as a Louisiana senator and secretary of state under President Andrew Jackson. Livingston's widow and daughter had decided to redesign Montgomery Place, their huge estate along the Hudson River in Dutchess County. Catherwood was commissioned to design the estate's conservatory. He created a seventy-foot-long structure of delicate framework and glazed glass fashioned in an arching neo-Gothic style.[48]

His most important project, however, was the design for his own panorama exhibit hall.[49] He had already tested the waters in 1837 in Boston, where he had exhibited the Jerusalem panorama with success. In the spring of 1838, "Catherwood's Panorama" opened at Prince and Mercer Streets, right off Broadway. The

Catherwood's Panorama in New York City; illustration on the poster is
believed to be drawn by Catherwood.

imposing brick and wood rotunda occupied ten thousand square feet and rose several stories. It was fitted with a circle of skylights for daytime exhibitions as well as two hundred gaslights for the evening shows. The exact cost of its construction is not clear, though according to Catherwood's account book it may have run as high as sixteen thousand dollars, an enormous sum at the time. It was insured for only half that value. To pull it off, Catherwood had teamed up with a New York bookseller and publisher named George William Jackson, who helped finance the project and eventually ran the business side of the venture.[50] It is likely Robert Burford invested as well.

Jerusalem provided the rotunda's first exhibit.[51] As it had been in London, the panorama was an immediate success. It did not bring in 140,000 visitors in a single season as it had in London, but it still drew large audiences, sometimes as many as three hundred people a day, each paying twenty-five cents, or the equivalent of about six dollars today.

Over the next year and a half, Catherwood would have little time for architecture. Panorama ads had to be placed in New York's newspapers, souvenir pamphlets giving historical background had to be written and sold at the exhibits. A panorama of Niagara Falls was created, probably from drawings by Catherwood. The partnership paid him a combined total of two thousand dollars for that canvas and the Jerusalem panorama. The business was so successful that at the end of 1838 he sailed to England with his four-year-old son, Frederick Jr., to retrieve more panoramas from Burford, including the canvas of Thebes, as well as one of Lima, Peru. Rome and New Zealand would follow. In addition, arrangements were made to set up showings in other cities, including Boston, Philadelphia, and Baltimore. And throughout this period, Catherwood delivered as many as four lectures a day at the rotunda, drawing from his personal experiences in Jerusalem and Thebes.

Sometime in the midst of this whirlwind of activity Catherwood met Stephens.[52] We have no record of their first encounter, but the two had certainly met by early 1838, when Stephens mentions Catherwood in his book *Incidents of Travel in Egypt, Arabia Petraea, and the Holy Land.* The Harper brothers were printing new editions of the book as fast as they could, and Stephens first refers to Catherwood in the fourth edition, which came out in February 1838, just before the panorama opened. Catherwood, he said, had brought with him from England "models and drawings of all the principal monuments in the Old World" and "a panoramic of Jerusalem . . . which it is hoped, will soon be exhibited here." In the eighth edition, published later that year, his comments reflected even greater familiarity with Catherwood. And his remarks were more generous, urging people to go to the new rotunda and see the exhibit, which, he wrote, "presents a vivid picture of the holy city." He added that when he visited Jerusalem he was "so fortunate as to find in the hands of a missionary a lithographic map made by Mr. Catherwood . . . with which he was in the habit of rambling about alone."

How familiar the two men were at that point is hard to gauge. But it's not hard to imagine a friendship forming quickly—they were kindred spirits with much common experience to unite them. Egypt and the Holy Land initially brought them together and sometime during the next year their mutual interests alchemized into a partnership. The shift in their discussions about Jerusalem and Thebes to Copán and Palenque must have been an easy one.

First, however, Catherwood had to return to England to get additional canvases from Burford. Gertrude was pregnant again and Catherwood was intent on putting his panorama business on a sound footing. Stephens, meanwhile, was as tireless and productive as ever. After the success of his first book, he dashed off a second on his travels through Greece, Turkey, Russia, and Poland. It went through three editions in two weeks and kept the printing presses at Harper Brothers humming.[53]

It is unclear when Stephens and Catherwood first discussed Central America or whose idea it was, but there are clues. Stephens had met a logging contractor named Noah O. Platt, who worked in Mexico and described visiting some ruins in the state of Chiapas. Then, not long after Stephens's book on Egypt and the Holy Land came out in 1837, the *Knickerbocker*, a New York monthly, published a series of articles on old Indian ruins in the United States and Central America.[54] Reminiscing twenty years later, the editor of the magazine, Lewis Gaylord Clark, recalled an encounter with Stephens right after the series was published. It was an autumn morning, Clark remembered, when Stephens stopped by for a chat. Clark recalled Stephens asking how he might contact the series' author. "I have become deeply interested in the subject," Stephens reportedly said, "and really I have half a notion to go upon that long-sleeping and deserted ground [of Central America], and examine it for myself."[55]

So important were Stephens's and Catherwood's later books on Central America that others also vied for the credit. John Russell Bartlett, a Rhode Islander who moved to New York in 1836, claimed the expedition south was his idea. With a partner, he opened a bookstore at Astor Place that became a famous center for the literati of New York. In his journal he wrote about an encounter with Stephens in 1838 during which he mentioned reports of mysterious ruins in Yucatán. He pointed out that it would be a natural follow to Stephens's book on Egypt and Arabia Petraea and gave him books on the subject.[56]

Meanwhile, Catherwood and Bartlett had also become friends. They were on such good terms that Catherwood offered him partial use of his residence on Houston Street while he went to London to retrieve more panoramas. "I am sorry I did not see you yesterday," he wrote Bartlett in November 1838, aware that Bartlett was looking for lodging. "As I shall probably take my little boy with me to England, Mrs. C does not feel inclined to live in a House by herself and I thought if you could not do any better you might occupy the House reserving one parlour and bedroom for Mrs. C and her baby. . . ."[57]

Sometime after Catherwood returned from London, whatever discussions he and Stephens earlier had about Central America began to jell into a plan of action. These talks came before Stephens's appointment as U.S. chargé d'affaires following the death of his immediate diplomatic predecessor, William Leggett. As Catherwood later recalled: "Our preparations were scarcely completed, when Mr. Leggett, who was on the point of setting out as United States Minister for that country, died suddenly, and upon application for it, Mr. Stephens immediately received the appointment. We had some misgivings lest this should interfere with our antiquarian pursuits. . . ."[58]

Yet Gertrude was eight months pregnant and Catherwood had two other young children and his business to consider. Stephens's offer of $1,500 in exchange for his artistic services helped, but it could not have been inducement enough to leave his young wife, children, and comfortable home for the wild, disease-plagued jungle in a region racked by civil war. But the chance to find old ruins again, to live outside the genteel constraints of urban and domestic life, to relive, in effect, what had been the most exciting time of his life, was simply too seductive. Indeed both men were primed for such an adventure. Decaying ancient ruins had become each man's raison d'être. They had been away from them too long. And it would not be the last time they felt compelled to go back.

Elizabeth Catherwood was born on July 8, 1839. It was decided that Gertrude, the newborn, and the other two children would return to England and live with Catherwood's mother while he was away in Central America. Gertrude left New York in early September.[59] That month the contract was signed between Catherwood and Stephens providing a guaranteed income to Mrs. Catherwood of twenty-five dollars a week, and no matter what, the full $1,500 to be paid even if they failed to return.[60] On the third of October 1839 the two men stepped aboard the *Mary Ann* and sailed away.

◄◄ PART THREE ►►

Archaeology

Journey into the Past

The massive volcanos of Aqua, Fuego, and Acatenango loomed over Stephens and Catherwood as they rode west out of Guatemala City for Mexico on April 7, 1840. Stephens's ministerial blue coat was packed and on its way home, his diplomatic mission over, and the two men were free at last to pursue the antiquities that had riveted them in New York and drawn them into chaos and turmoil of Central America. Their destination, Palenque, lay two hundred and fifty miles on a direct line from Guatemala City, but the winding up-and-down path through the mountains would add countless extra miles to the trail. "It would be less difficult to reach Palenque from New York than from where we were," wrote Stephens, noting that only water separated the docks of Manhattan from the Gulf of Mexico and Usumacinta River, the jumping-off point to Palenque. Coming from the Guatemalan capital, where Stephens's obligations had left them, they would have to pass over the highlands of central Guatemala, undulating terrain crisscrossed by deep ravines and mountain rifts, and then climb over two of the highest mountain ranges in Central America and Mexico. Awaiting them on the other side was the steep, dangerous descent into the jungles surrounding Palenque.

There would be crucial benefits, however, to the path they were taking, despite the terrain and the bands of agitated Indians still roaming the countryside. And it characterized the planning Stephens had put into their now-revived archaeological expedition. They were to pass through a series of old Indian ruins along their route. But unlike the stones of Copán and Quiriguá, these ruins were well known, were much more modern, and had been part of the history of the Spanish Conquest of Central America. They were the first Maya cities the conquistadors encountered, built by descendants of the ancient Maya, although neither Stephens nor anyone else had yet fully made that connection. Their route to Palenque, then, unknown to them, was to take them back through layers of the Maya past.

The first stop was Iximche,[1] which had been the capital of the Kaqchikel Maya Indians when the first Spanish conquistador, Pedro de Alvarado, and his invading army arrived on the scene in April 1524. The ruins lay less than fifty miles west of Guatemala City on a table of elevated land surrounded by deep ravines that gave the site an almost impregnable defensive position. By the time Alvarado approached, he had already defeated the powerful K'iche' Maya nation, the Kaqchikel's tribal enemy immediately to the west, in a series of savage, terrifying battles. Well aware of Alvarado's military prowess (the Kaqchikel had sent warriors to help the Spanish against the rival K'iche'), the chief lords of Iximche greeted Alvarado outside their capital, professed allegiance to the Spaniards, and invited them into the city. The Maya capital was only a little more than fifty years old, founded after the Kaqchikel broke away from the K'iche', but it was nonetheless impressive. Its central core consisted of two major plazas and two smaller ones, at least two temple pyramids, several courts where the ball games favored by natives throughout Mesoamerica were played, as well as other rudimentary palaces and residences. The construction consisted of well-cut stone; the streets were straight and crossed at right angles. Alvarado decided to make Iximche his center of operations. But the Spaniards' oppressive treatment of the Kaqchikel, including incessant demands for gold and other tribute, eventually led to a rebellion; in 1527 Alvarado razed the city.[2] The Spaniards then relocated their operational center to a site forty miles southeast, at the foot of Volcan Agua.[3]

This history was known to Stephens and Catherwood as they entered what was left of the old city through a narrow passage that took them up the side of a steep ravine to the tableland above. As they came out on top at first they did not see any evidence of ruins. Walking a short distance, however, they came upon a low wall beyond which they saw mounds of rubble. In contrast to the much older Copán,

Iximche was a major disappointment. Among the piles of stones, they could make out the foundations of what had been large structures. They found two sculpted stones but their features were so weathered they were barely visible. There was little else to see, and certainly no hint at the former glory of the once-powerful Kaqchikel Maya. There was nothing in the way of artwork or hieroglyphics that might establish a link to Copán or Quiriguá. The Spaniards had been efficient in their demolition. And during the intervening centuries, nearby inhabitants finished the job by carrying away much of the city's remnants to provide construction materials for their surrounding villages.

As Stephens and Catherwood continued west, they followed Alvarado's path backward, in the direction from which he and his army had come. When they arrived days later at Utatlán, the former capital of the K'iche' Maya, they were equally disappointed. Alvarado had destroyed and burned this city as well.[4] And again much of the rubble had been removed and reused by nearby villagers.[5]

Like Iximche, the K'iche' capital also sat on an elevated table of land surrounded by deep ravines that made it an effective stronghold during the K'iche's almost continuous warfare with the Kaqchikel and other neighboring Indian nations. Modern estimates put its founding in the early 1400s, and by the time the Spaniards arrived more than a century later, it had grown into one of the more impressive cities in Mesoamerica. Like Iximche, it had once had a ball court, palaces, gardens, royal residences, temples, and plazas. As Stephens and Catherwood wandered through the three-hundred-year-old ruins, it was clear that little of its sophistication was left. Corn grew among the mounds of stone, cultivated by a local family. There were remnants of walls, the hard floor of the plazas, and faint indications of decorative painting on the inside corners of some structures. In the center of the rubble stood a small, pyramid-shaped mound with steep steps on three sides. Breaking off pieces of stucco at the pyramid's corner, the two men discovered several more layers of stucco underneath, revealing a hint of the art that apparently had once flourished. On one layer they could make out the colored shape of what looked like a jaguar.

But where were the sculptures and carved hieroglyphs they found at Copán? Already the two men wondered if there was any link at all between Utatlán and what they had found in Copán and Quiriguá only 150 miles to the east.

> In our investigation of antiquities we considered this place important from the fact that its history is known and its date fixed. It was in its greatest splendor when Alvarado conquered it. It proves the character of the buildings which the Indians of that day constructed, and in its ruins confirms the glowing accounts given by Cortez and his companions of the splendor displayed in the edifices of Mexico. The point to which we directed our attention was to discover some resemblance to the ruins of Copán and Quiriguá; but we did not find statues, or carved figures, or hieroglyphics, nor could we learn that any had ever been found there. If there had been such evidences we should have considered these remains the works of the same race of people, but in the absence of such evidences we believed that Copán and Quiriguá were cities of another race and of a much older date.

The two men were just beginning to gather pieces of the puzzle. Clearly some of the Indian societies Cortés and Alvarado encountered during their conquests displayed advanced social and artistic achievements. And some of the impressive architecture they found, including that of the Aztecs in Mexico and Indians of Guatemala, even if demolished by the Spaniards, was at least preserved in vague descriptions written by the conquistadors themselves and the priests who accompanied them.

The Maya Indians who built Iximche and Utatlán were, in fact, of the same ethnic and linguistic group as the builders of the Classic-era cities of Copán and Quiriguá. Though the two Indian groups' exact origins are not clearly understood by today's scholars, at the time of the conquest some experts believe they had occupied Guatemala's western and central highlands for as long as a millennium, living on the southern fringe of the great Classic Maya heartland in the Petén.[6] Stephens and Catherwood were on to something but the connections were anything but clear.

Their initial perspective was also colored by the most prevalent scholarly theory of the time, which proposed that another race had landed in Mesoamerica hundreds if not thousands of years earlier, and had brought the seeds of Old World civilization with them, resulting in cities like Copán, Quiriguá, and Palenque. The so-called Lost Tribes of Israel were among most frequently mentioned candidates, along with the Phoenicians and other Mediterranean seafarers.[7] After all, they would have known about temples and pyramids, hieroglyphics, and other forms of writing invented by the Egyptian and other Middle Eastern civilizations. If the theory was true, then they could have built Copán centuries before, and the Indians who constructed Iximche and Utatlán were merely copying and carrying on this tradition hundreds of years later, even if they lacked the artistry and written language evident in the earlier, now-buried cities. The one explanation that nineteenth-century scholars found impossible to grasp was that the ancestors of the existing Indian tribes could somehow have created Palenque and other highly evolved cities completely on their own.

The "tribes of Israel" hypothesis had been advanced as far back as the sixteenth century by the Spanish bishop Bartolomé de Las Casas, who was known as the fervent "protector" of the native Indians in Mexico and Guatemala. Later, multiple versions of the "theory" were proposed down the centuries, including one variation incorporated in the Book of Mormon. But the version Stephens was probably most familiar with—and a good example of the speculation of the day— was put forward in a lecture given before the Mercantile Library Association in New York City in 1837 and published later that year, not long before Stephens left for Central America. The author, Mordecai M. Noah, was a prominent Jewish journalist and early Zionist who was active in New York City politics, and like Stephens was a published travel writer. Noah's lecture, which Stephens may have attended, advanced the two prevailing ideas concerning the Phoenicians and the tribes of Israel, and in a single stroke, combined them. He explained that the Phoenicians, or Canaanites as he also called them, sailed out from the Mediterranean and across the Atlantic to the New World more than two thousand years earlier. Meanwhile, the lost tribes went from Palestine in the opposite direction and traveled through Asia, eventually crossing the Bering Strait to North America, and moved south to Central America.[8]

We have no evidence Stephens knew of Noah, although it is likely, as the two men traveled in the same literary circles in New York. And before Stephens left for Central America, he was intent on finding and absorbing every scrap of information about the region—its antiquities and politics. He also refers in his book to the wide range of speculation then rampant among scholars that if any civilization existed in North America, it was brought by "the Jews, the Canaanites, the Phoenicians, the Carthaginians, the Greeks, the Scythians in ancient times; the Chinese, the Swedes, the Norwegians, the Welsh and the Spaniards in modern."[9]

At the other end of the spectrum stood the influential Scottish historian William Robertson, famous at the time for writing one of the first major histories of the Americas. Stephens noted that Robertson rejected entirely the idea that Old World travelers had brought any civilization to the New World. In his history, in fact, Robertson disputes there were any civilized people in the New World at all when Columbus arrived. "The inhabitants of the New World," Stephens quotes from Robertson, "were in a state of society so extremely rude as to be unacquainted with those arts which are the first essays of human ingenuity in its advance toward improvement." Robertson went on to argue in his history that the Spanish had simply exaggerated when they described the sophistication of the cities they encountered. The temples, he wrote, were nothing more than "a mound of earth" and the "houses were mere huts, built with turf, or mud, or the branches of trees, like those of the rudest Indians." Robertson based his argument on an account from a person who had traveled in every part of New Spain, and he concluded "there is not, in all the extent of that vast empire, a single monument or vestige of any building more ancient than the conquest."[10]

It was against this backdrop of wide-ranging assumptions and conjecture that Stephens and Catherwood had to work. Yet such speculations would not limit their thinking. Stephens took no sides. They were in Central America to see for themselves. And lawyer Stephens made clear that before he reached any conclusion he wanted to see the evidence—all the evidence.

It was not all single-minded antiquarian labor, however, not on an expedition led by John L. Stephens. He still had a book to write and there were other tempting sights to see. So they took a detour to Lago de Atitlán, a dazzling lake set high among Guatemala's volcanoes. "From a height of three or four thousand feet," he wrote, "we looked down upon a surface shining like a sheet of molten silver, enclosed by rocks and mountains of every form, some barren, and some covered with verdure, rising from five hundred to five thousand feet high. We both agreed that it was the most magnificent spectacle we ever saw. We stopped and watched the fleecy clouds of vapour rising from the bottom, moving up the mountains and the sides of the volcanoes."

Not content just to look from afar, they embarked upon one of the necessary "incidents" of his books' titles. They set out the next morning to sightsee along the lake's edge in a tiny dinghy, no more than a flimsy local fishing craft made of flat wooden boards and generously meant for one occupant. "As we moved away, the mountainous borders of the lake rose grandly before us," Stephens wrote. Then the trouble started. The huge lake was well known for its powerful and tricky winds, which began to blow them out toward the middle. Juan, the boatman, paddled furiously toward shore. "Mr. C was in the stern, I on my knees in the bottom of the canoe. The loss of stroke, or a tottering movement in changing places, might swamp her; and if we let her go she would be driven out into the lake, and cast ashore, if at all, twenty or thirty miles distant. . . . We saw people on the shore looking at us, and growing smaller every moment, but they could not help us." Finally, Juan maneuvered the boat under the cover of a bluff that cut the wind, and he was able to paddle the boat to the shore. The sightseeing was over, and Stephens admitted: "We had enough of the lake."

In Quetzaltenango, their next stop, politics emerged once again. They encountered everywhere the horror of Carrera's execution of the town's leaders. "The place was still quivering under the shock of that event," he wrote. They heard firsthand accounts of the massacre. "I was told that Carrera shed tears for the death of the first two, but for the rest he said he did not care. It was considered a blow at the whites, and all feared the horrors of a war of castes."

Quetzaltenango was Guatemala's second-largest city—handsome, the streets well paved with cobblestones, its seven churches dominating the skyline. And it was Easter week. Elaborate processions and other religious displays quickly overwhelmed everything else. The plaza was filled with Indians from the countryside; most of the white residents, terrified by the recent events, stayed away. The religious rituals and ceremonies Stephens and Catherwood witnessed were, he wrote, "so thrilling, so dreadfully mournful, that, without knowing why, tears started from our eyes." He added that even a descent from the cross on Good Friday that he had witnessed on Mount Calvary in Jerusalem did not compare to the religious fanaticism and frenzy he was now seeing.

Three days later, they were free of Central American politics for good, walking through yet another set of ruins outside the town of Huehuetenango, more than thirty miles to the north. The site was the third major Indian capital the Spanish overran during the early years of the conquest. Named Zaculeu, it was the royal ceremonial center of the Mam Indian nation. Like Iximche and Utatlán, it also sat on a plateau surrounded by ravines. It had been heavily fortified and the Mam Maya held off the Spanish for more than six weeks before surrendering to Alvarado's brother, Gonzalo, in 1525. The Spanish siege had succeeded in weakening the trapped Mam to the point of starvation before they finally gave in.[11]

Stephens and Catherwood found the site weathered and broken into a confused jumble of grass-covered stones, like the two previous sites. Later archaeological excavations, however, would determine it was much older than the K'iche' and Kaqchikel capitals, and had been originally settled almost a thousand years before the Spanish arrived. The two travelers met the owner of the property, who said he had bought the land from the Indians but that they continued to return, much to his annoyance, to perform ritual ceremonies on top of the sites' two remaining pyramid-like structures. He agreed to allow Stephens and Catherwood to dig into the pyramids and mounds if they promised to turn over to him any treasure they might find. They spent the next day with laborers from Huehuetenango excavating the site but found little more than fragments of bones and a few clay vases. Stephens wrote that he regretted not having more time to explore, but Palenque, the shimmering goal beyond the horizon, still beckoned.

In Huehuetenango, they received a surprise visit from an American named Henry Pawling, whom Stephens had met earlier managing a cochineal plantation south of Guatemala City. Pawling, who grew up in Rhinebeck Landing on the Hudson River north of New York City, had been traveling and working in Mexico and Central America for seven years. When he learned that Stephens and Catherwood were headed to Mexico, he left his job and set out to catch up with them. Four days of hard riding brought him to Huehuetenango. An earlier plan to go to Mexico had been thwarted by his lack of a passport, and he hoped he might attach himself to Stephens, whose venture carried the proper diplomatic papers. Pawling offered his services in any capacity in exchange. Stephens did not hesitate. Pawling was young, spoke fluent Spanish, was a fellow American—and a New Yorker. He was on the road and in need. It did not hurt that he had also brought with him a pair of excellent pistols, an ominous-looking "short double barreled gun slung to his saddle-bow," and a much-needed spare mule. "I immediately constituted him the general manager of the expedition," Stephens explained.

The reinforced team now headed north into the most rugged part of their journey—the Cordillera de los Cuchumatanes, a formidable mountain range whose peaks reached 12,500 feet, Central America's highest summits outside of the volcanos. The expedition now consisted of Stephens, Catherwood, Pawling, a cook and factotum named Juan, and a fugitive Mexican soldier named Santiago. An older, respectable muleteer acted as a guide.

The next four days brought discomforts and obstacles on a biblical scale. The first night, camping on a windswept ridge, was so cold that they woke the next morning covered in frost, their water frozen with a layer of ice a quarter inch thick. The next day, traveling along another ridge so narrow that a strong gust might blow them off, they found themselves suddenly surrounded by a raging forest fire. They hustled back down the trail to a nearby hamlet and barely escaped being consumed by the sheets of flame roaring up the sides of the ravines. Next, a swarm of giant flies escaping the conflagration descended on them and began attacking their mules. "Every bite drew blood," Stephens explained. "For an hour we labored hard but could not keep their heads and necks free. The poor beasts were frantic, and in spite of all we could do, their necks, the insides of their legs, mouths, ears, nostrils, and every tender part of their skin, were trickling with blood."

Despite their appreciation for the breathtaking beauty of the mountain views, they were relieved when their long descent finally brought them to the Río Lagartero and the border with Mexico and North America. Their only concern was that the Mexican army, searching for smugglers along the border, might detain them for lack of a Mexican passport. But they crossed the river without incident. Reinvigorated by a leisurely bath in the river's cool waters, Stephens felt he could ride clear across Mexico, up to Texas, and all the way home to New York. "Returned once more to steamboats and railroads, how flat, tame and insipid all their comforts seem," he wrote. "We were out of Central America, safe from the dangers of revolution, and stood on the wild borders of Mexico, in good health, with good appetites, and something to eat. We had still a tremendous journey before us, but it seemed nothing. We strode the little clearing as proudly as the conquerors of Mexico, and in our extravagance resolved to have a fish for breakfast."

Two days journey over mostly barren plains and hills brought them next to the Mexican town of Comitán, where they braced themselves for trouble for their lack of passports. In short order, however, Stephens's diplomatic status, evident in his Central American papers, once again won the day. He and his entourage were all granted the necessary documents to continue on. "I recommend," he wrote, "all who wish to travel to get an appointment from Washington."

In Comitán they learned that the difficulties they faced getting to Palenque would be far greater than anticipated. They knew the road would be rough but were told its rugged, dangerous ascents and descents made it much longer than it appeared on the map. And far from leaving political upheaval behind, they discovered for the first time they would be traveling through two Mexican states, Chiapas and Yucatán, that were also convulsed by revolution. Worst of all, they were told the Mexican government had issued orders that Palenque was off-limits to foreigners.[12]

A tough trail did not much worry Stephens, not after Mico Mountain and their recent jaunt over the Cuchumatanes. "As to the revolutions," noted Stephens with a touch of his usual bravado, "having gone through the crash of a Central American [one], we were not to be put back by a Mexican [uprising]." The ban on visits to Palenque, however, was not so easily dismissed. The options were not good. Stephens could travel north to Mexico City to argue his case, but that would add weeks or months to their timetable, assuming he was successful. If not, the game was over. Or they could chance it and sneak into Palenque.

They talked themselves into going ahead. Santiago, the fugitive soldier, left them but Juan remained. Now intrigued with seeing the ruins, Pawling decided not to go to Mexico City as planned but to continue on with them. They departed Comitán on the first of May more determined than ever to reach the destination they had dreamed about in New York, seemingly a lifetime ago.

The first leg of the journey was uneventful. After they arrived at a town named Ocosingo on the third day, a violent thunderstorm broke upon them, the opening volley of the new rainy season. Their effort to get to Palenque before the rains had failed. The lightning that thundered and crashed around them seemed ominous, given what they already had heard of the path through the mountains ahead.

Riding through Ocosingo, they saw along a church wall two sculpted statues they recognized immediately as cut in the style they had seen in Copán, though smaller. It was the first exciting hint they were entering new ground and had left behind the sculptureless ruins of the Guatemalan highlands. During his research Stephens had come across an account by a retired army captain named Guillaume Dupaix, who some thirty years before, in 1808, had passed through Ocosingo on his way to investigate Palenque at the request of the Spanish crown.

Told of ruins near Ocosingo, Dupaix visited them and his brief written description along with several illustrations lay undiscovered until
they were finally published in Paris in the 1830s.[13]

The ruins, known today as Toniná, lay eight miles east of town,
and the next day Stephens, Catherwood, and Pawling rode out to take
a look. Modern archaeologists have determined that between A.D. 600
and 900, during the height of the Classic Maya era, Toniná was the
site of a major military power that rivaled Palenque, located forty
miles to the north. At one point, in the year 711, according to hieroglyphs later deciphered at the site, Toniná's "Ruler 3" succeeded in
capturing and beheading one of Palenque's kings.[14] Despite its military prowess, however, Toniná never approached Palenque in the scale
and beauty of its architecture or art, as Stephens was soon to find out.
Stephens and his companions nonetheless found Toniná impressive.

As they approached they first glimpsed a stone building emerging
high above the canopy of trees. Coming out of the forest onto a grassy
plaza, they found two sandstone figures lying flat on the ground, their
faces turned upward. Though they appeared weathered and eroded,
Stephens noted that many of their features were still distinct. The
three men looked up. The ruins towered above them, rising more than
230 feet, embedded in the side of a hill connected to mountains
beyond. It looked like a fortress, wrote Stephens, an enormous pyramidal shape with numerous terraces, all faced with stucco still covering most of the stone construction beneath. They were able to ride up
through gaps in the terrace walls until they reached the third level,
where they tied their horses. The terraces were overgrown with grass
and shrubs. From the third level they were able to climb to a building
at the top. The structure was fifty feet wide by thirty-five feet deep,
with a single entrance in the front. Entering they found it divided into
five inner chambers. The stucco covering the stone walls had dropped
away in many places. Clearly visible above an inside portal was a huge
wing spread out on one side. The plaster on the other side, where the
other wing would have been, had fallen into piles of rubble along the
base of the wall. The doorway itself was topped with a lintel made of
a long, thick wooden beam. They were stunned. It was the first time
they had encountered any structural wood in the ruins, which they

thought incredible given the obvious ancient age of the structure. They would later find similar wooden lintels in other ruins and their discovery would affect Stephens's view of the age of the old cities. "It was so hard," Stephens wrote of the lintel, "that, on being struck, it rang like metal and was perfectly sound, without a worm-hole or other symptom of decay."

They had been told by Ocosingo's alcalde that there was a passageway in the ruins that served as a subterranean route leading all the way to Palenque. Nothing would have pleased them more than to find such a shortcut, Stephens noted. Their guide pointed to the passageway but refused to enter. Undeterred, Stephens took off his coat and lay on his stomach to crawl in.

"When I had advanced about half the length of my body, I heard a hideous hissing noise," he wrote. "And starting back, saw a pair of small eyes, which in the darkness shone like balls of fire. The precise portion of time that I employed in backing out is not worth mentioning." They braced themselves, pistols drawn, swords and machetes at ready, waiting for the beast to dash out. Pawling finally stuck a long piece of wood into the hole and "out fluttered a huge turkey-buzzard which flapped through the building and took up refuge in another chamber." Undaunted, Stephens worked his way through the tight entrance a second time, only to find that it opened into a chamber that led nowhere. However, its stucco walls were covered with figures exquisitely formed in bas-relief, including images of monkeys, and along the back wall two life-size humans in profile, facing each other. Catherwood crawled in to make some sketches but the light was bad, and the heat and the smoke from the candles soon drove the two men out. The three men explored several other buildings as they climbed from terrace to terrace up the hillside. From the top, Stephens observed that the site commanded a view of the surrounding countryside for a great distance, which would have made it difficult if not impossible for any enemy to approach unnoticed.

It was the most remarkable site they had visited since Copán, or in Catherwood's case, Quiriguá. Even though they were pressed for time, Stephens wanted to return the next day to make a more thorough examination. It was dark by the time they got back to Ocosingo.

But when they met with the alcalde, he said it would take at least two days to gather enough men to do the kind of excavation Stephens wanted. And there were few if any tools available, not even a single crowbar in the town. The issue was decided when another violent storm broke and the rain came pouring down again: they would leave the next day for Palenque.

"I am strongly of the opinion that there is at this place much to reward the future traveler," wrote Stephens, who had no idea just how prescient he would turn out to be. Later archaeological digs would turn up two ball courts, a great number of monuments and sculptures, and a wealth of glyphs. These have allowed scholars to piece together the city's history and relations with its neighbors, which Toniná subjugated with ruthless proficiency. Among the monuments found were figures sculpted in the round, a rarity among the Maya. Toniná was one of the final classic Maya city-states to fall and the site contains a monument on which is recorded the last known "long count" date, correlated to A.D. 909, which marks the end of the Classic Maya period.[15]

As they headed north toward Palenque in the morning, Stephens looked off wistfully to the east. He was told there were other stone remains lying half-buried in the almost impenetrable lowland jungles beyond Toniná. As archaeologists would later discover, Toniná (and Palenque) lay along the western edge of the Classic Maya heartland while Copán lay at the eastern edge. But in Stephens's time the thick jungle in between still hid the remains of a great number of spectacular Maya cities—Piedras Negras, Bonampak, Yaxchilan, Dos Pilas, and beyond them, the "New York City of the Maya," Tikal, with its skyscraping pyramids.

Stephens was focused, however, on getting his ragtag expedition quickly and safely to Palenque. The rains of the past two nights had filled them with "a sort of terror." It did not help that he had brought with him Captain Dupaix's account of his 1808 journey. Dupaix had warned:

> The journey is very fatiguing. The roads, if they can be so called, are only narrow and difficult paths, which wind across moun-

tains and precipices, and which it is necessary to follow sometimes on mules, sometimes on foot, sometimes on the shoulders
of Indians, and sometimes in hammocks. In some places it was
necessary to pass on bridges, or, rather, trunks of trees badly
secured, and over lands covered with wood, deserted and dis-
peopled, excepting a very few villages and huts. We had with us
thirty or forty vigorous Indians to carry our luggage and hammocks.[16]

Little had changed in the intervening thirty years. Palenque was
forty miles away in a direct line on the map, but the path snaked up
and down, more than doubling the distance. Although Dupaix's expedition had taken eight days, Stephens and company would make it
in five, but with no less toil and agony. They were apprehensive as
well about the local natives, given what they were told of their wild
nature. Dupaix had made the journey with a troop of dragoons.
Pawling's two extra pistols and double-barreled gun were more welcome than ever.

In the end, the terrain was so severe that a relay of four different
sets of Indians with fresh legs from intervening villages was needed to
haul the expedition's baggage. On the third day, the heat was crushing
and the path went straight up and down over one mountain ridge
after another. The trail headed straight down at an angle too dangerous to ride. When they started their ascent on the other side, riding
was again out of the question. Encumbered with swords, pistols, and
spurs, Stephens and the others led their mules up paths so steep they
had to stop and sit down every few minutes to catch their breath. Finally they reached the top, mounted, but rode only a hundred yards
before they had to descend again. "The descent was steeper than the
ascent," he said. "It was harder work to resist than to give way. Our
mules came tumbling after us; and after a most rapid, hot, and fatigu-
ing descent, we reached a stream covered with leaves and insects. It
was the hottest day we had experienced in the country." The intense
heat had left the foliage withered and desiccated.

The next day, they were informed, would be worse. By now they
were stripped of swords, spurs, and pistols, down to their shirts and

pants "as near the condition of the Indians as we could." Stephens was suffering violent headaches from the heat. Though it was customary for travelers in the region to be borne over the roughest terrain in armchairs strapped to the back of the carriers, Stephens wrote of his "repugnance to this mode of conveyance." But on the fourth day, his head splitting with pain, Stephens was ready to order up an armchair, repugnant or not, when they hit a particularly steep ascent. He climbed aboard the chair, which was strapped to the back of a thin Indian no more than five feet, seven inches tall. "Not to increase the labor of carrying me," he wrote, "I sat as still as possible." But he faced backward and could not keep from twisting around to see where they were headed. As they approached the edge of a precipice that dropped down more than a thousand feet, Stephens wanted to dismount but could not make himself understood by the Indians. The carrier shook as he carefully put one foot ahead of the other along the edge.

> I rose and fell with every breath, felt his body trembling under me, and his knees seemed giving way. The precipice was awful, and the slightest irregular movement on my part might bring us both down together. To my extreme relief, the path turned away; but I had hardly congratulated myself upon my escape before he descended a few steps. This was much worse than ascending; if he fell, nothing would keep me from going over his head; but I remained till he put me down of his own accord.

After hours of climbing, they finally made it to a hut where they hoped to stop for the night. But there was no water, and they were forced to push on. They continued the climb, reached the top, and started another horrible descent. Then a powerful wind swept over them, breaking off dried leaves and branches, and dark clouds dropped down over the mountain. They were desperate to get to the bottom before the storm broke. "Fortunately for the reader, this was our last mountain; it was the worst mountain I ever encountered in that or any other country, and, under our apprehension of the storm, I will venture to say that no travelers ever descended in less time."

They reached the plain, crossed a river, and arrived at an empty rancho. The storm now broke behind them on the mountain, but they were dry and safe in the small clearing. The rancho was no more than a thatched hut open on four sides. They had begun preparing a fire for dinner when all of a sudden they were assailed by a swarm of mosquitoes. They could barely eat, despite their ravenous appetites. They lit other fires and smoked tobacco to keep the mosquitoes at bay. In the darkness they discovered they were also surrounded by giant fireflies, which, unlike those back home that flashed intermittently, kept a constant light. They seemed like "shooting stars," Stephens wrote.

The travelers lay on the ground that night fully clothed against the mosquitoes. Pawling tried to rig cloth over his head but found he could not breathe in the heat. He went to lie on the banks of the river, where the Indians also rested. But at midnight, amid thunder and lightning, the rains poured down and everyone sought shelter under the thatched roof of the rancho. The sound of hands slapping mosquitoes punctuated the night. No one slept. Finally, before daylight Stephens walked down to the river and submerged himself along the shallow shoreline. "It was the first comfortable moment I had had. My heated body became cooled, and I lay till daylight." As day dawned, the mosquitoes, engorged, departed. But everyone was more exhausted than when they had arrived. And somehow in the restless night, Catherwood had lost his emerald ring, an object he greatly prized for sentimental reasons.

They mounted for the last day's journey. The trail was level but went through deep tropical forest. By midday, they reached a separate path that veered off through the jungle in a direction they believed led directly to the ruins of Palenque. It might be their best opportunity to sneak into the site. But they could not be certain and were unable to communicate with the Indian carriers. And at this point they had decided they were in much too "shattered" a state to take up immediate residence in the ruins. They would stay on the main path and take their chances in the town of Santo Domingo de Palenque, where they hoped to rest and stock up on provisions before continuing on to the ruins. They came out of the forest onto a broad plain and saw cattle grazing. It seemed almost a dream, the grass fresh from the first rains, a huge tree standing alone before them covered in yellow flowers. Stephens looked back at the dark peaks behind him. They had escaped the mountains and rain forests and unbaptized Indians. They had survived somehow and he knew that nothing now could keep them from the object of their desire—Palenque.

◁ **13** ▷

Palenque

More than twelve feet of rain fall every year on Palenque. The soil is fertile, the tropic sun fierce, and layer upon layer of irrepressible vegetation fight continually to bury the once-great city of the Maya. Deep within the blue-green shadows of the trees, laced with more than fifty streams and springs, the foliage battles for every speck of sunlight. The cackle of birds and drone of insects cut the wet air. Vapors drift like ghosts over the jumble of stones. Cortés and his army, during their horrifying march to Honduras in 1524, passed within twenty or thirty miles of the buried city, known in ancient times as Lakamha, or "Big Water," and they never heard a word of its existence. It still lay unearthed and forgotten 260 years later—as it had for nearly a millennium—when the president of the Royal Audiencia in Guatemala City ordered an inquiry into reports by local priests that there were "stone houses" in the forest.[1] Sent to investigate, the alcalde of nearby Santo Domingo de Palenque, José Antonio Calderón, slashed his way through the jungle in 1784 and spent three days at the ruins before being driven off by the rain. He reported that he found more than two hundred structures, including what he thought were some eighteen stone palaces. And the remains of Palenque officially entered the history books.

Calderón's report created a sensation within the Guatemalan court—and raised a number of questions. Could there be something new and different about these remains, as distinguished from the monuments erected by the Toltecs, Aztecs, and Incas, which were well known from the early days of the Conquest? And might these ruins answer the centuries-old question about the origin of the earliest in-

Temples at Palenque. (Carlsen)

habitants of the Americas and where they had come from? José Es-tacheria, the president of the Audiencia, decided to send his architect to investigate. When the commissioner returned, he confirmed much of what Calderón had found. Wondrous and strange, Palenque was emerging from the mists hundreds of years after the Conquest, plus an unknown number of centuries after its abandonment, and was about to earn a special place in the history of exploration. However, these first reports and later accounts that would eventually secure its fame were still decades from reaching the public.

News of the discovery made its way across the Atlantic to Spain through the secretive colonial bureaucracy, and orders for a compre-hensive survey and excavation came back directly from the royal court in Madrid.[2] King Carlos III had shown great interest in antiquities; as ruler of Naples, he had sponsored the first excavations at Pompeii and Herculaneum.[3] A Spanish artillery captain named Antonio del Río was selected for the job in Guatemala City and arrived at Palenque through a heavy fog in May 1787, accompanied by an artist named

Ignacio Almendáriz.[4] When they finally stumbled upon the stone buildings under the mass of foliage and creepers, Del Río understood immediately the immense effort it would take to clear the area. He returned from Palenque village a week later with seventy-nine Indians armed with axes and within two weeks the vegetation around the most intact group of ruins had been chopped down and burned. Finally they could breathe healthy air, Del Río wrote. Next they attacked the trees and foliage covering the tops of the structures and invading their inner recesses. Then, with the blunt force worthy of an artilleryman, Del Río began excavation.[5] It was as if a bomb had been set off in the middle of the site.

"Ultimately," he wrote, "there remained neither a window nor a doorway blocked up; a partition that was not thrown down, nor a room, corridor, court, tower, nor subterranean passage in which excavations were not effected from two to three yards in depth." With sight lines opened, Almendáriz went to work and produced twenty-six sheets of drawings, some providing the first reasonably accurate albeit cartoonish depictions of the figures and hieroglyphs that were carved into Palenque's walls or molded onto the structures in plaster.[6] He displayed considerable artistic license, however, simplifying the floor plans and stucco ornamentation.

Del Río, meanwhile, made a thorough examination of the central ruins. He took measurements, chipped off some hieroglyphs and parts of stucco figures, and collected flints, "earthen jars," and crystal objects, all sent back to Spain for further investigation. He included an elaborately sculpted leg from a stone table.

The extraordinary art at Palenque, however, either failed to impress him or his descriptive powers abandoned him, for his report ended up as flat and lifeless as it was brief, running less than a dozen pages. The no-nonsense artillery officer chose, instead, to rely heavily on numbered references to Almendáriz's drawings, in the hope, apparently, that the images would best convey what they had found. He formed an opinion, however, about the origin of the buried city. And like many who would follow him, Walker and Caddy included, he was trapped within the only frame of reference he knew—the classical. He wrote that the sculpted forms bore strong Roman and Greek influences:

For in their fabulous superstitions, we seem to view the idolatry of the Phoenicians, the Greeks, the Romans, and other primitive nations most strongly portrayed. On this account it may reasonably be conjectured, that some one of these nations pursued their conquests even to this country, where it is probable they only remained long enough to enable the Indian tribes to imitate their ideas, and adopt, in a rude and awkward manner, such arts as their invaders thought fit to inculcate.[7]

In the end, however, little came of Del Río and Almendáriz' work. It ended up unpublished, collecting dust in the archives of Guatemala and Spain, one more of Spanish America's secrets kept from the outside world.

It took twenty years before the next major expedition, this one under King Carlos IV. Retired captain Dupaix had a special interest in pre-Columbian sites and under a commission from the viceroy of New Spain traveled in 1808 to Toniná and Palenque. He was accompanied by a detachment of dragoons and José Luciano Castañeda, a drawing master from Mexico City. In the end, however, Castañeda's drawings and Dupaix's commentaries met the same fate as Del Río's report—they too were buried in the archives. These would lie forgotten in Mexico City during the next thirteen years of political upheaval, which resulted in Mexico's independence from Spain in 1821.

Castañeda, though more talented than Almendáriz, also had difficulty reproducing accurately much of what he had seen in Palenque. Dupaix, however, proved a careful observer, the first to make the break between what he had seen at the ruins and what he knew of classical Greek, Roman, and Egyptian art and architecture. In language far more imaginative than Del Río's, he proposed that Palenque was built by a people, he wrote, "endowed with their own genius, their own force of imagination, and that progressed over the course of centuries." He was not willing, however, to go so far as to attribute the palaces and temples to the indigenous tribes of Mexico and Central America, but instead to a race long since vanished: the people of legendary Atlantis.[8]

The palace at Palenque and its interior courtyard. (Carlsen).

Therefore, well into the 1800s the first discovered traces of the extraordinary glyphs, art, and architecture of the Maya civilization were known only to a small group of individuals associated with the royal Spanish court.[9] After the wars of independence from Spain, however, the ground shifted. Del Río's report was pulled from the archives by an English doctor living in Guatemala, brought to London, and published in 1822.[10] Next, Dupaix's account of his 1808 expedition was discovered in Mexico City and included in a folio published in 1831 by an eccentric Irishman named Edward King, otherwise known as Lord Kingsborough.[11]

Kingsborough was a wealthy young aristocrat from Cork who had become obsessed with Mexican and American antiquities. Before he died at the age of forty-two, he devoted his entire fortune to the publication of nine huge illustrated folios, one of which included Dupaix's and Castañeda's work.[12] The folios were filled with stunning hand-colored Mexican picture writing, and glyphs mostly copied from bark paper Maya "codices" or books, found and sent home to Europe by

Spanish conquistadors and explorers. He was convinced that the codices and the stone remains turning up in Central America and Mexico were the work of the "lost tribes of Israel."[13] Sadly, his publications bankrupted him, and he died of typhus in a debtor's prison in Dublin in 1837, two years before he was to inherit his father's rich estate.[14]

Kingsborough's volumes, *Mexican Antiquities,* along with the reports by Del Río and Dupaix, reignited the intellectual debate and deepened the mystery that Europeans—and later, Americans—had grappled with ever since Columbus returned from his first voyage to America.[15] The discovery of inhabitants on the American continents, some living in relatively advanced societies, baffled Western intellectuals and religious scholars—and threatened the biblical order of the world. Where did these natives come from, how old were their cities, and how did they fit into the long-accepted Egyptian, Greek, Roman, Old and New Testament narrative? Did these Indians populate the Americas before Noah and the great flood or sometime afterward? Encouraged by Dupaix's report and the paper codices of Maya hieroglyphs, Kingsborough's volumes included texts with speculative answers to these questions, linking the "lost tribes" with Mexico for example. Meanwhile, the French were not to be outdone. A publication in Paris in 1834, *Antiquités Mexicaines,* was also filled with scholarly tracts about the similarities between the Mexican ruins and those of Egypt, India, and other Old World civilizations.[16]

The on-the-ground reports from Del Río and Dupaix, undiscerning and biased, did nothing to upset this worldview. They only sharpened it. The discovery of an architecturally sophisticated site of possibly great antiquity simply prompted most of the faraway pedants and theorists to view Palenque as a single, unique colony that somehow found its way from the Old World to the New, thus leaving their basic historical narrative intact.[17] It would take Stephens and Catherwood, seasoned with their personal Old World explorations, to carefully examine all the evidence—the disparate and widely scattered ruins—and forge a new narrative.

In 1832, around the time of Kingsborough's publication, a new, larger-than-life character arrived on the scene. As Yale University archaeologist Michael Coe described it, "During the first half of the nineteenth century, Americanist research was replete with eccentrics: the dead hand of the academy had yet to stifle the unbridled enthusi- asms of a small band of amateurs in Europe and America."[18] Into Santo Domingo de Palenque rode "Count" Jean-Frédéric-Maximilien de Waldeck, a naturalized French citizen who at different times claimed as his birthplace Vienna, Prague, or Paris. He also gave his birth date as March 16, 1766, which, if true, would have put him in his mid-sixties by the time he arrived at Palenque. A man of hearty con- stitution and oversize, self-created legend, Waldeck made incredible boasts of his adventures—travel at the age of fourteen through South Africa, studies in neoclassical art in Paris, participation in the French occupation of Egypt and the Chilean fight for independence as well as friendships with Napoleon, Humboldt, King George III, Lord Byron, Marat, Robespierre—little of which could ever be documented.[19] Even his birth date is suspect, a potential blow to his reputation late in life in Paris, where well past the age of one hundred he purported to be a famous "admirer" of women. A tall, imposing figure with a rich baritone, Waldeck took the title of "count" based on a claim of noble birth into the Waldestein-Württemberg family.

For all his self-mythologizing, however, he was a talented artist. And in 1822, he claimed to have had a life-changing experience when he was hired in London to engrave the Palenque drawings for Del Río's book. Like Kingsborough he became obsessed with American antiquities. Then, after working for a silver-mining company in Mexico and as a portrait artist in Mexico City, he finally arrived at Palenque in May 1832. "From the moment I saw [Almendáriz's] pen and ink drawings [for Del Río's book]," he wrote the Société de Géog- raphie in Paris, "I suspected that they were less than faithful to the originals and I began to cherish a secret desire to go and draw them for myself."

Waldeck spent nearly a year traveling back and forth to the ruins from the village and lived four months in a hut at the foot of the so- called Temple of the Cross. He worked diligently sketching and paint- ing the ruins, enduring, for the most part alone, the heat, rain, and tormenting insects. Like Almendáriz and Castañeda, he struggled mightily with the intricate hieroglyphs, writing to a friend at one point that he had spent twenty days copying just 114 glyphs.[20] Finally, exhausted and running out of money, he made his way north to Yucatán. There he visited and worked in ruins that would become known as Uxmal.[21,22] Famously irascible and contentious, however, he somehow offended the Mexican authorities, who appeared at his door in the Yucatán capital of Mérida and confiscated his writings and drawings. Anticipating such a move, however, Waldeck had made copies and had sent much of his original work on to Jamaica. In another version of the story, Kingsborough, who had been funding Waldeck, intervened and had his artwork returned to him. Waldeck finally left for London in 1836.[23]

Though he was a gifted artist, much of Waldeck's work was infected by his neoclassical training and his own rich imagination. He often gave in to the temptation to idealize and romanticize what he had found.[24] He was also unable to escape from his belief that the ruins were the work of Old World colonists, and some of his illustrations looked more Egyptian and Greek than the Maya originals.[25] He created sculpted statues where none could later be found, his measurements were at times wildly inaccurate, and he drew imaginary elephants and turtles on walls and pavers. He also creatively restored parts of the ruins that were damaged. In one such fabrication he recreated Uxmal's largest pyramid—originally built in an oval shape—with four flat sides in the Egyptian fashion.[26]

Yet shortly after his return to London, he used a novel method to come the closest of anyone to calculating the true age of the ruins. In an appearance before the Royal Geographic Society in May 1836, he first dazzled members with his drawings and then stated flatly that the ruins were at least one thousand years old.[27] He based his claim, he said, on the trees he found growing in the ruins, explaining how he had cut down one of the trees and then counted 973 concentric rings on a cross section of the trunk. As he pointed out, the tree must have implanted itself after the building was already in ruins.[28]

Waldeck went on to Paris, where he published his work in a folio in 1838 made up almost entirely of illustrations of Uxmal and Yucatec Indian men and women in native dress. It included a single image of

View of Palenque Palace today from a nearby temple. (Carlsen)

Palenque. He would not publish his drawings of Palenque for another three decades.[29]

○○○

Stephens's first impressions of the ruins of Palenque mirrored those of Calderón, Dupaix, and Walker: lush tropical rain forest, dense undergrowth draped in lianas, mounds of stones, shapeless rubble over which their mules stumbled, then, finally, as they mounted first one terrace, then another, the large building and a tower through the trees that was, Stephens wrote, "unique, extraordinary and mournfully beautiful."

It was as if Del Río's "slash and burn" and the many clearings by others during the intervening decades had never happened. The jungle, resilient and automatic, had closed in and smothered Palenque once again. Thick vegetation reclaimed the top of the structure; roots snaked along its cornices and down the walls; trees edged in, their branches filling the doorways. Some of the walls had fallen but the elaborate ornamentation along the building's façade could still be seen through the foliage, along with strange stuccoed figures on its pilasters. The Indians accompanying them cried out "el palacio," the palace. Stephens, Catherwood, and Pawling scrambled up the last steps on foot and entered the palace's outer corridors. They took a quick look around then returned to the entrance and fired off four rounds each into the air. It was a celebration of pure joy. But, wrote Stephens, "It was intended too for effect upon the Indians . . . who, we knew, would make such a report in the village as would keep any of their respectable friends from paying us a visit at night."

Fearing rain, they wasted little time in setting up residence along the palace's corridor, which ran partway around the building. Juan, their cook, who had pleaded to stay behind in the village, set up a rudimentary kitchen on stones at the end of the passageway, Pawling constructed a table of stone from the rubble; branches were cut from the trees and fastened together to form beds. Clearing away some trees on the terrace, they realized the elevated height of the palace offered a view out over the immense jungle at their feet, across a broad, flat, forested plain all the way to the Gulf of Mexico. Deeply superstitious, their Indians carriers slowly melted away, refusing to stay at night in the ruins, and headed back to the village.

Just as Stephens and his companions sat down to supper, the sky darkened; looking out over the forest, they could see the trees bent down by the force of the wind. In an instant, the wind whipped through the corridors, followed by heavy rain. Their supper was drenched. The sky shook with thunder and lightning. It was a rude welcome—but only the beginning of the torments to come.

And yet there were moments of solace. The wind meant they could not light a candle as night fell, but Stephens discovered that hunkered down in a protected corner of the corridor his surroundings were so well illuminated by fireflies of such enormous size that the light from a single one allowed him to read an American newspaper that he had brought with him from Guatemala. "It was one of a packet, full of debates in Congress . . . and it seemed stranger than any incident on my journey to be reading by the light of beetles, in the ruined palace of Palenque, the sayings and doings of great men at home." His thoughts of home turned even more wistful as Catherwood, emptying the pockets of his shooting jacket, handed Stephens a Broadway omnibus ticket: "Good to the bearer for one ride."

In the morning they were soaked to the skin and there was not a dry spot to stand on. Worse, the tortillas were moldy. "As often before in time of trouble," Stephens wrote, "[we] composed ourselves with a cigar." Fresh tortillas soon arrived with the village butcher, who served as Santo Domingo's official guide to the ruins—the ban on visitors proving untrue—a service he had also provided to Waldeck, Caddy, and Walker. Without him, Stephens explained, they had no idea which direction to take because the jungle formed a solid curtain around the palace.

They spent the first full day getting their bearings and making a preliminary survey of surrounding temples. The next day the hard work began. Stephens and Pawling set about measuring the palace. Then, with the help of the few Indians who came daily, they cleared some of the trees and constructed scaffolding for Catherwood to set up his camera lucida. Their overriding objective was to allow for the utmost accuracy in the drawings. Moss, algae, and mold covered many of the stuccoed and carved stone reliefs, at times completely obscuring the sculpted figures and hieroglyphs beneath, and had to be scrubbed away. Courtyards within the palace were filled with trees and brush, so much so that it was impossible to see across them. All this vegetation had to be cleared.

In one courtyard, extracting the rubble revealed nine extraordinary figures, six feet in height, carved into limestone slabs below the corridor. "They are adorned with rich headdresses and necklaces but their attitude is that of pain and trouble," Stephens wrote. "The design and anatomical proportion of the figures are faulty, but there is a force of expression about them which shows the skill and conceptive power of the artist."

The rains came regularly at around three or four every afternoon but that became the least of their discomforts. Every night they were under siege from mosquitoes. The second night, in order to escape

TOP   Palace courtyard at Palenque. (Catherwood)
BOTTOM   Detail of sculptural relief in courtyard at Palenque. (Catherwood)

"these murderers of rest," Stephens took his bedding down a pitch-black passage at the foot of the palace tower and found a low crawl space where he could spread his mat. The dampness of the spot was cooling and bats whizzed overhead, snapping up and driving away most of the mosquitoes. He wrote that he had "twinging apprehensions of the snakes and reptiles, lizards and scorpions, which infest the ruins," but was finally able to fall asleep.

It proved only temporary relief; the next night was worse. Even an exposed fingertip was viciously attacked. But to stay completely under the sheets, the heat was unbearable. "In the morning, our faces were all in blotches," he wrote. Exhausted from the grueling labors of the day, they knew they would not be able to continue without sleep. Finally they struck upon a solution. They sliced open their sheets, which had been sewn together to form sacks. Using their straw matting as a base, they bent three branches to arch over their beds, stretched the sheets over, and sewed them down tightly all around. This left a small opening to crawl in. Each night, Stephens noted, "hosts were waiting for us inside." However, after they closed the opening behind them they hunted down each mosquito with the flame of a candle. There was a second advantage to the new arrangement: though they could not escape the spray of the rain, the damp sheet a foot or two above their bodies acted to cool the heated air within. "It is on occasions like this that the creative power of genius displays itself."

But there seemed no solution to a torment that finally did Stephens in. Like Caddy before him, he fell victim to an insect the Indians called a *nigua*. This tiny tick, according to Stephens, ate its way into the flesh and deposited its eggs, which quickly hatched and multiplied. He carried one in his foot for several days, not knowing what was wrong. Finally Pawling tried to pick it out with a penknife, leaving a large hole. Soon the foot swelled to the point that Stephens had to sit for a day with his foot up. It was attacked by a swarm of small black flies, which inflicted hundreds of punctures. The swelling increased such that on his tenth day at the ruins, Stephens decided he had to return to the village. The foot was too swollen to fit in the stirrup and he could not let it hang down without feeling that his pulsating blood would burst through his skin. Resting it on a pillow over

TOP Temple of
Inscriptions at Palenque.
(Catherwood)

RIGHT The temple
today. (Carlsen)

the pommel of the saddle, he managed to make his way slowly down through the forest to Santo Domingo.

He spent two days on his back in a house rented from the village alcalde. Finally, with the help of the expedition's medicine chest, the swelling went down enough for him to hobble around the town making various social calls, one of Stephens's favorite diversions. Feeling guilty, however, he bought bread, parts of a butchered hog, and enough other delicacies for a small feast, and as soon as he was able, returned to the ruins with his haul. He had been gone only a few days, but he was stunned when he saw Catherwood. "He was wan and gaunt," Stephens reported, "lame, like me, from the bites of insects; his face was swollen, and his left arm hung with rheumatism as if paralyzed."

The changes at the ruins were equally startling given the short time he was away. The rain had seeped into everything, the walls were slick with moisture, water dripped through crevices in the palace roof. The saddles, bridles, boots, anything made of leather, were green with mildew, the pistols and guns covered in rust. Time was running out. Yet somehow Catherwood continued to work. Within days they knew they had to leave. Each night brought ever more rain until they feared the thunder and lightning would bring the palace down on their heads. "On Thursday, the thirtieth of May, the storm opened with a whirlwind," Stephens wrote. "At night the crash of falling trees rang through the forest, rain fell in deluges, the roaring of the thunder was terrific, and as we lay looking out, the aspect of the ruined palace, lighted by the glare of the lightening such as I never saw in this country, was grand; in fact, there was too much of the sublime and the terrible."

In the morning, the courtyard and lower compartments of the palace were flooded. Catherwood worked on for another day. In less than three weeks of almost continuous labor, he had achieved the nearly impossible, capturing the essence of ruins on paper with more accuracy than anyone before him, especially the hundreds of hieroglyphic inscriptions. But he could go on no longer.

○ ◎ ○

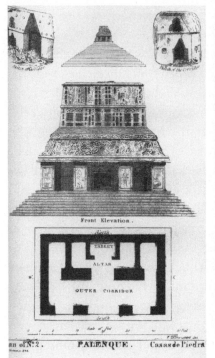

Two temples at Palenque. (Catherwood, left; Carlsen, right)

On May 31 he completed his last drawing. They packed up on Saturday, June 1, and "like rats leaving the sinking ship," Stephens wrote,
they left Palenque.

Catherwood was barely able to make it back to the village. The
trail was nothing but mud and gullies, the earlier streams swelling
now into small rivers. Climbing up the bank of one of the rivers,
Catherwood's mule fell backward and rolled onto him. Pawling was
able to pull him free. He was uninjured but badly shaken and faint.

Once in the village he collapsed, shattered and exhausted. He improved only gradually. Meanwhile, Stephens returned to his notebooks, which he had neglected for days. A month earlier, when they
arrived in Santo Domingo, they were gratified to learn that Walker
and Caddy had survived their journey and not been murdered. Stephens was also well aware of the earlier explorations of Del Río,

Dupaix, Galindo, and Waldeck, and he gave each his due in his book. In fact, he was determined to disclaim any credit for discovering Palenque and one of his first written comments about the ruins was to describe graffiti they found on the palace walls. Caddy's and Walker's names were there, and several others, including that of the logging entrepreneur Noah Platt, who had described the ruins to Stephens several years earlier.

Stephens would end up devoting two book chapters—thirty-six pages—solely to description of the Palenque ruins. But he understood it would be Catherwood's work that would make the difference, and elevate their book above all that had come before. "I uphold [Catherwood's] drawings against these costly folios," he wrote referring to Kingsborough's and the French volumes. "And against every other book that has ever been published on the subject of these ruins."

Thirty-four illustrations of Palenque would accompany Stephens's text, all of them engraved from Catherwood's drawings, sketches, maps, elevations, cross sections, and floor plans. One of Catherwood's most important achievements was the three pages he devoted to the large, complex hieroglyphic panels they found in a structure that would later become famous as the Temple of Inscriptions.[30] Double-page engravings would also show the lords of Palenque, large, imposing figures in elaborate, feathered headdresses carved into limestone slabs embedded in the walls of the other temples. Catherwood would give the world its best look at the beauty and strangeness of the great ruined city, and yet the truly sublime art of Palenque continued to defy two-dimensional representation on the page.

Palenque was not Copán. There Catherwood had been able to use his architect's eye, his skill at shading and perspective, to capture the great depth of the sculpting and the three dimensions of the large stelae, altars, and other monuments. At Palenque there were no monoliths, no stone pillars and stelae. The art was on flat surfaces. Stephens and Catherwood were only able to find a single three-dimensional statue, with one side unfinished, apparently fashioned to be set against a wall. Over the next century and a half, however, excavations at Palenque would yield a wealth of three-dimensional sculpture, astonishing ceramic and stone figures, heads, and incense holders, some formed in a naturalistic style almost unique in the Maya world. This naturalistic approach, so unlike the formulaic method of sculpture found at many other Maya sites, would bring Palenque's inhabitants to life, often revealing their distinctive personalities. In 1840, however, they lay buried under tons of earth and jungle. The bas-relief sculpting found on the walls by Stephens and Catherwood, though intricate and remarkably elegant, was simpler, the human form and face shown mostly in profile. It was accomplished on vertical surfaces in very shallow relief, a skill that reached an apogee at Palenque.

The artists did their work in two media: on limestone or with lime stucco or plaster. They perfected their carving technique on extremely fine-grained limestone, some of the densest and smoothest in Mesoamerica. The material allowed them to sculpt in exquisite detail with sharp edges. While the stone's hardness did not permit the depth of the sculpting in the softer stone of Copán and Quiriguá, the limestone's density allowed the hard-cut details of Palenque's art to survive more than a millennium of moisture, heat, and vegetative growth. Likewise, the very fine plaster they used, which hardened to concrete-like toughness, was built up only so far off the flat surface as if to replicate the limestone carvings, and it too was molded into reliefs of exacting delicacy. The meticulousness of the artists had reached such a level that in some cases each layer was painted even though it was to be covered over with another layer of plaster. "They dressed these figures," writes archaeologist Merle Greene Robertson, "as though they were real humans, first the underwear, then the jaguar skirts, aprons, loincloths, and last the beads and feathers. However, each piece of clothing was first painted with a thin layer of lime stucco and then color put on top, even when another garment was to cover the first."[31]

The hieroglyphs, masterfully carved and molded, and carrying within them a record of Palenque's dynastic history, must have presented the toughest challenge to the city's artists. As they fashioned the intricate glyphs into small oblong forms, similar to the Egyptian cartouche, the figures and shapes sometimes displayed only subtle differences. The glyphs were remarkably complex, a written language passed down through generations of scribes. Catherwood struggled just in outlining them on paper; it seems unimaginable to have carved

Bas relief inside a Palenque temple. (Catherwood)

or molded them. He had little more than two weeks to reproduce it all, not only the glyphs but also the stuccoed and carved figures, the temples with their complicated roof combs, the palace and its court-yards, and he did so with extraordinary accuracy. Still, the true magnificence of Palenque's art eluded capture. It would eventually take photography with dramatic lighting to even come close.

Stephens scrupulously documented what they had found. He could rhapsodize with the best romantics of his day, but he disdained factual exaggeration and inaccuracy. Palenque had been described earlier as an immense city, occupying miles of ground east and west of the palace. In one article in the United States, Stephens later noted that it had been reported the site occupied an area ten times the size of New York City; in another, that it was three times the size of London. With firsthand knowledge of the site, he believed there was no evidence for these claims. It was entirely possible, he wrote, that the city had indeed been large, especially if most of the populace lived, as such did in ancient Egypt, in "frail and perishable" huts similar to those occupied by the Indians in the nearby villages. As for other such remains covering a vast area, it was impossible to know or claim to know. "The whole country for miles around is covered by a dense forest of gigantic trees," he wrote, "with a growth of brush and underwood . . . impenetrable in any direction except by cutting a way with a machete. Without a guide, we might have gone within a hundred feet of all the buildings without discovering one of them."

Today, more of Palenque's remains are still being unearthed. In the years 1998 to 2000, fifteen hundred structures were mapped in the area surrounding Palenque's urban core, four times the number located only fifteen years earlier.[32] Stephens's guess was right that a large city was possible but no one could have known or claimed it in 1840.

But it was not the size of Palenque that struck wonder in Stephens. And within the bounds of what they had found, he felt free to let his imagination loose:

> What we had before our eyes was grand, curious and remarkable enough. Here were the remains of a cultivated, polished and peculiar people, who had passed through all the stages incident to the rise and fall of nations; reached their golden age, and perished, entirely unknown. We lived in the ruined palace of their kings; we went up to their desolate temples and fallen altars; and wherever we moved we saw the evidence of their taste, their skill in arts, their wealth and power. In the midst of desolation and ruin we looked back to the past, cleared away the gloomy forest, and fancied every building perfect, with its terraces and pyramids, its sculptured and painted ornaments, grand, lofty, and imposing, and overlooking an immense inhabited plain; we called back into life the strange people who gazed at us in sadness from the walls; pictured them, in fanciful costumes and adorned with plumes of feathers, ascending the terraces of the palace and the steps leading to the temples; and often we imagined a scene of unique and gorgeous beauty and magnificence.

Stuck in the village while Catherwood recovered, Stephens made the most of the extra time. He discovered that the six thousand acres surrounding the ruins was for sale by the state of Chiapas and had been for two years with no buyers, and to his amazement the offer included the ruins at no extra cost. The appraised value of the whole lot was estimated at fifteen hundred dollars. As with Copán and Quiriguá, Stephens's interest in Palenque ran deeper than just capturing it in words and images. He desired to put the Americas on the world map with a museum that rivaled the great institutions of Europe. Pieces from Palenque would provide an incredible start. Stephens was never able to suppress his American entrepreneurial instincts. "I would fit up the palace and re-people the old city of Palenque," he wrote excitedly, no doubt thinking of the dry season, a hotel or two, and a lemonade concession. Just how serious he was—it is never certain with Stephens—proved moot almost immediately. A "difficulty" arose that he could not easily surmount. In order to own land, a foreigner must be married to a "daughter of the country." Stephens looked around. Santo Domingo was a small place. "The oldest (available) young lady was not more than fourteen," he explained, "and the prettiest woman, who already had contributed to our happiness (she made our cigars), was already married."

There was another possibility. Two sisters occupied one of the best houses in town, which also happened to contain two carved stone tablets from the ruins. Stephens already had his eye on the house with the thought of renting it if he returned to spend more time in the ruins. Both sisters were about forty, one a widow and the other single, and both, he said, "equally interesting and equally interested." Ownership of the ruins, a nice house, and two extraordinary stone tablets was tempting. But since there were two sisters it was a very delicate situation. Then new information changed everything. He learned he could purchase the ruins in the name of the American consul in the nearby port town of Laguna de Términos. The consul, Charles Russell, already owned large properties through his Mexican wife. Stephens quickly made arrangements with Pawling, who agreed to act as Stephens's purchasing agent and return to Palenque from Laguna with the consul's authorization and Stephens's funds, assuming Russell was game. Pawling was also charged with returning with enough "plaster of Paris" to make castings of the ruins' carved and stuccoed reliefs and arrange for their transport to New York.

Catherwood, meanwhile, had recovered enough after three days that they were able to take their leave. They rode through the town saying their farewells and after a day's ride reached a convent and a tributary of the mighty Usumacinta River, which in the ancient past had served as the major water route between Palenque and the great Maya cities buried and unknown in the lowland forests to the east.

Their expedition, however, was headed the other way, northwest down the river to the Gulf of Mexico. Their final destination was Yucatán and they would take the sea route north to get there. But before stepping aboard the canoe and setting off, Stephens had one more goodbye:

> He had carried me more than two thousand miles, over the worst roads that a mule ever traveled. He stood tied to the door of the convent; saw the luggage, and even his own saddle, carried away by hand, and seemed to have a presentiment that something unusual was going on. I threw my arms around his neck; his eyes had a mournful expression, and at that moment he forgot the angry prick of the spur. I laid aside the memory of a toss from his back and ineffectual attempts to repeat it, and we remembered only the mutual kind offices and goodfellowship. Tried and faithful companion, where are you now? I left him, with two others, tied at the door of the convent, to be taken by the sexton to the prefect at Palenque, there to recover from the debilitating influence of the early rains, and to roam on rich pasture-grounds, untouched by bridle and spur, until I should return to mount him again.

◁◁ 14 ▷▷

Uxmal

There was nothing pleasant about the journey on the Usumacinta to the Gulf of Mexico. Clouds of mosquitoes patrolled the river and attacked the men at every opportunity; alligators watched ominously from the banks or floated just under the waterline. Frequent rain squalls compounded their misery. They were wet, crammed together in the bottom of the boat, and barely slept. It took several days but finally they floated through a vast flat swampland, crossed the Laguna de Términos, pulled into the Gulf port town of Laguna—and there found themselves in the middle of yet another revolution. Yucatán government leaders had just declared their state independent from the central authorities in Mexico City. But so far this revolt bore scant resemblance to the violent conflict they had left behind in Central America. In nearby villages and towns the insurrectionists drew little blood as they deposed central party officials. In the port of Laguna, the rebels of the Liberal party declared their allegiance to the new Yucatán state, then disarmed the Mexican army garrison and ran the soldiers out of town.

Despite the political turmoil, Stephens and Catherwood were greatly relieved as they came ashore. The town seemed like heaven, filled with shops, cafés, and cantinas, a thriving depot for the export of logwood from the country's interior to the United States and Europe. A dozen ships lay at anchor. It was an important enough settlement to merit a U.S. consul, and Charles Russell was sitting on his porch when Stephens and Catherwood strode up to greet him. "The wear and tear of our wardrobe [was] manifest to the most indifferent observer."

It had been more than seven months since they had seen the waters of the Caribbean. And New York felt closer than ever when a ship master sitting with Russell, who had just sailed in directly from New York, handed them some newspapers and passed along other news of the city. To Stephens's delight, he recognized the man, whom he identified only as Captain Fensley. He turned out to be another acquaintance from New York whom Stephens had consulted about Mexico before departing the year before.

Stephens and Catherwood's plan was to hire a bungo, a large sailing canoe, and head north up the coast to Yucatán seaport of Campeche, but they learned it was occupied by Mexican troops and under siege by the rebels. Captain Fensley, leaving soon to return to New York, agreed to take them beyond Campeche to the port of Sisal, where they could continue their journey to Mérida and their final destination, the ruins of Uxmal.[1]

Over the several days it took Fensley to ready his brig for the voyage, Stephens made financial arrangements with Russell, who agreed to help him buy Palenque and send parts of it to New York for his projected museum. Letters were drafted authorizing Pawling to return to Santo Domingo and act as their agent. And, as if matters were not going well enough, it also happened that the consul had a few extra barrels of plaster of Paris left from construction of his recently built house. Pawling now had all the materials he needed to make molds at the ruins. He accompanied Stephens and Catherwood out to Fensley's ship for final farewells. "We had gone through such rough scenes together that it may be supposed we did not separate with indifference," wrote Stephens in his best understated prose. Juan continued on to Sisal with them, where Stephens would make arrangements, as he had promised, to send him back to Guatemala.

In a few days they were anchored off Sisal. After briefly entertaining the idea of staying aboard the ship all the way to New York, now less than three weeks away by sea, Stephens and Catherwood resolved to press on to Uxmal, their final objective, even if it meant dodging their way through yet another revolution. They entered Sisal along a pier under an old Spanish fort and were immediately challenged for their passports by several armed soldiers. Yet little else told them a rebellion was under way. Instead, moderation appeared to be the rule of the day, something they had seen little of in Central America.

The next day they were in Mérida, a handsome city of thirty-five thousand residents, with a hotel on the main plaza that reminded them of the comforts of Europe. Stephens was hoping to meet another acquaintance from New York, a Mérida resident named Simon Peon, whom he had encountered the year before at a Fulton Street hotel where Stephens often dined. When Stephens had mentioned that he was soon heading south in search of ruins, Peon invited him to his hacienda, where some ruins were located—the remains of the old city of Uxmal.

Stephens and Catherwood went to pay Don Peon a visit and were taken aback to see that the Peon family lived in a mansion that took up nearly half of one side of the central Plaza de Armas. The building had been constructed hundreds of years earlier by Francisco de Montejo, the Spanish conquistador who subdued most of the Yucatán Peninsula in 1546, after nineteen years of bloody fighting. The entrance to the residence was one of the most imposing in all of Mexico. It was framed by Corinthian columns and topped by an ornate balcony. The Montejo coat of arms was set in the wall, flanked on each side by sculptured figures of two giant Spanish soldiers holding pikes and crushing under their feet the heads of four howling Indians.

Don Peon was not at home. His mother, Doña Joaquina, invited them in and explained that her son was at the Uxmal hacienda and due back in Mérida soon. When Stephens suggested they leave immediately in the hope of catching him there, Doña Joaquina offered to make the necessary arrangements and provide them with a guide.

The next day, while the arrangements were being made, Stephens and Catherwood had a chance to take in some of Mérida society. The scene around the plaza seemed remarkably normal considering the state was in the midst of rebellion. In fact, independence from Mexico now seemed assured and peace at hand, at least temporarily, after news arrived that the Mexican army garrison at Campeche had surrendered. There was a flurry of activity, including promenades under the arched corridors surrounding the plaza and a procession celebrating one of the church's biggest annual festivals, the Feast of Corpus

Christi. In Stephens's typical whirlwind fashion, in the space of a day, the two men were able to attend the service at the cathedral, take in the festival procession, call upon a lady with a beautiful daughter, pay a visit to Mérida's bishop ("a man several feet around," Stephens observed, "handsomely dressed, and in a chair made to fit"), and then finish with a night at the theater. At six thirty the next morning, they were on the road to Uxmal.

The two men quickly discovered that northern Yucatán was nothing like the lush, wet mountains surrounding Palenque 280 miles to the south. The peninsula was, instead, an immense, flat bed of carbonates, mostly limestone, created over millions of years from accumulated layers of coral and other sea sediment. Once underwater, the Yucatán plateau now barely rises above the warm shallow sea surrounding it. Its thin, stony topsoil is more like chalk than loam, adequate enough for cattle and a few hardy crops like hemp and corn, but bone-dry more than half the year. Low tropical "dry" forests of short trees and scrub scratch out an existence on a terrain devoid of any rivers or streams. Water collects during the rainy seasons in low depressions or soaks through cracks in the limestone into subterranean caverns and streams. Access to water during the dry season is mainly through cave entrances and sinkholes that open onto startlingly beautiful underground pools called cenotes, some many feet deep, scattered by the hundreds across the peninsula—or from man-made cisterns and reservoirs constructed to store rainwater.

The road the two men took was stony and rough; it cut through the scrub forest. Three miles out they came to the Peon family's first hacienda, a hemp plantation. The hacienda consisted of a large stone house, beside which sat a giant stone tank twelve feet deep and filled with much-needed water. Nine miles farther on they came to the next Peon hacienda, where they ate breakfast. The sun beat down mercilessly, and the heat became more and more oppressive with each mile. Each hacienda seemed more imposing than the last. This one had its own church, a large cross over the door. Fifteen hundred Indians lived as tenants on the property in a form of feudal bondage, dependent on the Peon family for their water during the dry season. Every hacienda was run by a majordomo, usually of mixed blood, who managed the operation for the Peons.

Their guide suggested the young mestizo majordomo call for a coach to carry them to the next stop, due to the heat. From the belfry of the church he put out a call, not unlike, Stephens noted, the call to prayer from a Muslim minaret. Within fifteen minutes two dozen Indians appeared and began hacking at nearby trees and shrubs with their machetes. They quickly laid down poles and bound them together with hemp until they had built two platforms covered by branches bent like bows above. Grass hammocks were hung from the poles and matting was stretched over the branches to block the sunlight. Six Indians were chosen as carriers for each coach. Stephens and Catherwood crawled inside and were soon on their way. "In the great relief we experienced," Stephens wrote, "we forgot our former scruples against making beasts of burden of men. They were not troubled with any sense of indignity, and the weight was not much. There were no mountains."

Many miles later they arrived at an immense hacienda, again surrounded by huge water tanks. Catherwood, still recovering from the Palenque ordeal, fell into his hammock in a large, empty suite of rooms while Stephens went off to investigate a natural pool nearby. Surprised to find a large opening in the ground—his first cenote—he sent immediately for Catherwood. "It was a large cavern or grotto with a roof of broken, overhanging rock," he wrote, "and at the bottom water pure as crystal, still and deep, resting on a bed of white limestone rock. It was the very creation of romance; a bathing-place for Diana and her nymphs." The two men plunged in with "feelings of boyish exultation" and swam around the basin until dark.

At dawn they were on horseback again, riding under a savage sun until midday, when they finally arrived at the Peons' Uxmal hacienda. They had covered fifty miles in two and a half days but Don Peon had already left for the city and somehow they had missed him along the way. They were so dehydrated and drained of energy that they took immediately to their hammocks for a siesta.

The hacienda was similar to the others, complete with chapel and water tanks, but it was much older and rougher in appearance, with an "unwholesome sensation of dampness," Stephens recalled. There were also two majordomos, one of whom was a young Spaniard who, to their surprise, had recently arrived from New York, where he had served as a waiter at Delmonico's, one of Stephens's favorite restaurants. Don Peon, while in New York, had persuaded him to come south, saying he would train him to manage several of his family's haciendas. However, the young man confessed to Stephens that he missed New York dearly, already nostalgic for the opera and Delmonico's, where a friend who accompanied him to New York still worked as head chocolate maker. Stephens began to feel Yucatán was so close to New York by water it seemed like a suburb of the city, if a stony and unbearably hot one. Now only Uxmal stood between them and their return home, and the ruins lay just a mile away.

Stephens was anxious to go. The two men set out on foot that afternoon, but Catherwood soon began to feel ill and turned back to the hacienda. When Stephens later breathlessly reported what he found— "mounds of ruins, and vast buildings on terraces and pyramidal structures, grand and in good preservation, richly ornamented, without a bush to obstruct the view, and in picturesque effect almost equal to the ruins of Thebes"—Catherwood, grumpy, and out of sorts with exhaustion and illness, brushed Stephens off as "romancing." The next day, however, he made the trek to Uxmal and pronounced Stephens's earlier description an understatement.

Both men were incredulous. Here was the fifth major set of ruins they had encountered, each one magnificent, each different, and yet somehow mysteriously similar. Another large, obviously civilized city, filled with sophisticated sculpture, ornate architectural wonders, and yet, Stephens noted, not a word of its history known.[2] The Peon family deed went back 140 years and the ruins were listed only as Las Casas de Piedra, the houses of stone. The current name of the ruins, Uxmal, had been taken from the hacienda.

Catherwood wasted no time getting to work. Fortunately the site was relatively open and the views unobstructed because the forest that had encroached on it had been cut down the year before, primarily to allow for the planting of corn. Some clearing may also have been ordered by Waldeck four years earlier. In one day, Catherwood managed to make an important series of sketches. The most detailed captured a broad vista of the ruins including a towering pyramid, which the Indians called "the house of the dwarf," based on a local legend, and a flamboyantly decorated nearby building they called "the Nunnery." He then explored the ruins' most imposing edifice, called the "House of the Governor" because of its massive size and elaborate stonework. He diagrammed the enormous platform on which the building stood and made a floor plan of the twenty-five rooms within the building, while Stephens measured and took down the dimensions. Late in the afternoon, Catherwood also made rough sketches of sections of the building's long façade, struggling again to capture new and entirely different kinds of stonework, incomprehensible mosaics the two of them had never seen before.

It was a promising start. That night, however, Catherwood was consumed by a violent fever, the symptom of a serious attack of malaria compounded by his already weakened and exhausted state. Later it would fall to Stephens to convey in words most of what they had found at Uxmal, barely aided this time by Catherwood's abbreviated work. At the moment, he was in fear for Catherwood's life. Although the fever broke the next afternoon, the two men decided to go back to Mérida immediately. They now understood how convenient Yucatán was to New York and agreed they could easily return later to complete the work at Uxmal and follow up on reports and rumors of other ruins on the peninsula. They also knew from an encounter they had at Sisal that a Spanish brig was due to sail within days for Havana. If they left early the next morning they might arrive at Sisal before it departed. They informed the majordomo of their intention and he climbed the belfry of the chapel. Soon Indians were busy piecing together a coach for Catherwood.

They left at three in the morning, Catherwood in the coach on the shoulders of Indian carriers and Stephens on horseback carrying a letter from the junior majordomo to his friend, the Delmonico chocolate maker. The moon was high as Stephens followed behind the coach. "The stillness broken only by the shuffle of their feet," he wrote, "and under my great apprehension for [Catherwood's] health, it almost seemed as if I were following his bier." During the morning they stopped at two villages for relief carriers, then set out the last twenty-seven miles to Mérida. They arrived in the city late at night after almost twenty-four hours on the road. The next morning they met with Don Peon, who was preparing to leave for Uxmal to meet them. Seeing Catherwood's condition, he promised that if they returned he would join them at Uxmal and help make a thorough investigation of the ruins.

At Stephens's request, Peon agreed to ship two items from Uxmal to New York. The first was a sculptured stone figurehead from above one of the doors of the Governor's House, "the face of a death's head, with wings expanded, and rows of teeth projecting," which today is on display at the American Museum of Natural History in New York City.[3] Peon had already removed it from the building with the intention of setting it up as an ornament at the hacienda. The second was a fallen wooden lintel that Stephens and Catherwood found leaning against the wall inside the Governor's House. Stephens considered the heavy beam invaluable because on it was carved a line of hieroglyphic characters similar to those they had seen at Copán and Palenque, providing a crucial link that tied the ruins at the three distant sites together. "There are at Uxmal no 'idols,' as at Copán; not a single stuccoed figure or carved tablet, as at Palenque," he later explained. "Except for this beam of hieroglyphics, though searching earnestly, we did not discover any one absolute point of resemblance." The wooden beam never made it to New York, for reasons unknown.

At dusk after a heavy rainfall, Catherwood and Stephens set out by carriage for Sisal. On the way they met a detachment of Yucatán soldiers who had just arrived from their victory at Campeche. A short time later they congratulated the victorious general and his officers trailing behind. The short revolution appeared to be a success. Just before dawn they arrived at the port and almost immediately boarded the Spanish brig *Alexandre*. Two hours later they were under way, headed for Havana. It was June 24, only a week short of nine months— what seemed a lifetime—since they had sailed out of New York Harbor.

Despite the hardships, physical obstacles, and threats of violence they had to overcome, Stephen and Catherwood knew they had accomplished an enormous amount, well beyond what they had imagined before the start of their journey. They had found Quiriguá, explored Copán, Toniná, and Palenque, and carefully recorded each in words and images. And even though their stay at Uxmal was frustratingly short, it was enough for them to weave its ruins into the pattern they saw emerging of a widespread, sophisticated civilization—still of unknown antiquity and origin—but an advanced society and culture no one knew existed. What else, they wondered, still lay out there undiscovered in the jungle? And how soon would they be able to return to find out?

Though Catherwood's health was compromised, they felt tremendous relief that only water now separated them from home. The captain told them they would be in Havana in a week, and from there the two men expected to find quick passage to New York. But after four days sailing in light winds along the coast of the peninsula, they had covered no more than 150 miles by the captain's reckoning. Then the wind stopped altogether.

> The sun was intensely hot, the sea of glassy stillness, and all day a school of sharks were swimming around the brig. From this time we had continued calms, and the sea was like a mirror, heated and reflecting the heat. On the Fourth of July there was the same glassy stillness, with light clouds, but fixed and stationary. The captain said we were incantado or enchanted, and really it almost seemed so.

They had hoped to celebrate the Fourth of July with the U.S. consul in Havana. But day after day the ship drifted on the open sea, not a speck of land on the horizon. It seemed impossible at this point, after so many months of hard travel, to be floating aimlessly, going nowhere. The two men worked their way through every book in the ship's library, mostly French novels translated into Spanish, with one exception they were not anxious to read: a history of "awful" shipwrecks. They idled the time away watching the sharks, eventually catching and eating two of them as provisions began to dwindle. On the July 12 the brig swung into a fast current, but the air remained a dead calm. The mate's soundings stopped at 120 fathoms, still short of the bottom. "At this time our best prospect was that of reaching Havana in the midst of the yellow fever season, sailing from there in the worst of the hurricane months, and quarantine at Staten Island." That is, if they ever got to Havana. The captain, a thirty-year veteran of the sea, sailed by reckoning and there was no chronometer aboard to take longitudinal readings. Catherwood's chronometer was old, badly beaten up from their journey and now unreliable. Only able to guess where they were, the captain was growing anxious that they had entered the Gulf Stream and would be carried beyond Havana and out into the Atlantic.

There were eight other passengers aboard, all Spanish, as well as nine crewmen and the captain. Food stores were running low, but the real concern was water. On the thirteenth they opened the last barrel. There were more sharks than ever, as if sensing time was running out.

Then, on the fifteenth, three weeks out from Sisal, a slight breeze came up, sending a jolt of hope through the ship.

A short time later salvation appeared as a tiny blip on the horizon. The captain headed leeward with all speed and slowly, ecstatically, they closed in on a sailing vessel bearing an American flag. They lowered the "jolly boat," and since the captain was unable to speak English, Stephens and Catherwood were dispatched. But the jolly boat's seams had opened while lying on the brig's deck in the scorching sun and water poured in. The boat was half-full in minutes. Stephens and Catherwood sat up on the gunwales watching the sharks "playing around us," and urged the crew to row harder. As they approached the American ship, its crew grew suspicious and claimed they were pirates. "But the captain," Stephens wrote, "a long, cool-headed down-easter, standing on the quarter with both hands in his pockets, and seeing the sinking condition of our boat, said 'Them's no pirates.'"

Once on board, Stephens could hardly believe it when the captain told them his ship was headed directly for New York. The vessel, named the *Helen Maria,* was carrying a full load of logwood out of Tabasco, but the captain agreed to take Stephens and Catherwood aboard. He had barely enough food for his crew, and now with two more passengers he had none to spare. Even so, he agreed to send a supply of water over to the *Alexandre.* He also provided the Spanish captain with the coordinates of their location. The Spaniard had miscalculated greatly. After twenty-one days at sea his brig was only two hundred miles from Sisal.

Stephens and Catherwood returned briefly to the *Alexandre* for farewells. They shook hands all around. "They were not sorry to get rid of us, for the absence of two mouths was an object," explained Stephens, who learned later that the brig made it to Havana safely, although in wretched condition and without a crumb of food aboard.

Sixteen days later, Stephens and Catherwood sailed into New York Harbor. They arrived just short of ten months from the day they had left.

◁◁ 15 ▷▷

"Magnificent"

Stephens and Catherwood were more than ready to embrace the civilized comforts of New York again. However, any relief the city might have provided Catherwood—his health uncertain—was short-lived. Waiting for him was a letter from his older brother James explaining that on the date he was living in the stone palace at Palenque, their mother, Anne, had died in London. There was more. It also appeared that his marriage was in some danger and James advised him to come to London as soon as possible. Catherwood booked passage and sailed for England sometime in August, less than a month after he landed in New York.[1]

When he arrived in London weeks later, there was an ugly confrontation with Gertrude. In his letter James had explained to his brother that during his time in Central America Gertrude had moved out of the family home at Charles Square as their mother's health declined and had taken up lodgings in Charlotte Street, Portland-Place. James added that she was also receiving visits from a notorious brawler and inebriate, Henry Beresford, the marquis of Waterford.[2] Catherwood remembered Beresford from their brief travel together in Palestine six years earlier. Apparently during his "Grand Tour" of the Mediterranean, the marquis had also become acquainted with Gertrude in Beirut. The two of them crossed paths again in London. Catherwood now demanded to know if they were lovers. What was spoken between them during their confrontation was never fully disclosed but, as his attorney later described it, Catherwood afterward was convinced of "his dishonor and her perfidy."[3] The news, however, was worse than Catherwood had imagined. Gertrude was having an affair not with Beresford but with a family member, his second cousin, Henry Caslon.

Catherwood must have reeled at the discovery. The Caslon and Catherwood families had been especially close: Frederick's father, John James, had been a partner in a letterpress foundry with the Caslons, who were related to the Catherwoods through James' and Frederick's mother, Anne.[4] James later testified that he had accompanied his brother to the Charlotte Street house for his meeting with Gertrude. He said he was not present for most of the conversation but did hear Gertrude tell his brother at the end: "You shall keep the children." She had no intention of breaking off with Caslon. At this, Catherwood gathered up his son and two daughters, one of whom he barely knew, and left for Charles Square. His long absence in Central America had cost him dearly and he must have weighed over and over whether the journey with Stephens was worth the neglect of his family and loss of his wife. But he was furious with his cousin, an emotion that would not leave him.

With reconciliation impossible, he had no intention of staying in London as his panorama business and his work with Stephens required he return to New York as quickly as possible. Devastated by the loss of the two women closest in his life, he sailed within weeks for New York, arriving in October with his three children and their nanny.[5]

Stephens, meanwhile, had plunged almost immediately into work on his book. He was a demon writer and the ferocious pace of his writing put intense pressure on Catherwood to begin work on the illustrations as soon as he got back. Stephens no doubt expressed great sympathy for Catherwood and his personal troubles; he may even have felt some guilt concerning them. Yet there was little time for Catherwood to brood, and returning to work may have been the best salve for his wounds. While Stephens had always been a fast and fluid writer, now he felt added urgency, fearing that another account of the Central American ruins, including illustrations, might be published ahead of theirs. Indeed, the two men were aware that Caddy and Walker had survived their return to Belize.

We have no account of Catherwood's physical health during this period but a friend described him as depressed. His anger so consumed him that in December he arranged for charges to be brought in London against Caslon, accusing him of "criminal conversation" with Gertrude, a Victorian-era euphemism for illicit intercourse. Such legal actions, similar to "alienation of affection" lawsuits in the United States at the time, permitted a husband or wife to bring charges against their spouse's lover for monetary damages. It would be a year before Catherwood's lawsuit would go to trial. Meanwhile, the upbringing of his children and work on the book were more than enough to preoccupy him. And while his panorama business must have taken up some of his time, it also appeared to be running smoothly under his partner's supervision.[6]

The book presented a serious challenge. For Catherwood, the priority was to make sure the illustrations represented the truest possible copies of the ruins as they had found them. He and Stephens were acutely aware of the ransacking force that tropical nature exerted on the ruins. They themselves had suffered its abuses. And they were aware also that the sites might be altered and even destroyed through excavations and removal, especially after their book was published. In fact, Stephens was already planning such removals with the justification that the artifacts and monuments would be better preserved if they were shipped to the United States and housed safely in a museum— and, of course, securely away from Europeans.

Yet even if their intention was to remain faithful to the ruins and preserve them for history, the two men were also creatures of their time. The overriding artistic impulse of the day was "romanticism," with its emphasis on infusing nature with emotion and drama. It was a filter from which they could not, like most artists of their era, entirely escape. It can be seen in some of Catherwood's backgrounds, where hills and volcanoes appear exaggerated, roots and vines take on snakelike qualities, and his dramatic use of light and dark in the forests leaves viewers with a feeling of ominous, enveloping decay. It was as if his emotional response to the lushness and menace of the jungle had freed him from the dry precision of his work in Egypt and the Holy Land. That precision, however, never left him when it came to the stone monuments and temples themselves, which he depicted with the utmost accuracy.

Stephens was not immune. He also was unable at times to keep emotions, especially feelings of sheer wonderment and awe, from invading his prose. But, all told, the degree to which both men indulged in romantic sentiments was minor and they labored hard to represent the actual ruins, the structures, glyphs, and idols, as true to their originals as possible.

For Catherwood the most difficult task came with the transfer of his artwork to engraving plates. In the field he had created innumerable pen and pencil sketches, other drawings with great exactitude using his camera lucida, and he painted many scenes in sepia and watercolor. These works had to be coordinated with Stephens's text and reduced to single book-size images for the engravers to copy. Stephens decided that the fidelity of the illustrations was so important that no expense should be spared, and so he authorized Catherwood to hire the finest engravers in New York and London. But after seeing the results produced by the professionals' engravings on wood, the perfectionist in Catherwood was not satisfied. "Though done with exquisite skill, and most effective as pictures," Stephens later explained in the book, "they failed in giving the true character and expression of the originals; and at some considerable loss of time and money, were all thrown aside." The surreal imagery of the stone monoliths, in particular their twisting, incongruous shadows, which Catherwood had captured with such depth and dimension at Copán, must have driven the engravers crazy.

A decision was made to have them re-engrave the illustrations on steel, which would create extremely fine lines. "And, in my opinion," Stephens wrote, "they are as true copies as can be presented; and, except the stones themselves, the reader cannot have better materials for speculation and study." In the end, the book contained seventy-nine engravings and lithographs, including a map showing their route through Central America.[7]

In Central America Stephens had filled notebooks with details, keenly aware of the material he would need when he returned. The corresponding scenes in the book emerge with startling immediacy. Though there is little question about his detailed descriptions of the ruins themselves, it is impossible to know how faithful his accounts are about people and events. Yet a reading of the book is likely to dispel any doubt about his commitment to get everything right—the people, landscapes, the interviews, and the "incidents." He traveled most of the time with Catherwood, sometimes with others, and described a variety of occasions when others were present, including such figures as Morazán and Carrera, all of whom could have contradicted or challenged his accounts if inaccurate. Indeed, as with Catherwood's illustrations, he openly professed the necessity to create as true an account as possible and was critical of others who took liberties or exaggerated what they found in travels and explorations.

In May 1841 the text was completed. Stephens had written nearly nine hundred pages of crisp, engaging prose in less than ten months, a remarkable achievement. He delivered the manuscript to the Harper brothers at 82 Cliff Street along with a brief preface expressing his appreciation to former president Martin Van Buren for making it all possible. Still struggling with his engravers, Catherwood approved the last of the illustrations the next month and the two-volume set began rolling off Harper's presses in July, less than a year after their return to New York.[8]

For a hefty double volume on a stuffy subject like antiquities, the work was a stunningly popular success. Edgar Allan Poe, for one, declared it "magnificent." In an abbreviated review published the month the book came out, he wrote that he had yet to receive a review copy but was so anxious to read it he borrowed and skimmed an advance copy from a friend. A bare-knuckled critic at times, Poe bowed before the clean, direct energy of Stephens's prose, praising the book as "perhaps the most interesting book of travel ever published."[9]

And despite its stodgy—though conventional at the time—title, *Incidents of Travel in Central America, Chiapas, and Yucatán*, the Harpers could not run their presses fast enough. "The appearance of the book," wrote the *United States Democratic Review*, "was hailed by an instantaneous rush upon its publishers, who were for many days literally unable to bind and deliver copies in sufficient quantities to supply the still increasing demand."[10] The book went through twelve printings in the first three months with estimates of up to twenty thousand copies sold by December, an incredible number at the time and far outstripping the

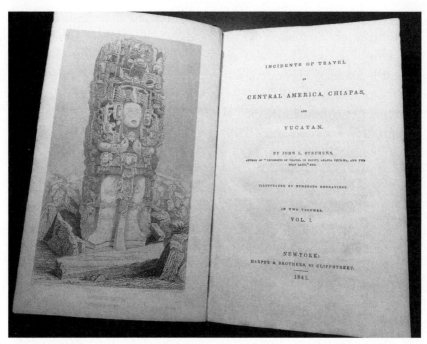

Title page from *Incidents of Travel in Central America, Chiapas, and Yucatán.*

great success of Stephens's previous books.[11] It was quickly published in Britain as well, and there, as in the United States, it received almost universal acclaim. By February of the next year a French translation appeared and a German one was in the works.

"We close this book with regret," wrote the reviewer in the *London Quarterly Review.* "From the first page to the last, the animation, the characteristic energy, and the buoyant spirit of the author remain undiminished. The political details . . . would in themselves be sufficient to render the work one of high interest and permanent value."[12] As they had with his earlier book on Egypt and the Holy Land, the critics succumbed again to the charm of Stephens's persona. "There is something exceedingly agreeable to a reader in the manner of Mr. Stephens," noted one reviewer; "there is a good humor, a *bonhomie* about him, which is irresistibly fascinating. He is the very Democritus of travelers, laughing at inconveniences, which would make some men gnash their teeth and tear their hair in anguish, making the best of everything that turns up."[13]

The accolades were not confined to the book reviewers—or to comments on Stephens's writing and persona. Historian William Hickling Prescott, then hard at work on his pioneering study of the Spanish conquest of Mexico, was greatly impressed. Four years earlier, publication of his book *The History of the Reign of Ferdinand and Isabella* had established him as a master of narrative history, renowned for his deep research, impartiality, and elegant writing. Publication of his *Conquest of Mexico* in 1843 would catapult him into the rank of one of the greatest historians of his time. Because of blindness he worked almost exclusively from his home in Boston, dictating his prose and relying on researchers in Spain. But he had traveled in 1838 to New York, where he and Stephens met for the first time right after Stephens's debut book appeared.[14] A friendship grew with their mutual interest in Spanish America.

In a quick exchange of letters following his return from Mexico, Stephens summarized for Prescott some of his findings, which the historian found invaluable for his own book. Stephens told him the quality of the Central American ruins were equal to "the finest of the Egyptians" and "the buildings at Palenque and Uxmal are very large and really one can hardly help speaking of them extravagantly."[15] Prescott replied, expressing his astonishment that the structures were "so well executed." He fully agreed with Stephens that the then-preeminent historian of the Americas, William Robertson, was probably wrong in his insistence that Native Americans were too primitive to have developed an advanced civilization.[16] When Stephens's book came out, Prescott dashed off a long letter to Stephens: "I cannot well express to you the satisfaction and delight I have received from your volumes. I suppose few persons will enjoy them more, as very few have been led to pay much attention to the subject. You have indeed much exceeded the expectations I had formed, which were not small."[17]

Prescott and other scholars were impressed with Stephens's conservative approach regarding the portrayal of the ruins: not exaggerating their size or age as others had done but describing and showing them just as he and Catherwood found them. Aside from the adventures and close calls of the rest of his story, in the end it was the ruins that most captivated his readers. "[Stephens] avows that he does not attempt to solve the great question of the history of Central America," wrote the *New York Review*, "but merely to furnish the as yet inexplicable and unexplained pages of that history . . . aided by the practiced eye and the obedient pencil of Mr. Catherwood."[18] The critics lavished praise on Catherwood, one calling him "one of the most accomplished and accurate draughtsman of the day."[19] Prescott wrote to Stephens that Catherwood's drawings "carry with them a perfect assurance of his fidelity, in this how different from his predecessors who have never failed by some over-finish or by their touches for effect to throw an air of improbability, or at least uncertainty, over the whole."[20]

At the end of his book, Stephens took great care in addressing the question of who could have built these grand, seemingly ancient cities in the jungle. As a lawyer, he knew that his readers, like jurors, wanted a good summing up, and he felt he had accumulated enough facts to lay out very basic conclusions. And like a good attorney he coolly and rationally argued his case from the evidence. "Much learning and research have been expended upon insufficient or incorrect data, or when a bias had been given [as] a statement of facts," he wrote. He insisted that he and Catherwood had come to the ruins with no preconceived bias and sought only to learn from what they found.

As a result, he said, he felt compelled to strongly refute the persistent arguments that the ruins they found were left by Romans, Greeks, Carthaginians, Egyptians, Jews, Chinese, or Hindus, who had somehow migrated to America in the distant past. Having traveled personally among Old World ruins, he argued that the Central American and Mexican remains bore no resemblance to any Greek or Roman works. And having extensively studied the ancient architectures of Asia, he found no similarities with those, either.

As for an Egyptian connection, he said, that theory was based primarily on the appearance of pyramidal structures in Egypt and the New World. But, he wrote, they are not the same. Egypt's pyramids are four-sided and smooth, and come to a point. He and Catherwood found no such structures in the jungle among the ruins. At Uxmal, the pyramid is oval—despite Waldeck's images—and in Palenque and Copán they appear as sloping terraced platforms with stairways up their sides and temples on top. He added: "The pyramidal form is one which suggests itself to human intelligence in every country as the simplest and surest mode of erecting a high structure upon a solid foundation." Each pyramidal type also served a different function, he argued: in Egypt as burial places for the pharaohs and other high-status people, and in Central America as platforms apparently for worship and sacrifice.

They also had found no columns in the ruins of Copán, Palenque, and Uxmal; in contrast, columns were a striking feature repeatedly used in the temples along the Nile.[21] And there was nothing to be found in Egypt like Copán's and Quiriguá's huge isolated monoliths or stelae portraying strangely feathered lords and covered with hieroglyphs—which also bore no resemblance to the cartouches of Egypt.

Eliminating the connection with the "Old World," there appeared only one remaining possibility, he declared. The monuments and pyramids of Central America and Mexico are "different from the works of any other known people, of a new order, and entirely and absolutely anomalous: they stand alone." Then Stephens drew his pioneering conclusion—a concept that flew in the face of prevailing scholarship, and that would prove prescient and ultimately correct:[22]

> Unless I am wrong, we have a conclusion far more interesting and wonderful than that of connecting the builders of these cities with the Egyptians or any other people. It is the spectacle of a people skilled in architecture, sculpture, and drawing, and, beyond doubt, other more perishable arts, and possessing the cultivation and refinement attendant upon these, not derived from the Old World, but originating and growing up here, without models or masters, having a distinct, separate, independent existence; like the plants and fruits of the soil, indigenous.

Native Americans had built the cities, created the art, raised the towers, temples, and pyramids, and fashioned their own unique system of writing. This conclusion would forever alter the understanding of human history on the American continents and provide new insight into human cultural evolution.

Stephens nonetheless remained cautious about the antiquity of the civilization he and Catherwood had found. Spanish explorers and conquistadors, after all, claimed to have seen large inhabited cities on Yucatán Peninsula as they first sailed along its coast in the early 1500s. And Hernán Cortés and his men reported in 1519 on the wonders of the Aztec capital of Tenochtitlán, the site of modern-day Mexico City. Could those cities have been the same age as the ruins they explored in the jungle?

Stephens focused also on the condition of the ruins themselves in questioning their antiquity. He said it was difficult to imagine the ruins surviving one or two thousand years in the face of the onslaught of tropical growth and decay. He was also puzzled by their discovery of wooden beams in the ruins, particularly the carved example he found at Uxmal "in a perfect state of preservation." Finally, he said, the hieroglyphs on the bark paper codices taken by Spaniards from New Spain and later discovered in the libraries of Europe by Kingsborough resembled the hieroglyphs on the monuments they encountered in the forests. "The inference," he wrote, "is that the Aztecs and Mexicans, at the time of the conquest, had the same written language with the people of Copán and Palenque."

Stephens based his speculations, however, on incomplete knowledge and unconnected data. He had no way of knowing, for example, that the Aztecs had no hieroglyphic written language, but only rudimentary pictographs. Or that the wooden beams they had found were made of rock-hard sapodilla wood, capable of holding up for more than a millennium.[23] But he deserves credit for not venturing beyond the evidence he had accumulated, even if it meant possibly diminishing the significance of their discoveries by assigning the ruins a more modern age.

> We began our exploration without any theory to support. Our feelings were in favour of going back to a high and venerable antiquity. During the greater part of our journey we were grop-

ing in the dark, in doubt and uncertainty, and it was not until
our arrival at the ruins of Uxmal that we formed our opinion of
the comparatively modern date.

However, he and Catherwood were uncertain.

Some (ruins) are beyond doubt older than others; some are
known to have been inhabited at the time of the Spanish conquest, and others, perhaps, were really ruins before; and there
are points of difference which as yet cannot very readily be explained.[24]

They had, after all, spent too little time at Uxmal, and too many
questions remained unanswered. Still, Stephens had expressed mixed
feelings to others about going back. Furthermore, following the enormously positive reception of his book, he was offered an appointment
as secretary to the U.S. legation in Mexico. He gave it serious thought
but declined.[25]

He still had not given up his dream of establishing a "National
Museum of American Antiquities" and received pledges totaling
twenty thousand dollars from well-off friends in New York to bring
back artifacts and monuments to fill it. But he had been frustrated in
all his attempts so far. The Payes brothers in Guatemala were still
holding out for a huge sum to ship to New York one or more of the
colossal monoliths at Quiriguá. He also received news that twenty-
eight plaster molds Pawling had laboriously cast at Palenque had been
confiscated by the Mexican authorities.[26] And the ten-foot wooden
beam carved with precious hieroglyphs from Uxmal, which Don Peon
in Mérida had agreed to send to New York, never arrived.

By late summer 1841, in the months after the book's release, he and
Catherwood were scheming again. The pull south was too powerful.
Catherwood would once more have to leave his children, who would
be sent back to London with their nanny to live with family members
on Charles Square.[27] Gertrude had disappeared from London with his
cousin. In the end it was as if Catherwood and Stephens had no

choice. They knew there was more. They had not finished what they started.

Their success was now their greatest enemy, as the book probably had excited rivals. They had not heard yet of Walker and Caddy, and Stephens especially feared expeditions from Europe. They made up their minds to leave quickly and quietly, no later than October. He told Prescott of their intentions but asked him to keep their confidence. "We wish to get off without any newspaper flourishes," he wrote Prescott in September, two weeks before they put to sea. "We wish to complete what we have begun before others can interfere with us."[28] And this time, they would carry with them an unusual apparatus, which may have added to their reasons for going. Technologically, they were on the cutting edge. This time they hoped to bring back more than words and drawings.

◄◄ 16 ►►

Yucatán

In their quest for lost worlds, Stephens and Catherwood could never seem to get enough hardship and danger. Faced once more with mosquitoes, ticks, disease, and political upheaval, they chose to sail south again into the heart of yet another hurricane season—as they had two years before—pressing to reach Yucatán for the start of the dry season. And they did so in classic Stephens and Catherwood fashion—aboard a ship carrying six hundred kegs of gunpowder.

They left New York on October 9, 1841, aboard the sailing ship *Tennessee*, bound directly for the Yucatán port of Sisal. The gunpowder belowdecks was headed for the newly independent Yucatán government in its fight with Mexico. The risk of hurricanes seemed like nothing to the two men now. On the fourth night out, they looked up to see lightning flash across the sky. With a storm approaching, Stephens wrote, long, jagged spears of light shot down to the sea "as if expressly to ignite our gunpowder." A quick meeting was called. "We discussed, though rather disjointedly, the doctrine of conductors and non-conductors, and advised the captain to put a few links of chain around the mainmast, and carry the end over the side. We had some consolation in thinking that six hundred kegs were no worse than sixty, and that six would do our business. . . ." The next morning the sea had calmed; they had survived once more.

Aboard ship with them was Dr. Samuel Cabot Jr., a young Boston surgeon who at the last minute had joined the expedition principally to indulge a passion for ornithology, but also to help investigate the ruins and practice medicine when the need presented itself.[1] A naturalist, physician, former top boxer at Harvard College, and master fencer, he seemed to have all the qualifications for the rough-and-tumble journey ahead—though whether he had Stephens and Catherwood's panache for life-or-death adventure was yet to be proven. What must he have thought when five days after barely surviving detonation from lightning, the *Tennessee* was being driven by gale-force winds straight at a treacherous range of coral in the Bahamas known as the Abaco reef. Their true peril became apparent when the captain appeared at breakfast, his forehead gleaming with huge drops of sweat betraying his distress. "We sat with the chart before us," Stephens wrote, "looking at it as a sentenced convict might look at an advertisement of the time fixed for his execution. The sunken rocks seemed to stand out horribly on the paper." Hours later and just in time, the wind shifted and Stephens and Catherwood survived one more in a seemingly endless series of close calls, much to Cabot's relief. Ten days later they were anchored off the port of Sisal.

While they waited for the custom officials to allow them ashore, Stephens wrote his father about the anxiety he felt over how he would be received: "I am not quite as confident as when I had a diplomatic commission. An hour on shore would enable me to advise you whether the people remember my former dignity and pay me the respect due to fallen greatness."[2] He need not have worried. Arriving in Mérida the next day, Stephens found himself a celebrity; news accounts of his book had preceded them. And since the book had described the generosity and grace of Yucatán society, he and Catherwood were welcomed warmly by their former acquaintances. Per usual they found themselves in the middle of a fiesta, the more positive of the two situations they routinely encountered in their travels, the other being revolution. As for the political revolt during their first visit and Yucatán's succession from Mexico, it was still afoot, though at such a low level as to be barely noticeable. The biggest news was Yucatán's recent alliance with the Republic of Texas against the Mexican government.[3] The nine-day Festival of San Cristobal was winding down, thus their first priority was to plunge in and enjoy it. Next a visit to the governor, then the social rounds, and finally they were ready for business.

They unpacked the new technology they hoped would help them capture exact images of the ruins. Two years earlier, the first photographic instrument, called a daguerreotype, was demonstrated in New York—exactly two days after Stephens and Catherwood left for Central America. Just before their current voyage, they were able to acquire one. Now they needed to figure out how to make it work. So they set themselves up in the living room of their rented house as Mérida's first ladies' portrait studio. "It was a new line for us," wrote Stephens, "but not worse than for the editor of a newspaper to turn captain of a steamboat; and, besides, it was not like banking—we could not injure anyone by a failure."

They practiced first on themselves, then invited the public. Since they were not asking for money, they reserved the right to pick their subjects—pretty young ladies, who began showing up at their door almost immediately. It was a difficult process, requiring perfect stillness from the young women for exactly ninety seconds while the camera lens was opened. Developing the images was equally delicate, a process of bathing the copper photographic plates with mercury and other chemicals in a darkroom. It was pioneering work at the leading edge of a new technology, but after a number of failures and successes over several days, Catherwood felt he had mastered the apparatus sufficiently that they could close up shop and head into the field.

There was one more venture before the expedition left for the ruins. They learned that many Méridanos suffered from an eye condition called strabismus, or cross-eyes, and Dr. Cabot offered to perform at no charge a new surgical technique that could correct the condition simply by cutting one of the contracted muscles of the eye. It is debatable how much practice, if any, Cabot had in performing the surgery. He would go on later to become one of Boston's most distinguished surgeons. But at twenty-six, he had finished advanced surgical studies in Paris only six months earlier. And in a letter his mother wrote to Cabot's brother, Elliott, she noted that young Samuel saw the Yucatán trip as an opportunity to operate on "some unlucky subject."[4]

When word got out that the doctor from the United States could cure cross-eyes, a number of "subjects" began lining up outside the house. An operating room of sorts was set up, again in their living room, which was large enough to accommodate local doctors, as well as the governor and a small crowd of other invited and uninvited luminaries. Using fine, Parisian-made scalpels, Dr. Cabot performed the surgeries without anesthesia. Stephens and Catherwood served as his assistants. After several operations, all successes, including one on the "oldest general in the Mexican service," who lived in Mérida in exile, Stephens had had enough: "My head was actually swimming with visions of bleeding and mutilated eyes." With the loss of his assistants, Cabot explained the surgery in full to the gathered doctors and offered to send them surgical instruments on his return to Boston. As Stephens said, "considering the thing fairly introduced into the country, we determined to stop."

Cabot was a local hero. "And I could but think how fleeting is this world's fame," wrote Stephens. "At first my arrival in the country had been fairly trumpeted in the newspapers; for a little while Mr. Catherwood had thrown me in the shade with the Daguerreotype, and now all our glories were swallowed up by Doctor Cabot's cure of strabismus."

The three men left Mérida on horseback on November 12, Stephens and Catherwood each armed with pistols and Cabot with a shotgun to bring down his ornithological specimens. They had no attendants or even a map, as there were no reliable maps available in the country. They would eventually produce one of their own by measuring distances by the hours traveled, taking compass bearings, and using a sextant Catherwood brought this time for latitudinal readings.[5] In contrast to the magnificence of the volcanoes and lush, picturesque valleys of Central America, Stephens grumbled that the road here was boring—flat, stony, and straight, and tightly hemmed in on both sides by thick low forest.

Their first goal had been to return to Uxmal. But while in Mérida they were told where they might find the remains of an old city named Mayapán—not far off the main road to Uxmal. They rode through haciendas and Indian hamlets until they finally reached a giant estate named Xcanchakán, which was owned by an acquaintance they had made in Mérida. The majordomo was expecting them and took them out into the forest. They found themselves stumbling over fragments of sculpted stone and broken walls. They had arrived at Mayapán. The

Hacienda Xcanchakán in Yucatán. (Catherwood)

remains of the city had never been formally explored, and the only person with any knowledge of the site was the majordomo, who said he had not visited it in twenty-three years. He explained that the ruins took up about three square miles and had once been surrounded by a strong wall.

Starting at Mérida and stopping first at Mayapán, then continuing on to Uxmal, the men were, without knowing it, journeying backward through time, in the same sense they had when they left Guatemala City on their long trek through Iximche and Utatlán to Palenque. Stephens was not totally in the dark. Before the journey, he had sought out every book he could find that contained information about the Spanish conquest of Yucatán.[6] He knew, for example, that Mérida had been built by the conquistadors over an Indian city called Tiho after the natives lost in a furious battle outside the city in 1542.[7] Following the battle, the Spanish tore down Tiho's step pyramids and temples and used the stones to construct their colonial capital.[8]

Stephens also learned from the Spanish chroniclers that Mayapán had been one of the last great Indian capitals and was destroyed during a rebellion only a hundred years before the Spanish arrived. (The word

Mayapán, near Mérida in Yucatán. (Catherwood)

Maya was originally used by the Spanish to describe the language of the Yucatán Indians and came to be used generally to describe the Indians in the early 1800s.) As the first archaeological explorer on the site, Stephens had no way to fit the ruins into the long chronological narrative of Maya history. Witnessing its extremely fallen condition, he theorized that Mayapán might have been founded long before Uxmal. Modern archaeologists, however, would come to categorize Mayapán as a "late postclassic" city and determine it was established centuries after Uxmal's founding.[9] They have now constructed a historical timeline in which Palenque and Copán flourished during the so-called Classic period of the Maya, from A.D. 400 to 900, Uxmal between 700 to 950, and Mayapán from 1000 to 1461. Tiho was one of the small surviving centers still occupied by the Maya at the time of the conquest, just as Iximche and Utatlán had been in Guatemala.

Nothing of this historical sequence was understood by the three men as they groped their way through the forest of Xcanchakán and ran almost head-on into a huge, square-shaped mound rising sixty feet from the ground. It had not been visible through the thick forest and was so covered with vegetation it looked like a small, steep, wooded

Present-day photo of Mayapán. (Carlsen)

hill. But they could make out the outlines of four grand staircases rising up each side to a flat platform at the top. They found sculpted stones of human figures or animals "with hideous features and expressions" scattered everywhere. Then they came upon a large unusual round building, something they had never seen before in their earlier explorations. From a large mound it rose to a height of twenty-four feet and was covered in layers of stucco still showing the remains of red, yellow, and blue paint. A single door led to a circular passageway inside, around a solid center. The opening was no more than three feet wide and they could not conceive of what purpose it had served. Next they discovered a platform protruding from a mound with what appeared to be a double row of broken columns, the first columns they had encountered among the ruins. While Catherwood went to work sketching the circular structure, Stephens and Cabot explored a nearby cenote that led down to a lime-encrusted pool of water.

It was nearly dark when they reached the hacienda of Xcanchakán, one of the finest on the peninsula with its giant water tanks, huge cattle yard, and cool residential corridors. The next morning they saddled up for Uxmal. Though they found many more mounds and intriguing fragments the day before, hinting at the vast dimensions of Mayapán, the site was so overgrown and buried they would need a battalion of workmen to help clear it. They were anxious to pick up where they had left off at Uxmal, which was so much more in the open.

At noon the next day, however, as they approached Uxmal they were startled by the change that had taken place over the last year and a half. The land surrounding the buildings had been cleared at the time of their first visit, but now they could barely see the ruins as they rode in. "The foundations, terraces, and tops of the buildings were overgrown, weeds and vines were rioting and creeping on the facades," wrote Stephens. "A strong and vigorous nature was struggling for mastery over art, wrapping the city in its suffocating embrace, and burying it from sight. It seemed as if a grave was closing over a friend."

Hacking their way through the weeds up a stairway and over several terraces, they took up housekeeping inside the so-called Casa del Gobernador, or Governor's House, an immense rectangular block edifice 320 feet long, 40 feet deep, and 26 feet high. The magnificent structure was cut with thirteen doorways and covered with an upper façade of incredibly intricate stone mosaics. Because the rain had continued longer than usual, they were warned in Mérida to delay their visit to Uxmal, considered one of the unhealthiest spots on the peninsula during the rainy season. As they entered the *casa* they realized they should have followed the advice. The air was so damp they could hardly breathe, and they were certain that if they did not do something fast they would fall victim again to the fever—malaria, or "bad air" in Italian—that had brought down Catherwood on their last visit. Their first order of business was to build a fire inside the stone building to dry it out.

Even with the addition of a doctor to the expedition they were no closer to understanding the cause of the disease; it would be another sixty years, during the building of the Panama Canal, until health experts identified mosquitoes as the guilty culprits. That night puffing away on their cigars before climbing into their hammocks, they talked smugly about how they had taken the offensive against the dampness and found a way to hold off the fever, possibly until the rains stopped altogether. But the massive elevated terraces on which Uxmal was built contained solid rock depressions where the rainwater collected, giving birth to their enemy. And just as they lay down to sleep, they suffered the first attack. "Our heads were hardly on our pillows," Stephens recalled, "before the whole population seemed to know exactly

where they could have us, and dividing into three swarms, came upon us as if determined to lift us up and eject us bodily from the premises." That would be the last night they slept without protective netting over each hammock, but it was already too late.

The next day they wasted no time getting to work. Indians arrived from the nearby Peon hacienda and started cutting away the vines and vegetation. As soon as vistas were cleared, Catherwood set up the daguerreotype. But he was not satisfied with the first images produced, as there was too much contrast between the parts of the ruins that fell in the sunlight and those in the shade. "They gave the general idea of the character of the buildings," Stephens wrote, "but would not do to put into the hands of the engraver without copying the views on paper." So Catherwood, meticulous as ever, began drawing each structure with his pencils and camera lucida, down to the smallest details. He created, Stephens reported, such "minute architectural drawings of the whole, and has in his possession the materials for erecting a building exactly like it." The daguerreotype, however, still proved useful. Stephens and Cabot operated it to create broader views to supplement Catherwood's drawings.

TOP Full view of the Governor's Palace at Uxmal. (Catherwood)
BOTTOM Désiré Charnay's photograph of the facade of Uxmal's nunnery.

Uxmal today: the Governor's Palace with the Pyramid of the Magician
in the distance. (Carlsen)

Tireless and in good health, Catherwood would work almost continually for the next six weeks to capture Uxmal's architectural and
sculptural wonders—the so-called Nunnery quadrangle, the "pyramid of the magician," the aptly named houses of the pigeons and the
turtles, as well as the Governor's House.[10] He created drawings that
took in sweeping vistas of the ruins as well as those capturing the
smallest fragments of their ornate façades. The results would prove to
be masterworks when he later published his own large-scale folio of
the ruins.

Stephens, soon satisfied that the clearing of the ruins was going
well, decided to ride west from Uxmal to see if there were other remains worth investigating. Traveling alone over the next six days with
guides he picked up at haciendas along the way, he visited vestiges of
what appeared to be several smaller Maya cities. At one site, nearly
forty miles to the west, he entered a chamber where he found a painting on a wall in bright primary colors, an image similar to a mask they
had found in Palenque. He was so focused on the work, however, that

TOP Catherwood's illustration of the front of the Pyramid of the Magician at Uxmal.
BELOW View of the back of the pyramid today. (Carlsen)

he failed to notice the thousands of *garrapatas* (ticks) crawling over him. He fled the chamber and changed clothes, scraping the ticks off his body before they could bury themselves in his flesh.

Days later, on his way back to Uxmal, he stopped at the village of Maxcanú, where he was directed to a nearby cave rumored to be made by human hands. Although a group of villagers traveled out to the cave with him, none would enter. Intrepid as ever, Stephens went in alone with string attached to his wrist so that he could find his way out. He carried a candle in one hand and a pistol in the other. The cave indeed proved to be man-made, with a series of narrow hallways that crisscrossed, doubled back, and formed an elaborate labyrinth. He was reminded of the passageways in the tombs and pyramids of Egypt, and he became excited at the thought he might discover a large room, a gallery, a royal tomb. Instead he was met with a rush of bats that swept past his head; the flaps of their wings nearly put out the candle. He was finally stopped by debris that completely blocked further passage. Back out in the fresh air, he looked up and realized that he had not been in a subterranean passage at all but had penetrated deep into a large pyramid. It was a revelation because he had always viewed these pyramids as solid masses. Now he believed this pyramid and others like it might hold secret chambers that could help in understanding who built them and why.

The villagers explained there were a number of other mounds nearby along with sculpted stones. Stephens was intrigued as the site began to take on the dimension of a sizable city. There were no recorded accounts of these ruins, and even the Indians of the village said nothing about them before they set out that morning. He wanted to return for a more thorough examination, but when the expedition finished at Uxmal they decided to travel in the other direction, south and east. The ruins, which would come to be known as Oxkintok, turned out to be a major Maya city with roots older than Uxmal's. It would be another a century before it was excavated and explored.[11]

By the time Stephens got back to Uxmal, he had visited seven locations with remnants of mounds, temples, and other stone structures, most of them at scattered minor sites. Seeing the monumental, intact artistry of Uxmal overwhelmed him once again. That night they made a large bonfire on the terrace in front of the Casa del Gobernador. "The flames lighted up the façade of the great palace," Stephens wrote, "and when they died away, the full moon broke upon it, mellowing its rents and fissures, and presenting a scene mournfully beautiful."

The rains started again but did little to stop them from investigating many underground dome-like chambers they found scattered around Uxmal. Stephens, daring as ever, disregarded the risk of scorpions and snakes and allowed himself to be lowered on a rope into some of the caverns. They were coated with hard plaster inside. Stephens theorized they may have been granaries but in the end, after examining several more of what the natives called *chultuns*, he realized they were cisterns used to store water from the rainy season through the dry season. Stephens and the others wondered how the builders of these cities, obviously with large populations, could survive the long dry season in a region bereft of rivers, streams, and lakes. The *chultuns* and cenotes provided one answer. Later they found man-made lakes, including one nearby at Uxmal, complete with plastered stone bottoms that proved the engineering sophistication of the original inhabitants.

Over the following days, as Catherwood kept drawing and Cabot hunted for bird specimens, Stephens continued to measure and explore. In one of the apartments of the palace he located the sculpted wooden beam they had found on their first visit, which was never shipped to New York. They had found other wooden lintels but this one was unique, the only wooden beam that was exquisitely carved with rows of hieroglyphs. Once again Stephens arranged to have the ten-foot beam carried to Mérida and sent to the United States, presumably with the consent of Don Peon, who had recently visited them at the ruins. Stephens planned to have it, along with the other artifacts they were collecting, transported eventually to Washington, D.C., for the national museum he still planned to create. "It left Uxmal on the shoulders of ten Indians," he wrote, "after many vicissitudes reached [New York] uninjured, and was deposited in Mr. Catherwood's Panorama."

In early December, Stephens found half-buried sculpted stones at the top of one of Uxmal's highest mounds, which he believed led to a

Masks of the rain god Chaac at Uxmal. (Catherwood)

doorway. Indian workman started digging and the characteristic emblem of Uxmal, "a hideous face with the teeth sticking out," slowly began to appear. But the stones started to totter and the workmen stepped back fearing they might topple on them. Stephens, who had been helping in the excavation, threw himself into the work alone, digging with all his strength, carried away by the thought he was about to enter a chamber that had been "closed for ages." But when he got below the cornice and thrust his machete into the earth where he believed the doorway to be, he hit a stone wall.

Crushed by the disappointment and covered in sweat, he reeled under the glare of the sun. "In descending the mound my limbs could scarcely support me," he recalled. "With great difficulty I dragged myself to our apartments. My thirst was unquenchable. I threw myself into my hammock, and in a few moments the fiery fever was upon me. Disease had stalked all around us, but it was the first time it had knocked at our door." He was again in the clutches of malaria.

After four days of violent fevers and chills, he was finally able to mount his horse and ride nine miles to a hacienda, where he collapsed. He was then carried on the shoulders of Indians in a makeshift "coche" to the large town of Ticul, some twenty miles from the ruins. There he was taken into the church's quarters by the town's priest, whom Stephens identified only by the name Carillo. Explosions of fireworks marked another fiesta under way, but in his current condition, Stephens noted, the sounds were "murderous."

Under the care of the priest, Stephens remained in bed the next three days. On the fourth he felt well enough to take a stroll with the priest around the grounds, and when they returned they found Dr. Cabot lying on a stretcher in the corridor, racked with fever. "I was startled by the extraordinary change a few days had made in his appearance. His face was flushed, his eyes were wild, his figure lank." It turned out Cabot had come down with the fever the day after Stephens left Uxmal and he had been in a state of delirium ever since. The next day, one of their regular helpers, named Albino, arrived shaking with chills and fever. With him was a note from Catherwood. He was now alone at Uxmal, he wrote, but would hold out for as long as he could. At the first sign of fever, he added, he would join them.

◅ 17 ▻

London

On the morning of December 11, 1841, magistrate James Scarlett gaveled court to order in London's medieval Guildhall, an imposing Gothic building on Gresham Street that had served as a stage for many of England's historic trials. One year had passed since Catherwood filed suit against his cousin Henry Caslon, and now as he labored alone in Uxmal thousands of miles across the Atlantic, a jury assembled at Guildhall to decide his case. The jurors were promptly sworn in by Scarlett, whose formal title was Lord Abinger.

When Catherwood had ordered his London solicitor to file the suit the previous year, his cousin and wife, Gertrude, had disappeared from London. It would have been highly unusual for Catherwood, a man of great personal reserve and privacy, to request a court trial that would expose his private life, and worse, an embarrassing affair between his wife and cousin, to public scrutiny. It is most likely, however, that he thought he could avoid a trial and win his case by default since the couple had vanished. But Henry and Gertrude had returned to London months later and began living openly as "man and wife" in the Caslon family home on Chiswell Street. The case had now become enough of a scandal that the trial attracted the attention of the London newspapers.[1]

As was legal custom, Mrs. Catherwood, as the purportedly ill-used spouse, was not named a defendant in the lawsuit, and it is not clear from the record if she was present in court. As the case opened, Caslon pleaded not guilty to the charge of "criminal conversation" with Gertrude. His attorney, Frederic Thesiger, then presented a novel legal defense, claiming that no crime occurred in Caslon's affair with Gertrude because the Catherwoods, in fact, were not married. They had not been legally wed in Beirut in 1834, he said, because the ceremony had been performed by an American Baptist missionary and not a clergyman from the Church of England, as required by English law.

This shocking contention was put aside by Lord Abinger, who judged it was such an unusual legal question that it could only be decided by an appellate court if an appeal was filed later. He then ordered the trial to proceed on the presumption that the Catherwoods were married. The principal question before the jurors was whether illicit relations occurred between Henry and Gertrude before Catherwood filed his lawsuit the prior December and therefore Catherwood had a legal basis to sue.

Though not directly representing Catherwood, Attorney General Frederick Pollock prosecuted the case as a criminal matter on behalf of the crown. To first establish the Catherwood marriage, he called Catherwood's brother, James, who testified that the Catherwoods had lived together as man and wife at the family home on Charles Square for several years and bore three children together.

Servants from Gertrude's London household on Charlotte Street were then summoned and gave testimony indicating that Henry had stayed with Gertrude through the night on several occasions during the crucial period in question.

Pollock also called Catherwood's old traveling partner from Egypt and Palestine, Joseph Bonomi, to further establish the legitimacy of the Catherwoods' marriage. Bonomi explained to the jury that he was present at the Beirut home of English consul Peter Abbott when the wedding took place on March 11, 1834. Gertrude's father, stepmother, and two sisters were present at the ceremony. He added that the wedding was performed according to rites of the Church of England. Soon after the nuptials, he said, the Catherwoods left to travel through Syria, and two or three months later he met them in Damascus. From there the three of them traveled to the ancient ruins at Baalbek, where they stayed for another month before the couple left for England. He described the newlyweds as affectionate and completely comfortable together.

Caslon's defense attorney, Thesiger, then took over and cross-

examined Bonomi about exactly who had performed the wedding ceremony in Beirut. Bonomi answered that it was an American
missionary. "I can't say that Mr. Bird was of the Church of England,"
Bonomi continued. "He wore no surplice."

Thesiger then worked to shift the focus of the trial from Henry
and Gertrude to Catherwood himself. He asked Bonomi what the
sleeping arrangements had been when he and the newlyweds traveled
through Syria together.

"At Baalbeck, I slept in the same tent with the plaintiff and his
wife," Bonomi replied, uncertain where Thesiger was headed.

Did Mrs. Catherwood object? Thesiger asked.

"She might have objected to this," Bonomi responded. "I don't
know that she did, but it was almost a matter of necessity, there being
but one tent. All the persons who traveled in that country had tents to
sleep in. It was the custom of the country. Society at Beirut and Acre,
and other places in Syria was what might be called very easy and familiar; very different to what it was in the cold northern climate of
England."

Thesiger did not let up. Under further questioning Bonomi admitted that they met Gertrude's father, Peter Abbott, at one of the ancient
sites, and that on that occasion Bonomi did not sleep in the same tent
with the Catherwoods. He slept under some ruins.

From newspaper accounts, Thesiger's questions appeared relatively
innocuous, leaving at most a vague insinuation that an improper
sexual relationship may have existed between the three of them. The
implications, however, may have been much clearer in the courtroom.
Bonomi apparently felt Thesiger's cross-examination had left a stain
on his honor.[2] In later correspondence with his own attorney, he insisted that a letter be included in the court record that he felt would
clear his name.

Thesiger also asked Bonomi if Gertrude's father had warned Catherwood to take extra precautions concerning his new wife because her
mother had been Spanish and because she had grown up mostly in the
East.

"Of course, the society of the East is much more free and easy than
in England," answered Bonomi. "Mr. Abbott might have cautioned

the plaintiff to take care of his wife on account of her blood and disposition." Mrs. Catherwood, he added, was "of a particularly lively and fascinating disposition. She had an Eastern education, and was of exceedingly pleasant and fascinating manners, lively temperament and of Spanish blood."

Then Thesiger called Catherwood's brother, James, and during his questioning attempted to show that Frederick had been a less-than-attentive husband. He asked James if his brother and Gertrude slept in separate beds or in separate rooms at Charles Square. James answered that he had never been aware of that, except perhaps during the last stages of her pregnancies. Thesiger made particular note of Catherwood's ten-month absence in Central America, a fact some jurors may already have known from the publication of Stephens and Catherwood's book.

Thesiger: Did not your brother, Frederick, tell you that his marriage to Mrs. Catherwood was not worth "a farthing"?

No, replied James.

In his summation, Thesiger tried to lessen any possible damages the jury might award Catherwood by portraying Mrs. Catherwood as a loose woman and Catherwood as a negligent husband. "It was not at all unlikely," he told the jurors, "with her peculiar blood and education, as well as the absence of her husband, that she had sinned ere she met the defendant. Such a wife, deserved the cautious guard suggested by her father to the plaintiff; but instead of adopting so prudent a course, he sends her home from New York alone, and exposes her to all the perils of neglect and desertion. This was an act of neglect so great as to deprive him of the shadow of a claim to compensation for anything that may have happened."

The jurors deliberated less than twenty minutes, returned a verdict in Catherwood's favor, but awarded him damages of only 200 pounds sterling. He had asked for 5,000.

Technically, Catherwood was vindicated. But his slender victory had come at considerable, mortifying cost. Questions had been raised about his moral character, as well his fitness and attentiveness as a husband, due in particular to his long absence in Central America.

In effect, his marriage to Gertrude was over. And there would be no divorce. The minimal award from the jury was overturned two years later when an appeals court ruled that his marriage had never existed. The case (*Catherwood v. Caslon*) would be cited as a precedent for years to come, the appellate justices ruling that marriages conducted outside the Church of England were not legal—and the award of damages to Catherwood was therefore vacated.

⊙⊙⊙

A month later a curious exhibit opened in central London a mile to the west, at Somerset House, between the Strand and the Thames River. Somerset House had once housed the Royal Academy's exhibition hall, where Catherwood previously showed his work. On January 13, 1842, Captain John Caddy displayed his drawings and paintings of Palenque for the first time publicly. The showing took place in the rooms of the Society of Antiquaries; the society's minutes note that the drawings had "the appearance of great accuracy, and varying as they do from others published by Lord Kingsbury and Mons. Waldeck, they are entitled to the particular attention to the English Antiquary. Captain Caddy supposes these ruins to be of Egypto-Indian origin."[3]

It had been more than a year and a half since Caddy and Patrick Walker had returned safely to Belize from their Palenque expedition. Since that time, Lieutenant Caddy had been promoted to captain and had sailed home on leave to England, where he was reunited with his wife and children. Meanwhile, Colonel Alexander MacDonald had sent ahead to the Colonial Office in London a copy of Walker's official Palenque report and Caddy's drawings. He was hopeful the documents would finally justify to his superiors his quick decision in 1839 to order the expedition without prior approval. The report and drawings were received by Lord John Russell, sometime in early 1841, around the time Caddy had landed in England.

In a return dispatch to MacDonald, Lord Russell praised Walker and Caddy, giving them "great credit for the zeal and spirit of enterprise." He called the drawings "very curious and interesting." At the time Russell was unaware that Stephens and Catherwood were in New York working to complete their book on the same subject. He said he wanted to relieve MacDonald of his concern over reimbursement for the Palenque expedition but noted that the colonel had not yet provided any accounting of the expenses. When you do so, he said, "I will, provided it shall appear that the expenses were moderate and reasonable, recommend to the Lords of the Treasury to relieve you from the responsibility."

At this point events took an ill-fated twist and the record of Walker and Caddy's tortuous Palenque expedition all but disappeared from the history books—thanks in part to Stephens and Catherwood but also to Britain's slow-moving, many-layered bureaucracy. It is unknown whether MacDonald's "military chest" was ever reimbursed. Instead the whole affair was quietly buried in the archives. More than a century later David Pendergast, who published the account of the Walker-Caddy expedition, discovered the reason why in a deft piece of detective work. He managed to disinter from the colonial records MacDonald's last letter to Lord Russell. On the cover of the dispatch Pendergast found an unsigned note, dated October 14. The author of the note had undoubtedly read Stephens and Catherwood's book, which had only recently arrived from the United States.

> An American named Stephens made the same journey, & has published a full account of Palenque with drawings & far more complete than any which were made by Captain Caddy and with a far more extensive range of general observation. I fear, therefore, that nothing can be done with this Despatch than to lay it aside.

Despite the recommendation to set it aside, the letter continued to wind its way up the bureaucratic ladder to a higher authority in the Colonial Office. The next officeholder, named, coincidentally, J. Stephens, appended a final note:

> Colonel Macdonald and Mr. Walker & Capt. Caddy executed this scientific mission with no previous sanction from the Treasury. The motive was merely that we might not be outstript in this case in scientific zeal by the Americans. This was not very wise, and the result is that we have been beaten by these new

rivals in scientific research, who will now boast over our inferiority instead of having to boast only over our comparative inactivity. After all the Drawings and Travel have not been published, and now it is hardly to be supposed that any Bookseller would hazard the publication. In short the whole affair has been a blunder, though a very well meant one.

No official publication or notice was ever made of the expedition. Lord Russell wrote MacDonald that he had forwarded Walker's report and Caddy's drawings to the Royal Geographic Society but the documents may never have arrived. The society shows no record of them. Instead, Pendergast found only Walker's report and expense record in the Colonial Office archives and none of Caddy's drawings. They apparently were returned to Caddy and ended up in the exhibit at Somerset House.

Caddy soon had other distractions. In early 1842, not long after his exhibition, his fifth child was born. There would be eight eventually. A few months later he left England with his family for a new military posting to the town of London in Ontario, Canada, not far from where he had grown up. Before long, Palenque would become a distant memory and like Private Carnick, the single casualty of the expedition, who lay buried somewhere in the Petén, all but forgotten.

◅◅ 18 ▻▻

Discoveries

By Christmas Day 1841, first Stephens, then Dr. Cabot, and finally Albino returned to Uxmal, all sufficiently recovered from their bouts of malaria. Catherwood, who remained healthy and alone at the ruins with nothing but work to keep him occupied, had completed most of the plans and drawings. Because he was the sole resident for weeks in the Governor's House, each night he rigged a spring-loaded pistol with a cord across the doorway to "bring down" any uninvited guests. Fortunately, none had appeared.

While Stephens was recovering at the convent in Ticul, he was able to make several short trips to the suburbs and surrounding forests. It seemed that everywhere he turned he came upon vestiges of old structures and temples, most of them brought down by local villagers who had carried off the stones for their own construction. And he was told by Carillo, the local priest, that not far to the south lay the remains of several other ancient cities. Stephens now began to realize that at one time this part of Yucatán must have been heavily populated and dotted with sophisticated cities and sacred centers.

During the last week of December the men wrapped up their work at Uxmal and prepared to head south toward the reported ruins. Before leaving, Stephens climbed one last time the rubble-strewn staircase of the great "House of the Magician" pyramid. It took him to the highest point above the ruins, and visible to the west, as far as he could see, lay flat green scrub forest. He stood at the top of the pyramid on a platform that jutted out dramatically, with a doorway that opened into the temple behind him, its entrance framed by ornate mosaics of stone. He flinched as he imagined the horror of the human

TOP   House of Pigeons at Uxmal. (Catherwood)
BELOW   The view today. (Carlsen)

sacrifices that were probably performed here, a practice described by the early Franciscan historian Diego López Cogolludo: the Maya priests would cut out the hearts of their victims to offer to their idols, and then throw the bodies down the stairway to the crowded court-yard below. Stephens wrote: "In all the long catalogue of superstitious rites that darken the pages of man's history, I cannot imagine a picture more horribly exciting than that of the Indian priest, with his white dress and long hair clotted with gore, performing his murderous sac-rifices at this lofty height, in full view of the people through the whole extent of the city."

Looking out over Uxmal he could see the man-made terraces and huge multilevel limestone platforms that formed the base of the city. Immediately before him was the quadrangle known as the Nunnery, named for the eighty-eight apartments or cells in the buildings sur-rounding its courtyard. On the far side of the court he could see one of the most intricate façades in Uxmal. The entablature above the doorways was covered with stone ornaments and an elaborate frieze that included two feathered serpents, entwined, running the entire length of the 173-foot-wide structure. A human head was clenched in the open jaws of one of the snakes.

Beyond the quadrangle to his left lay two long identical mounds, their serpent-covered façades facing each other seventy feet apart. Ste-phens wrote: "It was our opinion that they had been built expressly with reference to the two great rings facing each other in the facades, and the space between was intended for the celebration of some public games." They had guessed right again. Archaeologists would later de-termine that Uxmal's rings and slanted walls, like similar parallel walls found at ruins in Guatemala, Mexico, and as far away as Copán, were indeed courts used for ritual ball games. To the left of these courts Stephens could see the ragged skyline of the "house of pigeons," the Governor's House, and the other enthralling structures of Uxmal, perched at different levels on the site's broad terraces.

The next day, while taking final images of the Nunnery with the daguerreotype, Stephens received a note from Catherwood. The inde-fatigable artist had not escaped the fever after all. Gloom descended over them all. Heavy rains started again. Catherwood was bedridden

LEFT   Mosaic ornamentation at Kabah. (Catherwood)
RIGHT   Detail, present day. (Carlsen)

in the Governor's House, and then Stephens and Cabot, as if in sympathy, suffered relapses of chills and fever.

Two days later, miserable and sick, they finally summoned the energy to depart. As they did, Catherwood pointed out that it was the first day of 1842, New Year's Day. They had survived another year, but they were in no condition to celebrate and were even too weak to travel on horseback. The Indians from the hacienda improvised the stretcher-like coaches to carry the three men to the nearby village of Nohcacab.

◉ ◉ ◉

By the eighth of January they had recovered enough to ride south and arrived at a place the natives called Kabah, where they encountered a range of ancient structures that were stunning even to the experienced eyes of Stephens and Catherwood. Some of the buildings were in an excellent state of preservation and almost entirely complete. One edifice was covered with the most intricate set of stone mosaics they had yet seen. Almost rhythmic in effect, it gave the impression of a hundred eyes staring out from the wall. It was unique among the ruins because of its repetitious pattern of masks representing what would later be identified as the long-nose rain god Chaac. Nearby also stood a large ceremonial step pyramid. Hieroglyphics no different from those they had found at Copán could be seen carved on various structures, and several "comb-like" superstructures stood atop some of the roofs, similar to those at Palenque.

All in all, Kabah was of such artistic sophistication—equal in some respects to Uxmal, if smaller in scale—that it prompted the men to wonder again at the advanced level of organization and skill that must have been required to create each site. What surprised Stephens and the others the most was that such magnificent ruins were "absolutely unknown" except to the local villagers and farmers. And it was becoming clear to Stephens that they were on much larger ground than they had ever imagined two years earlier when they stumbled awestruck through Copán and Palenque. He and Catherwood now understood they were witnessing the far-flung remains of a highly refined and interconnected civilization that had existed centuries earlier, had sprawled over a territory now encompassing three modern nations, and had vanished mysteriously and apparently abruptly with none of its history known even to the local natives. The question that would continue to haunt them through the remainder of their journey, and one they could never resolve, was why. Why had these marvelous stone cities, constructed with such labor and artistry, been abandoned, and the great civilization they represented evaporated?

They spent a number of days at Kabah while Catherwood went to work with his pencils and paints and Stephens worked the daguerreotype. Although nothing was known about Kabah's history, nearby villagers told Stephens the city had once been connected to Uxmal in ancient times by a great paved road that could still be found in places in the jungle. It was constructed on a fifteen-foot wide raised bed of stone that had been stuccoed over, forming a smooth finish. The road was called Sacbe, or Sacbeob in the Mayan language, meaning "white way." Stephens and Catherwood never located the causeway, although they did discover a large archway at Kabah facing in the direction of Uxmal; Stephens said it reminded him of the ancient triumphal arches he had seen in Rome. Spanning fourteen feet, it stood alone in a clearing, its top fallen in—and, Stephens wrote, "disconnected from every other structure, in solitary grandeur." Had they done some digging, however, they would have found that it was not isolated at all: in fact, the stone road passed under it and ran twelve miles in a nearly straight line through the forest to a second monumental arch at Uxmal. And while it is now understood that the ancient Maya never had use of the wheel, the smooth white highway must have provided an efficient way for messengers and perhaps armies, as well as regular pedestrians, to travel quickly through the jungle from one city to the other.

At one point, some distance beyond the arch, they uncovered a group of mostly collapsed buildings buried in the forest, which even the native guides did not know about. Inside one of the buildings they found red handprints covering nearly an entire wall. The paint was bright and looked almost fresh. The broken and fallen structures, though unimpressive from the outside, also yielded another other important find. Above the doorway of one of the apartments, which was filled nearly to the top with rubble, Catherwood found an exquisitely carved wooden lintel or architrave. He had crawled in on his back to take measurements and looked up, and there was the full-length figure of a royal lord standing on a snake and wearing a feathered headdress. What was most remarkable was the figure's striking resemblance to the figures they had seen carved in the walls at Palenque. It was the first image they encountered in Yucatán that provided such a clear link between the two cities.

Stephens had to have it. He wanted to ship it to New York for display in his hoped-for museum. But the carving on the lintel took up two entire ten-foot beams embedded in the walls on each side of the doorway. He was also concerned that the villagers at Nohcacab would object, recalling the problems he had had getting even plaster casts out of Palenque. But the next day, he was able to assemble a crew of village men armed with crowbars who managed to dislodge the beams after a day of great labor. He then had the two beams carefully wrapped as he had the hieroglyphic-covered beam from Uxmal.

LEFT   Carved lintel at Kabah, shipped by Stephens to New York. (Catherwood)
RIGHT   Interior at Kabah. (Catherwood)

Catherwood would later depict the beams' departure from Kabah in a beautifully colored lithograph showing a rare image of Stephens. It is a dramatic illustration filled with movement, and in the background most of Kabah's principal ruins can be seen against the tropical Yucatán countryside.

Surprised to find the architrave in such a nondescript location, they now began to take much greater care in their investigations. But while they found wooden lintels in several buildings, none were carved. Stephens did, however, come upon two six-foot-high stone doorjambs, elaborately carved and buried in a pile of unassuming remains. Like the architrave, they showed royal lords in feathered headdresses, but this time towering over other figures kneeling before them, an artistic theme they had seen worked so successfully in bas-relief at Palenque. Stephens struggled along with Indian laborers for two days to remove them for shipment to New York.[1] Then he was struck down violently again with fever, as though the ruins had fixed a curse on him anytime he personally labored to disturb them. He mounted his horse for Nohcacab but could only get so far. He wrote, "I was obliged to dismount and lay down under a bush; but the garrapatas drove me away. At length I reached the village and this was my last visit to Kabah."

In a short time, Cabot, Albino, and this time Catherwood, too, joined Stephens in the village convent with relapses of fever. "Death was all around us," Stephens wrote. He meant it literally. A cemetery and charnel house abutted the convent, which allowed Stephens in his weakened state to indulge in one of his favorite themes: the melancholy impermanence of life. Rows of skulls lined the top of the convent wall. "The spectacle around was gloomy for sick men," he wrote. He never missed the incongruities of the moment. Even in the midst of this mortal gloom, he noted, another fiesta was under way.

Stephens was the only one well enough to attend the festival's final procession; he even helped carry the image of the town's saint through the village to the church. "An irregular troop of women followed, all in their ball dresses and bearing long lighted candles." Rockets and firecrackers were set off, and next came the village men, most of them half-drunk. The dance in the plaza started.

> The whole village seemed given up to the pleasure of the moment . . . there were pretty women prettily dressed; in all there was an air of abandonment and freedom from care that enlisted sympathetic feeling; and as the padrecito and myself returned to the convent, the chorus reached us on the steps, soft and sweet from the blending of women's voices, and seeming to spring from the bottom of every heart:
>
> > *"Que bonito es el mundo;*
> > *Lastima es que yo me muera."*
> > *"How beautiful is the world;*
> > *It's a pity that I must die."*

⊚ ⊚ ⊚

Finally, on January 24, they were again well enough to travel. They had gotten hold of excellent horses and decided to travel light, leaving the heavy baggage behind. Stephens listed the few items they packed in their saddlebags or with them on horseback: "the daguerreotype apparatus, hammocks, one large box containing our tin table service, a candlestick, bread, chocolate, coffee, and sugar, and a few changes of clothes." And, of course, Catherwood's fold-up camera lucida, his pencils, paints, and paper, plus Stephens's ever-present notebooks.

Over the next six weeks, they zigzagged their way south, discovering one set of ruins after another strewn across the countryside or buried deep in the jungle. They proceeded based solely intelligence they gathered from villagers and farmers about "old stones" in the forest. Albino proved indispensable as interpreter and scout. Some sites were no more than an isolated structure in the forest while others appeared to be the remnants of sacred centers or small cities like Kabah. The first two sites they encountered south of Kabah—called by the local Indians Sayil and Labna—were such locations. Each had well-preserved buildings, some impressively large and decorated. At both places they found startling temples perched on top of pyramids or mounds, made even taller by giant ornamental, Palenque-like roof combs.

At Labna, they spent an entire day examining a temple set atop an extremely steep fifty-foot-high mound that was almost impossible to climb without clinging to trees that had rooted in the fallen stones. At the top, the temple's decorative roof comb rose another thirty feet. It was, Stephens wrote, "once ornamented from top to bottom, and from one side to the other, with colossal figures and other designs in stucco, now broken and in fragments . . . a row of death's heads; underneath were two lines of human figures." Catherwood made drawings using different angles of the sun while Stephens and Cabot worked with the daguerreotype. The white stucco was so intense in the sunlight that it was painful to look at, and some traces of brightly colored paint remained, Stephens said, "defying the action of the elements."

Not far from the mound, they found a stunning, remarkably proportioned arched gateway covered with abstract designs and glower-

TOP Archway at Labna. (Catherwood)
BELOW Present day. (Carlsen)

ing masklike images that again showed the builders' refined artistry. Stephens and Catherwood, even with their experiences in Egypt, Greece, and Rome, could not recall any other culture that had employed the embellishments and overpowering imagery they were seeing or had mastered the intricacies of stonework in these strange and frozen images. It was obvious to both men that the façades were intended to produce a hypnotic, haunting, if not terrifying, effect on the viewer—and probably even more so when they were covered in their original paint. What must it have looked like hundreds of years ago? they wondered. Extrapolating from the few remaining traces of color, their imaginations conjured up a dreamlike vision—shimmering façades adorned with twisting, arabesque patterns in deep relief, punctuated by grotesque masks of lurid, glaring gods. The force of the imagery was staggering.

Over the next month, they passed through ruins with Indian names like Sabachtsche, Kewick, Xampon, Chunhuhu, Ytsimpte, Labphak—and dozens of smaller sites with no names at all. At each, they stopped long enough for Catherwood to capture them on paper, and the other two men, if the light was right, with the daguerreotype. They were in an almost constant state of astonishment. Each site was unheralded and unknown except to the small circle of nearby natives. How could they have remained so hidden from Yucatán society, they wondered, let alone the world at large? Stephens lamented that many of the remains, already desolated by time and nature, would not be around much longer—a prediction that later proved true, as some of them would become such formless rubble the expedition's illustrations and descriptions are the only documentary evidence of their existence. It was as if they were witnessing the last traces of this puzzling civilization dissolve before their eyes.

This apprehension motivated them to record every significant structure they came across and to try to carry back to New York the best, most portable of the artifacts—sculpted stones, clay figures, and painted vases. Today such removal would be illegal and internationally condemned, but Stephens was acting at least in part out of a sincere desire to preserve, observing that no one in Yucatán was at all interested in protecting such treasures. He was also candid about his desire

Village along Stephens and Catherwood's route in Yucatán. (Catherwood)

to possess them for the United States, just as France and England were acquiring ancient artifacts, sculpture, and monuments from Egypt, Greece, and Italy for their own national museums.

At the ruins outside the village of Kewick, for example, they found a striking image carved into a large stone that was embedded in one building's ceiling. It displayed a figure painted clearly in bright red and green wearing a wild headdress and surrounded by hieroglyphics. Without objection and with great effort, the local Indians broke through the roof and lowered the stone with ropes. Measuring eighteen by thirty inches it was so heavy the ropes broke, though the stone fell to the floor undamaged. Stephens wanted to take it to New York. But it weighed too much for a mule and the Indians refused to carry it to Mérida. Stephens agreed to leave it behind but only after persuading the proprietor of the nearby rancho to place it in a covered apartment to shelter it from the rain. He said he hoped another American traveler would "bring it away at his own expense, and deposit it in the National Museum in Washington."[2]

The rains finally began to taper off and the dry season struggled belatedly to assert itself. Mosquitoes gave way to *garrapatas*. The bites of the tiny ticks were torture. "Frequently," wrote Stephens, "we came in contact with a bush covered with them, from which thousands swarmed upon us, like moving grains of sand, and scattered till the body itself seemed crawling. Our horses suffered, perhaps, more than ourselves, and it became a habit, whenever we dismounted, to rasp their sides with a rough stick."

The mosquitoes, however, had left their legacy. When the expedition left Kewick for the next village, Catherwood complained of a headache and asked to slow down while Stephens and Cabot rode ahead. Later that morning at the next rancho the baggage carriers came up and announced that Catherwood was down. They had left him lying in the road. When Stephens got to him, the artist was on the ground under a tree, shaking with the chills and wrapped in all the coverings he could find, including his horse's saddlecloths. Albino was at his side. The sight shook Stephens, who recalled the severe episode that had so disabled Catherwood on their last visit. Soon the carriers came with the materials to make a covered coche and carried him to the rancho. When they arrived, Stephens found Cabot had also come down with the fever. Stephens himself began feeling the chill, and all took to their hammocks once again.

They returned to Ticul, where they rested and recovered. There Stephens met one of the few, if only, Maya scholars on the peninsula, Juan Pío Pérez, a former government official who had authored a monograph explaining the Maya calendar. Stephens would have long discussions with Pérez, who as a regional administrator had access to many old documents in the Mayan language and made one of the first studies on how the Maya computed time. Stephens would incorporate Pérez's research in the appendix to his book.

By mid-February the expedition was south again at ruins called Xampon, where Catherwood created one of his most dramatic illustrations. With a moon emerging dramatically from swirling dark clouds, he used deep contrasts of black and white to cast shadows over a half-

Moonlight bathing ruins at Xampon. (Catherwood)

buried building, its walls fallen away to reveal inner apartments and arched ceilings. In the foreground, two dogs are running through waves of grass, bringing down a deer. In spite (or possibly because) of his frequent fever attacks, Catherwood seemed each day to be reaching higher levels of artistry, finding new ways to express the extraordinary things they were seeing. At their next stop, Bolonchen a village near the southern frontier of inhabited Yucatán, they would encounter a wonder that would require every bit of Catherwood's artistic prowess.

Throughout their journey, water was a constant concern—how to find it in this stony land of no rivers, to slake their thirst and that of their horses. And, how had the ancient and current inhabitants survived in such terrain with its long dry season? They found several answers: the natural cenotes, the man-made subterranean *chultun*s and lakes of the ancients, and the deep wells and storage tanks of the haciendas and villages. They had earlier witnessed the human survival skills in the deserts of the Sinai and Egypt, and here they were equally impressed by the tenacity and resourcefulness of the Yucatec Indians.

The marvel of Bolonchen would exceed anything they had yet

seen. The village had nine wells but all eventually became waterless during the dry season. When that happened the villagers had to travel to an unusual cave located nearly two miles away. Stephens and his partners had to see it for themselves. An immense overhanging rock framed the cave's opening. Led by Indians with torches, they entered and descended several levels into the darkness, at one point climbing down a twenty-foot ladder. Finally they came to the edge of a huge cavern that dropped down at least one hundred feet. Sunlight streamed down from above through a hole in earth's surface.

To get to the bottom they had to descend a giant wooden ladder, much in need of refurbishing. Wrote Stephens: "It was very steep, seemed precarious and insecure." But Stephens was determined to feed his omnivorous curiosity and see what was below. And like the boat adventure out on windy Lago de Atitlán and the black passageways in tottering ruins he had entered with no more than candle and twine, this would be one more adventure to write about.

So down they went, the rickety dry wood snapping under their feet. They stumbled, hung on, and somehow made it to the bottom. The floor of the cavern, however, was not the end of the journey. Stephens and Cabot continued to descend ever deeper, climbing down a series of shorter ladders until they finally entered a grotto with a small basin of water. Covered with grime and black from their smoking torches, sweating in the damp heat, they could not resist. They stripped and took a quick dip. Their torches meanwhile sputtered and threatened to go out, and they were seized with fear they would never find their way out through the blackness. "We were then fourteen hundred feet from the mouth of the cave," wrote Stephens, "and at a perpendicular depth of four hundred feet."

On their way back up, one ladder collapsed beneath them. Fortunately Albino arrived with a rope to pull them up to the next level. They explored three side passages that led to other water basins. To their great relief, they finally reached the main cavern, ascended the great wobbly ladder, and eventually emerged exhausted into the sunlight. Stephens could not believe it when he was told the seven thousand residents in the town and surrounding countryside depended solely on the water in the cave for their survival four or five months out of the year.

While Stephens and Cabot explored the cave, Catherwood stayed behind in the cavern to draw the extraordinary scene before him. His final illustration, though not of a giant stelae or ancient pyramid, nevertheless ranks among his finest artistic achievements. With a master's eye, he caught in one stunning image the story of the Indians' determination to survive by going deep into the earth to obtain their water. The illustration succeeds not only in its vivid contrasts of light and dark, and the rigid horizontal and vertical lines of the wide, long ladder against the smooth swirl of the cavern wall behind, but in its portrayal of the unremitting human effort to carry the water upward, the Indians crawling antlike up the ladder with loaded water vessels on their backs—an image impossible to forget.

As they continued south to a site known as Labphak (today called Santa Rosa Xtampak), Stephens noticed changes in their surroundings. The paths were much less stony and the soil was deeper and richer in loam. They encountered their first sugar rancho. At the ruins of Laphak they found an immense building, one of the largest they had seen. The structure and its surroundings were overgrown with trees. Clearing away the foliage they found a "gigantic staircase" and a large number of doorways and apartments, terraces, and a grand courtyard. Stephens was struck by wall panels stuccoed in bas-relief, unlike the limestone mosaics of the north. And the panels displayed stylized images of royalty similar to the stuccoed art of Palenque.

> We were now moving in the direction of Palenque, though, of course, at a great distance from it; the face of the country was less stony, and the discovery of these bas-reliefs, and the increase and profusion of stuccoed ornaments, induced the impression that, in getting beyond the great limestone surface [to the north], the builders of these cities had adapted their style to the materials at hand.

Exploring the surrounding areas, they stumbled on another large building partially buried and a range of disconnected structures with ornamented façades, and they concluded that Labphak was probably at one time a good-size city. Later archaeologists would determine that as many as ten thousand people had lived in the area and the central precinct had a rich history as a regional capital going back to the classic period between A.D. 550 and 950. Stephens wanted to continue their investigations, but the Indians who helped with the preliminary clearing of the site abandoned them when a heavy rainstorm rolled from the north. With another recurrence of fever, Catherwood was too weak to work, and they decided to leave. "There was no place which we visited that we were so reluctant to leave unfinished," Stephens wrote.

Iturbide, their next stop to the south, was a new town at the edge of Yucatán's southern frontier and filled with Indian immigrants from the north. It had grown from twenty-five people to 1,500 in a period of five years due to the government's offer of free land to settlers. Given its rapid growth as a pioneer outpost, Stephens referred to it as the "Chicago" of Yucatán. (Today it is known primarily as Vicente Guerrero.) What had brought Stephens and Catherwood to Iturbide was, as usual, an account they picked up along the road of a set of ruins known today as Dzibilnocac, located near Iturbide. They found the remains worthwhile but Catherwood's continuing recurrences of fever left him too weak to work. A day later, he made the effort and stood drawing before the largest structure as a neighboring tobacco farmer held an umbrella over his head to protect him from the sun. Inside the structure they found remnants of paintings that reminded Stephens of those he had seen in Egyptian tombs, with the flesh of the figures painted red like those in Egyptian art. The paintings were too fragmented to be copied, Stephens wrote, "and seemed surviving the general wreck only to show that these aboriginal builders had possessed more skill in the least enduring branch of the graphic arts."

As Catherwood worked, Stephens and Cabot wandered around the site and counted thirty-three different mounds, all so overgrown with trees and vegetation that few features were visible. When they returned to the principal building, they found Catherwood lying down. He was too weak to continue. Stephens became so concerned for Catherwood and so disheartened by their constant struggles with illness that he suggested they call off the rest of the expedition and go home. Catherwood, however, would not hear of it and insisted they keep on.

Beyond Iturbide, however, lay nothing but wilderness, stretching all the way south to the lowland jungles of Guatemala's Petén. In the town they heard no reports of any further ruins in that direction, but Stephens was not convinced. "It may well be that wrecks of cities lie buried but a few leagues farther on," he wrote, "the existence of which is entirely unknown at the village of Iturbide, for at that place there was not a single individual who had ever heard of the ruins at Lab-phak, which we visited just before, until they heard of them from us." They decided, however, not to continue south. They had accomplished a great deal on their southern march, despite the recurring malarial fevers that had struck down each of them, Catherwood most seriously of all.

There was more to come in the north, perhaps much more. And they coveted one reportedly magnificent set of ruins that like Uxmal had been a principal reason for their return to Yucatán. It had always hovered on their horizon, in their plans, and they were determined now to explore it if they could only stay healthy enough to get there.[3]

◁ 19 ▷

Chichén Itzá

Now in early March, they had been on the road more than four months. From Iturbide they traveled one hundred miles north through several towns, visiting minor ruins along the way. After two weeks with several stops to allow Catherwood to regain his strength, they arrived at their long-anticipated destination: a dazzling group of ruins called Chichén Itzá. They already knew some history about the ruins, whose name means "Mouth of the Well of the Itzá" in Mayan. The conquistadors had briefly occupied the site in 1533 in an attempt to make it their capital, apparently attracted by its central location and its stone ruins to use as building material for their new city. In a large show of force, however, Maya warriors defeated the Spanish in a fierce battle on a plain outside the ruins. When the battle was over, 150 Spaniards lay dead and most of the remaining soldiers were wounded.[1] The surviving conquistadors were able to slip away during the night. It was one of the worst defeats suffered by the conquistadors and set back the Spanish conquest of Yucatán by years.[2] Stephens noted that it was therefore not a surprise that the Spaniards left very few details describing the site, considering their harried circumstances and defeat. But its existence was firmly established in the history books of the Conquest.

"Ever since we left home," he wrote, "we had had our eyes upon this place." They were told in Mérida that it would be difficult for any person to miss the ruins traveling from Mérida east to Valladolid, Yucatán's second-largest city. The taller structures were clearly visible from the road. But if they were known to the people of Yucatán, Stephens noted they were still virtually unknown to the outside world. Determined to remedy that, he and his companions spent more than

Cenote at Chichén Itzá. (Catherwood)

two weeks meticulously examining and recording the ruins' every crack and crevice.

The site had two large cenotes open to the sky whose water level remained the same year-round, indicating that they were being fed by a consistent subterranean water source. No doubt this was the reason the original builders had picked the location for their city. Though set amid stands of trees, which were dense in places, the main buildings were located in the middle of a large cattle ranch leased from the government by a man named Juan Sosa, who had built a hacienda nearby. Unlike many of the other sites they had explored, Chichén thus did not require laborious clearing. The cattle kept much of the underbrush down and created paths that made it easy to walk from one structure to another.

At this point Stephens and Catherwood had visited nearly forty separate Maya ruins and could not have been faulted if they had become a bit jaded. Stephens, however, irrepressible as ever, his zeal undiminished, declared Chichén Itzá "magnificent." Without doubt it was the most impressive site in Yucatán since Uxmal. Many of the structures were, like Uxmal's, imposing, built on a monumental scale and in a state of good preservation, which led Stephens to speculate, as he had with Uxmal, that these cities could have been inhabited by the Indians at the time of the Conquest. Spanish records, however, made no claim Chichén Itzá was a thriving city like Tiho, on which they later built Mérida. And modern studies indicate that both Uxmal and Chichén had already reached their peak and were abandoned hundreds of years before the Spanish arrived.[3]

Stephens, with none of the tools of modern archaeological science at his disposal, had vacillated about the age of the ruins from site to site. He struggled to remain open to all possibilities. "Chichen, though in a better state of preservation than most of the others," he wrote, "has a greater appearance of antiquity; some of the buildings are no doubt older than others, and long intervals may have elapsed between the times of their construction."[4]

Along with the cattle came an extra dose of *garrapatas*, but as intolerable as the pests were, the men found the clearing of much of the site by the cattle well worth it. Catherwood was able to get to work immediately. They would document Chichén Itzá as thoroughly as they had Uxmal, Palenque, and Copán, even though they knew they were not the first to investigate the site. They were aware that not long before their arrival the ruins had been visited by an Austrian diplomat and an American engineer working in nearby Valladolid.[5]

Their first discovery at Chichén set the tone. In the initial building they entered, called Akatzeeb ("House of the Dark Writing"), they found a tablet displaying the sculpted image of a royal lord or priest in bas-relief and rows of hieroglyphs. This once more confirmed the unity of art and writing they believed linked most of the ruins they had examined. In their travels they had now seen significant variations in architecture and exterior ornamentation, but the common denominators of a civilization—its artistic and cultural themes and its writing—were almost the same throughout. Chichén was particularly rich in hieroglyphs and bas-reliefs. It was clear to them that they had reached one of the northernmost points of the same unique and cohesive civilization they had been tracking since their visit to Copán, far to the south.

Yet Stephens, his skills of perception by now finely honed, sensed something different about Chichén. "In general," he wrote, "the facades were not so elaborately ornamented as some we had seen, seemed of an older date, and the sculpture was ruder"—especially compared to the delicately chiseled bas-reliefs they found at Palenque. But the sculptors of Chichén were working with much more porous stone, which did not lend itself to the detail that had so impressed them at Palenque. More than this, Chichén was clearly the most warlike site they had investigated. Carved images of warriors abounded—soldiers carrying spears and shields and decked out in elaborate war feathers. An entire platform wall in the center of the site's main plaza was made up of rows upon rows of sculpted human skulls impaled on lances.

Despite Chichén's clear cultural linkage to the sites in the south, in Chiapas, Guatemala, and Honduras, Stephens also saw that the Itzá, the people who had once ruled the city, seemed to have a closer connection with Mexico than they had seen at other sites. He detected strong similarities between one temple's colored murals—images of the Itzá armies overrunning cities and villages and destroying their enemies—and the Mexican "picture writings" published in Lord Kingsborough's giant volumes. He also observed that a "dance" of Itzá warriors carved on the wall of a second temple, each wearing headdresses of feathers and carrying bundles of spears, resembled images of soldiers carved into a giant "sacrifice" stone that had been dug up in the plaza of Mexico City near where one of the Aztec's temples had once stood. He knew too that the Aztecs and other Mexican societies worshipped the feathered serpent, and scattered around Chichén were many serpent sculptures and images. Chichén seemed to Stephens a mix of the Central American culture and the Mexican. And once again his observations would prove prescient. Archaeologists would later trace many central and coastal Mexican influences at Chichén, in part due to the Itzá Maya's success in coastal trade.

Although the bas-relief wall figures were simpler and "ruder" than those in the south, they found a group of structures that greatly resembled the gorgeously ornamented buildings at Uxmal, Kabah, and Labna. Segregated from the rest of Chichén's ruins in a separate section, these structures appeared so elaborate in their stonework and so elegant in overall form that they seemed constructed to imitate and

TOP   The so-called "Nunnery" at Chichén Itzá. (Catherwood)
BELOW   Detail, present day. (Carlsen)

TOP   Main pyramid at Chichén Itzá. (Catherwood)
BELOW   Main pyramid and grounds today. (Carlsen)

outdo the façades Stephens and Catherwood had found in southwest-ern Yucatán. These exterior decorations and mosaics are now known as the Puuc style. Had immigrants from Uxmal and Kabah settled at Chichén and replicated their style, or had the Itzá just stolen it? Or could this style have originated in Chichén and been taken south? One modern scholar has called the Puuc style "baroque," but a better analogy might be "rococo"—the florid, over-the-top European style of the eighteenth century. In any case, it was a form of ornamentation that seemed to be reaching for its own extreme end.

These structures were catnip for Catherwood, who lavished some of his best work on them. It was as if they had been built and deco-rated for no other reason than the pure aesthetic pleasure of looking at them, and Catherwood reveled in it, capturing them in all their brilliant intricacy.

All of Chichén Itzá offered a wealth of material for Catherwood to work with. The site seemed to have one of everything that they had encountered at the other ruins, and some in better condition. For ex-ample, they found again the two parallel walls that would later come to be identified as ball courts. Only here the walls enclosing the court were incredibly massive, as were the carved stone rings implanted in the wall directly opposite one another.[6] The rings were twenty feet from the ground, four feet in diameter, carved as "entwined serpents," and perfectly intact, unlike the rings at Uxmal, which they found fallen and shattered. They discovered a huge round building similar to the one they found at Mayapán. And not far north of it sat the one structure that seemed obligatory at almost every site: a pyramid. But here was one of the most impressive stepped pyramids they had yet seen. At one of the four staircases that rose to the temple on top, Ste-phens observed "two colossal serpents' heads" flanking the base, ten feet in length, with mouths wide open and tongues protruding.[7] Climbing up to the temple they found over the doorways intact carved beams—again made of rock-hard sapodilla wood—with stone door-jambs also beautifully sculpted with human figures in bas-relief.

But as they stood on the platform outside the temple looking down, they saw something through the trees they had never encoun-tered before.

Lightning strike over the ball court at Chichén Itzá. (Catherwood)

From this lofty height we saw for the first time groups of small columns, which, on examination, proved to be among the most remarkable and unintelligible remains we had yet met with. They stood in rows of three, four, and five abreast, many rows continuing in the same direction. . . . Many of them had fallen, and in some places they lie prostrate in rows, all in the same direction, as if thrown down intentionally. In some places they extended to the bases of large mounds, on which were ruins of buildings and colossal fragments of sculpture, while in others they branched off and terminated abruptly. I counted three hundred and eighty, and there were many more.

Chichén Itzá both amazed and confounded Stephens and Catherwood. The site displayed a stunning amalgam of styles, some extravagant and excessive, yet still containing clear threads of unity with the ruins they had explored earlier. The site was as vast as Uxmal and as grandiose, yet given the two cities' proximity—less than ninety miles apart—their differences left a seemingly unsolvable riddle. Far from

Photo taken from the top of the main pyramid at Chichén Itzá. (Carlsen)

helping to shed more light on the mystery of these old and wondrous cities, Chichén Itzá seemed only to compound their inscrutability.

The day before their departure they were drawn to Chichén's north cenote, which for centuries had been a sacred place of pilgrimage for Yucatán's Indians, and remained so. When they reached it through a thick forest of trees, a hawk was circling inside the huge, almost perfectly round cavity in the ground. They came to the edge and looked down into the water below. The cenote's ragged, layered limestone walls dropped straight to the green pool twenty feet below, leaving no path down to the water's surface—and no way up. Trees and shrubs cantilevered out over the sides and in one place along the edge the men came upon a stone structure. Standing on the brink looking down into the watery abyss sent a shudder through Stephens. According to legend, he explained, it was here that humans were thrown into the water below, as a sacrifice to the rain god.[8]

◅ 20 ▻

Tuloom

On March 29 they left Chichén Itzá and traveled due east to Valladolid, arriving ahead of their baggage. The city of fifteen thousand was founded very early in the Spanish era, and Stephens pronounced it run down and its seven churches "dilapidated." The whole place had an air of "melancholy," he wrote. Valladolid was their first stop on their way to the east coast of the peninsula, where, following up again on reports, they hoped to find the remains of a city described by the earliest Spanish sailors as stunning in size and splendor and—most intriguing of all—inhabited. The place was called Tuloom (Stephens wrote it phonetically but today it is spelled Tulum). They wanted also to sail across to the island of Cozumel, where the Spanish claimed to have discovered numerous stone temples.

The three men located lodgings in Valladolid, and as they settled in for the night, Albino came galloping into town and banged on the door to announce there had been a terrible accident. The horse carrying the daguerreotype broke and ran, smashing the apparatus to pieces. The device was a dead loss. The men consoled themselves with the thought that at least they had the images they had already developed on copper plates.

More disturbing than the loss of the daguerreotype was a sense of foreboding they felt in Valladolid. Earlier Stephens sensed a current of fear running through white Yucatecan society that in Valladolid seemed more palpable than anywhere else. In one of his frequent sociological asides, he had written that the peninsula's Maya Indians had suffered centuries of brutal subjugation, many working in feudal bondage to their white masters. He asked: "Could these be the descendants of that fierce people who had made such bloody resistance to the Spanish conquerors?"

Since the Conquest the natives had been barred from owning weapons, but Stephens now learned that in the recent revolt against Mexico, the whites relied heavily on the Indians to do their fighting. Indians had been recruited from the countryside and armed to help expel the Mexican garrison from Valladolid. He wrote: "What the consequences may be of finding themselves, after ages of servitude, once more in the possession of arms, and in increasing knowledge of their physical strength, is a question of momentous import to the people of that country, the solution of which no man can foretell."

While Stephens could not "foretell" the exact consequences, he understood the danger from his experience in Guatemala. Yucatán was, in fact, a time bomb. For once, Stephens and Catherwood's timing was propitious: they would leave soon and finally miss a revolution. This was one they may not have survived. In the years that followed, the peninsula exploded and Valladolid would be the center of hundreds of massacres of whites by the Indians. The Yucatec Maya, often attacking with only their machetes, rose throughout eastern and central Yucatán and mounted a revolt of such savagery that it made Guatemala's Indian uprising appear agreeable by comparison. By 1848, the Indians had swept from the east across Yucatán, surrounded Mérida, and nearly drove all the white inhabitants of the peninsula into the sea. What followed was eight years of conflict and fanatical slaughter that came to be known as the "War of the Castes." Before it was over as many as eighty thousand people would die, 16 percent of the population, and another 25 percent were driven from the peninsula. The Spanish conquistadors never entirely crushed the will of Yucatec Maya, who had endured centuries of oppression while waiting for their moment of retribution.[1]

The expedition was spared any violence but on the road east of Valladolid they met a large group of indigenous men whose appearance brought back memories of Guatemala. "Naked, armed with long guns, and with deer and wild boars slung on their back," wrote Stephens, "their aspect was the most truculent of any people we had seen. They were some of the Indians who had risen to the call [in the attack on the Mexican garrison in Valladolid], and they seemed ready at any moment for battle."

Stephens was also surprised when they were unable to find anyone in Valladolid who had heard of Tuloom. There was a settlement on the coast named Tancah, they were told, but they would need to proceed east to the town of Chemax to determine if there was even a road to it.[2] Chemax was located in a straight line between Valladolid and Tancah, and when they arrived they discovered that in fact they had reached what was effectively the eastern boundary of populated Yucatán. They were now at the frontier with nothing but forty-five miles of tangled jungle and wilderness between Chemax and the coast. And they were told Tancah was nothing but a "mere rancho." There was a way through the jungle, however—a little-used, heavily overgrown foot path.

Stephens also learned Tancah was a camp set up by a smuggler and pirate named Molas. Sometime earlier Molas had been sentenced to death in Mérida but he had escaped from prison in the capital and fled to the coast, where he and his family set up their lonely camp, "out of the reach of justice." When soldiers who were sent from Mérida to capture him reached Chemax and saw the jungle in front of them, they turned around and went back. Sometime later Molas was found dead on the footpath, though no one could explain why. "These accounts came upon us most unexpectedly and deranged all our plans," Stephens wrote.

Tuloom was believed to be the first city spotted by the Spanish when they arrived off the Yucatán coast in the spring of 1518, on an expedition from Cuba led by Juan de Grijalva. The four Spanish ships stopped first at a large island the natives called Cozumel, and then sailed across the channel to Yucatán mainland. The expedition's chaplain, Juan Díaz, described what came next: "We followed the coast day and night; on the following day . . . we sighted a city or town so large that Seville would not have appeared bigger or better . . . a very tall tower was to be seen there." When Stephens met Juan Pío Pérez the month before, he told Stephens an explorer named Juan José Galvez had recently sailed the same stretch of coast and reported finding two ancient cities not far down from Cozumel—Tancah and

Tuloom—and noted that the later was surrounded by a massive stone wall. How was it possible so little was known about these ruins? Stephens wondered.

The expedition had reached a crossroad. Tuloom appeared just out of reach, a siren's song floating from beyond the jungle. Stephens's final pair of shoes were so worn they would never survive a forty-five-mile footpath. But they were all now healthy and had come this far, and Tuloom, especially, loomed as an indispensable and probably final destination before the rainy season closed in on them and terminated the expedition. "Turning back formed no part of our deliberations," Stephens wrote. They huddled and came up with an alternate plan, unfortunately one that would add unexpected weeks to their itinerary. A road led northeast from Chemax all the way to the northern port of Yalahao. There they could take a boat around the northern tip of the peninsula known as Cape Catoche, and then south to Cozumel, Tancah, and Tuloom. "This would subject us to the necessity of two voyages along the coast, going and returning," Stephens admitted, "and would require, perhaps, a fortnight to reach Tancah, which we had expected to arrive at in three days."

It took them three days just to reach Yalahao, over a hard road of sharp stones. "It was desperately hot," Stephens wrote. "We had no view except the narrow path before us, and we stumbled along, wondering that such a stony surface could support such a teeming vegetation." At Yalahao they found an isolated mini-port of palm-thatched huts shaded by coconut trees, a former haunt of pirates, many of whom had now settled down to the respectability of smuggling or growing sugar at nearby ranchos. But memories were still fresh of the days when the place was notorious for its pirate law, and for plunder brought ashore and spread around in gambling and drunkenness. One canoa, or boat, lying offshore was pointed out to them as a former pirate craft. The location was ideal for pirating because the tiny port faced the broad channel between Yucatán and Cuba, allowing the buccaneers to prey easily on passing merchant ships. And when the pirates were pursued by larger, heavily armed ships, they escaped by sailing their shallow-hull vessels into the long, lagoon-like bay where the larger ships could not follow.

While Cabot was enthralled with the bird life along the coast, Stephens and Catherwood wasted little time hiring a small canoe and buying provisions. After two days they were ready. The plan called for their horses to be taken all the way back through Valladolid, then west to a port near Mérida called Silan. The men would then sail to Silan on their return from Tuloom. When the canoe was filled with food, casks of water, and "implements" for making tortillas, there was little room left for the expeditionary party. The open craft, named *El Sol,* was thirty-five feet long, six feet wide, carried two sailors besides the captain, had two sails, and had no keel. They boarded on April 7, and, Stephens wrote, "prospects seemed rather unpromising for a month's cruise. There was no wind; the sails were flapping against the mast; the sun beat down on us, and we had no awning of any kind, although the agent had promised one. Our captain was a middle-aged Mestizo, a fisherman, hired for the occasion."

They drifted the first two days, making little headway. The first night they were crammed together in the stern, sleeping side by side so tightly, Stephens wrote, "that if the bottom had fallen out we could hardly have gone through." Eventually they got around Cape Catoche, spent a night on a tiny island named Contoy, then the next day cruised the coast of Isla de Mujeres, an island that like Yalahao had been a notorious "resort" for pirates, including the well-known Jean Lafitte. *El Sol* sailed on, veering west to the mainland, and approached the empty sand hills of Kancune, today the major tourist resort of Cancún. They took time out to bathe along the shore and beachcomb for shells, but at sunset they found themselves running for their lives to the boat, "flying before the natives." "Swarms of mosquitoes," Stephens wrote, "pursued us with the same bloodthirsty spirit that animated the Indians along the coast when they pursued the Spaniards."

The next day they sailed to the island of Cozumel before a stiff breeze; the choppy seas broke over the gunwales, soaking them, their provisions, and their baggage. They anchored offshore for the night, and in the morning, after searching the thickly forested shoreline they spotted a small estate of abandoned thatched huts. They threaded their way through the reef into a small bay, went ashore, and took up residence in the empty rancho. Relieved from the wet, packed con-

Huts and encampment at Cozumel where Stephens, Catherwood, and
Cabot stayed. (Catherwood)

fines of the canoa, the three men stretched out in the shade of a coconut tree to take in the beautiful little bay. "With our guns resting
against the trees, long beards, and canoa costumes," Stephens wrote,
"we were, perhaps, as piratical seeming a trio as ever scuttled a ship at
sea."

Stephens had read accounts by Juan Díaz, Bernal Díaz del Castillo, and other conquistadors who had accompanied Grijalva, and
later Cortés, on their explorations at Cozumel; they had provided one
of the chief motivations for their journey. All the reports described a
populated island dotted with hamlets containing stone houses and
"towers" where the natives worshipped idols. So Stephens and his
companions were surprised to find the island seemingly uninhabited.
The rancho was hemmed by tropical jungle so overgrown and dense
that they realized it would be all but impossible to cut their way any
distance inland in search of ruins. They might pass within feet of an
old building and never see it. Cabot, however, found the island rich
with rare species and quickly went to work bringing down as many as
he could to add to his large and growing ornithological collection.

While inland exploration was ruled out, the next morning they
investigated a square stone building that had been visible through the

trees when they entered the bay. Small and squat, it little resembled the great structures they had seen at Chichén, Uxmal, and other sites on the mainland. But it bore the typical appearance of a small temple, built on a platform with steps all around, its four doors facing out to the four cardinal points of the compass. They found another ruin nearby, built on a low terrace, with vestiges of the original paint on its exterior walls. Not far away, buried in the jungle, they also discovered the remains of a Spanish church, possibly the one that Cortés had ordered built after landing on the island in 1519. The roof had collapsed but its walls still stood twenty feet high and a tree grew from the altar.

The next day was lost when a thunderstorm came up suddenly. The captain, to save his boat, quickly sailed out of the bay for safer anchorage, leaving the expedition party behind without baggage or provisions. With darkness coming on, Stephens feared for the boat's crew in the roiling waters. Then he wondered about their own fate. "If she never returned," he wrote, "we should be [four] Robinson Crusoes, all alone on a desert island." They took some solace in the fact that they at least had guns—then discovered they had little ammunition with them onshore. "As the storm raged our apprehension ran high, and we had got so far as to calculate our chances of reaching the mainland by a raft."

Such a measure proved unnecessary when the next day Stephens and Albino walked several miles over jagged rocks—strewn with old wreckage—and found the boat and crew safely ensconced in a protected cove. "Sails, luggage, Doctor Cabot's birds, and my copy of Cogolludo, were spread out to dry." When they left the following day, Stephens wrote, "a hawk mourning over its mate, which we carried away, was the only living thing that looked upon our departure." Unsuccessful on Cozumel, they now pinned all their hopes on finding the city "as large as Seville" on the peninsula's coast.

It took two days to sail back across the channel to the Yucatán mainland and south down the coast to the rancho at Tancah. Though the distance was not long, they had to fight rough seas, wind, and a strong northern current. Before landing at Tancah, they spotted in the distance high on a cliff the huge stone tower of Tuloom, and a charge of anticipation shot through the men. Here at last, they had reached their end point, the culmination of their long Yucatán journey. Stephens directed the captain to run *El Sol* onto Tancah's white sand beach. They found an abandoned hut, which they cleared and set up as a residence. Within a short time they received a visit from the pirate Molas's sons, two young men who had taken possession of the rancho after their father's death the year before. They were welcoming, no doubt happy to have company in their isolated state. Tancah itself was reputed to contain stone buildings that were once visible from the sea. The young men led them through the jungle to a cornfield, where they found a less than impressive collection of broken and fallen structures scattered about on stone terraces.

Their disappointment was short-lived. Tuloom, after all, was the endgame, their essential final prize. It lay three miles south and the next day they set off down the coastline, walking on white powdered sand and cooling their bare feet in the crystalline waters. The youngest Molas accompanied them as a guide. About halfway, they had to climb a series of steep cliffs. At the top of each, the distant tower, which was called "Castillo," or castle, came closer to view, a wild, dramatic sight, a stone fortress perched on a cliff looming high above the sea.

Climbing up the last ravine, they headed through thick jungle with old stone walls and ruined buildings barely visible through the trees, and finally they arrived at the foot of a grand staircase leading up to a temple at the top of the Castillo. Scattered trees grew out of the steps and the gloom of the forest hovered over them. Not since Copán, their first ruins, did they feel as engulfed by nature. "We had undertaken our long journey to this place in utter uncertainty as to what we should meet," Stephens wrote. "Impediments and difficulties accumulated upon us, but already we felt indemnified for all our labor. We were amid the wildest scenery we had yet found in Yucatán."

They cut their way up the imposing thirty-foot-wide stairway, bordered by massive balustrades, then hauled their luggage up, and took possession of two rooms in the temple. Stephens wrote: "We looked

TOP   Present-day photo of the so-called "Castillo," or castle, at Tulum. (Carlsen)
BELOW   The "Castillo" as seen from the coast. (Catherwood)

over an immense forest: walking around the molding of the wall, we looked out upon the boundless ocean." Standing on the ledge behind the temple poised high on the cliff, they stared down into the perfectly clear aquamarine water lapping at the coral sand below.

Knotted roots and vines snaked over the building and the men spent the first day clearing away as much vegetation as possible. As the foliage was pulled away, a structure of almost classical simplicity emerged, designed with Grecian symmetry. The façade faced west toward the jungle and the staircase dominated the middle, rising three stories to the square temple at the top. Large enclosed apartments on the second level spread out on each side from the stairway like identical wings, their roofs fallen in, platforms in front. Each wing had its own staircase down to the forest floor and thick columns framed the doorways. At ground level just below the apartments two small temples projected from the base on each side, both with single doorways leading to inner chambers. From the front, the entire structure had the appearance of a perfectly balanced, stepped layer cake. At its back—from out at sea—the blank sloping wall that formed the rear of the main building gave the impression of an impregnable citadel growing directly out of the cliff high above the water.

There was no daguerreotype for Tuloom. This time the images would be captured by Catherwood's pencils and brushes alone. And hours were spent clearing away enough of the surrounding jungle so that he could stand back with sufficient perspective to do his work. Then Cabot went hunting and Stephens took measurements.

He found a massive wall surrounding the site that was up to 26 feet thick and rose to a height of 16 feet in places. It formed three sides of a giant rectangle enclosing the whole precinct of Tuloom. The fourth side was the open cliff facing the sea. It would have been ideally defensible against enemies. They discovered five narrow gateways through the wall and two stone watchtowers built in the corners. From the beginning of the expedition they had heard of walls protecting the old cities but had only found remnants of them. Here the wall was almost entirely intact, suggesting to Stephens that Tuloom had been built more recently than other ruins, especially given the forces of nature all around them. He measured it by walking along its top.

Small temple at Tulum. (Catherwood)

"Even then it was no easy matter," wrote Stephens. "Trees growing besides the wall threw their branches across it, thorns, bushes, and vines of every description grew out of it, and at every step we were obliged to cut down the Agave Americana, which pierced us with its long, sharp points." From end to end it measured 2,800 feet, or more than half a mile. Young Molas told them that he had found a large number of scattered ruins outside the wall, which led Stephens to assume the buildings inside formed the religious and administrative center of a much larger city.

Catherwood continued to work at top speed. At one point, Stephens, looking down from the platform outside the temple doorway, watched him. The scene left in Stephens an indelible image of pure Catherwood stoicism. The artist had set up his camera lucida on a raised stone platform not far from the base of the Castillo's staircase. He stood shaded from the sun by overhanging branches. Stephens wrote: "The picturesque effect being greatly heightened by his manner of keeping one hand in his pocket, to save it from the attacks of mosquitoes, and by his expedient of tying his pantaloons around his legs to keep ants and other insects from running up."

On a number of scattered structures they found curious masks and other sculpted decorations over cornices and doorways, along with wall tablets carved with images similar to those at Labphak. Painted frescoes covered the inner walls of several buildings, most of them effaced beyond recognition. They discovered a cenote filled with brackish water just inside the north wall, obviously the source of water for Tuloom's inner sanctum.

And yet they were desperate to leave. Stephens's shoes had worn so thin he was now restricted to moving about only when absolutely necessary. And along with the natural beauty came the murderous mini-vampires. The mosquitoes were driving them out. Every night was torture. "We held our ground against them for two nights," Stephens wrote. The men were apparently without their netting. On the third evening they were finally forced out of the temple, only to be driven back in again, seeking relief but never able to find it. They had all but given up sleeping. "A savage notice to quit was continually buzzing in our ears and all that we cared for was to get away."

Catherwood had gotten down on paper the major structures and they were packing to leave when Cabot, in one last search for an ocellated turkey, cut his way into the jungle and stumbled on another group of remarkable buildings. They stood less than a hundred feet from the Castillo but had been entirely invisible in the density of the foliage until Cabot came directly upon them. A few feet to one side and he would have passed them without noticing. Even Molas knew nothing of them. Now there was no way they could escape until the trees and undergrowth were cleared and Catherwood had a chance to record them.

One of the structures consisted of twin temples, one on top of the other. The unique building was richly decorated with sculpted figures in niches above the doorways and the walls inside were covered in paintings. Unfortunately the murals were so coated in moss and mold, their subjects were impossible to make out. They also found two rounded stelae, somewhat like those at Copán and Quiriguá but much less ambitious. They stood little more than six feet high and the sculpting was worn and indistinct. Stephens does not record how many hours or days the new discoveries added to their stay but a substantial amount of clearing was necessary for Catherwood to complete his drawings.[3] Finally they were measured, drawn, and added to his site plan, and the men fled before their bloodthirsty, devoted antagonists.

They had come to the end. Tuloom was their last great ghost city, haunted with wonders no less astonishing than those of their first, Copán. Both places were victims of nature, lost to time, and, as with so much of what they had witnessed between, provocative and mystifying. It was by chance they had journeyed at the end to Tuloom, which by coincidence had been one of the final holdouts at the end of the once-great Maya civilization. Spanish chaplain Juan Díaz may have exaggerated when he reported in 1518 that Tuloom was "so large that Seville would not have appeared larger or better." But he was certainly correct that what he saw from the sea was a still-occupied city of impressive elegance and splendor. Later scientific investigations would show that Tuloom survived for decades after the conquistadors arrived because the Spaniards chose to invade Yucatán from the west, the Gulf of Mexico, avoiding the wild jungle they had seen along the east coast. Tuloom was never conquered but was gradually abandoned during the late 1500s as the diseases brought by the Spanish finally reached the site, breached the great wall, and scattered and killed its inhabitants. Stephens sensed the difference in Tuloom. He observed that the enormous wall was largely intact and many buildings in good preservation despite the blunt forces of nature.

Young Molas told them that he had heard of other great buildings "covered with paintings in bright and vivid colors" and located deep in the forest to the west. The men questioned an old Indian at the rancho who had reported stumbling upon them while hunting. But he was evasive and gave information too ambiguous for them to venture miles through the jungle in search of them, especially in Stephens's case, without shoes.

Yet even if they could not penetrate it, the forest intrigued them. The huge swath of land from the Molas rancho inland forty-five miles to Chemax was covered by tropical jungle watered by the trade winds and hurricanes that blew in from the sea. Not a road ran through it and white men never entered. Stephens was convinced, he said, "ruined cities no doubt exist." Eighty years later he would be proven right when archaeologists discovered the ancient city of Coba some thirty miles northwest of Tuloom. The city, which dates from the Classic Maya era, was one of the most populous and complex centers in Yucatán and its main pyramid one of the tallest in the Mayan world. What Stephens also could not know was that the vast wilderness, which extended far to the north and south, was virtually empty at the time of their visit but would soon be populated again. Within a decade it would become refuge to a large population of Indians who sought the safety of its forests at the end of the War of the Castes.[4]

The expedition had run out of space and time. The month of May, and along with it the rainy season, the final arbiter of all their explorations, were coming on fast. They were ragged and exhausted, and they still faced the long sea journey back to Mérida.

They left the Molas settlement at the end of April. With the current and wind working in their favor, they made good time sailing north. They spent their second night on the long, thin outcropping of rock and sand known as Isla de Mujeres, or Island of Women, where they visited two stone temples overlooking the sea. They rounded Cape Catoche and headed west back to Yalahao. "The old pirates' haunt seemed a metropolis," said Stephens. Continuing west with a strong wind, they arrived the next day at Silan, known today as Dzilam de Bravo.

They must have looked the role of shipwrecked Crusoes as they waded ashore. Their clothes were in tatters and their faces sunburned and covered with beards. As planned, the horses were waiting for them with their handler, identified by Stephens only as Dimas, who had heroically brought them more than 150 miles from Yalahao.

Cabot was in heaven. The coast near Silan was thick with bird life and they set out for two days in pursuit of flamingoes and roseate spoonbills.

It would be another week before they reached Mérida. Along the way they stopped to examine several large overgrown mounds, and though some were immense in size and complete with fallen temples, they were undistinguished. Many of them had been whittled down to provide building materials for townspeople. In the town of Izamal an imposing Franciscan church and monastery had been built three hundred years earlier on the site of a huge pyramid, which had been dismantled to provide stones for their construction. In the backyard of a nearby house, they found a gigantic head protruding from a stuccoed wall. Catherwood dutifully made a record and created a dramatic image of the sculpture for his later book of hand-colored illustrations.

Not far outside Mérida, they stopped for the night at a hacienda named Aké. In the morning they investigated the mound call "El Palacio." Following a grand stairway up to a broad platform they came upon thirty-six stone columns standing in three parallel rows, some fourteen to sixteen feet high, apparently at one time holding up a roof. The platform was overgrown and some of the columns had fallen. It was their last exploration, the end of their long journey. They would never see stone temples, pyramids, or ancient ruins again.

They spent several days in Mérida visiting friends and packing up artifacts and Cabot's enormous collection of bird specimens. The capital was on war footing again, and the chief of the Mexican government, Santa Ana, was threatening invasion. Although Stephens wanted nothing to do Yucatán's problems—he was already diverted by news from home about possible war with England and battles between Texas and Mexico—he still could not help himself. "I was in the Senate Chamber when the ultimatum of Santa Ana was read," he confessed. "The clouds were becoming darker and more portentous."

They made one last farewell "paseo" around Mérida's plaza. "A volcano was burning and heaving with inward fires," wrote Stephens, "but there was the same cheerfulness, gayety, and prettiness as before."

Unfortunately, the only ship available at the port of Sisal was the old *Alexandre*, the same vessel—becalmed and encircled by sharks—on which they had sailed during their last voyage home. There was no certainty about when another ship would arrive so they grudgingly ordered their baggage to Sisal.

They put to sea on the *Alexandre* two days later, on May 18. The voyage was long but this time uneventful. When they finally drew into Havana Harbor, they learned that yellow fever had just broken out in the city. But their luck held: they recognized an American packet ship, the *Anna Louise,* entering the harbor and learned it was sailing the next day for New York.

Stephens had already made arrangements in Mérida for shipment to New York of the two heavy, glyph-covered lintels they had taken from Uxmal and Kabah. But they still had with them a large number of valuable relics and artifacts they had accumulated during the expedition—sculptures, clay figures, painted vases—all of which were crucial for Stephens's long-dreamed-of National Museum of American Antiquities. These precious items, along with Cabot's bird collection, they had transferred to the *Anna Louise.*

That night, Stephens, Catherwood, and Cabot went ashore to visit the tomb of Christopher Columbus, the one man who had done more than any other to connect the Old World with New. The famous admiral died in Spain in 1506. Three decades later his remains were brought first to Santo Domingo and then in 1795 to Havana (a century later they would be returned to Spain). In June 1842, his bones lay in a marble tomb in Havana's cathedral, where the three men just off the *Alexandre* stood with a candle and their hats off to pay their respects.[5]

The next day they were at sea, and thirteen days later they sailed into New York harbor.

◁ 21 ▷

Home

At half past nine the night of July 29, exactly six weeks after he and Stephens had returned to New York, Catherwood locked the doors to his rotunda at Prince and Mercer Streets. As he turned to leave, he saw smoke. Within minutes flames shot up from within the cavernous wooden structure and a short time later firemen rushed to the scene and quickly set their hoses. They were able to preserve most of the exterior walls of the building, but within half an hour the roof fell in and flames from the inside flared into the sky with volcanic fury.

"Owing to the combustible state of the paintings and other materials in it," the *New York Herald* reported the next day, "the interior was entirely consumed including the splendid panoramas of Jerusalem and Thebes."[1]

Catherwood was ruined. His chief source of income—his panoramas—lay in ashes, his rotunda a shell. Worse, his dream with Stephens of a national antiquities museum was consumed in the flames as well. When they arrived in June, they had decided to store in the rotunda some of Catherwood's original illustrations and all the artifacts they had collected, including the two priceless hardwood lintels carved with hieroglyphs and images of feathered Maya royalty. Stephens wrote that he had intended to ship the entire collection—the lintels, "vases, figures, idols, and other relics"—to the "National Museum at Washington" as soon as the sculpted stones they had obtained at Uxmal arrived from Mérida.[2]

They found that nothing had survived the inferno. "I had the melancholy satisfaction of seeing their ashes exactly as the fire had left them," he wrote. "We seemed doomed to be in the midst of ruins."

Despite a statement by one witness that lightning touched off the blaze, in the end it was believed that one of the two hundred gaslights used to illuminate the rotunda gallery had caused the fire. The financial loss to Catherwood and his partner, George Jackson, was enormous; the loss of the artifacts was incalculable. Physical damages were put at over $20,000, a huge sum at the time, and the partnership was insured for only $3,000. The night of the fire Catherwood told the *Herald* reporter that he had tried to save the archaeological treasures, but that the firemen failed to follow his instructions on where to direct their hoses.[3] The losses were so devastating financially and psychologically, the rotunda was never rebuilt. And Catherwood would never create another panorama.

Miraculously, most of Catherwood's artwork from the expeditions survived. Apparently he kept many of his paintings and drawings in his nearby residence at 86 Prince Street and at the Harper Brothers' offices. These included at least some daguerreotype plates because Stephens noted later that the illustrations in their Yucatán volumes were based on daguerreotypes images as well as drawings Catherwood made "on the spot."[4] And Catherwood clearly had plenty of original material to work with when he later produced a beautifully illustrated book of his own on the ruins of Yucatán and Central America. His art now became his only lifeline connecting the great labors of his past with his work in the future. His former life had all but vanished; he had learned by now the humiliating details of the trial in London and knew there could be no reconciliation with his wife. His children and his collaboration with Stephens were all that he had left.

There is no way to gauge the full psychological toll the fire had on both men, but it must have been profound. The rotunda in ruins, their shared vision of a museum vaporized, they could only hurl themselves into work on the book, and at a frenzied pace that might help blunt the loss. As devastated as Catherwood was financially and no doubt emotionally, a pall descended over the ever-resilient Stephens that was to linger and become more evident as time went on. With the dream of his museum gone, some of the curiosity, restlessness, and ambition that had driven him over the last decade began to leave him as well.

In late August he took a break from the book and traveled to Massachusetts to consult with William Prescott, who was just finishing the monumental work for which he would become famous: *The History of the Conquest of Mexico.* Prescott at the time was staying at his summer home on the Nahant peninsula north of Boston and was eager to hear firsthand about Stephens's discoveries in the Yucatán.[5] Both men were intensely interested in the origins of the pre-Conquest civilizations in Mexico and Central America. They approached the subject from different perspectives but found common ground. Fieldwork was Stephens's specialty, while Prescott was a scholar who pored over Spanish chronicles, unpublished documents, letters, and manuscripts, many of which were being extracted for the first time from the archives in Spain. He rarely traveled beyond the Boston area and had never visited Mexico. Nearly blind, he depended instead on archival researchers and individuals like Stephens and other correspondents to serve as his eyes and ears. Stephens, meanwhile, relied heavily on Prescott for background information before and after his journeys, often borrowing Spanish histories and chronicles from him.[6] They had much to discuss. From all the disparate evidence the two men had gathered, they had come to the same conclusion, the one that flatly contradicted the prevailing theories of the time: the old ruined cities were not the work of people from outside America, from the Old World or Asia, but were wholly indigenous in their origin. Stephens's latest finding in the forests of Yucatán only confirmed it for both men.

On his way back to New York, Stephens stopped in Boston for several days to visit with Dr. Cabot and his parents. Cabot's mother later wrote to her younger son that Stephens was quite anxious to get back to New York to work on his book, but it had been "delayed by fevers." Suffered by whom—could Catherwood have had another recurrence on top of everything else?—she did not say.[7]

Despite the shock of the fire and a possible return of fevers, Stephens and Catherwood worked diligently through the fall and winter, and by the end of February 1843, only eight months after their return, the two-volume work—*Incidents of Travel in Yucatán*—was ready for the printers.[8] At 937 pages, it was slightly longer than their first Central America book and it included a greater number of engravings, 120 in all. The increase was due in part to the addition of the daguerreotypes but also to the greater number of ruined sites—an extraordinary forty-four—that they had explored. And unlike the first book, Catherwood added extra landscapes and scenes unrelated to the ruins, including his dramatic image of the ladder descending into Bolonchen cave.[9]

The book also differed from the first in the amount of material Stephens added as appendices—forty-seven pages of fine print—some of which would contribute significantly to future Maya scholarship.[10] They include statistics on the Yucatán, a short architectural treatise by Catherwood, and an ornithological memorandum by Cabot.[11] But the most important addition came from Pío Pérez, the only Yucatecan Stephens met who had made a scholarly study of the Maya. This material included the first manuscript ever published that attempted to outline the historical epochs on the peninsula stretching from A.D. 144 to the Spanish Conquest, and an essay by Pérez describing Maya terminology, their numbering system, and the complicated cycles of their calendars.[12] These additions indicate the seriousness with which Stephens sought to address the subject of Maya history.

Yet Stephens had been clear from the beginning that he was not interested in writing a lengthy, scholarly tract on the origins and culture of the Maya. He could never be confined that long to his desk. As his biographer Victor von Hagen observed: "He was no dry-as-dust scholar."[13] He was by nature a storyteller and what he craved was material—"incidents," action, evidence, fieldwork—surmounting all obstacles, relaying what he found and drawing the most concise and careful conclusions he could from those discoveries. And what he found in Yucatán surprised him: a vast range of ruins scattered across the peninsula, in great variety but also with an underlying unity in art, writing, and architecture—and the abject state of the contemporary Yucatec Indians. The evidence was now overwhelming, he wrote, and it reinforced what he had only guessed at in his first book: that a highly evolved indigenous civilization had existed across Central America and the Yucatán, well before the arrival of the Spanish. And based on the physical evidence, particularly at Uxmal and Tuloom, along with his reading of Spanish chronicles, those societies appear to have existed right up to the period of the conquest.

Then he posed the question: why conclude such a civilization had been created by the ancestors of the current Indians and not by some race now gone or by colonists from the Old World? He repeated the observations made in his first book that there was nothing about these ruins that resembled those of the Old World. Then, ever the lawyer, he took on the persistent counterargument, which he summarized as follows: "A people possessing the power, art, and skill to erect such cities, never could have fallen so low as the miserable Indians who now linger about their ruins." Stephens pointed out, however, that it was entirely possible given the brutality and ruthlessness of the Spaniards in their subjugation of the Indians after the conquest. And with an ingenious twist, he noted that the dramatic transformation of the Indians was no less visible in their Spanish conquerors:

> The Indians who inhabit that country now are not more changed than their Spanish masters. We know that at the time of the conquest they were at least proud, fierce, and warlike, and poured out their blood like water to save their inheritance from the grasp of strangers. Crushed, humbled, and bowed down as they are now by generations of bitter servitude, even yet they are not more changed than the descendants of those terrible Spaniards who invaded and conquered their country. In both, all traces of the daring and warlike character of their ancestors are entirely gone. The change is radical . . . and in contemplating this change in the Indian, the loss of mere mechanical skill and art seems comparatively nothing; in fact, these perish of themselves, when, as in the case of the Indians, the school for their exercise is entirely broken up.

As for how long the stone cities existed and from whence their builders and occupants had come, Stephens was much more circumspect. It was possible the structures and monuments had been built long before the conquistadors arrived, he wrote, but he seriously doubted that the period amounted to the several thousand years posited by Waldeck, who based his estimate at least partially on the number of concentric rings in trees he found growing on the ruins. Even Stephens's earlier explorations of Copán and Palenque, with their seemingly greater antiquity, never led him to suspect they had been abandoned many centuries before the Spanish arrived. The better-preserved condition of Uxmal, Tuloom, and the other Yucatec ruins, as well as the Spanish chroniclers' descriptions of teeming populations and towering temples, combined to convince him the civilization was more recent.

But if Stephens would turn out to be wrong with his more modern dating of the Maya ruins, it was because he was unable to grasp that the cities he (and the Spanish) found in Yucatán were the last vestiges of that civilization. Modern archaeologists would eventually place the best preserved of the Yucatec ruins in what they call the Terminal and Post-Classic periods, a time long after Classic-period cities like Copán, Palenque, and other southern lowlands sites had collapsed and were abandoned. Stephens, for all his observant wanderings among the ruins, had barely cracked the mystery of the Maya.

Other historical evidence added to the confusion. There were sophisticated Indians in Mexico, called the Toltecs, who lived hundreds of years before the arrival of the Spaniards, Prescott told Stephens. He explained that they built the city of Tula near present-day Mexico City sometime around the end of the eighth century. Picking up Prescott's thread, Stephens wrote that when their empire dissolved in the tenth or eleventh century, the Toltecs may have dispersed to the south and become the "originators of that peculiar style of architecture found in Guatemala and Yucatán."[14] But this meant the Maya cities and monuments would have been no more than four to five hundred years old when the Spanish arrived. Stephens had his doubts:

> It gives them much less antiquity than that claimed by the Maya manuscript [from Pío Pérez], and, in fact much less than I should ascribe to them myself. In identifying them as the works of the ancestors of the present Indians, the cloud which hung over their origin is not removed; the time when and the

circumstances under which they were built, the rise, progress, and full development of the power, art, and skill required for their construction, are all mysteries which will not easily be unraveled. They rise like skeletons from the grave, wrapped in their burial shrouds; claiming no affinity with the works of any known people, but a distinct, independent, and separate existence.

Based on the evidence he had found, Stephens sensed but still could not scientifically grasp the separate, full-fledged Maya civilization that future archaeologists would eventually flesh out in great detail. He understood he had uncovered a "lost" civilization, but he did not have the archaeological methodology (including meticulous excavation) to determine its long history or distinguish it from the later Indian societies to the north in Mexico. Listening to Pío Pérez, he felt he had stumbled onto something unique, a civilization older and more sophisticated, separate and distinct. Time would prove him right. Yet even if he was limited in his dating and full comprehension of the ruined cities he explored, his discovery of them and his carefully reasoned conclusion that they were indigenous in origin would mark him as the acknowledged progenitor of American archaeology.

◄ The Maya ►

Copán, the first ruins explored by Stephens and Catherwood, lay at the edge of the Maya civilization.[1] To its east and south lived simple hunter-farmers, some in scattered tribal settlements of which little is now known. To its northwest, however, teemed dozens of Maya cities in the tropical lowlands of the Yucatán Peninsula. Though it was in effect the Maya's far eastern outpost, Copán had nothing of a frontier town about it. By the early eighth century A.D., it was a glorious exemplar of the Maya civilization. It had magnificent stelae, pyramids, temples and palaces, exquisite art and hieroglyphics. Occupying a fertile valley in a temperate zone, Copán had flourished through three hundred years of dynastic rule under a dozen god-kings. It was stunningly beautiful—and powerful.

On December 29, 724, one of its greatest kings, known as 18 Rabbit, installed a young lord named Cauac Sky as king of a port city twenty-five miles north on the Motagua River. Though small, the city of Quiriguá was, because of its location, vital to Copán's trade not only because of the lucrative jade route along the river down to the Gulf of Honduras but also as a link with the city-states in the Maya heartland. For many decades Quiriguá had been under Copán's control as a client state. Then, less than fourteen years after his investiture, on April 23, 738, Cauac Sky captured 18 Rabbit in a battle. Six days later the great king of Copán was beheaded by his former vassal.

The defeat was staggering. As the thirteenth ruler of Copán's long dynasty, 18 Rabbit (known also as Waxaklajuun Ub'aah

K'awill) is credited by Mayanist scholars with taking his city to its greatest heights. During his forty-three-year reign he added more to Copán's art and architecture than any previous king. He built a temple called Esmeralda, which covered the tomb of his immediate predecessor, and another that rose like a mythic mountain out of the city's east court. He directed the reconstruction of one of the Copán's largest pyramids and created the original version of the city's now-famous hieroglyphic staircase. And after remodeling Copán's ritual ball court several times, he ordered up an entirely new one, flanked by buildings covered with multicolored sculptures of the great macaw bird deity.

His greatest achievement, however, was a program of sculptural art unmatched in Maya history. During his reign, he ordered seven monumental stelae erected in the city's Great Plaza, each sculpted by Maya artists at the zenith of their imaginative genius. All of the towering stone portraits—the same monuments that had baffled Catherwood when he first tried get them down on paper—represent 18 Rabbit in different divine manifestations, covered in mythic and cosmic symbolism. The hieroglyphs carved into each contain dynastic history and dedication dates timed to celestial events and important calendar cycles. The imagery evokes patron gods, bloodletting rituals, and the Maya creation story of rebirth from the otherworld. The works are masterpieces of three-dimensional realization, deeply carved with flowers, flint blades of war, ears of corn, double-headed serpents, seashells, crocodiles, macaws, cosmic turtles, the Jaguar God, fish monsters, and other supernatural symbols. On each, 18 Rabbit holds the royal scepter of divine power and wears a headdress so extravagant and towering it takes up nearly the top third of some of the massive blocks of stone.[2]

The great king's capture and beheading was deeply demoralizing for the city of Copán. Over the next seventeen years, not another monument was erected or construction project completed. And while 18 Rabbit was later followed by four more Copán kings and a short period of revitalization, a partially

Stela representing the king 18 Rabbit at Copán. (Catherwood)

completed royal sculpture dated 822 marked Copán's end. "For a city with such a passion for sculpture," observed scholars Martin Simon and Nikolai Grube, "it is poignant and fitting that this very moment of termination should be captured in stone. The valley had seen the last of its kings."3

Long before its final king, however, and even by the time of 18 Rabbit's inglorious end, Copán had already started its decline. At its peak, the city and surrounding valley maintained a population of nearly twenty thousand—its city center was the most densely populated of all Maya kingdoms—and it was far exceed-

ing the area's agricultural carrying capacity. So much deforesta-
tion had occurred that even the valley's upper slopes had been
cleared of trees and the resulting erosion was seriously damaging
its remaining growing fields. By the middle of the eighth century, malnutrition and disease had become more and more
common. With the end of the royal dynasty in 822, the city was
a shell, empty of all but a fraction of its former population. Yet
Copán was not unique. Its demise was emblematic of what was
occurring across the Maya heartland. Incessant wars, ecological
damage, overpopulation, and finally drought were strangling the
classic Maya civilization to death.

For all of Stephens's eloquently argued conclusions about the
builders of the ruined cities that he and Catherwood had found,
it was Catherwood who provided the most penetrating insight
into the ancient civilization that had created them. Writing in a
large folio of illustrations he published after their *Yucatán* book,
he reiterated the belief, which he shared with Stephens and
Prescott, that the builders of the lost cities were the ancestors of
contemporary Indians. But he went further, decoding the ruins
through the eyes of an architect and engineer:

> It is obvious that in the construction of these stupendous works,
> at a period when the mechanical resources of facilitating labour
> were imperfectly known, immense numbers of artisans must
> have been employed . . . that there must have been a supreme,
> and probably despotic power, with authority sufficient to wield
> and direct the exertions of a subordinate population to pur-
> poses subservient to the display of civil or religious pomp and
> splendour,—that, for the sustenance of the masses of people
> thus brought into contact, a certain progress must have been
> attained in the agricultural and economic sciences,—that many
> experiments must have failed, and many attempts made, before
> the degree of proficiency in building, sculpture, and painting,
> which we now see, was reached,—and that, in a country where

only the rudest means of transmitting knowledge from one generation to another was employed, it is probable the traditionary facts acquired by experience would be preserved by a sacred caste or tribe of priests, by whom, and for whose use, many of the buildings were undoubtedly erected.

The next 170 years of discovery, excavation, and research would prove each of Catherwood's observations prophetically on point. The prerequisites he outlined were known about ancient Old World civilizations, most notably Egypt's, which he and Stephens had studied firsthand in the rich agricultural lands bordering the Nile. What would turn out most striking, however, about the civilization created by the Maya was how improbable it was that it had emerged at all—rising on thin topsoils in dimly lit rain forests—and that it had reached the heights of refinement that it did.

For example, as early civilizations go, the Maya had few of the material and technological advantages found in Old World civilizations. First, unlike those societies, the Maya had no large domesticated animals and thus lacked not only the dietary protein they provided but the muscle power they brought to plowing, grinding, and transport. Second, archaeologists have found no evidence the Maya ever developed and used one of the most basic forms of technology: the wheel. Though they understood the concept (remains of wheeled toys have been found), they never employed pulleys or potter's wheels, carts and wagons, even though they built long, flat causeways on which they could easily have rolled. And finally, the Maya never developed the use of metal except in rare instances for personal ornamentation. Their tools (and weapons) were limited to bone, wood, sharp volcanic glass like obsidian, and hard rock like chert and flint.[4]Nonetheless, the Maya created a civilization of material and cultural sophistication at least the equal of those found in Egypt, Mesopotamia, and early Greece. How did they do it? How, asked scholars and archaeologists, could they have raised great city-states in the midst of the jungle and filled them with grand monumental architecture and art without the basic tools available to ancient Old World cultures?

In their two expeditions, Stephens and Catherwood's itineraries had taken them in a circle around what would later prove to be the core of the Classic Maya civilization: the dense lowland forests of the Petén, today the northernmost province of Guatemala. Remarkably, however, they had surveyed two of the greatest "golden age" Maya cities, Copán on the eastern fringe of the heartland and Palenque on its western perimeter. In between, waiting to be discovered, were more than sixty Maya cities and settlements from pre-Classic and Classic times—800 B.C. to A.D. 950—buried in a jungle no larger in square miles than the small U.S. state of Maryland. It was within this circumscribed, agriculturally unpromising environment that the Maya thrived, eventually growing east into today's Belize, west into Chiapas, and northward into the dry northern reaches of the Yucatán Peninsula to build Uxmal and Chichén Itzá, Labna, Kabah, and Tulum.

Agriculture presented their first fundamental challenge. Instead of rich cereal grains like wheat and barley, common in Eurasia but unknown in the Americas, the chief staple of the Maya was corn (maize), a protein-poor plant that Mesoamerican people selectively bred over thousands of years from a wild grass.[5] In the Petén the Maya faced severe seasonal rainfall, swamplands, long dry seasons, dense forest, and soils that in many places only thinly covered the limestone bedrock of the Yucatán Peninsula. To adapt, they alternated crops, fertilized their cornfields with the ash of burnt depleted stalks and rich muck from the swamps; they constructed raised growing beds in wetlands, stored and channeled water, and terraced slopes to capture silt. They carefully shifted and scattered crops under the canopies of thinned stands of protective rain forest, and kept household gardens of native avocados, papayas, and guava. They set aside fallow zones and grasslands for the hunting of deer, wild boar, tapir, and peccary to provide protein for their diets.[6]

By the tenth century B.C., family and tribal plots were producing enough corn and beans, peppers and squash to form a complete diet. The population began to increase quickly, hamlets grew into larger settlements and small chiefdoms, and the stage was set: enough of the populace was released from constant demands of farming and hunting to create the first stirrings of civilization—much as Catherwood had projected.[7]

Archaeological evidence now shows that the cradle of this civilization formed in a place known today as the Mirador Basin in northern Petén. Two key centers appear to have sprung up in a surprisingly short period of time, Nakbe and El Mirador, located eight miles apart and connected by a causeway made of crushed limestone. While Nakbe is now considered the oldest Maya ceremonial center and dates from about 800 B.C., El Mirador grew into one of the largest urban complexes in the world at the time, with a population by 200 B.C. estimated at between 60,000 to possibly well over 100,000 people. Its immense man-made platforms, bordering shallow lakes called *bajos*, supported palaces, pyramids, and temples, including a single architectural complex still considered among the most massive in the world, reaching 230 feet, or the height of an eighteen-story building. Constructed on multilevel terraces with millions of cubic meters of fill, the city's plazas and ceremonial structures were covered in plaster and coated in red paint made from cinnabar, along with yellows, blues, and greens. With up to a thousand surrounding structures and house mounds, the site covered seven to ten square miles. In addition to its central precincts, six causeways radiated out through the jungle to nearby smaller centers, one causeway measuring eighteen miles in length. These remarkable ancient thoroughfares, some still visible from the air today, rose from the swamps and forest floor ten or more feet in places, with widths of thirty to sixty feet. The superstructures in El Mirador were also planned: the temples are carefully aligned with the constellation Orion and are arranged in triadic patterns representing the three hearthstones in the Maya creation myth.

On discovering these two cities in 1960s through the 1990s, archaeologists were stunned. Here was material proof that an advanced civilization had sprung forth with amazing speed and much earlier than they had ever thought. They could only speculate at the social organization and the millions of man-hours of labor required to build a city as extraordinary as El Mirador. With its hundreds of structures, monumental architecture, and causeways, El Mirador has been described by one of its principal researchers, Richard Hansen, as the first well-defined political state in the Western Hemisphere.[8]

Though highly evolved, these first cities did not arise from the jungle fully formed and without assistance. Even though the Maya lived deep within the Petén, they were still in contact with surrounding Mesoamerican populations and cultures, some of which were also advanced. One of the most developed, the Olmec, flourished between 1200 and 350 B.C. along the Gulf coast near the modern-day Mexican states of Veracruz and Tabasco. During the culture's height, the Olmec constructed several large settlements complete with rudimentary ceremonial centers, earthen mounds, stylized pottery, and sculpture that included gigantic heads carved from volcanic rock. More important, there is some evidence, though not conclusive, that the Olmec created a so-called long-count calendar system, early logographic writing, the Mesoamerican ball game, and bloodletting rituals, all of which would become vital elements of Maya civilization. After the Olmec disappeared by 350 B.C., their influence continued to spread widely through other population groups, some with Maya roots located south of the Petén in the Guatemala highlands and along the Pacific coast.

Thus, following centuries of gradual agricultural development, the Maya civilization evolved rapidly from 800 to 200 B.C.—a precipitous ascent due in part to two abundant resources surrounding them and beneath their feet: wood and limestone.

First, the most significant innovation in the Maya's diet resulted from the immersion of corn kernels in water mixed with burnt-lime powder. The procedure began with the burning of limestone blocks on huge pyres of wood to reduce the stone to powder. Then the corn was soaked in the lime powder solution, a procedure called *nixtamalization,* which breaks down the walls of the kernels, frees calcium, lysine, and tryptophan, and greatly boosts corn's nutritional value and taste.[9] The resulting dough or masa was then easily worked into food staples like tortillas, a mainstay in the Maya Indian diet even today.

Second, when limestone was quarried (with stone tools) into blocks for use in architecture, the Maya discovered that burning large fragments—employing the same process used in the preparation of corn—also yielded a construction material essential for building structures on a grand scale. They combined the burnt-lime powder with water and fragments of mudstone, called marl, and produced a cement of tremendous strength. They also mixed the lime powder with water and binding agents such as sap from trees to create a light cream-colored plaster of great durability.[10] The plaster was then applied as stucco to create smooth surfaces over their stone temples and palaces, and to fashion sculptural art such as the colorfully painted zoomorphic faces of Maya deities that decorated their façades. One such mask at Nakbe measures sixteen feet high by thirty-five feet wide.[11] These innovative practices, as Catherwood had noted, no doubt took centuries of trial and error, failure and success.

By 200 B.C., most of the material components that would come to characterize Maya civilization, particularly its art and architecture, were in place. But there were essential cultural elements already at work as well. Digging near El Mirador in 2001, archaeologists uncovered a set of ruins, now known as San Bartolo, and found a stunning mural stretching across four walls of a buried vault. The vivid painting displays gods from the Maya's complex creation story, the mythological basis of a worldview that would bind and carry the Maya through the next millennium of their civilization. The well-preserved mural, intricately painted in black, red, yellow, orange, and blue, shows five gods next to the five sacred trees that in Maya mythology hold up the sky from the earth. It also includes images of the maize god, the deity at the center of the Maya's belief system, and royal lords practicing genital piercing, a ritual blood sacrifice symbolizing regeneration. The maize god also presides over the coronation of a king, the first visual portrayal so far found of the concept of divine right of kingship. Carbon dating has determined the paintings were made around 100 B.C., making them the oldest paintings yet found. The mural provided the first evidence that by that date the mythic gods had become intertwined and expropriated by Maya kings.

Also discovered at the site is the one of oldest known royal tombs, dating from 150 B.C., further evidence of the establishment of divine kingship, the central political principle that would govern all future Maya city-states. The archaeologists dug deeper and found a stone block painted with a hieroglyphic text believed to be the earliest identifiable Maya writing, carbon-dated from between 200 and 300 B.C.. One of the oldest ball courts, in which the Maya played ritual ball games, was also uncovered and may have been constructed as early as 600 B.C.. These recent finds at San Bartolo and the Mirador Basin have pushed back previous datings of the Maya civilization by hundreds of years. They have also blurred the lines between the pre-Classic (1800 B.C.–A.D. 150) and the Classic (A.D. 350–900) epochs, the broad categories archaeologists assigned the Maya civilization decades ago.

Indeed, in many ways, El Mirador and San Bartolo were more evolved than many classic Maya sites that developed hundreds of years later. Suddenly, however, a mysterious rupture in the Maya's development in the Mirador Basin occurred. Around A.D. 150 the cities of Nakbe and El Mirador and many of the surrounding centers were abandoned, and for many of the same reasons, archaeologists now believe, that the Classic-era Maya civilization would dissolve eight hundred years later.

Within a century of the Mirador collapse, however, the Maya were on the rise again. Dozens of small centers throughout the Petén began to grow in power and sophistication, initiating the first phase of a 650-year "golden age" that, according to archaeologist Michael Coe, "reached intellectual and artistic heights no others in the New World, and few in Europe, could match at that time."[12] And while the cosmology and belief in sacred royal power illustrated by the San Bartolo murals would unify the civilization, its political expression took the form of scores of independent kingdoms scattered across the lowlands, some of which would become the great city-states of Tikal, Calakmul, Caracol, Palenque, and Copán.

Belief in the supernatural and ancestor worship infused every aspect of Maya life, from the offerings of farmers to the rain god Chaac, to meticulously staged rituals played out before thousands gathered in plazas during temple dedication ceremonies or the investiture of their rulers. Pyramids, temples, sculpture, and art were created as statecraft to legitimize the royal lines. The kings themselves served as shamanistic intermediaries, the divine "vessel" and "axes of the universe," between the people and the gods.[13,14,15] Dressed in elaborate costumes and feathered headdresses, covered with jade pendants and earrings, they performed ritual dances on temple platforms to the accompaniment of flutes, drums, and trumpets, and engaged in self-mutilation, piercing their genitals with obsidian blades or stingray spines and running ropes through their tongues to summon the gods and regenerate the world with their blood.

With the rise of more and more separate city-states, conflict became inevitable. Maya kings, however, unlike our leaders, went into battle with their warriors, often carried on litters. In the early Classic period the wars were launched not for territorial gain but to capture the high nobles of the enemy, with the opposing king the ultimate prize. Each side carried royal battle standards and shields that they believed were invested with the spirits of their war gods, symbolized by animals such as serpents, jaguars, and owls. The earthly battles were fought on the supernatural plane as well, and a loss by the defeated king was considered a humiliating spiritual failure, and at times resulted in ruin for his entire kingdom.

As David Freidel, Linda Schele, and Joy Parker described in their book, *Maya Cosmos*:

Maya kings and their noble vassals put not only their bodies but also their souls in jeopardy every time they clashed. It is no exaggeration to say that they lived for those moments of truth, those trials of the strength of their spirits. Every major political activity in their lives—the dedication of every public text, image, and building of royal and community importance—required the capture and sacrifice of rival peers. Only in this way could the proper rituals of sanctification be fulfilled, the gods nourished, and the portals of communication opened between the human and the divine.[16]

Captured nobles and their kings were sacrificed by the victors following ritual ball games (captured common soldiers often became slaves). Virtually every Maya center of any size had a ball court—a long alley set between two sloping parallel walls open at both ends. The game was played with a large, hard rubber ball. The ball courts were considered a portal through which the Maya interacted with the spirit world; the games were ritual re-creations of the Maya creation story, in which humans, represented by mythological "Hero Twins," had defeated the underworld lords of death in a ball game. Scholars studying Maya art and inscriptions believe that the ball games, as ritual battles between good and evil, were used as reenactments of the defeat and capture of the rival lords, in which the captives were again defeated and then beheaded.[17,18]

Human sacrifice took other forms as well in the veneration and deification of the Maya lords. Archaeologists have found skeletons, sometimes of adolescents and children, buried in royal tombs beside their kings, a practice also found in Egypt, where retainers were sacrificed to continue to serve the pharaohs in the afterlife.

Every war, festival to the gods, temple dedication, and coronation was timed to important dates in the complex Maya calendar, reflecting the culture's obsession with time. The scribes kept the calendars and recorded the movement of the sun, moon, and stars, keeping track with 260-day and 52-year cycles along with the solar year. They were able to predict celestial events and eclipses with great accuracy. They also refined and perfected a second ancient Mesoamerican calendar called the "long count." It recorded a great cycle of time, restarting every 5,126 years to celebrate the continual re-creation of the universe. Long-count dates are commonly found with hieroglyphic inscriptions on monuments and paintings. And since Mayanist scholars now have broken the hieroglyphic code and worked out the correlation between the long count and our Gregorian calendar, they are now able to determine to the exact day when events occurred and to put together entire historical records of the Maya kings and queens and their dynasties.

By at least A.D. 300 the scribes had perfected writing, crucial to the transfer of knowledge between generations, as Catherwood noted, but also essential in the Maya world to establish sacred royal lineage and to legitimize the elites' authority. Their hieroglyphic inscriptions were the only true writing system in the pre-Columbian Americas, which meant the Mayan language could be transcribed phonetically as spoken, as well as through logograms or symbols for whole words or names. More than a thousand years later the Aztecs and Incas, for example, had not developed a system of phonetic writing (a transcription system common in the West today in alphabetic form). Experts estimate that thousands of Maya texts were written in accordion-like books made of pounded bark paper that have since perished in the tropical climate of the lowlands.[19] But the Maya left behind enough of their history chiseled in stone and painted on pottery and murals that scholars have been able to piece together the stories of individual kings and queens, the weak and the powerful, the rise and fall of the city-states, political intrigue, alliances, and wars.

We know now, for example, that on January 31, A.D. 378, a lord named Fire Born (Siyaj K'ak') arrived at the already powerful city of Tikal, undoubtedly accompanied by warriors, and established a new dynasty with strong if not direct ties to the dominant city in Mesoamerica at the time, Teotihuacán, located

Maya scribe god holding paint brush, drawn on a clay vessel.

in central Mexico. On the same day, the seventh ruler of the old
Tikal dynasty met his death, either in battle or possibly by sacri-
ficial beheading. For the next half century, Teotihuacán would
hold sway over not only Tikal but a large swath of central lowland kingdoms as well.[20]

Teotihuacán's influence stretched all the way to the Maya's
southeastern frontier, where a lord named Great Sun First Quetzal Macaw (K'inich Yax K'uk' Mo') arrived in A.D. 427 at the
pre-Classic settlement that would become Copán. If not Mexican himself, he brought with him many of the trappings and
artistic symbols of the Teotihuacán culture, probably from Tikal.
He went on to found the dynasty in Copán that would last seventeen generations.[21] Stephens and Catherwood would later
stand before a large square altar in the Copán forest that was
wrapped with the sculpted figures of sixteen of the seventeen
holy rulers. Yax K'uk Mo', the founder, is shown handing off the
scepter of power to Copán's penultimate ruler, who dedicated
the monument in A.D. 776. Though unaware of their signifi-

Altar to the sixteen kings of Copán. (Catherwood)

cance, Catherwood made sure he captured the figures on all four sides of the altar and the rows of glyphs engraved on its top.

Eventually, the Maya would reassert political control by slowly absorbing the foreigners into their society, most likely through marriage. But some artistic styles and other influences from Teotihuacán, with its powerful cult of the warrior, its militaristic symbols and gods, would enter Maya culture and linger for centuries.

The inscriptions also tell the story of the great rivalry between two of the largest and most formidable of the Maya kingdoms, Tikal, at the center of the Petén, and its giant northern neighbor, Calakmul, located in today's Mexican state of Campeche. Both had developed into regional superpowers through alliances with smaller cities or by binding them as vassal states. The sixth and seventh centuries saw a succession of wars between the two giants as well as their satellite cities. First Tikal suffered major military defeats in 562 and 657, a period when the once-great city went into steep decline. Then on August 5, 695, Tikal exacted its revenge when its ruler Lord That Clears the Sky (Jasaw Chan K'awiil) delivered a decisive military victory over the king of Calakmul, marking the resurgence of Tikal and a gradual end of Calakmul's dominion over a large number of lowland cities. It appears from the inscriptions that at least one of Tikal's kings lost his head in the earlier wars, possibly in a ball court sacrifice. Whether Calakmul's king, Fiery Claw (Yuknoom Yich'aak K'ak'), was taken captive during Tikal's victory and was sacrificed is not clear. What is known is that a battle effigy representing one of Calakmul's great gods was seized along with two important Calakmul lords. In November 695, three months after the defeat, a new ruler named Split Earth took the throne in Calakmul, likely installed by Tikal.[22,23]

Stephens and Catherwood had no way of knowing, when they surveyed Copán and Palenque, that each city's king had also suffered ignominious defeat. In fact in Copán's case, during his lone visit to Quiriguá, Catherwood saw tangible evidence of Copán's defeat not comprehending its significance. Quiriguá's king, Cauac Sky, enriched by his victory over Copán in 738, had gone on a building spree and reconstructed Quiriguá's acropolis. Then, with the intention of not just emulating but surpassing his former overlord, 18 Rabbit, he set about creating a series of the tallest and most massive stelae in the Maya world—each sculpted in his image no doubt by captive Copán artists. Catherwood sketched two of them, including one now known as Stela F, which stands twenty-four feet tall and weighs thirty tons.[24]

Palenque and its southern neighbor Toniná were also both cloaked in mystery when Stephens and Catherwood visited them in 1840. But as more and more art and inscriptions have been unearthed and interpreted by epigraphers, or glyph experts, a fractious and violent history between the two rival states has emerged, one that resembles to a small extent the ancient Gre-

Gigantic stela representing the king Cauac Sky at Quiriguá. (Photo by Alfred Maudslay)

cian wars between Athens and Sparta. While Palenque's kings (Athens) worked for centuries to create one of the most artistically and architecturally beautiful cities in the Maya world, the smaller Toniná (Sparta) was using its energy and talents to become a military force to be reckoned with. One of Toniná's chief sculptural programs focused on depictions of bound prisoners, some of which are arrayed on one of Toniná's two ball courts. They represent captured rulers of obscure outlying centers over which Toniná and Palenque were fighting for control, and presumably the ball court was where they met their end.

Despite its seeming preoccupation with art over war, Palenque nevertheless exerted powerful military and economic influence over Maya cities to the east. And in September 687 it drove south, attacked, and overwhelmed Toniná. Though the record is unclear, indications are that Toniná's king, known only as Ruler Two, was captured and likely beheaded in Palenque's ball court. The struggle between the two cities continued for another twenty-four years. Finally, in 711, Toniná struck back, entering the heart of Palenque's sacred precincts and seizing the city's sixty-six-year-old king, Precious Yellow Tied Peccary (K'an Joy Chitam II). Though his exact fate has not been recorded, a gracefully engraved sandstone panel found at Toniná shows him crouching with his arms bound and the paper strips worn by the condemned threaded through his earlobes. The defeat was a crushing blow, for it left Palenque with a ten-year dynastic gap before a new king ascended to the throne.[25]

○◎○

All was not war, however, and during intervening periods of peace, Maya rulers, their families, and nobles flourished. The common people may have prospered as well, especially if they were able to share in some spoils of war. Soldiers, for example, were able to take lower-class captives as slaves. But the lives of the non-elites were never easy. They worked the milpas, or cornfields, that provided food for their families and the elite, and during the off-season developed crafts or were conscripted in corvées that built their city's causeways, public spaces, and ceremonial centers. During war they were pressed into service as common soldiers.

Because Maya art and inscriptions were exclusively the domain of the elite, little was depicted of the daily life of the lower classes. We know about their food, grinding stones, and cooking from excavations, their nutritional levels from examinations of their bones, their degree of "wealth" from pottery sherds and crude ornaments, small figurines uncovered in the remains of their dwellings. If they show up in painted murals or vases at all, it is as war captives or court servants. Unlike the elaborate costumes worn by their lords, their dress was simple, men in white cotton loincloths, sometimes wearing a cloak for warmth,

Bas relief of a king at court in Yaxchilan with captive below.

and women in white sacklike shifts. The men kept their hair long and tightly braided, usually pulled back and bound or wrapped around their heads. Women's hair was also worn long in a variety of styles. Simple deer-hide sandals with hemp straps protected their feet (the elite wore a range of intricate bindings) and if a commoner could afford it, they added anklets, wristlets, and necklaces of shells or animal teeth. Both sexes decorated themselves with nose plugs and earrings of bone or wood. According to histories recounted to Spanish chroniclers after the conquest, lower-class marriages were monogamous.

The non-elites' residences were huts constructed with wood poles, dried mud walls, and roofs woven with thatch. The structures were usually built on raised mounds around family court-yards (as many of today's millions of Maya Indians still live).[26] And when they weren't working in the fields, household gardens, or on civic projects, they took their crafts and any surplus food to marketplaces for barter.

The same household clusters were replicated on all levels of society, with courtiers, scribes, and artists living around family courtyards but in larger structures, made of stone with stone-corbeled roofs, finely plastered floors, artifacts of jade, pottery, and sculpture. At every level ancestors and family dead were venerated and believed to be intercessors with the spirit world. Shrines were often found in family courtyards. The bodies of the dead, elite and common people alike, were buried below their dwellings, sometimes, for nobles, in rich tombs. Kings and queens were entombed beneath the pyramids and temple complexes. The household clusters spread out from the city's sacred and civic core in unplanned fashion, often to satellite centers, and as the density of the population thinned, the growing and hunting fields filled the uninhabited spaces.

For the ruling classes, especially the kings, a great deal is known because of the record left in Maya art and hieroglyphs. We know the holy lords lived polygamous lives surrounded by wives and courtiers in royal palaces. They sat on thrones covered with jaguar pelts, commanding their subjects, dispensing justice, and greeting emissaries, royal allies, and foreign merchants. In scenes chiseled into limestone and sandstone, on painted murals and polychrome pottery, they wear finely dyed textiles with geometric designs and flamboyant headdresses heavy with the long iridescent feathers of the quetzal and other tropical birds. They drink a frothy brew made from the cacao bean (and gave the world chocolate). They prized exotic goods brought from the coasts and the mountains in trade or tribute: marine shells, stingray spines, coral, finely cut chert, obsidian, pyrite polished into mosaic scepters and mirrors—and, most of all, jade from the Motagua Valley and its surrounding mountains. Control and display of these prized goods reinforced their status and power.

But nothing demonstrated their supremacy like their ability to mobilize mass labor forces, corps of engineers, artisans, and artists, to build and embellish monumental centers devoted to their reigns and dynasties. Though the ceremonial complexes played a ritualistic role in the Maya's interaction with the gods, in the end they were dedicated and inscribed to the divine kings and queens who lay buried beneath. The building projects increased in size, scope, and beauty through the Classic era and each passing century required more and more investment of resources and human labor.

The Maya lords were never satisfied. Each generation commissioned new monuments and pyramids, building one new acropolis on top of another, burying layer on layer of Maya history. Archaeologists tunneling into structures have found the remnants of the early pyramids and temples, some completely intact. The dedication of each new stratum of royal self-aggrandizement was always timed to important calendar cycles and played out by the kings in age-old, operatic rituals—human sacrifice and genital piercings. Each new cycle of construction yielded ever more refined and exquisite art. Artists, like the scribes, were esteemed by the kings, whose second and third sons sometimes joined their ranks.

By the end of the eighth century the population in the Petén—its inhabitants numbering in the millions—had reached its peak.[27] Cities, even those small in scale, overflowed with extraordinary art. Important centers with such names as Dos Pilas, Piedras Negras, Naranjo, Seibal, Cancuén, Yaxhá, Bonampak, Altar de Sacrificios, Yaxchilan, and dozens more filled the landscape. The Maya had achieved such success that its civilization, which had so brilliantly adapted to the rain forests for more than a millennium, was now living beyond its means. Newer cities in north—Uxmal, Kabah, Sayil, Chichén Itzá—began to swell in stature and population, fed by immigrants from the south.

In the Maya heartland, royal excess had taken its toll. Vast sections of the protective forests had been devoured to produce more and more plaster and cement. The lower classes scavenged for wood to cook their food and in some places scoured nearly every inch of arable land for growing fields. Wars increased in number and intensity and became almost continuous in certain regions. Burgeoning ranks of nobles—many of them heirs and relatives of the polygamous kings—formed kingdoms of their own and now fought each other for space and power. No longer limiting battles to the ritual capture of rivals, the lords went to war over land, trade routes, and for tribute or sheer domination over competitors. Increasingly, defensive walls and fortifications were erected around cities and even small hamlets.

By the first decades of the ninth century, the Maya lords were losing their hold on their people. Military defeats had shattered their aura of infallibility, devastated their cities, and set in motion large-scale emigration that depopulated their kingdoms and put great strains on neighboring areas. The kings' intercessions with the gods were no longer working. Then long periods of drought, the worst in hundreds of years, deepened the crisis. One such drought started in 810 and lasted nearly a decade, corresponding closely with the abandonment of a number of Maya cities, including Palenque.[28]

The political and spiritual authority of divine kingship, the unifying force that had created and sustained the Maya civilization for more than a millennium, was dissolving. Ever-larger pyramids, theatrical pageants and ritual events, even distracting wars and ball court sacrifices, were no match against forced emigrations, drought, and famine. And one by one, the great cities of the Maya heartland emptied out.

The so-called collapse of the Maya civilization did not happen overnight or in all places at the same time. Cities like Tikal and Calakmul, perhaps because of their great size, hung on to some form of weakened kingship for decades, even in the face of another major drought in 860. Toniná, a late survivor possibly due to its military prowess, recorded the last known "long count" inscription on the back of a stela—January 18, 909. The reasons for the demise of each city were multiple and complex and are still a subject of contention among archaeologists. Overpopulation, environmental degradations, and drought, followed by famine and disease, created a "perfect storm" to bring down the great lords and their kingdoms. By the end of the ninth century, the holy lords and their courtiers, scribes and the remarkable artists in the Maya heartland were gone. Finally, only squatters eked out a subsistence living among the remains of the once-great cities.

Remarkably, despite the severe droughts—another occurred in 910—Maya cities to the north, including the two greatest visited by Stephens and Catherwood, Uxmal and Chichén Itzá, were able to continue on due probably to accessible groundwater through cenotes and better-engineered reservoir systems. But by the middle of tenth century, following the death of one of Uxmal's greatest builders, Lord Chak (Chan-Chak-K'ak'nal-Ahaw), all monumental construction ceased at Uxmal and it too was in decline.[29] Chichén Itzá would hang on for another 250 years.

Chichén Itzá remains one of the last great mysteries of the Maya civilization. There is no clear consensus among Mayanist scholars on exactly where the so-call Itzá Maya came from and how much they were influenced by the Toltec, a militaristic society based in central Mexico. Some experts are convinced Toltec invaders took over Chichén Itzá, while others believe the Itzás' proximity to the Gulf of Mexico had simply made them a true international state that exchanged and incorporated influences from across the region. There is no question, however, that the city is filled with militaristic motifs, feathered serpent symbolism, and distinctive architecture associated with Toltec.

Stephens sensed Chichén Itzá was different. He described its mix of structures, some similar to the mosaic-covered Maya buildings they had seen in Uxmal and cities to the south, and others, though well preserved, seemingly older, "ruder," and not so elaborately ornamented. In these, what he was seeing was more simplistic but in fact more modern: warlike Toltec symbolism overlaying the final flowering of the Maya civilization.

Stephens and Catherwood, though keenly observant and prescient, still were unable to fathom what they had found in their journeys through Central America, Mexico, and Yucatán. Chichén Itzá, and especially Tulum, were the most modern, Copán and Palenque among the oldest. Stephen never felt he could accurately date them, but observed: "These cities were, of course, not all built at one time, and are the remains of different epochs." What the two men never imagined was just how far into the past those epochs stretched. What they had discovered was the last generation, the final layer of fluorescence of the Classic and post–Classic Maya civilization—the ultimate, artistically dazzling veneer of a civilization, archaeologists would find, extending back through time nearly two thousand years.

PART FOUR

Friends

◁ 22 ▷

Views of Ancient Monuments

Stephens and Catherwood's *Incidents of Travel in Yucatán* drew rapturous reviews, though by the time the critics' articles came out the book was already a huge popular success. Some reviewers pointed out that the book was so eagerly anticipated, and so many copies had been bought before they had a chance to comment, that they were at a loss about what they could say that readers did not already know. One commentator groaned:

> Who has not curiously scanned the multitudinous engravings in which the skill of Catherwood and the marvelous fidelity of the daguerreotype have given perpetuity, in representation at least, to those magnificent relics of ancient American architecture and art which the terrible energy of tropical vegetation is hurrying so rapidly to destruction? Who has not accompanied the adventurous author and his companions through all the dangers and privations of their devious route among crumbling ruins, underground vaults, caves, ranchos, desert islands, convents, haciendas, casas reales, fleas, moschetoes, garraputas, wild Indians, luxurious padres, bischos, black-eyed senoritas, tunlers, gamblers, smugglers, black ants and revolutions? . . . Oh that Stephens had lived and written his book a hundred and fifty odd years ago! That we, with patient research and gainful good fortune, might resuscitate him, as it were, and give knowledge of his rich treasures to the forgetting million.[1]

The *Knickerbocker* magazine went so far as to declare that "his volumes on Yucatán will take their stand, at once, as among the foremost achievements of American literature, not only in the estimation of his own countrymen, but in that of the enlightened world."[2] Stephens and Catherwood were acclaimed, famous. An English edition had already gone through 2,500 copies and it was reported that Queen Victoria was "among Stephen's enthusiastic readers." *Yucatán* would eventually be translated into six languages. As Harper & Brothers' best-selling author, Stephens was able to command the best possible publishing agreement.[3]

While the book ran through edition after edition, Stephens turned his attention to Catherwood. Unlike their first journey in 1839, no record exists of the monetary arrangement the two men made for the Yucatán trip. Yet Catherwood was suffering financially from the loss of his rotunda, so he and Stephens conceived of a project they hoped would help get him back on his feet. Over the preceding decade, an ornithologist-artist named John James Audubon had produced a set of giant prints under the title *Birds of America*, which won him great celebrity on both sides of the Atlantic. Sparing no expense to achieve the highest-quality reproductions, Audubon had financed the expensive project through exhibitions and advanced subscriptions.[4] With Catherwood's portfolio bulging from their two expeditions, Stephens reasoned that they might be able to do something similar. Money for Catherwood was certainly a large part of the motivation. But Stephens also felt that the small black-and-white, page-size engravings in their books had not come close to doing justice to Catherwood's enormous talents.

He laid out the ambitious plan in a long letter to William H. Prescott in late March 1843, accompanied by a copy of his just-published *Yucatán* book.[5] He had obviously given considerable thought to the idea for he calculated they would need 900 subscribers—libraries, learned societies, and wealthy individuals—each willing to pay $100 in advance to cover the expense of the oversize work. He told Prescott there would be up to 120 illustrations printed in large-scale "folio" in four quarterly volumes, which would be "creditable to the country as a work of art." Accompanying the images would be monographs in English and French by four eminent authorities, including Alexander von Humboldt and Prescott himself if he would agree to it.[6] Stephens added that he expected no gain for himself. "Nine hundred subscribers will save me from loss, which is all I care for," he told Prescott. The historian replied four days later that he would be pleased to contribute to the "noble" project.[7]

Raising that large a sum in subscriptions, however, was a daunting mission. Yet Stephens was optimistic. With the publication of *Yucatán*, he and Catherwood were the shining lights of New York City. The high point came in the May meeting of the New-York Historical Society. As a member of the executive committee, Stephens arranged for an exhibit of twelve of Catherwood's full-size illustrations, which drew lavish praise from society members.[8] No money was solicited; Stephens asked only for approval of a resolution allowing him to publish the folio under the "auspices" of the society. Several members urged passage of the resolution, one noting that the project "will have important bearing upon the character and reputation of our country," adding somewhat smugly that "Europeans have at present little access to anything coming from the Western hemisphere." The resolution passed unanimously.[9]

When it came to actually raising the money, however, the subscription campaign began to falter. The Harper brothers stepped forward and offered to publish if only three hundred subscribers could be found. Catherwood, meanwhile, followed the lead of Audubon and took his small exhibition on the road, organizing showings to solicit subscribers in Boston in June and probably in Philadelphia as well.[10] But Stephens and Catherwood had miscalculated. Due to the project's grandiose ambition and cost—and no doubt because demand was tempered by so much of the material already appearing in their *Yucatán* and *Central America* books—the project failed to bring in a sufficient number of subscribers.[11]

Frustrated by the failure, Catherwood left for London in July to try his luck there. Prescott drafted a letter of introduction for him to his friend Edward Everett, the U.S. ambassador to England. "A literary project of some magnitude is set on foot here by Messrs. Stephens and Catherwood," he said, referring Everett to the "magnificent drawings made by Mr. Catherwood."[12] Despite Everett's endorsement, however, Catherwood failed soon after arriving to get an audience with Queen Victoria and Prince Albert. He also had little luck with London publishers. England was in the midst of an economic depression and reeling from a humiliating defeat of its army in Afghanistan. Catherwood wrote Prescott in August: "It would seem nowadays that nothing is successful here with the rich and aristocratic without the patronage and sanction of royalty which ill accords with my loco foco notions." (The term *loco foco* refers to the radical working-class faction of the Democratic Party then active in New York.)[13] Catherwood put his political inclinations aside, however, and a short time later "had the honor"—according to the *Times* of London—of submitting some of his drawings to Prince Albert and visiting French royalty.[14] Whether they agreed to help him financially is not clear.

He was back at 21 Charles Square, which was still home to his brother Dr. Alfred Catherwood and their unmarried sister, Caroline. It was his first visit since his confrontation with his wife nearly two years earlier. There is no mention in his correspondence of his children, but they were apparently living in London with his family. Nor are there any surviving records concerning his wife, who presumably was still living with his cousin.

In December, he wrote Prescott that he had gotten hold of a copy of the historian's just-published book, *The Conquest of Mexico*. "I devoured it as I have formerly done a new and interesting novel," he wrote, "not leaving off until I had finished." But it is clear from the letter that the grand project he and Stephens envisioned had again collapsed for lack of subscriptions. He explained that he now planned to publish on his own a limited set of large-scale tinted and colored illustrations. "I am grateful for the mention of my name in [*Conquest*]," he continued, "and I have taken the liberty of sending you a few proofs of my work through Mr. Stephens. Mr. Stephens has kindly offered to write an introduction and the descriptions, but I fear they will scarcely be in time, as I am endeavoring to get out by the beginning of March."[15] Unfortunately, none of his correspondence with Stephens has survived.

In February 1844, Catherwood met with colleagues at the Royal

Institute of British Architects, where he exhibited his drawings and read a paper on the "antiquities of Central America." It was a nuts-and-bolts session in which he talked about the ancient Mayans' "perfect knowledge of stone cutting . . . various kinds of mortar, stuccoes, and cements." He also went into detail also about the unusual "Mayan arch," which he likened to that used by the Greeks, Egyptians, and ancient Etruscans, who had not yet developed the so-called Roman arch. "[Central American builders] were, in fact, so far as the mechanical part went, accomplished masons," he said. "Large masses of excellent concrete are found in many of their buildings." He explained also that he was greatly impressed with the painting he saw on the interior walls of some of the ruins, particularly in Chichén Itzá. "Their painting is indeed superior both to their architecture and sculpture and they went even beyond the Egyptians in the blending of colors, approaching more nearly to the paintings found at Pompeii and Herculaneum."[16]

He did not make his March deadline, but he may have achieved a more polished result because of the delay. His "imperial folios" (21x14¼ inches) appeared in late April 1844 under the title *Views of Ancient Monuments in Central America, Chiapas and Yucatán*.[17] The oversize books included a twenty-two-page introduction written by Catherwood and twenty-five extraordinary illustrations along with a map tracing all of the ruins he and Stephens had explored. He had hired the finest lithographers in England to engrave the work. In all, only three hundred were produced, at great cost, in London and New York. In 250 of the volumes the lithographs were tinted in browns, blues, and grays. Fifty were hand colored. Catherwood spared no expense in his pursuit of quality and perfection, hiring Owen Jones, a close friend and one of England's foremost visual designers, to create an elaborate multicolored frontispiece. Jones also printed the London edition.[18] Though the book contained only about a fifth of the illustrations proposed in the original plan, the project nonetheless cost a small fortune. How Catherwood was able to carry it off remains a mystery.[19]

Along with his introduction, Catherwood wrote descriptive text for each illustration. His introduction summarized much of the

ground Stephens had covered but he included the list of prerequisites he believed had been necessary for the Maya civilization to develop. He expressed himself most eloquently with his art, however, and the illustrated plates in his folio are masterworks. Here he is unbound from the small black-and-white engravings of Stephens's books. His use of lighting and contrast remains extraordinary but with the addition of color, the images spring to life. It is the work of a perfectionist yet one who has escaped the monk's cell into the sunlight. He is not completely free of the Romantic period in which he lived, exaggerating some landscapes and the gloom of the jungle to create a sense of mystery and desolation. And he has filled his scenes with exotic Indians, dogs, snakes, and even a jaguar, in part employing the old artist's trick to give proper scale to the ruins. Yet the monuments themselves, the idols, the hieroglyphs, ornaments, and temples, with only slight reconstructions, remain indisputably accurate. And, slyly, he also slips in his famously indistinct images of himself, Stephens, and Cabot.

Freed from the dominance of Stephens and Robert Hay, the modest, self-effacing Catherwood had finally produced a book entirely his own. And yet as extraordinary as it turned out, he was still not satisfied. When Prescott asked for advice on choosing an illustrator for one of his books, Catherwood replied: "In such important undertaking I really do not feel myself equal to it. It was this feeling which made me feel glad when I had my work entirely to myself, for I am sure I should not have pleased Stephens, nor have I pleased myself, but this is of little consequence."[20]

There is no record of how many copies Catherwood sold. The folios would have been prohibitively expensive for the average book buyer of the day. He set the price of the tinted editions at $30 and double that for his hand-colored ones.[21] Though it is difficult to translate prices from Catherwood's era to those of today, the tinted version might have cost the equivalent of as much as $750 in 2015 dollars and the colored edition $1,500. The original folios are now so rare they sell at book auctions for amounts ranging from $50,000 to $125,000, depending on their condition. If Catherwood had been able to sell all 300 books he would have earned more than $10,000, but how much he had paid the engravers and for the cost of printing is not known. Unlike the target audience for Stephens's relatively inexpensive and popular books, the buyers of the folios would have been universities, learned societies, libraries, and, the very anathema to his "loco foco notions," aristocrats and well-heeled collectors—the very subscribers Stephens had sought in the first place.

Catherwood reported to Prescott that the book was "doing very well" in London but was not sure how the New York edition would fare. Of the hand-colored volumes, he noted: "I have sold considerably more than I expected." And as it turned out, he had achieved some luck with royalty after all. Many years later, it was reported in the English newspapers that Prince Albert had sent a copy of Catherwood's book to Alexander von Humboldt in gratitude for a copy he had received of Humboldt's book *Kosmos*.[22]

But what of Stephens? After publication of his book and his campaign on behalf of Catherwood, he had all but disappeared. The failure of his subscription effort was one sign something was wrong, as was his belated offer to write the introduction for Catherwood's book. Around the time Catherwood's book was published, the two men discussed another grand adventure. This time, according to Prescott, they were considering a trip to Peru to seek out remnants of the Inca civilization. "This is my ground," Prescott wrote Catherwood in April, referring to the next book he was planning on the conquest of Peru. "But I suppose it will not be the worse for you mousing into architectural antiquities, and I wish I could see the fruits of such a voyage in your beautiful illustrations."[23]

The expedition never happened, but the prospect of such a journey leaves a tantalizing question. Given the two men's uncanny ability to sniff out pre-Columbian ruins, it is possible they would have found Machu Picchu, the now-famous "lost city" of the Inca. The ruins high in the Andes Mountains had never been found by the Spanish but were known to local Indians. Like the ruins of the Maya, no one had yet seriously explored the remnants of the Inca Empire, which had flourished in the fifteenth and sixteenth centuries before its conquest by the Spanish. Stephens decided against another long expedition, however, and the magical citadel of Machu Picchu would remain safely lost for another sixty-seven years, until it was "discovered" in 1911 by a Yale University lecturer named Hiram Bingham.

But why had Stephens declined to go while Catherwood appeared ready and willing? Was Stephens simply exhausted? Or had a breach opened between the two men? Not, apparently, on Catherwood's part for he had written the dedication in his folio to "my good friend John L. Stephens."

In the absence of any surviving correspondence between the two men during this period, the only clues we have of Stephens's state of mind come from Prescott. But the Boston historian's brief observations in several letters leave more questions than answers. In a comment on the proposed trip to Peru, for example, Prescott told Catherwood: "Stephens says he is not up to the enterprise and cannot leave his father. He is still labouring under depression from the heavy loss in the family circle. . . ."[24] Who or what Prescott was referring to is a mystery. If a death had come to the Stephens clan, it was not within the author's immediate family, according to available records. However, some illness may have befallen his father, based on further comments by Prescott. In July, in a second letter to Catherwood, he wrote:

Stephens I have not heard from lately, but Cabot saw him the other day in New York and said his spirits seemed pretty good. I thought him rather under a cloud when I saw him there in April last. He shows great depth of feeling certainly. I think while his father lives he will not much be disposed to ramble again, at least so he told me. And in the meantime he is taking care of his own and his father's property and courting the law; but it is not easy to win much professional business when it is known that a man does not need it.[25]

Stephens would not "ramble" again for some time, until his restless spirit took him south again to face a new jungle with a very different purpose in mind. Over the next years, he nearly vanished from the record books while "courting the law."

◁◁ 23 ▷▷

Steam

On a late summer morning in 1807, spectators packed the docks along the Hudson River to witness artist-engineer Robert Fulton maneuver a long, narrow craft with a comically tall black smokestack out into the river. No doubt the Stephens family, whose home was only a few blocks away, watched from the shore with two-year-old John Stephens in tow. The vessel had been dubbed "Fulton's Folly" by skeptics who stood by waiting smugly for the contraption to explode. Described as "an ungainly craft looking precisely like a backwoods saw-mill mounted on a scow and set on fire," the so-called "steam-boat" traveled a short distance from its launch, then stopped and sat dead in the water.[1] Jeers and catcalls floated out from the riverbank and the suspense grew palpable. Finally, an agitated Fulton disappeared belowdecks, made several mechanical adjustments, and the paddle wheels along the boat's sides started to churn through the water once again. Spewing fiery cinders and billows of black smoke, the boat slowly turned north up the river and two days later arrived in triumph at the state capital, Albany.

While the *Clermont* was not the first steam-driven vessel ever built, the boat's ensuing runs between New York and Albany became the world's first successful use of steam power in transportation. In an instant, with people little realizing it, the world had changed and the industrial age had come to America. The great epoch of steamships and railroads had begun. Stephens and Catherwood would grow up with the revolution and over the course of their lives witness every technological advance. Now, four decades after the launch of "Fulton's Folly," the unstoppable steam juggernaut was about to roll over them.

Catherwood was the first to succumb. He never gave up his yearning for old ruins but after Stephens decided against Peru, it was as if a curtain had dropped around their past and the men rarely spoke of antiquities again. With his book finished, Catherwood decided on a new direction, another personal transformation. Within a year of its publication, the artist-architect formerly known as "Catherwood, archt." added new initials to his name, "C.E.," for civil engineer. Now, at the age of forty-six, with children still to feed and educate, he re-emerged as a railroad man.

There is no record of his first move. For more than a year he dropped from sight, leaving us with another elusive hole in his life. He may have returned to the United States.[2] According to credentials he submitted for a British railway job, he claimed to have worked on railroads in America.[3] His latest makeover was well timed. Railroad engineers were in great demand in England. In 1845–46 a speculative craze in railroad stocks engulfed Britain in what came to be known simply as "the Railway Mania," one of the great technological booms in history.[4] Rails crisscrossed England as fast as steel for them could be manufactured. And the demand to invest in new railway projects had grown so overwhelming it spilled over into Britain's overseas colonies.

Riding the crest, Catherwood found a position as chief "practical" engineer of the Demerara Railway Company. Demerara was a jungle region studded with sugar plantations along the northeast coast of South America. The company seemed to know little about Catherwood's past—his panoramas, his antiquarian proclivities, his artistic talents—or cared even less. "The (management) committee considers that they have been particularly fortunate," reported company chairman Charles Cave to shareholders. "Mr. Catherwood, the gentleman they have engaged, resided for some years in North America, where he was employed upon railroads and extensive public works; and at the time his services were offered to the Company, he was professionally engaged upon a railway in this country." No mention was made of his familiarity with tropical forests, though perhaps he had used that as a selling point. Catherwood signed a one-year contract and left for Demerara, located in British Guyana, on November 17, 1845.[5]

There are no letters or any other accounts to explain why he left his children once again for such an extended period when he could easily have found work in Britain. Money may have been a factor. He would later write Stephens more than once about how seriously he took the responsibility of providing for his children. The loss of his New York rotunda was a serious setback even if he could claim some financial success with the sale of his folios. The job in Guyana may have offered him more freedom, salary, and control than was available in England. But by now a clear pattern had also emerged. He had spent much of his life wandering the Mediterranean and Near East, gone twice with Stephens to Central America and Yucatán, and had been ready for another long expedition to Peru. Work for him seem to justify a habitual restlessness. And Gertrude, calamitous as their marriage turned out, was no longer there to provide any anchor.

During the next five months, he surveyed sixty miles of coastline for a railway project to connect coastal plantations with Georgetown, Guyana's capital. Then he sailed to Jamaica to examine a railroad between Kingston and Spanish Town that presented conditions similar to Guyana's. Impressed, he would report to his board: "I could not help feeling, that if the Jamaica Railway was successful, with scarcely any but passenger traffic, how much more so ought be the Demerara line, with its vast amount of actual and prospective goods traffic, in addition to a large amount of passengers." After a stop in the United States to investigate locomotive and rail "manufactories" (and a likely stop in New York to visit Stephens and his family), he returned to London. There he presented his report to the company in October 1846. Pleased with his projections, the railroad board extended his contract and sent him back to Guyana to superintend the construction of the line, the first to be built in South America.

Meanwhile, in New York, Stephens appeared almost idle by comparison. In 1843, the year the *Yucatán* book was published, he had set up an office at 67 Wall Street, but no documents exist to show that he practiced law from there. The year before, in a report on New York City's wealthiest citizens, Stephens's father, Benjamin, was estimated to be worth $500,000, a fortune that would equal millions in today's dollars. "A carpenter of a New Jersey family," the report continued, "he was very industrious, a good workman, and has made all his money by hard toil and shrewd management. He built the old state prison in this city, and was a large contractor for building." John L. Stephens, "the distinguished Traveler," was listed next with a separate fortune of $100,000.[6] Both amounts were almost certainly exaggerations. Some of the best-known and wealthiest financiers of the day were worth no more than $500,000, and Benjamin Stephens, though rich, was not in that category. John Stephens certainly was not, though revenues from his books continued to pour in. Records from this period indicate he kept busy with investments. Besides speculating in uptown lots as the city spread rapidly north through Manhattan, both father and son were acquiring and renting properties in upstate New York, New England, and as far away as Ohio and Michigan.[7]

For the years immediately following publication of *Yucatán*, little is known about Stephens's personal life. He almost certainly lived with his father, with whom he usually stayed when he was in New York. They shared a comfortable four-story home with an elegant granite façade at 13 Leroy Place, a federal style row house that had an unusual ten-foot setback from the street. It was located in an elite section of the city one block off Broadway in what had once been the village of Greenwich, until it was overtaken by the city.[8]

By the summer of 1844, Stephens had apparently shaken off the mysterious depression that Prescott had noted. And if he was not actively practicing law, he may simply have been savoring the fruits of his eight years of hard travel and prolonged periods at his writing table. His literary and archaeological work had drawn him into the top ranks of the city's intelligentsia. He was seen frequently at the nearby offices of the *Evening Post*, where he visited the paper's editor, well-known poet William Cullen Bryant.[9] Described by a journalist at the paper as "a small sharp, nervous man," Stephens had joined Bryant on the management committee of the Century Association, a private club they helped organize in 1847. The association was limited to one hundred members, some of whom dreamed it would become the American equivalent of the French Academy. While its initial members were writers, artists, scientists, and other men of talent and intellectual achievement, it evolved within a few years into an association also of "bankers, railroad executives, insurance officials, leading lawyers and physicians."[10] And by then Stephens had become a fixture in both worlds.

He was also a regular at Bartlett & Welford's bookshop, located in Astor House, across from City Hall.[11] One of the owners, John Russell Bartlett, had concentrated much of his early book buying on Mexico and claimed to be the first to encourage Stephens to investigate the ruins in Mexico and Central America. His shop carried rare books and antiquarian tomes and was a meeting place for the city's savants and literati. Bryant, Washington Irving, Albert Gallatin, Edgar Allan Poe, and James Fenimore Cooper were regulars. Bartlett along with Gallatin founded the American Ethnological Society in 1842, which was devoted to "inquiries into the origins, progress and characteristics of the various races of man." Stephens and Catherwood were charter members.[12] Bartlett & Welford in 1844 also published the American edition of Catherwood's *Views of Ancient Monuments*.

During this period Stephens made a minor foray into politics. He was elected in 1846 as a delegate to a state convention to revise New York's constitution. He was a lifelong Democrat but was so popular he was picked as a consensus candidate by both the Whigs and the Democrats.[13] Through a sweltering summer in Albany, despite his fiery Tammany Hall past he avoided most of the spirited political debates, spoke little, and limited his efforts to court reforms.[14] The experience did not appear to spark any deeper interest in a political career. He was later urged by friends to run for the state senate but declined.[15]

Instead, like Catherwood, he gave in to the consuming force of the steam age. That same year he joined a group of investors putting together America's first transatlantic steamship company. Their plan was to build four large paddle-wheel steamers to carry cargo, mail, and hundreds of passengers regularly between New York and Bremen, Germany.[16] But unlike Catherwood, Stephens came in at the top. He was made vice president of the Ocean Steam Navigation Company.[17] And by the spring of 1847, when the first ship was ready, he agreed to accompany it on its maiden voyage, his first trip abroad since returning from Yucatán five years earlier.

The 230-foot wooden steamer was constructed in the New York

shipyards of Westervelt & MacKay, and its giant "side-lever" steam engines built at nearby Novelty Iron Works.[18] The vessel was also equipped with sails to provide auxiliary power. On June 1, 1847, the three-deck SS *Washington,* the potent symbol of America—a figurehead of the first president—on her bow, departed New York carrying Stephens, First Assistant U.S. Postmaster Major Hobbie, and 125 other passengers to the cheers of thousands lining the docks. While not a canal across Nicaragua, Stephens was still determined to expand America's (and New York's) reach and connect nations in his fervent belief that only good could come of it. America itself was in the middle of its greatest expansion since the Louisiana Purchase, annexing Texas and on verge of taking full control of the Oregon Territory. "We are bound to go ahead," enthused the *New York Herald,* reporting on the ship's launching. "And steam is the agent of the age."[19]

The *Washington* arrived in Bremen more than two weeks later, greeted by cannon salutes, musical bands, and thousands of citizens lining the city's wharves. Over the next days the *Washington'*s crew and passengers were showered with banquets and other festivities. Stephens spoke briefly at a formal dinner where the Americans were welcomed by the foreign secretary of Prussia. After a round of toasts, he read a letter from the directors of the company asking that Bremen accept a model of the *Washington.* In marched eight Bremen natives, now citizens of the United States who had returned for a visit, carrying on their shoulders a six-foot replica of the steamship. "This was received with a storm of enthusiasm," a spectator reported.[20]

Finally Stephens was able to slip away and board a train for Berlin, where he arrived on July 1 in the "mellow twilight" of midsummer. "I had but a day for Berlin," he noted, before he had to catch the *Washington* back to New York. "There was but one object in it I had any special desire to see, and that was—Humboldt."[21]

Baron Alexander von Humboldt, who had been reported in ill health, lived at the court of King Frederick Wilhelm IV in Potsdam, fifteen miles away. Stephens decided to take a chance and left immediately for Potsdam. The seventy-seven-year-old Humboldt, one of the king's closest counselors, lived in the royal palace, a splendid rococo residence called San Souci, set among hundreds of acres of manicured gardens. After boldly knocking at the door of Humboldt's apartment, Stephens was told the baron was not receiving visitors that day. Discouraged and with time running out, he left a letter of introduction from the former Prussian ambassador to the United States and his card, noting that he would call again at two o'clock. When he did he was ushered into the apartment's salon. A short time later Humboldt greeted him in heavily accented but fluent English, saying that no letter of introduction was necessary and that he was more than familiar with Stephens's writings and his famous travels.

Stephens was stunned. He could scarcely believe Humboldt, his boyhood hero, was standing before him praising his work. "Nearly half a century ago, he had filled the first place in the world of letters," Stephens wrote, "sitting as it were, upon a throne, lighting a pathway of science to the philosopher, and teaching the school-boy at his desk." Though ill, the baron appeared much younger than his years. He was dressed in a simple suit of black, the same simplicity reflected in his apartment.

They spoke briefly about the ruined cities of America, but the conversation turned quickly to the advantages of trade between the United States and Prussia when Humboldt learned of Stephens's connection with the steamship line to Bremen. Humboldt had just completed the first two volumes of his monumental work on the unity of all natural phenomenon, titled *Kosmos,* but Stephens noted that he was just as consumed by the current politics of Germany and Europe.

From European politics the conversation shifted to Mexico, whose ruins Humboldt had investigated not long before Stephens was born. Humboldt praised Prescott's *History of the Conquest,* adding that "there was no historian of the age, in England or Germany, equal to him." Then he surprised Stephens with the extent of his interest in the recent war between the United States and Mexico.

"He was full of our Mexican war," Stephens wrote. For all his liberal views, he added, Humboldt was still a native of Prussia, a state steeped in militarism. "In Prussia," Stephens continued, "war is a science, and according to the leading policy of Europe, to be always ready for war, every male in Prussia, the highest nobleman's son not excepted, is compelled to serve his regular term in the army." Even given that, Stephens was startled to learn that Humboldt, the king, and his military council often huddled around Humboldt's maps to follow the course of the Mexican War with every news dispatch from across the Atlantic. According to Humboldt, they had "followed General [Zachary] Taylor from his encampment at Corpus Christi . . . through the storming of Monterey, and the bloody scenes of Buena Vista. They had fought over all his battles, and with his positions all marked on the map."

Stephens said he was aware the American army had won the respect of much of Europe and that the army's success in Mexico had raised the nation to the ranks of a "first rate" power. But he had no idea until his conversation with Humboldt just how much it had also upset the "whole doctrine" in Europe, and especially Prussia, of standing, professional armies. "In the teeth of all settled opinions," he continued, "General Taylor, with a handful of regulars, and a small body of volunteers who had never been in battle, had stood up for a whole day against the murderous fire, and had finally defeated four times their number. Field marshals and generals of Prussia, among them veterans who had studied the art of war on the great battlefields of Europe, were struck with admiration at the daring and skill displayed at Buena Vista; and this admiration, Baron Humboldt said, they expressed without reserve, freely, publicly, and everywhere."

The two men had been talking for more than an hour when a servant entered and called the baron to dinner—with the king. Humboldt asked if Stephens might remain several days and accept a letter of introduction from him to several important gentlemen in Berlin with whom Stephens should become acquainted. "Circumstances did not permit me to deliver the letter," he wrote. "But I had the satisfaction of bringing it home with me, written in German, in a strong, firm hand, as an autograph of Humboldt, and a memento of one of my most interesting incidents of travel."

Seven weeks later, at a board meeting of Ocean Steam Navigation Company, Stephens moved that one of the next two steamers being built by the company bear the name "SS *Humboldt*." A letter to that effect was sent to Humboldt through the Prussian minister in Washington and in a reply, dated September 21, 1847, the baron agreed.[22]

The next month a three-page article titled "An Hour with Alexander Von Humboldt" appeared in a Boston periodical called *Littell's Living Age*. It would be Stephens's last published work—but not his last adventure. He would soon travel again, drawn once more into the jungle. However, this time steam and the gathering power of America's ambition in the world, not antiquities, would be the driving force.

◁ 24 ▷

Panama

The SS *Humboldt* would never be built. Even with the help of a lucrative U.S. mail subsidy, the company was never able to raise the capital needed to complete its grand four-ship plan. And by the spring of 1848, when the company's second and last steamship, the 235-foot SS *Herman* was launched, Stephens's energy and attention were elsewhere. He had gone south on another journey of discovery. Though very different from his explorations with Catherwood, this adventure would nevertheless reunite the two of them and consume the final years of Stephens's life. He was in Panama. He had gone under an agreement reached with William Henry Aspinwall.

How and when the two men met is unclear. Both their fathers were successful New York merchants and investors, and by the time Stephens became a director of the Bremen line, he and Aspinwall were traveling in the same business and social circles. Aspinwall came from a seafaring family that traced its lineage to the Pilgrims. He was born in 1807 in New York, educated at local schools, and went to work as a young clerk for his uncles Gardiner and Samuel Howland in their shipping firm. His grasp of the import-export business came so readily that by the age of twenty-five he was a partner. The company, which started with the Caribbean trade, had grown rapidly to include routes to England and the Mediterranean. A few years later, when the two senior partners retired, Aspinwall, then only thirty, and his cousin took over management of the company under the name of Howland & Aspinwall.[1] At the time, the firm had grown into the preeminent shipping line in New York, operating as far away as South America and China. For young Aspinwall, soft-spoken and modest but driven with ambition, it had been a meteoric ascent.[2]

At that point, with the company on firm financial footing, Aspinwall turned his attention to ship design and hired a pioneering naval architect named John Willis Griffiths.[3] A chronic risk taker, Aspinwall took a chance on Griffiths.[4] What Aspinwall wanted was speed. He knew that fresh tea leaves from China would sell at a premium in New York. So Griffiths designed for him what came to be known as the first "extreme" clipper ship, called the *Rainbow*.[5] He followed quickly with one of the most beautiful sailing vessels ever built, the *Sea Witch*, a black-hulled China clipper launched in New York in 1846. In March 1849, under billowing clouds of canvas, a golden dragon head thrust from her bow, the *Sea Witch* sailed into New York harbor 74 days and 14 hours out from Hong Kong, a sailing record not broken for the next 154 years.[6] At auction a short time later, the tea leaves carried in her hull made Howland & Aspinwall enough money in one trip to cover the cost of her construction. The long, sleek Aspinwall-Griffiths model, with its stacks of sails, would dominate the perishable cargo trade for decades. Yet even as the *Sea Witch* appeared over the horizon in 1849, clipper ships and speed records no longer consumed the restless Aspinwall. Ever farsighted, he had already moved on. He knew the steam engine was transforming the world, and it was racing forward at a speed even the *Sea Witch* would never be able to keep up with.

Given their background and close age—Stephens was two years older than Aspinwall—and the compact world of New York business, the two men's paths inevitably crossed. They made an odd pair: Aspinwall's smooth, doughy features and quiet demeanor a contrast to Stephens's sharp intensity and volubility. Both men possessed quick intelligence, yet Stephens remained an idealist in the face of Aspinwall's mercantile pragmatism. It was, in fact, a powerful combination. The two men found they shared a single compelling vision, which was about to draw them into deep alliance. Sometime in late 1847, not long after Stephens's return from Germany, they got together to talk about Panama.

Only a short time before, Aspinwall had completed his most audacious move yet, the culmination of a sequence of events that started in 1846 when the United States settled a long-running dispute with Britain over the Oregon Territory. The two countries signed a treaty that gave the land below the 49th parallel, with the exception of Vancouver Island, to the United States. Then, a year later, as the U.S. government prepared to take over California following its victory in its war with Mexico, it offered subsidies to shipping firms in exchange for carrying the U.S. mail from the east coast down to Panama and from Panama on to Oregon and California. Aspinwall grabbed the mail contract for the Pacific route, a subsidy worth $199,000 a year.[7] With a small group of business associates he set up the Pacific Mail Steamship Company and began building three steamships to send around South America to the Pacific coast.[8]

Hearing the news, a number of fellow capitalists in New York looked on in disbelief, wondering if Aspinwall had lost his mind. They pointed to the fact that almost no infrastructure for steamship repairs and coaling existed along the west coast, and with California and Oregon so distant and undeveloped, they questioned how the company could ever expect to turn a profit on its investment.[9] Aspinwall, however, had taken the long view, convinced California and Oregon held great promise. He also had a much more enterprising plan in mind. Panama was the key, he believed, to vast commercial transactions east and west, stretching from Europe to Asia, and he had now captured one link in the network.

So when he and Stephens, the expert on Central America, sat down to talk, it was about how visibly enticing the narrow Isthmus of Panama looked. The United States was now a continental empire with its annexation of California, Oregon, and half the western territories, and had emerged as the dominant force in the Americas. But it had also become a broad, sprawling nation with two distant coasts to connect. France and England had both shown strong interest in the isthmus. For Stephens, however, just as he had felt about the Maya antiquities, Panama must be kept within the compass of United States' control. Was it feasible, however, for a few New Yorkers with only private capital behind them to break through a narrow strip of land that had foiled plotters and dreamers for hundreds of years?

In January 1848, he arrived on the isthmus to find out. He was accompanied by an engineer named James Baldwin, hired to help him assess whether a railroad could be built coast to coast. It must have been an odd moment. Here was John L. Stephens, famously identified with unearthing the rain forest antiquities of Central America, returned to the jungle to plot a course for modern steam engines to divide and conquer the unforgiving wilds of the Isthmus of Panama.

Landing at the mouth of the Chagres River, the two men found out quickly what they were up against. The Caribbean side of the isthmus was a solid wall of jungle and mangrove swamps, not much different from the coast of Guatemala as Stephens and Catherwood had approached it nine years earlier. The only crossing to the Pacific was by canoe up the winding Chagres as far as the rapids in the middle of the country. Several nights had to be spent in huts or camped on the river's banks amid crocodiles, screeching macaws, snakes, and the unsettling basso roars of howler monkeys. As familiar as it was to Stephens, it remained unnerving. Leaving the river at the central villages of Gorgona or Cruces, the only way over the continental divide to the Pacific was on one of two ancient, rarely used trails, both in serious disrepair. Panama's long spine of mountains, the Sierra de Veraguas, formed a low saddle at this point. Travelers descended the final twenty miles to Panama City over painfully rugged terrain either on foot or mule.

The entire journey, though only some fifty miles, took days, even a week or more, depending on the season. During the rainy months, May through November, the Chagres was a plunging torrent filled with fallen trees, snags, and debris, while the trails to the Pacific became virtually impassable with mud. During the dry season, the twisting river ran so low through parts of the jungle that only shallow-draft canoes, or bungos, could clear the obstructions to make any headway upstream. And regardless of the season, clouds of mosquitoes swarmed out of the swamps carrying malaria and dengue fever. The route was so miserable and deadly that the year Stephens visited, fewer than four hundred people passed over it from the Caribbean to the Pacific.[10] Most people preferred taking their chances sailing south around the tip of South America despite the fact that it added months to the journey and posed its own serious dangers.

Even though they crossed the isthmus during the dry season—the healthy season—Baldwin got sick, probably with malaria. Stephens wrote his father that he himself had never felt healthier but was disheartened by the conditions they had found. "The country is very rough and broken and the survey much more difficult and will occupy more time than I expected."[11] Yet he forced himself to remain upbeat. "I think this is to be a point in the movements of the world and a great thoroughfare for travel. From this point there are to be great transactions with the whole coast of the Pacific up and down."

At some point the two men reached a "Eureka!" moment. Baldwin had recovered and found a pass through the continental divide that measured only three hundred feet above sea level. They realized then that with proper grading a rail bed could be laid across that would allow locomotives to pass ocean to ocean.[12]

When Stephens returned to New York in June, Aspinwall was ecstatic at the news. He had meanwhile acquired a third partner for the possible railroad venture—Henry Chauncey, one of the investors in the Pacific Mail Steamship Company. The fifty-three-year-old businessman was an obvious fit. Descended from an old New England family (his grandfather has been an early president of Harvard College), Chauncey was a partner through marriage in a commercial firm with interests on the Pacific coast of South America. Years earlier he moved with his wife and children to Peru and Chile, where he spent ten years in business, accumulating a small fortune.[13] With his connections between New York and South America, he brought to the partnership firsthand knowledge of trade in the region.

Meanwhile, during Stephens's and Baldwin's absence, the first Pacific Mail steamer, the SS *California,* was launched in New York. After sea trials it left for Cape Horn and the Pacific coast, followed not long after by the company's two other new ships, the *Panama* and *Oregon*. When the *California* left New York in October, it carried very few passengers.[14] It would be the last time any vessel departed for the Pacific coast empty.

In December 1848, President James Polk reported in his annual address to Congress that gold had been discovered California. "The accounts of the abundance of gold in [California] are of such an ex-

Founders of the Panama Railroad: Aspinwall (TOP); Stephens (BOTTOM LEFT),
and Chauncey (BOTTOM RIGHT).

traordinary character," the usually understated Polk explained, "as
would scarcely command belief were they not corroborated by the
authentic reports of officers in the public service who have visited the
mineral district."[15]

The news sent an electric jolt through America. Even before the
president's words had time to settle in, a public display in the War
Office in Washington of a small chest of gold brought back from California stoked gold mania to a fever pitch.[16] Advertisements for transport around the Horn or across Panama to the gold fields filled every
newspaper—and the now-legendary mad dash for California was on.[17]

Aspinwall's gamble on his Pacific Mail Steamship line was about
to pay off beyond anyone's imagining.[18] Yet no one quite grasped the
full dimensions of what was happening. Stephens and his two partners had spent the last half of 1848 working out a careful plan for their
railroad. They had arrived in Washington, hats in hand, to seek a large

government subsidy almost simultaneously with Polk's message to Congress. Despite the news from California they kept on lobbying, and even met with Polk personally. They were invited to dinner at the White House with the president, members of his cabinet, and a dozen senators and congressmen. However, Polk made no mention of the railroad in his December 14 diary entry, noting only that the dinner was attended by Aspinwall and "Stevens—of New York, the later the traveler."[19]

Over the next weeks, the partnership asked for five millions dollars over twenty years—after their railroad was operational—in exchange for free transportation across the isthmus for U.S. mail, government agents, and military troops, equipment, and munitions.[20] It was a preposterous sum of money, given the situation in California and the great profits that the railroad was certain to derive from it. Yet Congress almost went along. Senator Thomas Hart Benton of Missouri supported the idea (with a reduced subsidy), noting the three men had the capital, experience, and motivation to complete the project. "One of them, Mr. Stephens," he said, "is known throughout the reading world for his travels in a part of South America lying near the country over which this road is to run."[21]

In the end, President Polk would have none of it. After some in his cabinet urged him to support the enterprise, Polk wrote in a diary entry dated January 30, 1849: "I cut them off and said no such power existed in the Constitution. I stated that I considered the proposition of that bill as little better than a proposition to plunder the treasury. … If it passed, I told the cabinet I would veto it."[22]

The gold discovery, however, had already altered the calculus. On December 28, 1848, with passage of the legislation still pending, the three partners signed a formal agreement in Washington with New Granada (today Colombia, which at the time included Panama) giving them the exclusive right for forty-nine years to construct and operate the railroad across Panama.[23] Despite its favorable terms—Granada was to get a mere 3 percent of the net profit from the railroad's operations—the contract also carried serious risks. It depended entirely on Stephens's and Baldwin's initial assessment of the isthmus. On the basis of their survey, the partners put up $120,000 as security, which would be lost if the railroad was not completed within six years following ratification of the concession by New Granada's congress. Outwardly at least, the partners appeared confident they could pull it off. But Stephens, having seen the isthmus firsthand, must have swallowed hard and summoned every drop of his deep-rooted optimism before he signed.

Four months later the Panama Railroad Company was incorporated by the New York legislature.[24] The company's stock prospectus was wildly optimistic. As a result of the gold rush, it declared that "already the Isthmus of Panama has undergone a change extraordinary and almost unprecedented in the history of the world. It is no extravagance to suppose, that the whole country is, at no distant day, to be occupied by a thriving population, and that large cities, destined to hold a conspicuous and important place in the commerce of the world, are to rise up suddenly on either sea." The prospectus contained glowing reports from surveyors the partnership sent down in early 1849 to lay down the line of the railroad's crossing. The rainy season was portrayed as a minor problem. The famous unhealthiness of Panama's climate and swamps was downplayed. "That fevers do prevail is not to be denied," wrote Dr. Halsted, who had been sent to care for the surveyors during their work. "But they are not by any means as difficult to cure as those so common in our northern cities." And even swamp-filled Manzanillo Island, projected as the railroad's Caribbean terminus, which would later give the railroad builders unthinkable nightmares, was described in rosy terms as "beautifully situated . . . luxuriant with trees and shrubbery. The land is about ten or fifteen feet above high water mark, generally level, and well-watered with springs"—almost none of which later proved true.[25]

The plan was to raise an initial amount of $1 million at $100 per share. When the subscription list was opened on June 28, 1849, the entire allotment was taken by 3 P.M. A substantial amount of stock was transferred to Aspinwall, Stephens, Chauncey, and their original backers in exchange for signing over to the company their concession from the Republic of New Granada.[26] On July 2 the company directors met for the first time in New York and a prominent insurance executive named Thomas W. Ludlow was elected president. John L.

Stephens was named vice president.[27] The future glittered like a pot of gold. Two days later, the past showed up as Stephens's door.

◎◎◎

Earlier that year, in May, after working steadily for more than two years in British Guyana, Catherwood lost his position as chief engineer of the Demerara Railway Company. His contract was terminated in a cost-saving move by the company; other disputes with the railroad's local committee probably played a role as well.[28] Only one segment of rails along the Guyana coast had been finished and the project was well behind schedule. The year before there had been a ceremonial event to allow several railcars of dignitaries to run down a completed section. The inspection tour ended when a cow jumped onto the track, derailing the locomotive and causing the deaths of two passengers, including a Georgetown municipal officer.[29]

The disaster was only one problem that had plagued the railroad after Catherwood returned as chief engineer in March 1847. Recruiting labor proved difficult and there were numerous stoppages for lack of capital. Disputes with the landowners over the cost of acquiring sections of their property for the road also slowed the project. And even though Catherwood was able to open a large section of rails for traffic in November 1848, tensions escalated until finally in May the work was handed over to an assistant engineer willing to work for less pay.

Two months later Catherwood arrived in Philadelphia by way of the Turks Islands in the Caribbean.[30] A few days afterward he was in New York celebrating the Fourth of July with Stephens.[31] Neither man has left an account of the reunion but after so many years apart it must have been an especially warm one. It must also have felt like a homecoming since the Stephens clan had always been a second family to Catherwood. The last certain date he had been in New York was six years earlier, in July 1843, when the subscription effort for his folio had foundered. He may have come back to the city after the folio's 1844 publication in London and also visited Stephens in 1846 on his first return from Guyana to England, although we have no records confirming those trips.

During their years apart there was no hint of a break in their friendship or any falling-out between them. After Stephens rejected the idea of going to Peru, it appears that events had simply taken them on different paths. It is very likely they kept corresponding during this period, given what we have of their later letters, but such correspondence has been either lost or destroyed. Catherwood's departure for England in 1843 was clearly motivated by a desire to publish a work of his own and no doubt to reunite with his children and family. But it may also have been prompted by a need to disengage from Stephens, who had been the dominant force in their travels and publications. Now, in New York once again, he was at loose ends. He spent most of July there. Certainly the old traveling partners had a great deal to talk about, their conversations undoubtedly filled with railroads. Stephens likely described his time in Panama, and Catherwood his experiences— and frustrations—building South America's first railroad, which like Panama was located a notch above the equator and not very far to the east of the isthmus. Coincidentally, but perhaps irresistibly, both men had been drawn into tropical jungles once again.

In August, Catherwood was back with his family in Charles Square. He made the trip home aboard Ocean Steam Navigation's SS *Washington,* the same steamer that had carried Stephens two years earlier to Bremen. Possibly Stephens had wrangled a good stateroom for him because Catherwood commented on how pleasant the passage had been in a letter to Stephens dated August 18, 1849.[32] "My children are well," he continued. "My boy who is as tall as myself and a good scholar and arithmetician I intend to bring up as an engineer." But his plans were still uncertain, he said. For the moment he was handling some business for a wealthy New Jersey shipbuilder and railway executive he met on the *Washington.* He wrote that he was also in touch briefly with Aspinwall, who was then in London looking for shareholders to place $250,000 in Panama Railroad stock. Catherwood implied that he was considering a job with the railroad and wanted to discuss the matter further with Aspinwall. "The cholera may have driven him from London," he added. "No word from him."

When he wrote Stephens again in October, he still had not heard from Aspinwall, and the letter reflected a growing sense of frustration. He noted that due to mismanagement, the Demerara Railway had not laid a single rail in the months since his departure. "The company still owes me about a thousand pounds and I tremble for it," he explained. "And I consider myself very lucky in having safely put by as much as I have." He mentioned that he had sent a proposal to the Harper brothers offering to open a branch of their publishing house in London with one of the Harpers' sons, but he was not optimistic about the prospect. Then he asked Stephens outright if there was any chance of an appointment as "Surveyors of the Lands" for the Panama Railroad. "It is absolutely necessary that I should be doing something and my children are growing up around me."[33]

In most of his letters to Stephens (we have none of Stephens's replies), Catherwood made a reference to antiquities and Central America—like an aging athlete dwelling on earlier days of glory. He appeared unable to let go of their shared exploits and what had been one of the most extraordinary times in his life. At one point Stephens agreed to buy a set of very large Central American lithographs Catherwood had printed, possibly to help him out financially. Catherwood noted that there were seventeen in all and he would send them to Stephens for only the cost for their printing and framing, minus the ten British pounds that he owed him. "They occupy a good deal of space," he explained, referring to their large size. "To display them to advantage the room ought not to be less than 26 to 30 feet long and 16 to 18 feet wide and of good height." He had also been approached by a bookseller, he said, to put out a small volume on Central America, by which he assumed the seller meant a cheap two-shilling version of Stephens's book. "I informed him that I did not know how to write a book and further that I could not attempt anything of the kind without your sanction and approbation." He said he was more inclined to put out another version of his own book. "I find there is some demand for my work on Central America and having the plates still by me, I am thinking of publishing a cheaper edition at half the price of the former."[34] But it was clear with each letter that he was running out of money and angling more and more for railroad work with Stephens in Panama rather than betting on dubious publishing schemes.

Aspinwall, meanwhile, was having some success in placing the company's stock in England. The powerful London banking firm of

Baring Brothers & Company was willing to buy in if the British government agreed to join the United States in guaranteeing the neutrality of the isthmus. Aspinwall wrote Stephens in early October urging him to go to Washington to press President Zachary Taylor's administration to support the move.

In the same letter, he said that Catherwood had approached him for work and he asked Stephens for his opinion.[35] The company had already settled on two contractors to build the railroad, so it was unclear what role Catherwood could take on. "Catherwood is anxious to go to the isthmus, especially in your company," Aspinwall wrote. "And he would go with you on very reasonable terms. This he desired of me to understand particularly." A short time later, Catherwood wrote Stephens saying that he understood the company was not in a position to pay high salaries. His annual expenses, he explained, were between $1,500 and $2,000 and for the moment "I am obliged to travel on my capital, which of course is anything but desirable."[36]

Finally, in November, Aspinwall agreed to hire Catherwood, arranging a one-year, $1,500 contract along with payment for his travel expenses to Panama and back. Catherwood was to leave immediately for New York, Aspinwall wrote Stephens, where he was to meet the company directors before traveling to Panama with Stephens.[37] But Stephens appears not to have received Aspinwall's letter in time and left alone for Panama, where he arrived on December 10.

"I am in an iron house belonging to the railroad company with dozens inside and cannot step outside without stumbling over a body," he wrote to his father, describing the primitive settlement that had materialized at the mouth of the Chagres River as steamship after steamship arrived with gold seekers. "There is great confusion and distress. This afternoon between 500 and 600 were planted on the bank with luggage of all kinds, anxious, bargaining for canoes in mud and rain."[38]

Catherwood arrived the next month and joined Stephens in Panama City. The two old comrades were together again—only this time amid the chaos of a city overrun by thousands in the grip of gold fever. And on this occasion, their time together would be over almost before it started.

◅ 25 ▻

Crossing the Isthmus

The master plan for construction of the railroad was a simple one. It was designed to both accommodate and take advantage of the multitudes now descending on Panama. Based on the engineering survey performed earlier in the year, the project called for the railroad work to start in the middle of the isthmus at Gorgona, with the tracks to be laid from there over the Sierra de Veraguas to Panama City. It was expected this section would take no more than a year and that the railroad could then start transporting fare-paying passengers and freight coming up the Chagres River. Then, fortified with this infusion of additional cash, the company would pivot and begin the much more formidable task of laying tracks through the dense jungle on the Caribbean side. Meanwhile, a temporary plank road, if it could be built quickly enough along the route, would also bring in extra cash. The company was also in the process of building small, shallow-draft steamers to be sent to Panama and put into commercial service on the Chagres to transport passengers up the river to Gorgona. The steamboats would also ferry materials and labor crews up to the railroad work in the middle of the country. When the first half of rail line was finished, according to the plan, the company would then be able to provide comfortable transport by boat, covered wagon, and train across the isthmus in a day or two, and then on Pacific Mail steamships between Panama City and San Francisco, a voyage of no more than three weeks. Then entire journey between New York and San Francisco could be made in relative comfort and safety and reduced to little more than a month.[1] The scheme was perfect—on paper.

In October the company hired two veteran American engineers

with experience working in the tropics along New Granada's Caribbean coast. When they arrived on the isthmus at the beginning of 1850, they realized almost immediately they had a serious problem. The first of the shallow-draft steamboats had arrived for duty and it was clear that during the dry season, when most of the construction was to take place, even with their minimal drafts they could not make it up the Chagres in the low water.[2] The company would have to alter its plan immediately as pressure mounted from competing enterprises already planning Pacific crossings farther north through Mexico and Nicaragua. If those ventures gained a foothold, they could siphon off enough traffic from the isthmus to bankrupt the railroad before it was completed.[3]

Down the coast from the mouth of the Chagres lay the Bay of Limon, also known as Navy Bay, the name originally given to it by Columbus on his third voyage to America. It lay alongside a coral-rimmed island named Manzanillo, located a short distance from the mainland. The company's survey called for the railroad's Caribbean terminus to be built on Manzanillo because Limon Bay provided a well-sheltered deepwater harbor capable of accommodating oceangoing steamships. The contractors now realized that, like it or not, they would have to start construction from that point.

Stephens, meanwhile, had crossed to Panama City, where the company had set up its office. He wrote his father at the end of December that he had been detained five days on the river by late season rains. It had been a year and a half since he and Baldwin surveyed the isthmus and he marveled at the changes. Almost every day, he wrote, steamships emptied hundreds at the mouth of the Chagres. "All of which indicates the necessity of our road but at the same time increases the difficulties in making it." He called the changes in Panama City the most extraordinary. Where he had paid eight dollars a month for lodging earlier, he said, he now had to pay more than a hundred dollars for the same place. The city was a madhouse, jammed with people waiting for ships to California. He added that he was anxiously awaiting Catherwood as there was an enormous amount of railroad business to take care of before he left for Bogotá, the capital of New Granada. The concession between the railroad and the republic had

Map of Central America in 1850 with Panama (New Granada) at lower right.

not yet been ratified and the national congress was scheduled to vote on it in early spring. It was essential, Stephens wrote, that he be there. "I leave for Bogotá by steamer of the 27th of January and am afraid I shall not see Catherwood until my return."[4]

His old friend, however, showed up a short time later, bringing with him a bundle of company documents and letters. "I received your letter by Catherwood and am glad to learn you are well," he wrote his father. "I am at all times full with business." He had found decent lodgings with fresh ocean breezes, he explained, but was sick again. As bad as his old nemesis malaria was, the strain of work was also taking its toll and the irritation showed. "By the way," he grumbled in a rare rebuke aimed at his apparently tight-fisted father, "I wish you would not write on such little scraps of paper but on letter sheets and under an envelope. It makes no difference if the sheet is not filled."

He also told his father that he should have asked the company directors for a bonus if his trip to Bogotá was successful.

But I do not mean to complain for they did all that I asked and have sent me a power of attorney so absolute in its terms as I should hardly be willing to give to any living man, in fact putting the whole company absolutely and without any qualifications into my hands. Engineers, captains and everybody and thing under my control, showing a degree of confidence in my capacities and integrity which imposes on me a heavy responsibility, having to consider and decide alone matters of more importance than which in New York required two or three sittings of the board.[5]

Before leaving for Bogotá, he handed over a large part of the company's pressing administrative work and correspondence to Catherwood. They had not had much time together but looked forward to catching up when Stephens returned from Bogotá.

⊙ ⊙ ⊙

The city of Bogotá lay more than eight hundred miles inland from the Caribbean, perched on a table of land nearly nine thousand feet high in the Andes Mountains. It has been described by one historian who has written about the period as "one of the most inaccessible cities on the face of the earth."[6] The trek from Panama by boat and mule in the nineteenth century was a torturous trip of three or four weeks. In the final ascent to the city up a steep mountain track, Stephens fell from his mule and severely injured his back. He arrived in the capital in terrible pain and was immediately confined to his bed. Only with great difficulty was he able to continue railroad negotiations with the government. In mid-March, he wrote his father that despite the "severe journey" he was slowly recovering. "The cholera is all around us, and yesterday is said to have entered the city. But this does not disturb me, except so far as it may have an effect upon my business."[7]

In the middle of April, the congress ratified the railroad contract. Stephens was nonetheless unable to leave the capital for another five weeks, delayed by a serious illness. Whether it was related to his back injury, cholera, or his old malarial fevers is not clear. But a friend later remarked that after his accident near Bogotá he never fully recovered his health.[8] Many months later he reported still using a crutch. In the meantime, word of his injury and illness had spread to the newspapers in New York, causing great concern among his friends and family. Aspinwall expressed much uneasiness when he heard the news, writing Stephens in May: "I am glad that Catherwood has been on the isthmus and the fact must have also been a relief to your mind whilst forced to be absent. One thing keep in view—you must come home."[9] The seriousness of his condition was also evident in a letter Stephens's sister, Amelia Ann, wrote at the end of May mentioning "poor pa's anxiety" and urging him to come home immediately. She knew from the past that her brother rarely complained, especially of illness. "From your own account," she wrote, "you must have suffered dreadfully, and we know you must have been ill indeed when you speak of having suffered. You have been often absent, my dearest brother, but I never experienced so much uneasiness on your account before."[10]

Stephens was finally well enough to leave Bogotá in May, more than three months after he had been carried into the city. In spite of his debilities, his mission had been an unqualified success. Besides the ratification, extra modifications expanded the concession's land grants and added Aspinwall's wagon road.[11] And despite his injury and illness—he was confined to bed in one position for some period of time—he apparently had lost none of his charm. He won a number of friends among the government officials, whose later letters were filled with deep affection and respect for him. And while still convalescing he received a personal invitation from the president of the republic to dine with him at the government palace.[12] At the end, he still had to be carried down the mountains in a specially designed and cushioned chair to the Magdalena River for the journey back to Panama—no doubt reminding him of his brief but terrifying ride on the back of an Indian over the Sierra Madre mountains to Palenque.[13] In the coastal city of Cartagena, he met George Totten, one of the railroad's two contractors, who was recruiting workers, and the two men traveled together by steamer with forty laborers to Panama.[14]

Catherwood, who had been anxiously awaiting Stephens's return, was now also seriously ill in Panama City. He wrote Stephens that he had contracted his illness from "exposure" as he traveled by foot across

First shanty constructed in a Panama swamp for railroad workers.
(*Harper's New Monthly Magazine*, 1859)

the isthmus surveying the route for the plank road.[15] Neither man was in any condition now to make the trip across the isthmus to meet, especially with the rainy season upon them. "I am greatly disappointed at your not being able to reach Panama [City]," Catherwood wrote. "The last Fourth of July we passed together in New York . . . and I looked forward with peculiar pleasure to our passing another fourth together, though under very different circumstances. Capt. Liot tells me you did perfectly right not to attempt it as the road in some places is very bad." As for his own health, he said, "I don't remember where I had a more severe attack than my last."[16]

Before he boarded a steamship for New York, Stephens went to Navy Bay for the first time to observe the initial stages of construction. What he saw was utterly dispiriting. Manzanillo Island was nothing like the idyllic tropical paradise portrayed by the company's surveyors in the sunny stock prospectus. Ringed by coral, the square mile of its interior was mostly at or below sea level, a slimy patch of blue-black mud, swamp, and mangroves crawling with crocodiles, snakes, sand flies, and mosquitoes—and with no fresh water anywhere to be found. It was uninhabited and uninhabitable. But there was no choice. The bay itself was ideal and the railroad had to start from there.

Totten's contracting partner, along with James Baldwin, who now served as their chief assistant, had gone ashore the month before with a small force of workers and began cutting through the mangrove trees to clear enough space to construct a storehouse on piles.[17] When Stephens arrived, the men were still housed in a small brig anchored just offshore. It was impossible to sleep on the island at night because of the incessant attacks of the insects. Even aboard the brig, the crowded conditions belowdecks, the intense humidity and heat, and mosquitoes drove most of the men onto the deck even if it meant sleeping in the pouring rain. Most of the workers were sick with fever, and many who possessed enough energy were packing up to cross the isthmus and head to California. Stephens arranged for an abandoned steamship to be towed from Chagres to Navy Bay to provide the remaining workmen with better quarters.[18] When he left for New York at the end of June, the clearing of Manzanillo continued under sweltering, torrential rains with a minimal crew.

As depressing as conditions in Panama were, the railroad continued to move forward in New York on sheer momentum. When he arrived home, Stephens was elected the company's new president, a development that must have felt as much a burden as a distinction. After his visit to Navy Bay, and his many trips across the isthmus, he knew intimately the enormous obstacles that lay ahead.

With the full weight of the company now officially upon him, he would not be able to return to the isthmus for another six months. During the interval, his life was consumed by work: arranging contracts for locomotives, ordering rails, creating strategies to attract workers (they were offered contracts for six months, three months, even six weeks or less—with guaranteed passage home or to California). Everything had to be bought or built in the United States—with the exception of iron rails, most of which came from England—and then transported to Panama aboard steamers. Even the housing for the hundreds of workers now converging on the isthmus was prefabricated and sent down for assembly, along with thousands of pounds of food and medical supplies. Doctors were hired and a hospital was under construction on-site. Steam pile drivers, wooden pilings, railroad ties, tools—in short, everything necessary for the construction of a railroad—all had to be bought and transported to Panama at great expense.[19]

Stephens had now become, in effect, king of one of the greatest construction projects of his day, a monumental undertaking equivalent in its way to the great works of the Maya. He had to retake the jungle and remake its landscape, and if he had even a moment to see the parallels, he would certainly have appreciated the challenges and natural forces the Maya—lords and laborers alike—had to overcome with far fewer tools and resources than were at his disposal. It's doubtful such a thought would have been of any comfort, however. His health still compromised, the work never-ending, he had no choice now but to somehow summon up the energy to keep the dream of the first intercontinental railroad in the Western Hemisphere alive and moving forward.

After his experience in Guyana, Catherwood's goal was to get in and out of Panama as fast as possible, especially now that Stephens was no longer with him on the isthmus. Like the thousands of others who were thronging across Panama to the Pacific, his head was filled with dreams of California. He had made no secret of his plan in his negotiations with Aspinwall. And he told Stephens the year before that he had no desire to dig for riches but instead saw California as a gold mine of another sort—an opportunity to use his architectural and engineering skills in the rapidly developing American west coast. Under a new arrangement with Aspinwall, it was agreed that he would spend only six months on the isthmus because of his ill health, and the remainder of his contract year working for Aspinwall at the maintenance depot of the Pacific Mail Steamship Company in the town of Benicia, near San Francisco. Extra responsibilities in Stephens's absence and illness, however, delayed his departure for California until August. Before he left Panama City, he sent a request to Stephens:

. . . as my salary has been very small, that I have been delayed two months on the isthmus beyond my time, and that my services have been approved by Mr. L[udlow] and Mr. Aspinwall, that the board should grant me such a sum beyond my salary as they may think proper. I hope it will be $1000, which might be of great service when at San Francisco. I pay now $625 a year insurance on my life for the benefit of my children in case of my death and this alone is a heavy item . . . $1500 a year and three children to support at school. In fact, this year without some aid, I shall have to encroach on my capital which is small enough.[20]

When he finally landed in San Francisco in late August, his antiquarian yearnings caught up with him again. In a letter after his arrival, he informed Stephens he had learned about new "Indian ruins" in California during his passage north and that he hoped to track them down and investigate. "The source is very reliable," he added. He had also hoped, he said, that San Francisco would help him restore his health but complained about the city's "horrible," notoriously cold summer weather.[21] In October, two months later, he was singing the city's praises as "delightful, warm in the day but the evenings deliciously cool and invigorating, nor has any rain fallen for six or seven months," which must have been a shocking relief after Panama.[22]

Stephens, meanwhile, arranged for his friend's additional salary. Catherwood thanked him for making him "$1,000 richer," adding he was forever indebted to him for his "kindness and friendship." Unfortunately, Stephens's letters to Catherwood have never turned up, and we have only Catherwood's half of their correspondence. So it is difficult to know why Stephens did not reply to Catherwood's next several letters. Catherwood complained repeatedly that he received nothing personal, nothing about Stephens's family in New York, nothing about their mutual friends. Finally, exasperated, he wrote in January 1851: "I have no doubt the duties of your office occupy so much of your time as to leave small space for mere chit chat correspondence, but still I trust you will in your next and soon make some amends for your long silence."[23]

He was anxious about Stephens's health and tried to convince him to leave Panama for California, at least to join him and his nephew, Pratt Stephens, for a visit. Pratt had arrived earlier that year and wrote to his uncle from San Francisco: "Catherwood is on his way to this country and intends to induce you if possible to accompany him. I want you to become acquainted with this perfectly original place."[24] Catherwood went further, urging Stephens to consider a political career in California. "What a pity that you have not turned your steps to California and been a candidate for U.S. Senate," he wrote. "Even now it is not too late and you would have an excellent chance of success. A new man and a man of note would carry all before him. What say you?"[25]

Across the continent in New York, politics was the last thing on Stephens's mind, and his lack of response to Catherwood's letters was, as his friend suspected, more likely due to his crushing workload than anything else. Moreover, in early 1851, when Catherwood was grumbling about his long silence, Stephens was in Panama again, deeply enmeshed in the seemingly endless difficulties that were delaying the railroad's construction.

On his arrival he found a grim situation. The work crews were mired in what was said to be the worst swampland in Central America. Totten and Baldwin had waded with their men up to their chests through the swamps and succeeded in clearing and building their way off Manzanillo Island and onto the mainland. What they thought was the hardest part was only the beginning. The two men, who suffered alternating bouts of dysentery and malaria, now faced virgin tropical forest and mile after mile of quicksand, muck, and swamp in some places so deep that when they dumped in tons of rock and earth to support the railbed, they had difficulty reaching the bottom.[26] To move forward at all, they had to build a framework of pilings over the swamps to support the rails, and backfill or "crib in" the beds later. Meanwhile, the workmen were dying by the dozens, if not the hundreds.

"The climate stood like a dragon in the way," wrote Tracy Robinson, a company man who arrived in Panama several years after the road was completed. "To this day it seems astonishing that any soul survived to tell the tale."[27] Much of the work through the swamps was performed by natives brought in from the districts around Cartagena. They, along with several hundred blacks recruited from Jamaica, were considered by Totten the best and hardiest of the workers because they were accustomed to the climate. They were soon joined by Irishmen from New Orleans, and later directly from Ireland. Carpenters, mechanics, and assistant engineers poured in from the United States. By early 1851, when Stephens arrived, nearly a thousand men had joined the workforce, some putting up housing, hospitals, and stations on patches of high ground located at intervals nearly twenty miles inland along the survey line. But most were stuck laying the railbeds through the intervening swamps, where sometimes the work, especially in a section called the "Black Swamp," came to a frequent halt because of illness and death.

"The white men withered as cut plants in the sun," wrote Robinson, who had read firsthand reports. At times more than half the workforce was sick and unable to work. Of one group of forty-five carpenters, Totten recalled, after two months "only three or four of them were at work, or able to work. They were laid up with fever and ague." Those judged by the doctors unable to resume work, he wrote, were sent home by every steamer. One early group of workers agreed to work for one hundred days. But, according to Totten, only ninety out of the original three hundred completed their contract. In addition, hundreds of other men simply put up their tools and melted into the endless stream of humanity flowing across the isthmus for California.[28]

It was a life-and-death struggle, a war complete with battlefield commanders, casualties, and deserters; in the end, it was not clear how many lost their lives building the railroad.[29] The company never kept accurate records, which may have been deliberate. It publicly downplayed the accidents and illnesses—the malaria, dengue, typhoid fevers, dysentery, hepatitis, and cholera.[30] Many reports of the fatalities were gross exaggerations, such as the celebrated rumor that there was a dead man for every railroad tie laid across the isthmus, which would have placed the number of deaths at more than ten times the number of men who actually worked on the railroad. But the men were clearly dying at an intolerable rate, even for the times. Totten, the railroad's

Stephens's cottage overlooking the Chagres River.
(*Harper's New Monthly Magazine*, 1859)

chief engineer and later its superintendent, conceded that between 800 and 1,200 men lost their lives out of the more than 6,000 who worked the line during the five years it took to complete.[31] Other accounts stated that as many as 40 percent died. And these counts did not include the additional hundreds who became too sick to work and went home to early deaths, their health destroyed by the tropical diseases.

When Stephens arrived, the fatalities were only beginning, and he, too, was quickly sick again, probably with malaria and its all-too-familiar fevers and chills. Learning of his illness, a friend wrote in March pressing him not to stay on the isthmus during the coming rainy season: "Health is beyond price, recollect, and despite your mental energy, you have had a warning not to trifle with it."[32] Aspinwall also had gotten word. "Now for heaven's sake," he wrote him in April, "remember your promise—my dear fellow—not to remain on the isthmus at any exposure to yourself. I cannot tell you how I am concerned lest that spirit of yours should carry you beyond the bounds of prudence and I would give anything now to have you quietly at home again. I hope you will without fail return on the [steamship] *Georgia*."[33]

Stephens ignored them. He remained in Panama until July, well into the rainy season.[34] The agonizingly slow pace of the project only drove him deeper into work. It was growing depressingly possible that the primeval, unyielding Panamanian jungle might swallow the railroad whole and Stephens with it, just as nature had devoured the great cities of the Maya. Every timetable they set had to be revised, all their plans constantly recalculated and adjusted. And after long and hard lobbying, he failed to convince enough officials from Granada to grant the company title to the whole of Manzanillo Island, which he insisted was essential to create a port city for the railroad.

In addition, as company president, he knew money was running out, as the railroad was approaching the end of its shareholders' initial investments. Moreover, the prospects for raising new funds were diminishing with every report reaching New York of the deaths and sicknesses, the intolerable swamps and working conditions, and the company's inability to keep men under contract. Skeptical investors claimed the railroad would never be completed. And hanging over the company like Damocles' sword was the growing success of a transport company crossing Nicaragua set up by Cornelius Vanderbilt, the famously ruthless "Commodore," who was also eager to cash in on the gold rush. He had already put several steamers on the San Juan River, which flowed from Lake Nicaragua to the Caribbean. From the lake west it was only a short distance overland to the Pacific, a route Stephens knew well from his explorations there ten years earlier for a possible canal.

Finally, in July, Stephens returned to New York, where the original projectors of the railroad were focusing all their energies on raising new money. To buy more time, bonds were floated. Stephens kept his head down, suppressed his doubts, and pushed on with his work. He returned to the isthmus four months later, in November 1851. "It was a most fortunate circumstance that I came down as I did," he wrote his father in January. "The work had run down to its lowest point, and never looked darker. But the whole aspect is now changed. We are now in the last swamp, a terrible place it is for working in, but have dry weather and a good force, and two weeks will carry us safe over."[35]

Totten and Baldwin had refused to give in and pushed the road to the village of Gatun on the Chagres River, seven miles inland from Manzanillo. The entire enterprise, however, still faced the abyss of financial collapse.

Then the gods showed mercy: the very natural forces that had bedeviled the project unexpectedly turned in their favor. In early December foul weather forced several steamships to abandon the dangerous mouth of the Chagres River and seek shelter in Navy Bay. There hundreds of passengers swarmed onto Manzanillo Island and insisted they would pay almost any price for transportation to Gatun. "We offered to fit up our gravel cars for the conveyance of the passengers," wrote Totten, "which was gladly accepted: and thus, seated on rough boards or on their trunks, in the gravel cars, twelve hundred as jolly passengers as ever traveled, inaugurated the opening of the first seven miles of the Panama Railroad."[36]

At Gatun the passengers transferred to the native dugouts to continue the rest of their passage up the Chagres. Within weeks, virtually every arriving steamship had switched from the Chagres to Navy Bay, where a ride on the railroad cut two days from the trip over the isthmus. The decision by Stephens and Totten to take on the passengers, even at the risk of further construction delays, brought in a large transfusion of cash that helped save the railroad. Over the succeeding months, hundreds more workmen were recruited and the construction increased rapidly as the railbeds rose out of the swamps onto higher, firmer ground. Nearly twelve hundred men were working at points along the line in early 1852, which allowed Stephens to predict they would reach and cross the Chagres at the village of Barbacoa— halfway across the isthmus—by the end of the year. When word of the new developments reached New York, investors were again clamoring to climb aboard.

On February 22, 1852, matters had improved enough that the company held a ceremony to lay a cornerstone for Manzanillo's first brick building. Located next to the railroad's docks, the large structure would become the company's future offices. Nearby, an untidy slapdash town was quickly rising out of the old mangrove swamp as

Port of Aspinwall. (*Harper's New Monthly Magazine*, 1859)

hotel owners and storekeepers rushed to transfer their businesses from Chagres. Every day more of the island was filled in and streets laid out. Stephens arranged transport of fresh water by aqueduct from a river located miles away. And he was finally on the verge of convincing New Granada to grant the company full title to the island. The time had come to give the place a name.

Present for the cornerstone dedication was Granada's new ambassador to the United States, Victoriano de Diego Paredes. In a short speech he proposed the new city be named *Aspinwall,* in honor of the company's leading founder.[37] The recommendation was immediately taken up by George Law, one of the railroad company's wealthiest directors, who had just arrived to inspect the road. Then Stephens, speaking briefly as company president, formally adopted the name

The Stephens Tree, under which he was reportedly found unconscious.
(*Harper's New Monthly Magazine*, 1859)

(years later the Colombian government would change it to *Colón,* for Christopher Columbus), and three cheers went up from the crowd of spectators.[38] As the applause faded, it would have appeared to anyone lingering on the scene that it was John L. Stephens, famous chronicler of the ancient Maya civilization, who was, in fact, lord of one of the monumental undertakings of his age.

◎◉◎

What happened next is unclear. According to a popular account, Stephens was found a month later in the jungle near Lion Hill, lying unconscious along the railroad tracks under a giant ceiba that came to be known later as the Stephens Tree. He was reportedly carried in a coma aboard a steamer leaving for New York.[39] Certainly Stephens had fallen ill repeatedly in Panama.[40] And he did return to New York in April 1852.[41] But this account is possibly apocryphal. He was described by his friend, the Reverend Francis L. Hawks, as in "good if not better health than usual" when he arrived home.[42]

Ten years had passed since he stepped off the *Anna Louisa* with Catherwood and Cabot on their return from Yucatán, and he had spent almost half of the last four years of his life in the jungles of Panama. There was little question his accumulated travels had affected his health. At the age of forty-six he himself wondered aloud at times whether he would live to see completion of the railroad he was so determined to build. "I have had a hard siege," he conceded in a final letter to his father not long before he left Panama.[43]

On arrival in New York, he checked into the Delmonico Hotel, located just steps from the railroad's offices at 78 Broadway.[44] Aspinwall wrote to Stephens in March that the company's directors were anxiously awaiting his return to consult on the building of the long bridge that was to span the Chagres River at Barbacoa. The enterprise had turned the corner. The road now extended over half its planned route, spanning the worst, most tortuous part of the isthmus. The company was now planning to hand off the remaining construction to associates of George Law who had signed a contract to construct the Barbacoa bridge and lay the rails over the summit and the final distance to Panama City. "I think I see daylight," Stephens had written his father from Panama.[45]

In May, nearly three hundred people crowded into a banquet hall at Astor House for a dinner honoring George Law. His share of the Panama route, his mail steamship line between New York, Charleston, Havana, Chagres, and now the port of Aspinwall, had won great popular acclaim and a good deal of commerce for the merchants of the city. During the banquet, there was much praise for the Panama Railroad Company, on whose board Law sat as a prominent director. When Law rose finally to speak, he turned to Stephens, who was sitting nearby on the dais, and he raised his glass in a toast: "It is this gentleman who has been connected for a long time conveying passengers from here to California. It is he, I repeat, that commenced this enterprise. Everyone knows that work, and you all know John L. Stephens, president of the Panama Railroad." The crowd erupted in cheers.

Then Stephens rose and disavowed any claim to being the originator of the railroad. It was to William Aspinwall that honor was due, he said, setting off another round of cheers. He admitted, however, that after conducting the original survey of the isthmus several years earlier, he thought how impossible it would be that "the whistle of a locomotive would ever be heard in that country." He then turned and toasted Law for carrying forth the remainder of the railroad work, added toasts to the rival ventures crossing at Nicaragua and Tehuantepec, Mexico, and in a final rousing lift of his glass, exclaimed: "Success to the great American enterprise which is to connect the Atlantic and the Pacific Oceans."[46]

◁◁ 26 ▷▷

Together Again

A year earlier, a rich vein of gold-bearing quartz had been discovered in the foothills of the Sierra Nevada mountains in a place called Grass Valley.[1] Word of the discovery traveled 125 miles to San Francisco and set off a new, small-scale gold rush. Hundreds of gold seekers stormed the district, and among them was Frederick Catherwood.[2] He had once more decided to reinvent himself, this time as a mining engineer. In spite of his remarks to Stephens about avoiding the mines, the possibility of making a small fortune had simply proved too powerful.

Arriving in Grass Valley at the same time in April 1851 was an artist and writer named Alonzo Delano, who with a partner had purchased a claim on one of the hills in the valley. While working his dig, he befriended Catherwood, who by then had become part owner of a mine on nearby Gold Hill. Delano would go on to publish a number of sketches of characters he encountered during the gold rush. His brief depiction of Catherwood, written in a letter to a friend in August 1851, remains one of the only portraitures of Catherwood in existence. But much like Catherwood's earlier "self-portrait" in the ruins of Tulum, Delano's description leaves us again with blurred edges and Catherwood's mystique largely intact:

> Notwithstanding the horde of villains who throng in our midst, the high character of the miners and operatives for intelligence and various acquirements still deservedly continue. Among them I have for a neighbor and friend, Mr. Frederick M. Catherwood, celebrated the world over as an artist and

traveler. You would little dream that modest, quiet man, standing by that puffing, stamping, noisy crushing mill, without a particle of ostentation in his manner, dressed in a plain, coarse, drab corduroy dreadnought coat and pants, with high coarse leather boots reaching above his knees, his head covered with a broadbrim California hat and his somewhat prominent nose bridging a pair of spectacles, was the artist who illustrated the admirable works of Stephens's *Petraea* and *Yucatán*, with drawings taken on the spot. It is even he, and if you would make him blush, [. . .] speak to him of his works. He has too much modesty to intrude himself on your notice, but if you will draw him out you will find him a gentleman as well as an artist, and he is the president of his company and one of the proprietors of the mill.[3]

The Gold Hill Quartz Mining Company was a success, clearing between $800 and $1,000 a day during one early period, and Catherwood seemed finally to have achieved the financial security he had long sought.[4] He wrote Stephens that he remained cautious, however, and had invested no more than $5,000 of his capital in the operation.[5] His engineering skills were undoubtedly called on in the design of the millwork needed to separate the veins of gold embedded in the quartz. Steam engines drove the stamping machines that crushed the ore. The noisy steam age had come to the quiet Sierra foothills.

"Unfortunately California does not improve on acquaintance," he wrote Stephens. "I do not mean the country which is well enough but the state of society. To young men who are fond of certain kinds of excitement it may have its attractions, but to a sober plodding old fellow like myself it is peculiarly distasteful and nothing but direct money gain makes it bearable."[6]

In January 1852, when Gold Hill declared a 10 percent dividend, Catherwood was back with his children in London, where he had taken samples of Gold Hill's quartz to drum up new investors in the company. We have no date for his departure from California but it is probable that he left sometime in the fall of 1851. On his return to England he landed in Acapulco, then crossed through Mexico and not Panama.

In February 1852, while Stephens spoke at the cornerstone-laying ceremony on Manzanillo Island, Catherwood addressed members of the London's Banking Institute in Threadneedle Street. Members were concerned about the inflationary effects of the gold discoveries in California and, more recently, Australia. He described the overall situation in California and told the bankers that an estimated 180,000–200,000 men were currently working in the mining districts, averaging about seven or eight shillings a day.[7] Then, no doubt seeking investors among the bankers, he displayed samples of the gold-veined quartz he had brought from the Grass Valley mine.

In April he wrote Stephens from Charles Square asking if he was interested in investing in Gold Hill. He said he would understand if Stephens was cautious about such a speculative operation. "But I think it will turn out alright," he said, pointing out that he had already collected his first 10 percent dividend. He was trying to arrange a merger of Gold Hill with another mining operation, he explained, and he and others were working to raise new capital for the combined companies. "Let me know before all the stock is sold."

Then he mentioned again the Indian ruins he had heard about in California but had not yet had a chance to visit. Where exactly they were he didn't say, but he claimed they were "remarkable antiquities" of "massive and important character."[8] Only three or four others knew of them, he added, and he was anxious to get to the site before they did. (The reference is a mystery, as no ruins similar to those of the ancient Maya are known to exist in California.)

"My idea was to have made my careful drawings and then to have passed a month or so with you getting out a little addenda to a new edition of your work. How does that idea please you?"[9] Stephens may have welcomed the idea now that the weight of the railroad was slowly lifting from his shoulders with the new construction contract arranged by Law. Unfortunately we have no letters from Stephens to Catherwood to tell us.[10]

At the end of June, Catherwood learned from Stephens that he was back in New York and wrote how relieved he was to know he was safely home again. He wrote about coming to New York but indicated the merger negotiations were delaying his travel. Then he struck an apprehensive note. While he had been positive about his mining venture in April, now he was not so sure about its prospects. He indicated something may have gone wrong in California because financial accounts from Gold Hill were not being regularly sent to him. Then he added, ominously:

> You must not be surprised if I should once again come to you for employment in connection with the Panama railroad, and I think it well to ask you in advance whether you can give me a berth on it should I be obliged eight or ten months hence or possibly sooner to look out for a situation. I have embarked $13,000 in the mine, and I should not be surprised if I were to lose the greater part of it. Of course this is between ourselves. It annoys and worries me beyond expression, on account of my children, for as to myself I care nothing.[11]

Then silence. The June letter is the last to be found among the correspondence between the two men.

Since May's banquet, Stephens's health had gone into steady decline. Then sometime during the summer, the exact timing is not certain, he grew seriously ill. Because of the heat and humidity in the congested city, he left Manhattan for Long Island, possibly to the country home of a family member or friend. But he was not so ill that he did not follow closely all the business of the railroad as well as other news. "I have seen Mr. Lawrence [the U.S. ambassador to England]," Aspinwall wrote in a short note to Stephens on July 13, "and had a pleasant talk with him which I will communicate to you when I come up to see you. Glad to hear you are easier."[12]

Francis Spies, the secretary for the railroad, wrote him regularly concerning company business and the progress on the isthmus, which had slowed to a crawl during the peak of Panama's wet season. Spies visited with Stephens every chance he could get out of the office. "I have been trying to get down this week and see you but so far without success," he wrote on August 18. "I must come down on Saturday."[13] And whenever a steamer arrived from the isthmus, Spies

The SS *John L. Stephens*.

brought out the latest news, some of which must have weighed heavily on Stephens and added to his sense of urgency in finishing the road.[14]

One report told of a U.S. Army regiment that had been dispatched from New York to cross Panama and take up garrison duty in California and Oregon. Accompanied by their wives and children, 550 soldiers landed at the railroad's docks at Aspinwall on July 16, then traveled more than twenty miles over the company's existing rails to the center of the isthmus, where the construction was continuing. From there most of the men continued on foot over the mountain to Panama City while the women and children waited with the baggage as a young lieutenant in charge, Ulysses S. Grant, struggled to round up enough mules for the final descent. The delay, which lasted more than a week, proved fatal. By the time Grant got the rest of the party to the Pacific coast, their ranks had been decimated by cholera. The future general and U.S. president estimated that one out of three in his group had died. During the following weeks, many more in the regiment succumbed while quarantined in an abandoned ship in Panama Bay. By the time the regiment sailed for San Francisco at the end of August, Grant wrote his wife, they had "lost one hundred persons, counting men, women and children."[15]

Stephens's condition wavered. He had beaten back fevers before and there were periods of improvement. At one point Spies dashed off a note, undated, mentioning that he had heard from a mutual friend that "you appeared to be much more comfortable yesterday" and at last "the doctors are on the right track."[16]

But while his doctors by now understood the likely cause of Stephens's disorder, there was little they could do about it. He was diagnosed with a diseased liver, the result of hepatitis and an accumulation of tropical diseases picked up on the isthmus and at Bogotá. On August 31, the *Long Island Farmer and Queen County Advertiser* carried a short item: "John L. Stephens, esq., well-known traveler and artist, is said to be lying dangerously ill" in Hempstead, New York, a village not far from New York City on Long Island.

At this point Aspinwall, deeply affected by his close friend's illness, decided to name his latest Pacific Mail steamship in Stephens's honor. The 274-foot vessel, a magnificent state-of-the-art wooden side-wheeler, was in the final stages of construction at the Smith & Dimon shipyard on the East River. The ship was being fitted out with luxurious, wood-paneled staterooms, large glass portholes, improved ventilation system, tanks for twenty thousand gallons of fresh water, and an extensive suite of baths for its nine hundred passengers and crew, complete with hot and cold water. Aspinwall arranged for the steamer's launch and christening to take place on September 21, attended by Stephens's father, family, friends, and the public. Stephens was not well enough to join them. He had been moved to his father's house at 13 Leroy Place, where he could be cared for more easily by his doctors and family.

At two o'clock in the afternoon on the last day of summer—a "muggy" day, according to one newspaper—a large crowd gathered at the east end of Fourth Street. It had been forty-five years since two-year-old John Stephens and his family stood on the other side of Manhattan and watched the launch of the *Clermont* by steamboat pioneer Robert Fulton. Now, at half past three the enormous hull of the *John L. Stephens* slid into the East River and cheers went up from the spectators. At the time, New Yorkers gathered by the thousands to witness such launchings. "She is a very sharp, handsome craft and the beauty of her model was a matter of remark among the large assemblage present to witness her enter the water," the *New York Herald* reported the next day.[17] The *John L. Stephens* was the fourteenth steamship in the Pacific Mail line, its largest and most lavish. And standing that day in the thick of the "assemblage," almost certainly, was Frederick Catherwood and his son, Frederick, Jr.

Stephens was home again on quiet tree-lined Leroy Place, not far from the playing fields of his youth: the promenade along New York's Battery, the Bowling Green, where he dared to climb the iron fence in defiance of city elders to retrieve the balls that got away.[18]

A growing abscess had taken hold in Stephens's liver. Doctors in the mid-nineteenth century had almost no resources to deal with such a condition, no antibiotics or other medicines to treat the infection. Short of surgery, which in the pre-antiseptic age was just as likely to kill as cure a patient, they could at best offer only opiates and other palliative concoctions. And Stephens may have been delirious when Catherwood showed up at Leroy Place.

We know from Catherwood's own account that he and Stephens met at least once again after their brief time working together in Panama. Catherwood mentioned being separated for two years in a short profile of Stephens that he later published. We have no details, however, no records, no eyewitness accounts or descriptions of any kind for Stephens's final days. But we know from ship manifests that Catherwood and his son left Liverpool on September 4 aboard the steamship SS *Pacific* and arrived in New York on September 20, the day before the launch of the SS *John L. Stephens*.[19] The Stephens family, to whom Catherwood was devoted like a son and brother, would have been his first stop. Did he learn then for the first time the seriousness of Stephens's illness and the steamship's launch? Or had he found out while still in England and rushed to New York to be at his old friend's side? Without surviving letters or other accounts we will never have the answer. We know only that he arrived just in time.

The appearance of Catherwood and his son standing at his bedside

Burial vault of John L. Stephens at New York City Marble Cemetery,
with detail of Maya glyph sculpted from an image by Catherwood.

must have seemed to Stephens like a figment of his imagination, an
apparition, a fevered dream. Now seventeen years old, Frederick Jr.
had been no more than six or eight when Stephens last saw him. And
what did Catherwood see—and feel? Lying before him was his dearest friend, his old fellow traveler, the man with whom he had shared
hardship and daring, a partnership of near madness and genius. They
had endured severe illnesses together and yet Catherwood would have
been shocked to see his old companion's emaciated body, his eyes
sunken and skin yellow with jaundice. Just two years earlier, writing
from Panama to an unnamed person, probably Stephens's father,
Catherwood had been reassuring. "Knowing the strength of his constitution and how rapidly he recovers from attacks of the fever," he
said of Stephens's accident and sickness in Bogotá, "I trust to find him
in good health when we meet."[20]

   But this was no relapse of fever. Stephens's great heart and indom-
itable spirit were now overwhelmed by disease and deadly toxins. He

was dying. No amount of rebounds the two men had known before could be reassuring now.

Had Catherwood arrived too late? Was Stephens too distracted and feverish, his brain too confused for the two men to communicate? Or in their last hours together did they have time to talk—and remember? Talk of making books, railroads, of Egypt and Jerusalem? Recall the tormented ride up through the mud of Mico Mountain? Relive the moment the angry mob burst into the *cabildo* in Camotán and pointed muskets at their hearts; laugh again at the gold-dollar eagle pressed into the hot sealing wax? In his delirium, did Stephens gape once more with Catherwood, looking in utter wonder at the phantasmagoric Mayan lords towering over them in the Copán forest—the monoliths that changed their lives?

Did they remember their anxiety at traveling apart through Central America and their relief upon falling into each other's arms when they met again in Guatemala City? Were they able to share the memory of drifting perilously from the shore on the startling blue lake of Atitlán, feel the freezing cold nights, dodging the swarms of insects and fire along the trail as they crossed the Cuchumatanes range? Conjure up the giant fireflies at night in the palace at Palenque while they watched the black sky pierced by lightning as rain clouds swept toward them across the bent treetops? Did they recall the sharks circling their becalmed ship in the Gulf of Mexico, the daguerreotype sessions in Mérida and fumbling eye surgeries? Feel the cool, lime-infused crystalline water of the cenotes, where they swam at the end of long hot rides across stony Yucatán, relive one last time the descent on the rickety giant ladder at Bolonchen, their endless fevers and chills, their brief bearded sojourn on the palm-shaded sands of Cozumel Island, the murderous attacks of the mosquitoes at Tulum, and over and over and over again the haunting, perplexing beauty of the stone cities they had found together, buried so deep in the jungle?

The great arc of their extraordinary journey and long, close friendship came to an end on Tuesday evening, October 12, 1852.[21] Stephens died at his father's home on Leroy Place at the age of forty-six.

○◉◎

Stephens's body was taken by horse-drawn hearse three days later to St. Thomas Church, where an Episcopal service was performed. The rosewood coffin was then brought to Marble Cemetery at Second Street. Among the pallbearers was Samuel J. Tilden, a close friend of Stephens who would later become New York's governor and win the popular vote for the U.S. presidency in 1876, only to lose a disputed Electoral College vote to Rutherford B. Hayes.[22] Stephens's remains were put temporarily in an unmarked vault set aside for his brother-in-law. They were transferred nearly a century later to a large vault, where they remain today, marked by a Maya glyph with the appearance of a scribe copied from an earlier Catherwood illustration.[23]

◁ 27 ▷

Missing

Stephens had been Catherwood's best friend, his anchor, the man he had trusted and loved more deeply than any other, and whose loss must have pierced him grievously. And there were signs, too, that he was losing his equilibrium.

He had been under great pressure to get to California as fast as possible to salvage his mining investment. But within days of his return his merger plan began to unravel. Arriving in San Francisco, he demanded "immediate payment of a large sum" from the new partners on top of the amount that had been agreed on in England. The company's agent refused and the joint venture collapsed.[1] Catherwood's seemingly inexplicable demand may have been justified as the other company was already negotiating for other mining claims before he arrived.

What this meant for Gold Hill is not clear. During his absence in England an election of company officers took place and he was not reelected president.[2] Even if these events somehow undermined his personal investment, as he had hinted to Stephens might happen, the mining company itself continued to thrive financially for at least another year.[3] But Catherwood's name never came up in connection with Gold Hill Mining again. Instead he found himself a railroad surveyor once more, hired to help lay out a hundred-mile line from Marysville, near the mining districts, to Benicia, near San Francisco Bay.[4] The project was delayed by winter rains but completed by March 1853.[5]

Then Catherwood dropped from sight once again, only to reappear a year later in London with the publication of a revised edition of his first book with Stephens: *Incidents of Travel in Central America,*

Chiapas, and Yucatán.[6] The book, which went on sale in March 1854 for twelve shillings, turned out to be the inexpensive, single-volume reprint that Catherwood earlier declined to publish without Stephens's "sanction and approbation."[7]

"In preparing the present Work for publication in a cheap form," Catherwood wrote in the book's preface, "I have not omitted any of the illustrations that appeared in the American Edition, and have given some additional ones, which are now published for the first time."[8] And while he had augmented his own work, he explained that he had "curtailed a portion" of Stephens's narrative in order to reduce the book to a single volume. Yet the abridgements were minor and the new British edition still took up 548 pages—in smaller letter type. Catherwood's edits were also judiciously made in a way that kept the narrative force of the two-volume original.

Catherwood also made two significant additions to the work. The first was a portrait of Stephens, engraved "from a daguerreotype," in which a stern-looking Stephens glares from the page with intense, burning eyes, a shock of thick black hair swept from his high forehead, his chin and jaw firmly set, framed by his beard. The selection is a curious one from the person who knew Stephens and what he looked like probably better than anyone—an image that Catherwood may have felt captured Stephens's determined, unwavering spirit, but one also at odds with the few other, softer, more flattering portraits of Stephens that still exist.

The other addition was a two-page "biographical notice" by Catherwood briefly covering the high points of Stephens's life and the two men's partnership over more than a decade. It ends with a one-sentence tribute in Catherwood's characteristically formal—almost repressed—phraseology: "As his fellow-traveler and intimate friend, I may be permitted to bear testimony to his kindly disposition, and the many excellent qualities of head and heart which endeared him to a large circle of friends and connexions." He added that if the new edition was well received in England, it would be followed by a "continuation of our travels in Yucatán in the years 1841, 1842." That volume would never be published.

Six months later, on September 20, 1854, Catherwood boarded the

SS *Arctic* in Liverpool, bound for New York, this time traveling alone. The *Arctic* was the pride of the so-called Collins Line, based in New York, which had been battling its English rival, the Cunard Line, for several years for supremacy in the transatlantic packet trade.[9] Packets were steamships that ran on regular schedules, unlike most sailing ships, which were dependent on favorable winds and full cargo holds.

The "Great Atlantic Race," as it came to be known, stirred patriotic passions on both sides of the Atlantic. The *Arctic* was launched in 1850 in New York to great fanfare. At 284 feet and 2,856 tons, like the SS *John L. Stephens*, she was among the largest, most luxurious, and most powerful ships afloat. And within two years she had broken several records, steaming from New York to Liverpool in less than ten days.

When she left Liverpool for New York in 1854 on the last day of summer, she was filled to capacity, carrying 233 passengers, 175 crew members, and six lifeboats capable of carrying a maximum of 180 people. On board with Catherwood were dozens of New York society's most prominent members, who were returning home from summer travels in Europe, including the wife and two children of Edward Knight Collins, the principal owner of the Collins Line. Also aboard were three grown children of James Brown, part owner of the largest investment bank in North America, and George Allen, partner in Novelty Iron Works, the company that built the *Arctic*'s giant steam engines, who was returning to New York with his wife and small son.[10]

Seven days out from Liverpool, the *Arctic* steamed full ahead through a thick fog sixty miles south of Newfoundland. Approaching from the opposite direction was a smaller vessel called *Vesta,* an iron-hulled, propeller-driven steamship carrying more than a hundred sailors and fishermen on their way home to France following the fishing season on the Grand Banks. Though it was twelve noon, lookouts on each ship failed to see the other through the fog until the last moment. In an explosion of screeching metal, the 152-foot *Vesta* tore into the starboard bow of the *Arctic,* then continued on alongside and past the larger ship. When the *Arctic*'s captain, James Luce, ran out on deck and surveyed the damage he could see that the *Vesta,* whose bow was completely gone, was doomed to sink in a matter of minutes. Thinking that his much larger ship was not seriously damaged, he ordered the *Arctic*'s helmsman to circle the French ship in order to render all assistance necessary to save its passengers and crew. But within a short time it became clear the *Arctic* had also sustained serious damage along its starboard side, with a gaping hole below the waterline where much of the *Vesta*'s twisted iron bow now protruded. The *Arctic* began filling with water. Over the next hours, working frantically, the crew and passengers failed in every attempt to stop the inward rush of the sea.

Drifting away from the *Arctic* in the fog, the crewmen and fishermen aboard the *Vesta* fought to buttress the ship's forward bulkhead against the incoming water. They then shifted cargo to the stern and raised the ship's bow enough to enable them to keep the vessel afloat long enough to make it to the Newfoundland coast three days later.

On the *Arctic,* however, panic began to set in when it became clear that the ship was slowly settling deeper in the water and would not make it to the coast. Captain Luce, in a heroic effort, tried to get all the women and children on board into the ship's few lifeboats. With several loyal officers he fought off crew members, some of them firemen and coal tenders who rushed up on deck as the rising water below doused the fires under the ship's boilers. In a pitched battle that followed, they overwhelmed Luce, and along with some male passengers commandeered the boats. With the six lifeboats gone, most not even filled to capacity, the remaining crew and passengers ripped up planks and threw overboard spars from the ship's masts, doors—anything that floated—in an effort to lash together a large raft. Four hours after the collision, as the *Arctic* sank deeper into the sea, many of its passengers climbed praying and crying onto the roof of the deck house. Then the huge steamship went down, the sea swallowing virtually all of its passengers, including the captain, his eleven-year-old son, Willie, the Collins, Brown, and Allen families—and Frederick Catherwood.

Captain Luce, gripping his son, was sucked deep into the watery vortex but somehow managed to fight his way back up to the surface. A few moments later, one of the large round wooden covers that curved over the *Arctic*'s side paddle wheels broke free from the ship and, full with air, shot up through the surface. An edge left a deep gash across the captain's head. When the half-circle box fell back into the water, it crushed the skull of his son, killing him instantly. Luce

The sinking of the SS *Arctic*.

struggled for some time blinded by his own blood. Nearby George Allen, the partner of the Novelty Iron Works, had also surfaced alive. The two men clung to the floating paddle-wheel box, eventually pulling themselves into it. Twelve others made it through the freezing water and into the box, but only Luce, Allen, and another man were still alive two days later when they were rescued by a passing ship. Seven other passengers and crewmen who had also climbed onto large pieces of debris from the ship survived long enough to be found. In the end, seventy-six others in three lifeboats were rescued or made it to the Newfoundland coast. Fifty-nine were members of the crew and seventeen were passengers, not one of them a woman or a child. Of the original 408 passengers and crew aboard the *Arctic,* only 86 survived. Catherwood was not among them.

Horrifying accounts of the SS *Arctic* tragedy from the survivors, and an official report from Captain Luce, filled the newspapers in New York, London, and other cities for weeks. Obituaries for many of the *Arctic*'s most prominent passengers were published. But there was not one mention of Catherwood. Many days later the name "Mr.

Newspaper account of the tragedy of the SS *Arctic*.

Catherwood" finally appeared, a single line in a list designated: "Missing."

Six months afterward, in San Francisco, a note appeared in the April 15, 1855, edition of the *Daily Alta California*. It announced that a letter of credit from the Union Bank in London issued for Mr. Frederick Catherwood in the amount of 950 pounds sterling had been stopped—"Mr. Catherwood having perished in the *Arctic*."[11]

No obituaries ever appeared in London or New York or San Francisco. The blurred and elusive identity, the modesty and facelessness that had lingered around Catherwood all his life, followed him even into death.

Epilogue

The Petén sun, a huge bubble of molten gold rising off the edge of the world, lights up the old stones that jut through the jungle canopy. The stark, isolated temples of the Maya are the only objects visible above a sea of green. Standing for centuries atop their pyramids, glowing scarlet and saffron in the dawn, the stones have triumphed over nature for another day. The ancient city beneath the trees, originally called Yax Mutal and today Tikal, was the one place Stephens and Catherwood had most wanted to visit. A priest they met on their way to Palenque told them of it. The cleric said that as a young man he had climbed to the summit of the Cordilleras in the center of Guatemala, looked out over the immense forest extending to Yucatán and the Gulf of Mexico, and saw at a great distance "a large city spread over a great space, and with turrets white and glittering in the sun."

"We had a craving desire to reach the mysterious city," wrote Stephens.[1] But it lay in the middle of uncharted lowland jungle, where no white men entered, and they had to get to Palenque before the start of the rains. "We had difficulties enough in the road before us," he added, and they rode on to Palenque around the seemingly impenetrable Petén forest. They remained haunted, however, by the cleric's vision of magnificence and splendor; they were convinced also that other cities lay buried in the Petén waiting to be unearthed. And it would not be long, they believed, before they were.

Their speculations proved prescient but the timing wrong. Years would pass before Tikal was discovered and decades before other cities scattered throughout the Petén were found and their monuments, temples, and palaces laid bare. Deciphering the Maya's hieroglyphic

Tikal temples rising above the jungle canopy in El Petén, Guatemala. (Carlsen)

code would take more than another century. And today ruins still lie covered by the jungle.

Stephens had always been concerned about rivals, and he was certain that others would quickly follow in his path. But his books, despite their blazing rush of popularity, did not send an immediate surge of explorers into the heart of Central America. And he was in large part responsible. His vivid descriptions of Central America's rugged topography and unforgiving jungles were daunting enough. But he had also, if unintentionally, set people's teeth on edge with his repelling accounts of the political violence that permeated the region as well.

For Americans in particular, whose daring Stephens had hoped to inspire, there were other powerful dynamics at work. The United States was in the throes of a great westward expansion, "Manifest Destiny," aided and abetted by the gold rush and Stephens and Catherwood's second great adventure: the Panama Railroad, completed in 1855. As the nation shifted west, it also turned inward, its interests and energies consumed by settlement and improvements across its vast inner spaces. Then, in 1861, the country was swallowed whole—by civil war.

Stephens's books nonetheless remained extremely popular. New editions rolled off the presses year after year and stirred deep interest in Europe in particular. Rival England especially had been caught off guard, stung by Stephens and Catherwood's success. After all, an

American with the help of a "*yankified* English artist" had bested the British in finding a lost civilization in Central America right under their noses—even though Walker and Caddy had reached Palenque first.[2] Sluggish under the weight of its bureaucracy, the British government did nothing for more than a decade after publication of Stephens's books. It finally took the trustees of the British Museum to wake the Foreign Office from its slumber. Just as Stephens had feared, they decided it was essential that the great museum possess Maya antiquities for their collections—a desire no doubt aroused by the 1850 opening in Paris of an American antiquities gallery at the Louvre displaying artifacts from Mexico and Peru.[3]

Therefore, in July 1851, while Stephens was struggling to hold together his railroad company in Panama, Lord Palmerston sent a dispatch to Frederick Chatfield in Guatemala stating "it would be desirable to obtain for the British Museum some specimens of the sculptures" from the ruins at Copán.[4] The message was quite specific. The museum wanted the sculptures described and illustrated in pages 134 to 144 of Stephens and Catherwood's first volumes on Central America.[5] The request was remarkably ambitious given that these ruins constituted some of the largest statues and monuments in Copán. But after several years and innumerable dispatches back and forth between Belize, Guatemala, and England, nothing was done.[6]

Central American officials, meanwhile, had also read Stephens. In 1848, after being alerted by a *chiclero,* or gum gatherer, who said he saw stone structures towering above the jungle, Petén's governor, Colonel Modesto Méndez, ventured deep into the forest and found the overgrown, skyscraping temples of Tikal. The discovery resulted in the first official recording of the now-famous site. Méndez's report was published in a Berlin journal in 1853, a year after Stephens's death.[7] Then the discovery faded into almost complete obscurity.

For years no new explorations were made. Then gradually, over the next fifty years, starting in the late 1850s—twenty years after Stephens and Catherwood's first expedition—individual explorers began arriving in Chiapas, Yucatán, and Guatemala—nearly all of them Europeans. Each one carried well-worn copies of Stephens's books along with hundreds of pounds of cumbersome photographic equipment.

Alfred Maudslay working in Chichén Itzá.

Funded by American tobacco magnate Peter Lorillard, a Frenchman named Désiré Charnay was one of the first serious photographers of the ruins; in 1888 Harper & Brothers published his *Ancient Cities of the New World*. Alfred P. Maudslay, an English explorer, started out in 1881 with *Incidents of Travel* in hand and followed the exact route taken by Stephens and Catherwood up the Río Dulce to the town of Izabal, then over Mico Mountain to Quiriguá and Copán. By the time he completed his seventh and final trip through the region thirteen years later, he had meticulously documented Quiriguá, Copán, and Palenque and had penetrated deep into the lowland Petén jungle to record Tikal, Yaxchilan, and other previously unknown buried cities. He created an extraordinary record of the ruins using large-format cameras to produce beautiful, high-resolution black-and-white photographs. He also made maps, drawings, plans, and plaster casts.[8]

TOP   Fallen monument at Copán. (Catherwood)
BELLOW   The same fallen monument at Copán photographed by Alfred Maudslay.

Maudslay was quickly followed by Austrian explorer Teobert Maler, who would unearth more cities and expand the record to include ruins at Piedras Negras, Naranjo, and Seibal.[9]

Then, what had been a trickle in the late 1800s became a flood of new exploration in the first half of the 1900s. The ancient world of the Maya was coming to life once again. Every year it became more evident that the "Classic" civilization the Maya had created a millennium and a half earlier had been larger, more densely populated, and more highly advanced than anyone had imagined.

On-site photographs of the ever-growing number of ruins, as well as Catherwood's and others' precise drawings, became enormously helpful. The Maya's hieroglyphic inscriptions, along with their art and architecture, could be studied carefully and comfortably outside their difficult jungle environment. And while it would take decades before the hieroglyphic code was broken, scholars more quickly decoded the Maya's numbering system and complicated calendar. They deciphered the dates on the monuments, correlated them with our Gregorian calendar, and calculated the exact age of the ruins and their inhabitants. The history of the ancient dynasties inscribed in stone slowly began to emerge, and just as Stephens had predicted, the stern-faced, brooding statutes became real people with real histories.

At the beginning of the twentieth century, the old "antiquarianism" of the nineteenth century had transformed itself, writes archaeologist Ian Graham, from "not much more than the cataloguing of curiosities into a nascent scientific discipline."[10] And if Mayanist exploration belonged to the Europeans during the last half of the nineteenth century, Americans charged into the field in the twentieth, quickly dominating the subject in a way that Stephens had always hoped. The Peabody Museum at Harvard, the Carnegie Institution of Washington, the National Geographic Society, and a large number of universities and museums sent teams of archaeologists, ethnographers, and epigraphers to Mexico and Central America and worked with a growing number of local archaeologists. They scoured the forests, found and excavated new sites, and scrupulously documented and reconstructed many of the great ruined cites. Then slowly, in fits and starts at first, and finally with help from a Russian linguist named

Yuri Knorosov, key breakthroughs in the 1950s through 1990s allowed epigraphers to crack the hieroglyphic code and unscramble the Maya's remarkable system of writing.[11]

Stephens and Catherwood would have been astonished only by how long it took. "One thing I believe," wrote Stephens about the first towering stela he and Catherwood found in Copán in November 1839, "is that its history is graven on its monuments."

Today the ancient Maya are recognized for having achieved one of the most sophisticated early civilizations on earth. Tourists by the millions, from every part of the globe, annually descend on Maya ruins in Mexico, Guatemala, Honduras, and Belize. They are drawn by the unusual beauty of the art and architecture but also the myths and legends, real and imagined, that still shroud the Maya in mystery. Their civilization has taken powerful hold in the popular imagination, stimulating interest in shamanism, creation mythology, new age cosmology, and the discovery of different ways of understanding our place in the universe. The Maya have also inspired dozens of books and films linking them, not with Egypt, the Phoenicians, and Lost Tribes of Israel as in the past, but with visitors from outer space. Doomsayers most recently claimed the Maya's "long count" of 5,126 years, which ended (and started again) on December 21, 2012, meant the arrival of a cataclysmic apocalypse, a doomsday prediction that prompted Columbia Pictures to release a $200 million disaster movie titled *2012*.

Much still remains to be discovered about the ancient Maya, scientifically and archaeologically; new ruins continue to be found. And if we pay attention, the still-emerging story of their civilization has the power to teach us about another kind of apocalypse: environmental degradation, drought, war, and the dangers of overpopulation and overconsumption that threaten our world today. Their stone cities speak from across the centuries and tell us of the riches of great success and the risks of great failure—the very human story of kings and lords, their understanding of the cosmos, their sense of time, astronomical observations, mathematics, calendars, and language, as well their extravagance, overuse of resources, dynastic rivalries, conflicts and conquests. The glowering stone lords of the forest that so startled and mesmerized Stephens and Catherwood were not all-powerful gods but humans, and the ancient ruins surrounding them have now come to life—as Stephens wrote—with "orators, warriors, and statesmen, beauty, ambition, and glory."

◎ ◉ ◎

On January 27, 1855, work gangs on the rail line from the port of Aspinwall and the line running from Panama City met at the top of the continental divide. In driving rain at midnight, under the light of whale oil lanterns, the last rail of the Panama Railroad was laid and the final spike pounded into place. The next day the first train passed from sea to sea.[12] Though Stephens did not live to see it, his dream had become a reality.

"From its inception to its consummation, it is purely American," crowed the editor of the *Aspinwall Courier* several days later. "American genius conceived the plan; American science pronounced it practicable; American capital has furnished the sinews; American energy has prosecuted the gigantic enterprise to its completion in spite of the most formidable difficulties."[13]

The construction of the forty-seven-mile rail line had cost hundreds, if not thousands of lives. It was per mile the most expensive railroad in the world, at a final cost of $6,564,553 (at least $250 million in today's dollars). "The real wonder was that the road had been built at all," wrote Tracy Robinson, who later served as an official on the line. "One cannot pass from ocean to ocean, and see from the car windows the dense masses of tangled verdure on either side, forming in many places green walls apparently impenetrable, without a sense of the marvelous."[14]

For years the railroad was the most profitable in the world, and at one point its shares at $295 were the highest-priced stock on the New York Exchange. Then, on May 10, 1869, the Atlantic and Pacific coasts of the United States were joined in Utah with the laying of the last rails of the Central Pacific and Union Pacific railroads; the profits of the Panama Railroad fell dramatically. The company was sold ten

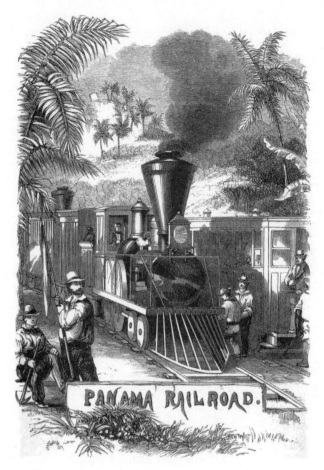

The Panama Railroad, four years after its completion.
(*Harper's New Monthly Magazine*, 1859)

years later for $25 million to a French enterprise that unsuccessfully attempted to build a canal across the isthmus following the same line as the railroad.

The United States took the railroad over in 1904 and it played a key role in the construction of the Panama Canal.[15] Today, after reconstruction in the late 1990s of much of the original route staked out by John L. Stephens and James Baldwin a century and half earlier, the railroad still hauls passengers and freight across the Isthmus of Panama.[16]

Acknowledgments

The genesis of this book came about through a perfect storm of co-incidents. In the late 1990s I was living in the Spanish colonial town of Antigua, Guatemala, when a friend named Jane Binaris one day handed me a copy of John Lloyd Stephens's *Incident of Travel in Central America, Chiapas, and Yucatán*. At the time, I had made the acquaintance of Edwin Shook, who had retired in Antigua after a long career as one of the world's great Maya archaeologists. Aware that I was soon returning to my home in San Francisco, he asked if I would help him sell a small library he had assembled of Central American books and periodicals to the Bancroft Library at the University of California, Berkeley. I agreed and before I left, as a reward, he carefully laid on his work table the extremely rare hand-colored originals of Frederick Catherwood's *Views of Ancient Monuments*. At the time I was in the thrall of Stephens's fresh, vivid account of his adventures with Catherwood, and I was stunned by the beauty of the images before me. Though I was unable to interest the university in Shook's collection, to my surprise I discovered that the Bancroft Library had in its archives Stephens's personal letters and papers. The synergy of these events inspired me to write *Jungle of Stone*, and my deepest appreciation for making it possible belongs to the late Edwin Shook and my dear friend Jane Binaris, who I regret did not live to see it in print, and to the Bancroft Library, where by coincidence I had worked as a student library page decades earlier.

It is difficult to heap enough praise on the books of John L. Stephens, whose brilliant, accessible writing and delightful companionship has won legions of fans over the last century and three-quarters. If *Jungle of Stone* is one tenth as well-written, interesting, and entertaining as his work, I should be extremely fortunate, and I strove throughout its writing to do him at least a small measure of justice. And if this book does nothing else than bring readers to Stephens, I would consider it a success. The vast rewards of his writing lay well beyond the pinched perimeter of this book.

As every author knows, no book is written in a vacuum, and for this book the vacuum is filled with experts, friends, and colleagues who helped give it life. Only one biography has been written about Stephens and another about Catherwood, both by the late Victor Wolfgang von Hagen, and to him I owe the biographical bones of this volume. Many scholars informed my understanding of the history and politics of Central America, but none better than Ralph Lee Woodward, Jr., whose remarkable *Rafael Carrera and the Emergence of the Republic of Central America, 1821–1871* stands as a comprehensive and compelling tale of the woes that befell the region in the mid-nineteenth century. For my modest comprehension of the ancient Maya, I owe a great debt to innumerable authorities, but several stand out: Robert J. Sharer, Arthur Demarest, Michael D. Coe, Simon Martin, Nikolai Grube, Ian Graham, David Freidel, Linda Schele, Joy Parker, Peter Mathews, and Richard Hansen.

One author in particular helped me fill in the broader story of the search for the ancient Maya. David M. Pendergast and his wonderful *Palenque: The Walker-Caddy Expedition to the Ancient City, 1839–1840* brought out of the shadows a little-known expedition that made the adventure richer and more exciting, and allowed me to step back and explore the wider theme of the British Empire versus American individual enterprise. And even though there was a wealth of detail in the newspaper accounts of the sinking of the SS *Arctic*, David W. Shaw's riveting *The Sea Shall Embrace Them: The Tragic Story of the Steamship Arctic* brought the horrifying tragedy vividly to life.

Tracking down and reproducing the original hand-colored *Views of Ancient Monuments* by Catherwood would not have been possible without the help of John Weeks, head librarian of the University of Pennsylvania Museum Library, and Alessandro Pezzati, museum archivist. I am also deeply grateful to my friend Alec Dubro, who unselfishly gave me an 1843 first edition of *Incidents of Travel in Yucatán*, which allowed me the opportunity to view and reproduce the fine-line original black-and-white engravings of Catherwood's work.

In my early research, I found important primary documents at the New York Historical Society, where my appreciation goes to Loraine Baratti in the manuscript department. *Jungle of Stone* could never have been written without the help of the staff at the University of California Library, Berkeley, and the university's special research collections at the Bancroft Library. In addition, my thanks go to archaeologist Richard C. Bronson, who provided me with historical information on Guatemala's Rio Dulce and the town of Izabal where Stephens and Catherwood landed and started their journey. I also owe a debt to three people in Britain, who personally aided me in my research into the life of Frederick Catherwood. Fiona Hodgson and Julie Redman, descendants of the Catherwood family, provided me with a family tree and information on Catherwood's early life in London. And I am grateful to Selwyn Tillet, whose research on Scotsman Robert

Hay turned up an important letter that shed light on the trial of Catherwood's cousin, Henry Caslon.

My friends Neil Friedman, Stephen Magagnini, and especially Ed Gilmore deserve awards for their generosity in reading parts and the whole of my manuscript and providing advice and crucially needed encouragement. I am grateful to so many of my friends for their support over the years. But for their constant belief in me and their ever-patient encouragements, I especially wish to thank Ellen Retter, who took me to see Stephens's tomb in New York City, Rick Carlsen, Chris Carlsen, Dorothy May, Barbara Arbunich, John Pearlman, Mark Liss, Bonnie Burt, Kathi McPherson, and Terry and Joanne Dale. And this book would never even have been contemplated if it were not for Carol DeRuiter, who took a fifteen-year-old boy and introduced him to the glories of the written word (and rigors of English grammar), and to her husband, Peter DeRuiter, who made me believe I could accomplish anything if I put my mind to it.

To my agent, Geri Thoma at Writers House, thank you for believing in this project from the beginning, and to Genevieve Gagne-Hawes for such superb editing that the book actually became a reality. For my editor, Peter Hubbard, I reserve my deepest appreciation for seeing the potential in *Jungle of Stone*, and understanding where it was weak and where it was strong. At my publisher William Morrow and HarperCollins, I am indebted to the hard work of Nick Amphlett, Lauren Janiec, Kaitlyn Kennedy, Paul Lamb, and Owen Corrigan. Thank you to cartographer Nick Springer, and I must express my awe at the skill and stamina of copy editor Tom Pitoniak.

And for literally keeping me alive and never giving up on me, for bearing the weight of endless monologues about Stephens and Catherwood, Morazán and Carrera, with encouragement and astonishing patience and grace, for being the pillar and love of my life, I will never be able to sufficiently express the depths of my gratitude to Kathie O'Shea. Moreover, few people are as fortunate as I have been to have had the constant companionship of Rosalita and Roxanne, who literally had my back throughout the writing of *Jungle of Stone*.

Finally, for their incredible beauty, dignity, and resilience, I will hold in my heart always the extraordinary Maya people—the descendants of the ancient Maya—whom I have had the good fortune to meet throughout my journeys through Guatemala, Honduras, Yucatán, and Chiapas, Mexico. May you forever keep your rich culture alive for the benefit of us all.

Selected Bibliography

PERIODICALS AND DOCUMENTS

The American Monthly Magazine. New York. (1833).

The Literary Gazette and Journal of the Belles Lettres, Arts, Sciences, &c. London. (1835).

The Annual Register, or a View of the History, Politics, and Literature of the Year 1835. London. (1836).

The Family Magazine. New York. (1837).

Times. London. (1841).

The Christian Examiner and General Review. Boston. (1842).

The United States Democratic Review. New York. (1843).

Littell's Living Age. Boston. (1847).

Mechanics' Magazine. Museum Register, Journal, and Gazette. London. (1847).

Panama Rail-road Company, charter. New York Public Library. (1849).

Railway Meetings. *Daily News.* London. (1849).

Sacramento Transcript. (1851).

Daily Alta California. San Francisco. (1852).

Banking Institute. *Daily News.* London. (1852).

West Mariposa Gold Quartz Mine Company. *The Times.* London. (1852).

Sacramento Daily Union. (1853).

The Times. London. (1854).

New York Daily Tribune. (1854).

Letter of Credit # 7185. *Daily Alta California.* San Francisco. (1855).

The Knickerbocker; or, New-York Monthly Magazine. (1859).

National Academy of Design Exhibition Record 1826–1860. New York: National Academy of Design. (1860).

Obituary, William H. Aspinwall. *New York Times.* (1875).

Ocean Steam Navigation. *New York Times.* (1864).

The Alexander von Humboldt Digital Library. (2006).

BOOKS

Aguirre, R. D. *Informal Empire: Mexico and Central America in Victorian Culture.* Minneapolis: University of Minnesota Press, 2005.

Aitken, J. *John Newton: From Disgrace to Amazing Grace.* Wheaton, IL: Crossway Books, 2007.

Almendáriz, R., A. d. Río, et al. Coleccion de estampas copiadas de las figuras originales, que de medio y baxo relieve, se manifiestan, en estucos y piedras, en varios edificios de la poblacion antigua nuevamente descubierta en las immediaciones del pueblo del Palenque en la Provincia de Ciudad Real de Chiapa, una de las del Reyno de Guatemala en la American Septentrional, 1787.

American Anthropological Society. *American Anthropologist.* Berkeley: University of California Press, 1900.

American Ethnological Society. *Transactions of the American Ethnological Society*. New York, Bartlett & Welford, 1845.

"The Antiquities of Central America." Book review. *United States Democratic Review* 9, no. 38 (August 1841), http://digital.library.cornell.edu/cgi/t/text/pageviewer-idx?c=usde;cc=usde;rgn=full%20text;idno=usde0009-2;didno=usde0009-2;view=image;seq=00172;node=usde0009-2%3A1.

Architects, R. I. o. B. "Antiquities of Central America." *Civil Engineer and Architect's Journal, Scientific and Railway Gazette* 7 (1844): 92–94.

Architectural Publication Society. *The Dictionary of Architecture*. London: Richards, 1852, 1887.

Arundale, F. *Illustrations of Jerusalem and Mount Sinai: Including the Most Interesting Sites Between Grand Cairo and Beirout*. London: H. Colburn, 1837.

Bancroft, H. H. *History of Central America*. San Francisco: A. L. Bancroft, 1882.

———. *The Native Races*. New York: Arno, 1967.

Baradère, H., G. Dupaix, et al. Antiquités mexicaines. Relation des trois expéditions du capitaine Dupaix, ordonnées en 1805, 1806, et 1807, pour la recherche des antiquités du pays, notamment celles de Mitla et de Palenque. Paris: Bureau des Antiquités mexicaines impr. de J. Didot l'aîné, 1834.

Barnhart, E. L. Palenque Mapping Project, 1998–2000 Final Report. Foundation for the Advancement of Mesoamerican Studies, 2000.

Bartlett, W. H. *Walks About the City and Environs of Jerusalem*. London: George Virtue, 1846.

Beach, M. Y. Wealth and pedigree of the wealthy citizens of New York City comprising an alphabetical arrangement of persons estimated to be worth. New York: Sun Office, 1842.

Bernal, I. *A History of Mexican Archaeology: The Vanished Civilizations of Middle America*. London and New York: Thames & Hudson, 1980.

Bishop, J. B. *The Panama Gateway*. New York: Scribner's, 1913.

Bourgoyne, C. Mémoire sur la possibilité, les avantages, et les moyens douvrir un canal dans l'Amérique septentrionale, pour communiquer de la mer Atlantique, ou du Nord, à la mer Pacifique, ou du Sud. Ca. 1785.

Brown, S. *Joseph Severn: A Life: The Rewards of Friendship*. Oxford: Oxford University Press, 2009.

Brunhouse, R. L. *In Search of the Maya: The First Archaeologists*. Albuquerque: University of New Mexico Press, 1973.

Burrows, E. G., and M. Wallace. *Gotham: A History of New York City to 1898*. New York: Oxford University Press, 1999.

Burton, W. E. *The Gentleman's Magazine*. Philadelphia, 1837.

Cabello Carro, P. *Política investigadora de la época de Carlos III en el área Maya: descubrimiento de Palenque y primeras excavaciones de carácter científico: según documentación de Calderón, Bernasconi, Del Río y otros*. Madrid: Ediciones de la Torre, 1992.

Carpenter, W. *Peerage for the People*. London: W. Strange, 1837.

Catherwood, F. Engineers Report. Demerara Railway Company. British Library, 1847.

Cebulski, F. J. "Letter from William Hickling Prescott to John Lloyd Stephens." Typescript (seminar paper), ca. 1967, 33 leaves.

Chamberlain, W. H., and H. L. Wells. *History of Yuba County, California with illustrations descriptive of its scenery, residences, public buildings, fine blocks and manufactories*. Oakland, CA: Thompson & West, 1879.

Clark, A. H. *The Clipper Ship Era: An Epitome of Famous American and British Clipper Ships, Their Owners, Builders, Commanders, and Crews, 1843–1869*. New York: Putnam's, 1910.

Coe, M. D. *Breaking the Maya Code*. New York: Thames & Hudson, 1992.

———. *The Maya*. London: Thames & Hudson, 2011.

Cohen, P. E., and R. T. Augustyn. *Manhattan in Maps, 1527–1995*. New York: Rizzoli International, 1997.

College of St. Gregory. *The Downside Review*. Bath, England, 1889.

Columbia University, and W. J. Maxwell. Catalogue of Officers and Graduates of Columbia University from the Foundation of King's College in 1754. New York: Columbia University, 1916.

Colvin, H. *A Biographical Dictionary of British Architects, 1600–1840*. New Haven, CT: Yale University Press, 2008.

"Congressional Summary." *American Whig Review* 9, no. 14 (1849): 208–16.

Coy, O. C. *The Great Trek*. Los Angeles: Powell, 1931.

Crosby, A. W. *The Columbian Voyages, the Columbian Exchange, and Their Historians*. Washington, DC: American Historical Association, 1987.

Crowe, F. The gospel in Central America containing a sketch of the country, physical and geographical, historical and political, moral and religious: A history of the Baptist mission in British Honduras, and of the introduction of the Bible into the Spanish American republic of Guatemala. London: C. Gilpin, 1850.

Danien, E. C., R. J. Sharer, et al. *New Theories on the Ancient Maya*. Philadelphia: University Museum, University of Pennsylvania, 1992.

Delano, A. and I. McKee. *Alonzo Delano's California Correspondence: Being Letters Hitherto Uncollected from the Ottawa (Illinois) Free Trader and the New Orleans True Delta, 1849–1952*. Sacramento, CA: Sacramento Book Collectors Club, 1952.

Delgado, J. P. *To California by Sea: A Maritime History of the California Gold Rush*. Columbia: University of South Carolina Press, 1990.

Demarest, A. A. *Ancient Maya: The Rise and Fall of a Rainforest Civilization*. Cambridge and New York: Cambridge University Press, 2004.

Demarest, A. A., P. M. Rice, et al. *The Terminal Classic in the Maya Lowlands: Collapse, Transition, and Transformation*. Boulder: University Press of Colorado Press, 2004.

Denevan, W. M. *The Native Population of the Americas in 1492*. Madison: University of Wisconsin Press, 1992.

Diamond, J. M. Guns, Germs, and Steel: The Fates of Human Societies. New York: Norton, 2003.

Dickinson, D. S., J. R. Dickinson, et al. *Speeches, correspondence, etc., of the late Daniel S. Dickinson of New York. Including: addresses on important public topics: Speeches in the state and United States Senate, and in support of the government during the rebellion; correspondence, private and political (collected and arranged by Mrs. Dickinson), poems (collected and arranged by Mrs. Mygatt), etc.* New York: Putnam, 1867.

Downing, A. J., and Making of America Project. *A treatise on the theory and practice of landscape gardening adapted to North America; with a view to the improvement of country residences. With remarks on rural architecture*. New York: Putnam, 1853.

Edison, P. N. "Colonial Prospecting in Independent Mexico: Abbé Baradère's Antiquités Mexicaines." *Proceedings of the Western Society for French History* 32 (2004): 195–215.

Eissler, M., and G. M. Toten, G. M. "The Panama Canal." *Scientific American Supplement* 14 (1882).

Evans, R. T. *Romancing the Maya: Mexican Antiquity in the American Imagination, 1820–1915*. Austin: University of Texas Press, 2004.

Exman, E. *The Brothers Harper: A Unique Publishing Partnership and Its Impact upon the Cultural Life of America from 1817 to 1853*. New York: Harper & Row, 1965.

Fahmy, K. *All the Pasha's Men: Mehmed Ali, His Army, and the Making of Modern Egypt*. Cairo and New York: American University in Cairo Press, 2002.

Fischer-Westhauser, U. "Emanuel von Friedrichsthal: The First Daguerreotypist in Yucatán." *Photoresearcher* (European Society for the History of Photography) 10 (2007).

Fowler, W. C. *Memorials of the Chaunceys, including President Chauncey, His Ancestors and Descendants* [and Appendix]. Boston: H. W. Dutton, 1858.

Freidel, D. A., L. Schele, et al. (1993). *Maya cosmos: three thousand years on the shaman's path*. New York, W. Morrow.

Garcâia de Palacio, D., E. G. Squier, et al.:Letter to the King of Spain: Being a description of the ancient provinces of Guazacapan, Izalco, Cuscatlan, and Chiquimula, in the Audiencâia of Guatemala, with an account of the languages, customs, and religion of their aboriginal inhabitants, and a description of the ruins of Copán. Culver City, CA: Labyrinthos, 1985.

Gibson, A., and A. Donovan. *The Abandoned Ocean: A History of United States Maritime Policy*. Columbia: University of South Carolina Press, 2000.

Graham, I. "Juan Galindo, Enthusiast." *Estudios de cultura maya*, Universidad Nacional Autónoma de México, Facultad de Filosofia y Letras, Seminario de cultura Maya, vol. 3 (1963): 11–35.

Graham, I. *Alfred Maudslay and the Maya: A Biography*. Norman: University of Oklahoma Press, 2002.

Grant, U. S. *Memoirs and Selected Letters: Personal Memoirs of U.S. Grant, Selected Letters 1839–1865*. New York: Library of America, 1990.

Grant, U. S., and J. M. McPherson. *Personal Memoirs of U.S. Grant*. New York: Penguin Books, 1999.

Graves, A. The Royal Academy of Arts; a complete dictionary of contributors and their work from its foundation in 1769 to 1904. London, H. Graves, 1905.

Greene, A. A Glance at New York: Embracing the city government, theatres, hotels, churches, mobs, monopolies, learned professions, newspapers, rogues, dandies, fires and firemen, water and other liquids, &c., &c. New York: A. Greene, 1837.

Griffith, W. J. "Juan Galindo, Central American Chauvanist." *Hispanic American Historical Review* 40, no. 1 (1960): 25–52.

Grutz, J. W. "The Lost Portfolios of Robert Hay." www.saudiaramcoworld.com, March/April 2003.

Hall, C., H. Pâerez Brignoli, et al. *Historical Atlas of Central America*. Norman: University of Oklahoma Press, 2003.

Hall, H. *America's Successful Men of Affairs. An Encyclopedia of Contemporaneous Biography*. New York: New York Tribune, 1895.

Haug, G. H., et al. "Climate and the Collapse of the Maya Civilization." *Science* 299 (2003): 1731–35.

Hawks, R. "The Late John L. Stephens." *Putnam's Monthly Magazine of American Literature, Science and Art* 1 (1853): 64–68.

Hemstreet, C. *Literary New York: Its Landmarks and Associations*. New York and London: Knickerbocker Press, 1903.

Herzog, R. "Über Henry Westcars Tagebuch einer Reise durch Ägypten und Nubien (1823–24)." *Mitteilungen des Deutschen Archäologischen Instituts, Abteilung Kairo* 24 (1969): 201–11.

Hoskins, G. *A. Visit to the Great Oasis of the Libyan Desert.* London, 1837.

Humboldt, A. v., and A. Bonpland. *Personal Narrative of Travels to the Equinoctial Regions of the New Continent During the Years 1799-1804.* London, 1814.

Humboldt, A. v., and H. M. Williams. *Researches, concerning the institutions & monuments of the ancient inhabitants of America: With descriptions & views of some of the most striking scenes in the Cordilleras!* London, 1814.

Humboldt, A. v., and J. Wilson. *Personal Narrative.* New York: Penguin Books, 1995.

Hunt, F., T. P. Kettell, et al. *Merchants' Magazine and Commercial Review.* New York, 1847.

"Incidents of Travel in Central America, Chiapas and Yucatán." *London Quarterly Review* 69 (1842): 52–91.

Jackson, K. T., and D. S. Dunbar. *Empire City: New York Through the Centuries.* New York: Columbia University Press, 2002.

Johnson, R. and J. H. Brown. *The Twentieth Century Biographical Dictionary of Notable Americans.* Boston: Biographical Society, 1904.

Juarros, D., and J. Baily. A statistical and commercial history of the kingdom of Guatemala, in Spanish America containing important particulars relative to its productions, manufactures, customs, &c. &c. &c. London: J. Hearne, 1823.

Kandasammy, L. "From Georgetown to Mahaica: A Brief History of South America's First Railway." *Stabroek News,* Georgetown, British Guyana, 2006.

Kark, R. *American Consuls in the Holy Land, 1832–1914.* Detroit: Wayne State University Press, 1994.

Keith, A. Evidence of the truth of the Christian religion: Derived from the literal fulfillment of Prophecy, particularly as illustrated by the history of the Jews, and by the discoveries of recent travellers. Edinburgh: Waugh & Innes, 1834.

Kemble, J. H. *The Panama Route, 1848–1869.* Berkeley: University of California Press, 1943.

Kingsborough, E. K., A. Aglio, et al. Antiquities of Mexico: Comprising fac-similes of ancient Mexican paintings and hieroglyphics, preserved in the royal libraries of Paris, Berlin and Dresden, in the Imperial library of Vienna, in the Vatican library, in the Borgian museum at Rome, in the library of the Institute at Bologna, and in the Bodleian Library at Oxford, together with the monuments of New Spain by M. Dupaix, with their respective scales of measurement and accompanying descriptions. London: Robert Havell, 1831.

Kuhnke, L., and eScholarship. *Lives at Risk: Public Health in Nineteenth-Century Egypt.* Berkeley: University of California Press, 1990.

Laing, A. *The Sea Witch: A narrative of the experiences of Capt. Roger Murray and others in an American clipper ship during the years 1846 to 1956.* London: Thornton Butterworth, 1933.

Lewis, O., and J. B. Goodman. Sea Routes to the Gold Fields: The Migration by Water to California in 1849–1852. New York: Knopf, 1949.

Lewis, W. J., F. Catherwood, et al. *Report of the Engineers on the Survey of the Marysville and Benicia National Rail Road.* Marysville, CA: California Express, 1853.

Lilly, L., C. S. Henry, et al. *The New-York Review.* New York: George Dearborn, 1837, 1841.

List, T. S. "The American Steam-ship 'Washington.'" 2012. http://www.theshipslist.com/1847/washington.html.

Lockey, J. B. *Diplomatic Futility.* Durham, NC: [n.p.], 1930.

López Cogolludo, D., F. d. Ayeta, et al. *Historia de Yucathan.* Madrid: Jvan Garcia Infanzen, 1688.

Lovell, W. G. *Conquest and Survival in Colonial Guatemala: A Historical Geography of the Cuchumatán Highlands, 1500–1821*. Montréal: McGill-Queen's University Press, 1992.

Madox, J. *Excursions in the Holy Land, Egypt, Nubia, Syria, &c. including a visit to the unfrequented district of the Haouran*. London: R. Bentley, 1834.

Manning, W. R., and United States Department of State. *Diplomatic Correspondence of the United States*. Washington, DC: Carnegie Endowment for International Peace, 1932.

———. Diplomatic Correspondence of the United States Concerning the Independence of the Latin-American Nations. New York: Oxford University Press, 1925.

Martin, S., and N. Grube. *Chronicle of the Maya Kings and Queens: Deciphering the Dynasties of the Ancient Maya*. London and New York: Thames & Hudson, 2000.

McCullough, D. G. *The Path Between the Seas: The Creation of the Panama Canal, 1870–1914*. New York: Simon & Schuster, 1977.

Means, P. A., A. s. d. Avendano y Loyola, et al. *History of the Spanish Conquest of Yucatán and of the Itzas*. Cambridge, MA: The [Peabody] Museum, 1917.

Metropolitan Museum of Art. Bulletin of the Metropolitan Museum of Art 7 (1912).

Miceli, K. L. "Rafael Carrera: Defender and Promoter of Peasant Interest in Guatemala, 1837–1848." *The Americas* 31, no. 1 (1944): 72–94.

Miller, M. E., S. Martin, et al. *Courtly Art of the Ancient Maya*. New York: Thames & Hudson, 2004.

Moorhead, M. L. "Rafael Carrera of Guatemala: His Life and Times." Ph.D. diss., University of California, Berkeley, 1942.

Morison, S. E. *William Hickling Prescott, 1796–1859*. Boston: Massachusetts Historical Society, 1958.

Morley, S. G. *The Inscriptions at Copan*. Washington, DC: Carnegie Institution of Washington, 1920.

Morrison, J. H. *History of American Steam Navigation*. New York: W. F. Sametz, 1903.

Nelson, W. *Five Years at Panama: The Trans-Isthmian Canal*. New York and Chicago: Belford, 1889.

Nevins, A. *The Evening Post: A Century of Journalism*. New York: Boni & Liveright, 1922.

New-York Historical Society. *Proceedings of the New-York Historical Society*. New York: Press of the Historical Society, 1844.

New York (State). Report of the Debates and Proceedings of the Convention for the Revision of the Constitution of the State of New York. 1846. Albany: Evening Atlas, 1846.

Nichols, T. L. *Forty Years of American Life*. London: Longmans Green, 1874.

Noah, M. M. Discourse on the evidences of the American Indians being the descendants of the lost tribes of Israel: Delivered before the Mercantile Library Association, Clinton Hall. New York: J. Van Norden, 1837.

Norman, B. M., C. C. Moore, et al. *Rambles in Yucatán, or, Notes of travel through the peninsula: Including a visit to the remarkable ruins of Chi-Chen, Kabah, Zayi, and Uxmal*. New York: J. & H. G. Langley; Philadelphia: Thomas, Cowperthwait; New Orleans: Norman, Steel, 1843.

Odlyzko, A. "Collective Hallucinations and Inefficient Markets: The British Railway Mania of the 1840s." University of Minnesota, January 15, 2010.

Oran. "Tropical Journeyings." *Harper's New Monthly Magazine* 18 (1859): 145–69.

Otis, F. N. Isthmus of Panama: History of the Panama railroad; and of the Pacific Mail Steamship Company. Together with a travellers' guide and business man's handbook for the Panama Railroad and the lines of steamships connecting it with

Europe, the United States, the north and south Atlantic and Pacific coasts, China, Australia, and Japan. New York: Harper & Brothers, 1867.

Palmquist, P. E., and T. R. Kailbourn. *Pioneer Photographers of the Far West: A Biographical Dictionary, 1840–1865*. Stanford, CA: Stanford University Press, 2000.

Peck, D. T. Yucatán: From Prehistoric Times to the Great Maya Revolt. [N.p.]: Xlibris, 2005.

Pendergast, D. M. *Palenque: The Walker-Caddy Expedition to the Ancient Maya City, 1839–1840*. Norman: University of Oklahoma Press, 1967.

Perez-Venero, A. *Before the Five Frontiers: Panama, from 1821–1903*. New York: AMS Press, 1978.

Philbrick, N. *Sea of Glory: America's Voyage of Discovery, the U.S. Exploring Expedition, 1838–1842*. Waterville, ME: Thorndike Press, 2004.

Philological Society (Great Britain). *The European Magazine, and London Review*. London, 1782.

Podgorny, I. "'Silent and Alone': How the Ruins of Palenque Were Taught to Speak the Language of Archeology." *Comparative Archaeologies*, part 2 (2011): 527–53.

Poe, E. A. "Review of New Books." *Graham's Magazine* (1841): 90–96.

Polk, J. K., and M. M. Quaife. *The Diary of James K. Polk During His Presidency, 1845 to 1849*. Chicago: McClurg, 1910.

Prescott, W. H. *History of the Conquest of Mexico, and History of the Conquest of Peru*. New York: Modern Library, 1936.

Prescott, W. H., and C. H. Gardiner. *Literary Memoranda*. Norman: University of Oklahoma Press, 1961.

Prescott, W. H., and R. Wolcott. *The Correspondence of William Hickling Prescott, 1833–1847*. Boston and New York: Houghton Mifflin, 1925.

Reed, N. A. *The Caste War of Yucatán*. Stanford, CA: Stanford University Press, 2001.

Restall, M., and F. G. L. Asselbergs. *Invading Guatemala: Spanish, Nahua, and Maya Accounts of the Conquest Wars*. University Park: Pennsylvania State University Press, 2007.

Rhodes, R. *John James Audubon: The Making of an American*. New York: Knopf, 2004.

Ridgely-Nevitt, C. *American Steamships on the Atlantic*. Newark: University of Delaware Press; London: Associated University Presses, 1980.

Río, A. d., and P. F. Cabrera. Description of the ruins of an ancient city: Discovered near Palenque, in the kingdom of Guatemala or, A critical investigation and research into the history of the Americans. London, 1822.

Roberts, J. L. "Landscapes of Indifference: Robert Smithson and John Lloyd Stephens in Yucatán." *Art Bulletin* 82, no. 3 (2000): 544–67.

Robertson, W. *The History of America*. London: A. Strahan, 1803.

Robinson, T. *Panama: A Personal Record of Forty-Six Years, 1861–1907*. New York: Star and Herald, 1907.

Rodríguez, M. *A Palmerstonian Diplomat in Central America: Frederick Chatfield, Esq.* Tucson: University of Arizona Press, 1964.

Salmon, F. "Storming the Campo Vaccino: British Architects and the Antique Buildings of Rome after Waterloo." *Architectual History* 38 (1995): 146–75.

Schele, L., and P. Mathews. *The Code of Kings: The Language of Seven Sacred Maya Temples and Tombs*. New York: Touchstone Books, 1998.

Schlesinger, A. M. *The Age of Jackson*. Boston: Little, Brown, 1945.

Severn, J., and G. F. Scott. *Joseph Severn: Letters and Memoirs*. Burlington, VT: Ashgate, 2005.

Seward, W. H., and F. W. Seward. *Autobiography of William H. Seward, from 1801 to*

1834 with a memoir of his life, and selections from his letters from 1831 to 1846. New York: Appleton, 1877.

Sharer, R. J., and S. G. Morley. *The Ancient Maya.* Stanford, CA: Stanford University Press, 1994.

Shaw, D. W. *The Sea Shall Embrace Them: The Tragic Story of the Steamship Arctic.* New York: Free Press, 2002.

Spears, J. R. *Captain Nathaniel Brown Palmer, an Old-Time Sailor of the Sea.* New York: Macmillan, 1922.

Starkey, P., and J. Starkey. *Travellers in Egypt.* London and New York: Tauris, 1998.

Stephens, J. L. *Incidents of Travel in Central America, Chiapas, and Yucatan.* New York: Harper & Brothers, 1841.

———. Incidents of Travel in Egypt, Arabia Petraea, and the Holy Land. Norman: University of Oklahoma Press, 1970.

———. *Incidents of Travel in Greece, Turkey, Russia, and Poland.* New York: Harper & Brothers, 1838, 1854.

———. *Incidents of Travel in the Russian and Turkish Empires.* London: R. Bentley, 1839.

———. *Incidents of Travel in Yucatan.* New York: Harper & Brothers, 1843.

———. John Lloyd Stephens Papers, 1795–1882. BANC MSS Z-Z 116, The Bancroft Library, University of California, Berkeley.

Stephens, J. L., and F. Catherwood. *Incidents of Travel in Central America, Chiapas and Yucatan.* London: A. Hall, Virtue, 1854.

Stephens Family Papers, New York Historical Society.

Stevens, J. A., B. F. DeCosta, et al. *The Magazine of American History with Notes and Queries.* New York: A. S. Barnes.

Sutcliffe, A. C. Robert Fulton and the "Clermont"; the authoritative story of Robert Fulton's early experiments, persistent efforts, and historic achievements. Containing many of Fulton's hitherto unpublished letters, drawings, and pictures. New York: Century, 1909.

Thomas, H. *Conquest: Montezuma, Cortés, and the Fall of Old Mexico.* New York: Simon & Schuster, 1993.

Tillett, S. *Egypt Itself: The Career of Robert Hay, Esquire, of Linplum and Nunraw, 1799–1863.* London: SD Books, 1984.

Tomes, R., and Making of America Project. *Panama in 1855: An account of the Panama rail-road, of the cities of Panama and Aspinwall, with sketches of life and character on the Isthmus.* New York: Harper & Brothers, 1855.

United States. Board of Consulting Engineers on Panama Canal, J. F. Wallace, et al. *Report of the Board of Consulting Engineers for the Panama Canal.* Washington, DC: U.S. Government Printing Office, 1906.

United States. Congress., F. P. Blair, et al. *The Congressional Globe.* Buffalo, NY: Hein, 2007.

United States. Department of State. Mediation of the Honduran-Guatemalan boundary question, held under the good offices of the Department of State, 1918–1919. Washington, DC: U.S. Government Printing Office, 1919.

———. Message from the President of the United States, transmitting, in response to the resolution of the Senate of the 18th ultimo, a report of the secretary of state, with accompanying papers, in relation to the capitulations of the Ottoman Empire. Washington, DC: U.S. Government Printing Office, 1881.

Von Hagen, V. W. John Lloyd Stephens Collection, 1946–47. New-York Historical Society, Von Hagen Papers, New York.

Von Hagen, V. W. *F. Catherwood, archt. (1799–1854).* New York: [N.p.], 1946.

————.*Frederick Catherwood, archt.* New York: Oxford University Press, 1950.

————. *Maya Explorer: John Lloyd Stephens and the Lost Cities of Central America and Yucatan.* Norman: University of Oklahoma Press, 1947.

Waldeck, J. F. M., M. Mestre Ghigliazza, et al. *Viaje pintoresco y arqueológico a la provincia de Yucatán (América Central) durante los años 1834 y 1836.* Mérida, Mexico, 1930.

Wallace, D. R. *The Monkey's Bridge: Mysteries of Evolution in Central America.* San Francisco: Sierra Club Books, 1997.

Weed, T., H. A. Weed, et al. *Life of Thurlow Weed Including His Autobiography and a Memoir.* Boston and New York: Houghton, Mifflin, 1883.

Whitmore, S. D. "Lord Kingsborough and His Contribution to Ancient Mesoamerican Scholarship: The Antiquities of Mexico." *PARI Journal* 9, no. 4 (2009): 8–16.

Wills, G. *Henry Adams and the Making of America.* Boston: Houghton Mifflin, 2005.

Wollam, P. F. "The Apostle of Central American Liberalism: Francisco Morazan and His Struggle for Union." M.A. thesis, University of California, Berkeley, 1940.

Woodward, R. L. *Rafael Carrera and the Emergence of the Republic of Guatemala, 1821–1871.* Athens: University of Georgia Press, 1993.

Notes

PROLOGUE

1. Much of the material describing the building of the railroad was drawn from numerous letters in Stephens's personal papers housed in the Bancroft Library at the University of California, Berkeley. Other background material was found in the following: Otis, F. N. (1867). *Isthmus of Panama: History of the Panama railroad; and of the Pacific Mail Steamship Company. Together with a travelers' guide and business man's hand-book for the Panama Railroad and the lines of steamships connecting it with Europe, the United States, the north and south Atlantic and Pacific coasts, China, Australia, and Japan* (New York: Harper & Brothers, 1867); J. H. Kemble and J. B. Goodman, *The Panama Route, 1848– 1869* (Berkeley: University of California Press, 1943); O. Lewis and J. B. Goodman, *Sea Routes to the Gold Fields: The Migration by Water to California in 1849–1852* (New York: Knopf, 1949); J. L. Schott, *Rails Across Panama: The Story of the Building of the Panama Railroad, 1849–1855* (Indianapolis: Bobbs-Merrill, 1967); G. Mack, *The Land Divided: A History of the Panama Canal and Other Isthmian Canal Projects* (New York: Octagon Books, 1974); D. Mc-Cullough, *The Path Between the Seas: The Creation of the Panama Canal, 1870–1914* (New York: Simon & Schuster, 1977).

2. John Lloyd Stephens Papers, 1795–1882, University of California, Berkeley, Bancroft Library.

CHAPTER 1: SOUTH, 1839

1. All quotes and paraphrases as well as the general narrative of the Stephens-Catherwood 1839–42 journeys to Central America and Mexico are taken from J. L. Stephens, *Incidents of Travel in Central America, Chiapas, and Yucatan* (New York: Harper & Brothers, 1841), and J. L. Stephens, *Incidents of Travel in Yucatan* (New York: Harper & Brothers, 1843).

2. With the exception of what would become known as Brazil, which was granted to Portugal in the famous 1494 Treaty of Tordesillas.

3. W. R. Manning and U.S. Department of State, *Diplomatic Correspondence of the United States* (Washington, DC: Carnegie Endowment for International Peace, 1932).

4. V. W. von Hagen, *Maya Explorer: John Lloyd Stephens and the Lost Cities of Central America and Yucatan* (Norman: University of Oklahoma Press, 1947).

5. Catherwood arrived in New York City on June 7, 1836, on the ship *Barque Union* from London, England. National Archives Microfilm Publication, M237, roll number 30, list number 447. Stephens arrived in Alexandria, Egypt, on May 11, 1836. See the final page of J. L. Stephens, *Incidents of Travel in Egypt, Arabia Petraea, and the Holy Land* (Norman: University of Oklahoma Press, 1970). His arrival in London would have been many weeks after Catherwood left England

(sometime around the middle of May) and was already in New York. Stephens landed in New York on September 6, 1836, arriving on the ship *Hiberia* from Liverpool, England. National Archives Microfilm Publication.

6. Architectural Publication Society, *The Dictionary of Architecture* (London: Richards, 1852).
7. Stephens, *Incidents of Travel in Egypt, Arabia Petraea, and the Holy Land.*
8. The original contract is among Stephens's papers at the Bancroft Library at the University of California, Berkeley.
9. The contract added in stilted legalese: "It being understood that all the money which shall so be paid to Mrs. Catherwood and family shall be deducted from the above-said sum of $1500 or otherwise taken into the amount of a final settlement as so much paid to the said Catherwood."
10. There is one vague sketch Catherwood made of himself in the ruins of Tulum, Mexico, but with so few details as to leave the mystery of his appearance largely intact.
11. W. M. Denevan, *The Native Population of the Americas in 1492* (Madison: University of Wisconsin Press, 1992). The reference to the slaves owned by Judge John Lloyd (Stephens's maternal grandfather) is found in letters to Stephens's father, Benjamin Stephens, from his sister-in-law, concerning the disbursement of Judge Lloyd's estate: John Lloyd Stephens Collection, 1946–47, New-York Historical Society, Von Hagen Papers.

CHAPTER 2: UPRIVER
1. J. B. Lockey, *Diplomatic Futility* (Durham, N.C.: [N.p.], 1930).
2. Manning and U.S. Department of State, *Diplomatic Correspondence of the United States.*
3. "De Witt, Charles Gerrit, 1789–1839," Biographical Directory of the United States Congress. Suicide referenced in Lockey, *Diplomatic Futility,* p. 281.
4. A. M. Schlesinger, *The Age of Jackson* (Boston: Little, Brown, 1945).

CHAPTER 3: MICO MOUNTAIN
1. John Lloyd Stephens Collection, 1946–47, New-York Historical Society, Von Hagen Papers.
2. N. Philbrick, *Sea of Glory: America's Voyage of Discovery, the U.S. Exploring Expedition, 1838–1842* (Waterville, ME: Thorndike Press, 2004).

CHAPTER 4: PASSPORT
1. R. L. Woodward, *Rafael Carrera and the Emergence of the Republic of Guatemala, 1821–1871* (Athens: University of Georgia Press, 1993).
2. D. M. Pendergast, *Palenque: The Walker-Caddy Expedition to the Ancient Maya City, 1839–1840* (Norman: University of Oklahoma Press, 1967). Pendergast includes Caddy's personal diary of the expedition and his description of the ruins at Palenque, as well as Walker's official report, all of which form the basis of this narrative. He also uncovered the crucial dispatches between Colonel MacDonald and the Colonial Office and the story from the *Belize Advertiser.*
3. Ibid. See illustration after p. 32.

Chapter 5: Monkeys like the Wind

1. D. R. Wallace, *The Monkey's Bridge: Mysteries of Evolution in Central America* (San Francisco: Sierra Club Books, 1997).

2. C. Hall, H. Perez Brignoli, et. al, *Historical Atlas of Central America* (Norman: University of Oklahoma Press, 2003).

3. Philbrick, *Sea of Glory*.

4. H. Thomas, *Conquest: Montezuma, Cortes, and the Fall of Old Mexico* (New York: Simon & Schuster, 1993).

5. Europe's population to the Ural Mountains was estimated at 80 million at the time, according to Alfred Crosby. See *The Columbian Voyages, the Columbian Exchange, and Their Historians* (Washington, DC: American Historical Association, 1987), p. 19.

6. Ibid.

7. The Indians were not without some form of payback in what is now referred to as the "Columbian Exchange." It is believed that they infected the Europeans with syphilis, although some controversy remains about whether the disease existed in Europe unrecorded prior to 1492. The first recorded case in Europe was reported in 1495.

8. C. Mann, *1491* (New York: Knopf, 2005); H. Dobyns, "An Outline of Andean Epidemic History to 1720," *Bulletin of the History of Medicine* 37 (1963): 493–515.

9. There is still controversy among scholars about whether Capa and his heir's death were caused by smallpox. As with so much of the speculation surrounding the Spanish Conquest of the Americas, few adequate records have been found, leading to arguments and counterarguments over the degree to which Old World disease impacted the New World. For example, since the attacks on the World Trade Center on September 11, 2001, and the subsequently heightened concern about terrorists' potential use of smallpox as a weapon, scientists have debated just how quickly the disease can spread and how infectious it really is. Some have pointed out that it is not as infectious as often claimed; some have used that information to argue that smallpox was not the sweeping scythe of death in the Americas that historians have made it out to be. What is often missed in the debate over details, however, is that the Europeans brought with them multiple deadly viruses and pathogens. Taken together, they would have been devastating. In addition, there is a multiplying effect from interruptions to farming and hunting that affected entire generations, leading to malnutrition and starvation. Few experts today argue that the totality of the disease impact was anything less than demographically catastrophic for Native Americans. For a sampling of a counterargument concerning smallpox, however, see Francis Brooks,: "The First Impact of Smallpox: What Was the Columbian Exchange Rate?" in *Columbus and the Consequences of 1492,* edited by A. R. Disney (Melbourne: La Trobe University, 1994).

10. Hall, Perez Brignoli, et al., *Historical Atlas of Central America*.

11. U.S. Department of State, *Mediation of the Honduran-Guatemalan boundary question, held under the good offices of the Department of State, 1918–1919* (Washington, DC: U.S. Government Printing Office, 1919), pp. 62, 172.

STEPHENS

1. Alexander von Humboldt Digital Library, 2006.
2. Ibid.
3. A. v. Humboldt and J. Wilson, *Personal Narrative* (New York: Penguin Books, 1995).
4. Ibid.
5. Ibid.
6. Ibid.
7. Alexander von Humboldt Digital Library.
8. A. v. Humboldt and A. Bonpland, *Personal narrative of travels to the equinoctial regions of the New continent during the years 1799–1804* (London: Longman Hurst Rees Orme and Brown, 1814).
9. Humboldt and Wilson, *Personal Narrative*.
10. A letter from John L. Stephens's mother, Clemence, to her sister Mary Hendrickson, sent from New York City to Middleton, New Jersey, indicates that by March 11, 1907, when the letter was written and John would have been fifteen months old, the family was living in New York. The letter is in the Victor von Hagen Papers at the New-York Historical Society.
11. E. G. Burrows and M. Wallace, *Gotham: A History of New York City to 1898* (New York: Oxford University Press, 1999).
12. In fact over the next decade, three-foot, nine-inch-long stone markers—1,549 of them—indicating every future street corner were placed all the way up the island. P. E. Cohen and R. T. Augustyn, *Manhattan in Maps, 1527–1995* (New York: Rizzoli International, 1997), p. 104.
13. K. T. Jackson and D. S. Dunbar, *Empire City: New York Through the Centuries* (New York: Columbia University Press, 2002), p. 119.
14. Burrows and Wallace, *Gotham*, pp. 333–34.
15. Records of Benjamin Stephens's early business transactions starting in 1796 can be found in the Stephens family files at the New-York Historical Society. Denevan, *The Native Population of the Americas in 1492*.
16. J. L. Stephens, *Incidents of Travel in Greece, Turkey, Russia, and Poland* (New York: Harper & Brothers, 1854). "The Bowling Green was associated with my earliest recollections. It had been my play-ground when a boy; hundreds of times I had climbed over its fence for my ball, and I was one of a band of boys who held on to it long after the corporation invaded our rights" (p. 282).
17. G. Wills, *Henry Adams and the Making of America* (Boston: Houghton Mifflin, 2005), pp. 223–45.
18. Denevan, *The Native Population of the Americas in 1492*.
19. Burrows and Wallace, *Gotham*, pp. 424–28.
20. BANC MSS ZZ 116, John Lloyd Stephens Papers, 1795–1882, Bancroft Library, University of California, Berkeley. Hereinafter referred to as BANC MSS ZZ 16.
21. Edgar Allan Poe Society of Baltimore, "Poe's Criticisms from *Southern Literary Messenger*," January 1837.
22. R. Hawks, "The Late John L. Stephens," *Putnam's Monthly Magazine of American Literature, Science and Art* 1 (1853): 64–68.
23. Von Hagen, *Maya Explorer*, p. 14.
24. Columbia University and W. J. Maxwell, *Catalogue of Officers and Graduates of*

Columbia University from the Foundation of King's College in 1754 (New York: The University, 1916).

25. Von Hagen, *Maya Explorer,* p. 15.

26. BANC MSS ZZ 116.

27 John Lloyd Stephens Collection, 1946–47, New-York Historical Society, Von Hagen Papers.

28. Hawks, "The Late John L. Stephens."

29. Stephens, *Incidents of Travel in Greece, Turkey, Russia, and Poland.*

30. Ibid.

31. It may have been that Stephens sent the letters directly to Hoffman, who traveled in the same circle as Stephens in New York and may have been a friend. So that their publication was more calculated and less a surprise than he let on. His only comment came on page 122 of his second book, *Incidents of Travel in Greece, Turkey, Russia, and Poland.*

32. *American Monthly Magazine,* October 1835, p. 91.

33. J. L. Stephens, *Incidents of Travel in the Russian and Turkish Empires* (London: R. Bentley, 1839), p. 200.

34. Ibid. P. 216.

35. L. Kuhnke and eScholarship, *Lives at Risk: Public Health in Nineteenth-Century Egypt* (Berkeley: University of California Press, 1990).

36. Stephens, *Incidents of Travel in Greece, Turkey, Russia, and Poland.*

37. Stephens, *Incidents of Travel in Egypt, Arabia Petraea, and the Holy Land.*

38. A. Keith, *Evidence of the truth of the Christian religion: Derived from the literal fulfillment of Prophecy, particularly as illustrated by the history of the Jews, and by the discoveries of recent travellers* (Edinburgh: Waugh & Innes, 1834).

39. A. Greene, *A glance at New York: Embracing the city government, theatres, hotels, churches, mobs, monopolies, learned professions, newspapers, rogues, dandies, fires and firemen, water and other liquids, &c., &c* (New York: A. Greene, 1837), pp. 149–66.

40. Stephens makes a reference to the hard times in the preface to the fourth edition: "And, in reference to the whole, [the author] can only say, as before, that in the present state of the world it is almost presumptuous to put forth a book of travels."

41. Burrows and Wallace, *Gotham,* pp. 571–617.

42. T. L. Nichols, *Forty Years of American Life* (London: Longmans Green, 1874), p. 343.

43. E. Exman, *The Brothers Harper: A Unique Publishing Partnership and Its Impact upon the Cultural Life of America from 1817 to 1853* (New York: Harper & Row, 1965), p. 93.

44. Ibid., p. 93.

45. J. A. Stevens, B. F. DeCosta, et al., The Magazine of American History with Notes and Queries (New York: A. S. Barnes), pp. 29–30.

46. T. Weed, H. A. Weed, et al., *Life of Thurlow Weed Including His Autobiography and a Memoir* (Boston and New York: Houghton Mifflin, 1883), pp. 435–36.

47. L. Lilly, C. S. Henry, et al., *The New-York Review* (New York: George Dearborn, 1837), pp. 351–67.

48. *Southern Literary Messenger,* August 1839.

49 W. H. Seward and F. W. Seward, *Autobiography of William H. Seward, from*

1801 to 1834 with a memoir of his life, and selections from his letters from 1831 to 1846 (New York: Appleton, 1877).

50. D. S. Dickinson, J. R. Dickinson, et al., *Speeches, Correspondence, etc., of the Late Daniel S. Dickinson of New York* (New York: Putnam, 1867).

CHAPTER 6: RUINS

1. J. W. Griffith, "Juan Galindo, Central American Chauvanist," *Hispanic American Historical Review* 40, no. 1 (1960): 25–52.

2. I. Graham, I. (1963). "Juan Galindo, Enthusiast," *Estudios de cultura maya México* 3 (1963): 11–35. Griffith and Graham give well-researched and complementary accounts of Galindo's involvement in Central America both politically and archaeologically.

3. Ibid. See miniature in Figure 2.

4. S. G. Morley, *The Inscriptions at Copan* (Washington, DC: Carnegie Institution of Washington, 1920).

5. Galindo's guess about the phonetic basis of the hieroglyphic writing is curious. He gave no basis for his supposition, which would seem to follow French savant Jean Champollion's partially phonetic decipherment of the Rosetta Stone ten years earlier, which had famously unlocked the written language of the Egyptian hieroglyphs. But Galindo in his limited learning seems unaware of Champollion's phonetic breakthrough, for Galindo wrote in his report: "This [Mayan] writing is hieroglyphic-phonetic, representing sounds, and is greatly superior to the paintings of the Mexicans, and the symbolic hieroglyphics of the Egyptians, which only represented things." For the next century epigraphers stubbornly refused to believe the Mayan hieroglyphs had phonetic components, and in fact were no more than calendar references, until finally in the latter half of the twentieth century it was proven to be a fully realized phonetic writing system.

6. Galindo was wrong on a number of counts as well. For example, he believed that Copán was founded around the eleventh century A.D. and that it was still flourishing, like the Aztecs, when the Spanish arrived.

7. D. Garcia de Palacio, E. G. Squier, et al., *Letter to the King of Spain: Being a description of the ancient provinces of Guazacapan, Izalco, Cuscatlan, and Chiquimula, in the Audiencia of Guatemala, with an account of the languages, customs, and religion of their aboriginal inhabitants, and a description of the ruins of Copán* (Culver City, CA: Labyrinthos, 1985).

8. Ibid.

9. Galindo was very hopeful for recognition, as well as a gold medal offered by the Société de Géographie in Paris for the best description of ruins found in the Americas.

10. Morley, *The Inscriptions at Copan.*

11. One scheme involved bringing his father from England to set him up as profitable head of a port in Boca de Toro, in what is now a part of Panama. The project failed miserably and only served to provoke New Granada, the nation today of Colombia, to send armed forces to claim the area.

12. Griffith, "Juan Galindo, Central American Chauvanist."

13. R. T. Evans, *Romancing the Maya: Mexican Antiquity in the American Imagination, 1820–1915* (Austin: University of Texas Press, 2004). Evans discusses

Stephens's unabashed nationalistic position at the time that Americans should be custodians of the archaeological treasures and that Latin Americans were too ignorant or uninterested to preserve them (pp. 54–62).

14. J. L. Roberts, "Landscapes of Indifference: Robert Smithson and John Lloyd Stephens in Yucatán," *Art Bulletin* 82, no. 3 (2000): 544–67. The author discusses in some detail the perceptual problems Catherwood faced and how he dealt with them.

CHAPTER 7: CARRERA

1. W. R. Manning and U.S. Department of State, *Diplomatic Correspondence of the United States Concerning the Independence of the Latin-American Nations* (New York: Oxford University Press, 1925), vol. 2, doc. 741, pp. 22–23.
2. M. Rodríguez, *A Palmerstonian Diplomat in Central America: Frederick Chatfield, Esq.* (Tucson: University of Arizona Press, 1964).
3. Ibid.
4. Graham, "Juan Galindo, Enthusiast."
5. Rodríguez, *A Palmerstonian Diplomat in Central America.*
6. Jose Rafael Carrera y Turcios would continue rule Guatemala as military leader and conservative dictator for twenty-two of the next twenty-five years. He was declared Guatemala's "president for life" in 1854 and died in 1865 at the age of fifty-one.
7. Pendergast, *Palenque.* Walker's official report and Caddy's journal are found in full in Pendergast's book.

CHAPTER 8: WAR

1. Woodward, *Rafael Carrera and the Emergence of the Republic of Guatemala, 1821–1871.* This is an extraordinary, deeply researched account of the period.
2. P. F. Wollam, "The Apostle of Central American Liberalism: Francisco Morazan and His Struggle for Union" (M.A. thesis, University of California, Berkeley, 1940); Woodward, *Rafael Carrera and the Emergence of the Republic of Guatemala, 1821–1871.*
3. Woodward, *Rafael Carrera and the Emergence of the Republic of Guatemala, 1821–1871,* p. 484.
4. Ibid. p. 49
5. K. L. Miceli, "Rafael Carrera: Defender and Promoter of Peasant Interest in Guatemala, 1837–1848," *The Americas* 31, no. 1 (1944): 72–94. Woodward and Miceli give the most complete description in English of the conditions that led to the 1837 insurrection. Woodward, *Rafael Carrera and the Emergence of the Republic of Guatemala, 1821–1871,* pp. 37–55; Miceli, "Rafael Carrera," pp. 72–75.
6. M. L. Moorhead, "Rafael Carrera of Guatemala: His Life and Times" (Ph.D. diss., University of California, Berkeley, 1942).
7. Ibid., p. 18.
8. Manning and U.S. Department of State, *Diplomatic Correspondence of the United States.*
9. H. H. Bancroft, *History of Central America* (San Francisco: A. L. Bancroft, 1882).

10. Manning and U.S. Department of State, *Diplomatic Correspondence of the United States.*
11. Ibid.
12. Ibid.

CHAPTER 9: MALARIA

1. Ibid.
2. There is no written record of communication from the State Department to Stephens asking him to investigate the feasibility of the canal location. His instructions were explicit: complete the treaty negotiation and close down the legation in Guatemala City. However, instructions were given to an earlier U.S. envoy to Central America, William Jeffers, to examine and discuss with the republic the construction of the canal across Nicaragua. Charles De Witt mentions in a dispatch to Forsyth that he considered those instructions to be "standing" orders incorporated into his formal instructions, so Stephens may well have assumed the same obligation when he decided to travel to Nicaragua. However, he also noted in a later letter to Forsyth that he made the trip at his own expense, indicating that he saw the matter as unconnected with his official duties. Nonetheless, Stephens delivered all his notes and observations, as well as the canal surveys that he copied, to the U.S. government in Washington on his return. Of course, he also used some of the key material in his book and he may well have considered his firsthand inspection in Nicaragua valuable if he decided to link up with New York friends who were then considering such a canal project.
3. Jefferson had known about the Nicaraguan route as early as 1785, when he received a French manuscript written by Chevalier Bourgoyne concerning the route. He presented the manuscript to the library of the American Philosophical Society in Philadelphia in 1817.
4. Other heads of state were equally intrigued by the Nicaragua route. The king of Holland in 1830 won the exclusive right from the new Republic of Central America to construct a canal along San Juan River. Writing from Guatemala five years later, however, Stephens's predecessor De Witt informed Secretary Forsyth that the Dutch project had fallen through. He added that the opportunity was now ripe for the United States to take on the project.
5. United States Congress., F. P. Blair, et al., *The Congressional Globe* (Buffalo, NY: Hein, 2007).
6. Manning and U.S. Department of State, *Diplomatic Correspondence of the United States.*
7. Pendergast, *Palenque.*
8. Don Juan also acted as a guide for Jean-Frédéric Waldeck in the early 1830s and for Stephens and Catherwood.
9. Pendergast, *Palenque.* Pendergast writes that Caddy's formal report was meant to accompany his portfolio of drawings and was to serve as an adjunct to a scientific presentation that he later made in London. It is unclear whether it accompanied Walker's official report to the Colonial Office. His personal diary, by contrast, which Pendergast includes in his book, was apparently never meant

for publication or for official eyes.

CHAPTER 10: CRISIS AT HAND

1. Griffith, "Juan Galindo, Central American Chauvanist." Stephens reported that in the account he heard, Galindo was killed by Indians. "After the battle," Stephens wrote, "in attempting to escape, with two dragoons and a servant-boy, he passed through an Indian village, was recognized, and they were all murdered with machetes." Stephens's *Incidents of Travel in Central America*, vol. 1, p. 423. However, in a dispatch, Frederick Chatfield wrote: "Colonel Galindo was shot at a village in the state of Honduras called Aguanqueterique . . . he was endeavouring to find his way to San Miguel, after the defeat of his chief Cabañas, when he fell in with a party of Honduran troops, who instantly destroyed him." Graham, "Juan Galindo, Enthusiast," pp. 21–22.

2. Galindo did receive the recognition he had long desired. Unfortunately, it came after he died, when he was awarded a silver medal from the French for his discoveries.

3. Woodward, *Rafael Carrera and the Emergence of the Republic of Guatemala, 1821–1871*, p. 120.

4. Bancroft, *History of Central America*, vol. 13, p. 141.

5. There are a number of reports describing of this historic battle, but Stephens, who spoke with eyewitnesses not long after the battle took place, gives the most vivid account recorded in English. Stephens, *Incidents of Travel in Central America, Chiapas, and Yucatan*, vol. 2, pp. 110–15.

6. Morazán, in contrast, had a reputation for treating prisoners well. See Bancroft, *History of Central America*, vol. 13, p. 141.

7. Ibid., pp. 141–2; F. Crowe, *The gospel in Central America containing a sketch of the country, physical and geographical, historical and political, moral and religious: A history of the Baptist mission in British Honduras, and of the introduction of the Bible into the Spanish American republic of Guatemala* (London: C. Gilpin, 1850), p. 147.

8. Jose Francisco Morazán Quezada returned to Central America from exile in South America less than two years after his defeat by Carrera. After attempting to raise an army to form a new Central American union, he was captured in Costa Rica in 1842 and executed by firing squad. His death at forty-nine ended all serious attempts to unite the Central American states in a republic.

CATHERWOOD

1. An outline of Frederick Catherwood's life has emerged from public records, a few existing letters, rare references to him by some of his contemporaries, his own small canon of writings, an account book, Stephens's narratives, and a key legal case involving his marriage. Of course, Catherwood's greatest legacy has been his artwork, but even much of that, particularly his work in Egypt, has been lost.

2. See http://www.british-history.ac.uk/report.aspx?compid=98247.

3. V. W. von Hagen, *"F. Catherwood archt" (1799–1854)* (New York: Oxford University Press, 1946), fn. 8, pp. 145–46. Von Hagen's biography mistakenly identified Nathaniel Catherwood as Frederick's father. But birth, baptism, and

church records identify his father and mother as John James Catherwood and Anne Rowe. Information relating to Frederick Catherwood's family came from correspondence with Fiona Hodgson and Julie Redman, who are descendants of the Catherwood family and have carefully traced their family tree.

4. J. Aitken, *John Newton: From Disgrace to Amazing Grace* (Wheaton, IL: Crossway Books, 2007), pp. 273–74.

5. Correspondence with Fiona Hodgson and Julie Redman.

6. J. J. Scoles, "Catherwood," *The Dictionary of Architecture* (London: Richards, 1852), pp. 53–92.

7. S. Brown, *Joseph Severn: A Life: The Rewards of Friendship* (Oxford: Oxford University Press, 2009), fn. 35, p. 29.

8. A. Graves, *The Royal Academy of Arts; A Complete Dictionary of Contributors and Their Work from Its Foundation in 1769 to 1904* (London: H. Graves, 1905), p. 14.

9. J. Severn and G. F. Scott, *Joseph Severn: Letters and Memoirs* (Aldershot, England, and Burlington, VT: Ashgate, 2005).

10. Von Hagen, *"F. Catherwood archt" (1799–1854)*.

11. F. Salmon, "Storming the Campo Vaccino: British Architects and the Antique Buildings of Rome after Waterloo," *Architectural History* 38 (1995): 146–75.

12. American Ethnological Society, *Transactions of the American Ethnological Society* (New York: Bartlett & Welford, 1845), p. 487.

13. *National Academy of Design Exhibition Record 1826–1860* (New York: National Academy of Design, 1860). His tempera of Mount Etna is one of the few surviving original paintings from the early period of his life.

14. P. Starkey and J. Starkey, *Travellers in Egypt* (London and New York: Tauris, 1998), p. 48.

15. H. Colvin, *A Biographical Dictionary of British Architects, 1600–1840* (New Haven, CT, and London: Yale University Press, 2008), s.v. "Scoles," p. 908.

16. *The Annual Register, or a View of the History, Politics, and Literature of the Year 1835* (London: Longman, Rees, Orme, 1836), p. 202.

17. K. Fahmy, *All the Pasha's Men: Mehmed Ali, His Army, and the Making of Modern Egypt* (Cairo and New York: American University in Cairo Press, 2002), pp. 95–96.

18. J. Madox, *Excursions in the Holy Land, Egypt, Nubia, Syria, &c. Including a Visit to the Unfrequented District of the Haouran* (London: R. Bentley, 1834), vol. 2, p. 28.

19. *Times* (London), August 25, 1824. The newspaper printed an extract from a letter sent from Ghenney on April 21, 1824, reporting that Catherwood, Parke, and Scoles had arrived from their "scientific excursion" and were "in good health."

20. R. Herzog, "Über Henry Westcars Tagebuch einer Reise durch Ägypten und Nubien (1823–24)," *Mitteilungen des Deutschen Archäologischen Instituts, Abteilung Kairo* 24 (1969): 201–11.

21. J. W. Grutz, "The Lost Portfolios of Robert Hay," www.saudiaramcoworld.com, March/April 2003.

22. Starkey and Starkey, *Travellers in Egypt*, p. 131.

23. Severn and Scott, *Joseph Severn: Letters and Memoirs*.

24. V. W. Von Hagen, *Frederick Catherwood, archt* (New York: Oxford University

Press, 1950), p. vi.

25. Architectural Publication Society, *The Dictionary of Architecture*.

26. *Downside Review* (Downside Abbey, Bath, England) 8 (1889): 115–16.

27. Graves, *The Royal Academy of Arts*, p. 14.

28. Its original name in the Punic era was Thugga. Catherwood called the area Dugga and today it is known as Dougga. It has become a tourist attraction because of numerous Roman ruins found there.

29. *Transactions of the American Ethnological Society*, pp. 474–91.

30. For a time Catherwood believed that he was the monument's discoverer. Later, however, he learned that the same inscriptions had been copied two hundred years earlier by a French traveler named D'Arcos.

31. When Sir Thomas Reade, the British consul in Tunis, learned of Catherwood's discovery, he ordered the inscriptions cut from the façade and sent to the British Museum and in the process destroyed much of the tomb. The monument, today called the Lybico-Punic Mausoleum, was reconstructed at the beginning of the twentieth century by French archaeologist Louis Poinssot. A six-foot-long sculptured stone representing "a charioteer driving four horses at full speed," which Catherwood dug up at the monument's base, was reattached to its top. Based on the structure's "earliest and most primitive" style of the Greek columns and capitals and the purely Egyptian architrave and cornices, Catherwood estimated that it was erected close to the founding of Carthage around 900 B.C. Modern experts, however, place the date closer to 300 B.C.

32. Starkey and Starkey, *Travellers in Egypt*, pp. 132–33.

33. G. A. Hoskins, *Visit to the Great Oasis of the Libyan Desert* (London, 1837).

34. Ibid. Hoskins described the journey in great detail. The villages they visited are today known as El-Kharga, Baris, Bulaq, and Ezbet Dush.

35. F. Arundale, *Illustrations of Jerusalem and Mount Sinai: Including the Most Interesting Sites Between Grand Cairo and Beirout* (London: H. Colburn, 1837).

36. W. H. Bartlett, *Walks About the City and Environs of Jerusalem* (London: George Virtue, 1846). The account by Catherwood is on pp. 161–78.

37. Arundale, *Illustrations of Jerusalem and Mount Sinai*, p. 69.

38. It was built at approximately the same time that the Mayan cities of Palenque and Copán were thriving in Central America during their peak Classic period.

39. Arundale's diary ends with their arrival at Beirut, so the details of what exactly followed are unknown.

40. Gertrude Catherwood lists this as her name in Frederick Catherwood's will.

41. U.S. Department of State, President Garfield, et al., *Message from the President of the United States, transmitting, in response to the resolution of the Senate of the 18th ultimo, a report of the secretary of state, with accompanying papers, in relation to the capitulations of the Ottoman Empire* (Washington, DC: U.S. Government Printing Office, 1881), p. 35.

42. R. Kark, *American Consuls in the Holy Land, 1832–1914* (Detroit: Wayne State University Press, 1994), p. 85.

43. Bonomi's account of the wedding of Gertrude Abbott and Frederick Catherwood, and their travel afterward, was described in testimony given by Bonomi in a trial in 1841.

44. Correspondence with Fiona Hodgson and Julie Redman.

45. S. Tillett, *Egypt Itself: The Career of Robert Hay, Esquire, of Linplum and*

Nunraw, 1799–1863 (London: SD Books, 1984), pp. 68–71.

46. *The Literary Gazette and Journal of the Belles Lettres, Arts, Sciences, &c.* (London: W. A. Scripps, 1835), p. 380.

47. Von Hagen, *Frederick Catherwood, archt*, pp. 43–45.

48. A. J. Downing, *A treatise on the theory and practice of landscape gardening adapted to North America; with a view to the improvement of country residences. With remarks on rural architecture* (New York: Putnam, 1853). Includes an illustration of Catherwood's conservatory at p. 452, one of the only illustrations of a structure designed by him. Also see Downing's "Rural Essays," p. 201, and Haley's "Montgomery Place," p. 13, for more information.

49. Catherwood's panorama was not the first in America. One had been built in 1818 by the artist John Vanderlyn on land leased from New York City at the northeast corner of City Hall Park. However, it went into bankruptcy eleven years later. *Bulletin of the Metropolitan Museum of Art* 7 (1912).

50. The bound account ledger that recorded the panorama's expenses and income from 1838 through 1842 is preserved in the New-York Historical Society archive. Except for the bookkeeper who kept the accounts, it is difficult, if not impossible, to determine how Catherwood and Jackson apportioned between them the costs and income over the four years recorded in the ledger, and how profitable the business actually was. It was a complicated enterprise with panoramas sent off for exhibitions in Boston, Baltimore, Toronto, Philadelphia, and other places, for which there is no record of income. In addition, books relating to the panoramas were sold to customers, a small but seemingly thriving sideline. The account book, however, does give the raw numbers for daily income from the New York exhibits, as well as the amount due monthly for renting the land on which the rotunda sat—owned by the Astor family— salaries, publishing expenses, gas bills, taxes, and the cost of renting the panorama canvases themselves.

51. There is evidence that Catherwood took his Jerusalem panorama to Boston to exhibit in 1837. *Christian Examiner and General Review* 23 (1842): 261.

52. Victor Wolfgang von Hagen, biographer of Stephens and Catherwood, wrote that the two men met in London at Burford's panorama of Jerusalem, an assertion that has been many times repeated. However, an encounter between the two in England would have been physically impossible. Maritime passenger records show that Catherwood and his family were aboard a ship for New York when Stephens was traveling from Beirut to Alexandria, Egypt. Stephens arrived in New York on September 6, 1836. Catherwood and family had arrived three months earlier, on June 7, 1836.

53. Exman, *The Brothers Harper*, p. 121.

54. *The Knickerbocker; or, New-York Monthly Magazine* 54 (1859).

55. Ibid., pp. 318–19.

56. S. E. Morison, *William Hickling Prescott, 1796–1859* (Boston: Massachusetts Historical Society, 1958).

57. Von Hagen, *Frederick Catherwood, archt*, n. 4, pp. 152–53. Von Hagen quotes from John R. Bartlett Correspondence, John Carter Brown Library, Brown University. A copy of this letter is also in the file of the Victor von Hagen Papers at the New-York Historical Society.

58. "Biographical Notice," in the London edition of *Incidents of Travel in Central*

America, Chiapas, and Yucatan, published by Catherwood in 1854.
59. "Court of Exchequer," *Times* (London), December 11, 1841.
60. BANC MSS ZZ 116, contract between Stephens and Catherwood.

CHAPTER 12: JOURNEY INTO THE PAST

1. Bancroft, *History of Central America*, ch. 25. The capital has been called various names. Stephens referred to it as Patinamit. And the name given it by the Mexican warriors who accompanied Alvarado on his conquest was Quauhtemala, which was later transformed to the general name for the country, Guatemala.

2. M. Restall and F. G. L. Asselbergs, *Invading Guatemala: Spanish, Nahua, and Maya Accounts of the Conquest Wars* (University Park: Pennsylvania State University Press, 2007). This excellent book offers a *Rashomon*-like version of the conquest of Central America, with English translations of records, letters, and other accounts of the invasion by the conquistadors, including those of Pedro de Alvarado and his brother, Jorge, the Mexican Indians who accompanied them, and the conquered Indians themselves.

3. R. J. Sharer and S. G. Morley, *The Ancient Maya* (Stanford, CA: Stanford University Press, 1994), pp. 737–41. Bancroft, *History of Central America,* also gives a detailed account of Alvarado's conquest of Central America (chs. 22–27). As has been mentioned, the Spanish capital, called Santiago, was relocated several times. It went from the foot of Volcan Agua, following a huge mudslide that buried much of the town, to the nearby Panchoy Valley, where it remained for several centuries, until 1773, when this city too was destroyed, this time by an earthquake. The remains of that city came to be known as La Antigua when the capital was moved for the last time to its current location and eventually named Guatemala City. Today the town of Ciudad Vieja, or Old City, occupies the site at the foot of Volcan Agua. And La Antigua, with its lovely colonial-style houses, churches, and cobblestone streets, is a UNESCO World Heritage Site.

4. It should be noted that the K'iche' and the Kaqchikel Maya were no pushovers in the face of the Spanish onslaught. The Maya fought heroically but their warrior class was already decimated by the Old World diseases, principally smallpox, which had spread rapidly from the Europeans and preceded the invasion. The Spaniards, though small in numbers, were tough and disciplined. And they were aided significantly by thousands of Tlaxcan warriors and other Indian groups sent from Mexico on the Conquest, along with the often-mentioned technological superiority of Spanish firearms, artillery, steel weapons, armor, and horses, terrifying animals that the Indians had never seen before.

5. Utatlán, however, was one of the better documented of Guatemala's Indian sites. As it had done with Galindo's investigation of Copán, the liberal Guatemalan government under Galvez had also commissioned Miguel Rivera y Maestre in 1834 to make a thorough examination of Utatlán, or what remained of it. Stephens met Rivera y Maestre in Guatemala City and described him as "a gentleman distinguished for his scientific and antiquarian tastes." He gave Stephens a copy of his government report, in addition to a small clay statue of a seated Mayan figure that he had extracted from the ruins.

6. See http://pages.ucsd.edu/~gbraswel/docs/Braswell%20CV_
   Peer%20Reviewed%20Chapters%20&%20Articles/Braswell%202003f.pdf.
7. The ten Lost Tribes of Israel were originally located in the Northern Kingdom
   of Israel and were exiled during the Assyrians' invasion of the Kingdom in 722
   B.C. Their disappearance ever since has prompted centuries of speculation
   concerning where they went.
8. M. M. Noah, *Discourse on the Evidences of the American Indians Being the
   Descendants of the Lost Tribes of Israel: Delivered before the Mercantile Library
   Association, Clinton Hall* (New York: J. Van Norden, 1837)0, pp. 21–29. Noah
   wrote: "Mexico and Central America abound in curiosities, exemplifying the
   fact of the Asiatic origin of the inhabitants, and it is not many years ago, that
   the ruins of a whole city, with a wall nearly seven miles in circumference, with
   castles, palaces, and temples, evidently of Hebrew or Phoenician architecture,
   was found on the river Palenque. The ruins of this city near Guatemala, in
   Central America, are described by Del Río in 1782, [and] when taken in
   conjunction with the extraordinary, I may say, wonderful antiquities spread over
   the entire surface of that country, awaken recollections in the specimens of
   architecture, which carry us back to early pages of history, and prove beyond the
   shadow of a doubt we who imagined ourselves to be the natives of a new world,
   but recently discovered, inhabit a continent which rivaled the splendor of Egypt
   and Syria, and was peopled by a powerful and highly cultivated nation from the
   old world."
9. E. K. Kingsborough, A. Aglio, et al., *Antiquities of Mexico: Comprising fac-
   similes of ancient Mexican paintings and hieroglyphics, preserved in the royal
   libraries of Paris, Berlin and Dresden, in the Imperial library of Vienna, in the
   Vatican library, in the Borgian museum at Rome, in the library of the Institute at
   Bologna, and in the Bodleian Library at Oxford, together with the monuments of
   New Spain by M. Dupaix, with their respective scales of measurement and
   accompanying descriptions* (London, 1831). Kingsborough included in his
   volumes several essays by scholars who speculated on the origins of New World
   natives, their cities, and ancient civilization. They included: "Comparison of the
   Ancient Monuments of Mexico with Those of Egypt, India, and the Rest of the
   Ancient World," by Alexandre Lenoir, and "Discourse on Two Questions
   Submitted to the Historical Congress of Europe, the Value of Documents
   Relating to the History of America, and to Decide Whether There Is Any Link
   Between the Languages of the Various American Tribes and those of Africa and
   India," by Charles Farcy.
10. W. Robertson, *The History of America* (London, 1803). Most of Robertson's
    discussion on the state of Native American Indians can be found in vol. 2, Book
    IV, pp. 13–32.
11. W. G. Lovell, *Conquest and Survival in Colonial Guatemala: A Historical
    Geography of the Cuchumatán Highlands, 1500–1821* (Montréal: McGill-Queen's
    University Press, 1992), pp. 61–64. Bancroft, *History of Central America,* also has
    a vivid account of Gonzalo de Alvarado's campaign against the Mam Indians
    (pp. 695–704).
12. In fact, wrote Stephens, three Belgians, who reportedly were sent not long
    before by their government on a scientific expedition to Palenque, had applied
    for permission to visit the ruins and were turned down.

13. Kingsborough, Aglio, et al., *Antiquities of Mexico*. See Dupaix's report.
14. S. Martin and N. Grube, *Chronicle of the Maya Kings and Queens: Deciphering the Dynasties of the Ancient Maya* (London and New York: Thames & Hudson, 2000), pp. 177–89.
15. Ibid.
16. Here Stephens quotes Dupaix in translation in *Incidents of Travel in Central America*, pp. 262–63.

CHAPTER 13: PALENQUE

1. The ruins had been known to the local natives for decades, maybe centuries, simply as "las casas de piedra," the houses of stone, without any history attached to them. The earliest discovery of Palenque by Europeans is still a mystery. Writing in his history of Guatemala, published in two volumes, 1808–18, Domingo Juarros described Palenque: "This metropolis . . . remained unknown until the middle of the eighteenth century, when some Spaniards having penetrated the dreary solitude, found themselves, to their great astonishment within sight of the remains of what once had been a superb city, of six leagues in circumference; the solidity of its edifices, the stateliness of its palaces, and the magnificence of its public works, were not surpassed in importance by its vast extent; temples, altars, deities, sculptures and monumental stones, bear testimony to its great antiquity." See D. Juarros and J. Bailey, *A Statistical and Commercial History of the Kingdom of Guatemala, in Spanish America containing important particulars relative to its productions, manufactures, customs, &c. &c. &c.* (London: J. Hearne, 1823), pp. 18–19. Juarros does not name the Spaniards but there were oral reports that a parish priest named Antonio de Solis, from nearby Tumbala and Santa Domingo del Palenque, had visited the ruins of Palenque as early as 1746. One of his relatives, Ramon de Ordonez y Aguiar, heard a family account of the visit and became the prime instigator of future government surveys of the site. Although Ordonez y Aguiar, a priest living in Ciudad Real (present-day San Cristobal de las Casas), apparently never visited the site himself, he succeeded in prompting two local officials from Ciudad Real, Fernando Gomez de Andrade and Esteban Gutierrez, to visit the ruins in 1773. Ordonez y Aguiar drafted a "memoria" on what was found and alerted the authorities in Guatemala City about the discovery. But it took another eleven years before José Estacheria, the president of the Audiencia of Guatemala, ordered José Antonio Calderón, the mayor of Santo Domingo, the hamlet closest to the site, to investigate in 1784. A full discussion of the involvement and actions of Ramon Ordonez y Aguiar and José Estacheria, as well as the reaction of the royal courts in Guatemala and Spain to the discovery is outlined in Jorge Cañizares-Esguerra's excellent *How to Write the History of the New World* (Stanford, CA: Stanford University Press, 2001), pp. 321–46.
2. P. Cabello Carro, *Política investigadora de la época de Carlos III en el área Maya: descubrimiento de Palenque y primeras excavaciones de carácter científico: según documentación de Calderón, Bernasconi, Del Río y otros* (Madrid: Ediciones de la Torre, 1992). This work provides copies of the correspondence and other documents concerning Palenque, including the reports of Bernasconi and Calderón that passed between Guatemala and the Royal Court in Spain.
3. There appears to be no direct orders from King Carlos. There are, however,

documents located in Spain and the British Museum indicating that the royal historiographer of Spanish America, Juan Bautista Muñoz, corresponded from Spain with the president of the Royal Audiencia in Guatemala, José Estacheria, about the several expeditions to Palenque. See Cabello Carro, *Política investigadora de la época de Carlos III en el área Maya*. In dispatching the expeditions the two men drafted a list of questions that they wanted answered, such as the scope of the ruins, their age, who were the founders, and the reason for its abandonment.

4. E. C. Danien, R. J. Sharer, et al., *New Theories on the Ancient Maya* (Philadelphia: University Museum, University of Pennsylvania, 1992). Ignacio Almendáriz has also been identified by the name of Ricardo Almendáriz (p. 5).

5. There is some speculation that Del Río, like the original conquistadors, was looking for gold and other treasures.

6. R. Almendáriz, A. d. Río, et al., *Coleccion de estampas copiadas de las figuras originales, que de medio y baxo relieve, se manifiestan, en estucos y piedras, en varios edificios de la poblacion antigua nuevamente descubierta en las immediaciones del pueblo del Palenque en la Provincia de Ciudad Real de Chiapa, una de las del Reyno de Guatemala en la American Septentrional* (1787).

7. A. d. Río and P. F. Cabrera, *Description of the Ruins of an Ancient City: Discovered Near Palenque, in the Kingdom of Guatemala or, A critical investigation and research into the history of the Americans* (London, 1822), p. 19.

8. Evans, *Romancing the Maya*, pp. 23–32.

9. Domingo Juarros published a history of the Kingdom of Guatemala in 1808 in which he briefly described Palenque: "The hieroglyphics, symbols, and emblems, which have been discovered in the temples, bear so strong a resemblance to those of the Egyptian as to encourage the supposition that a colony of that nation may have founded the city of Palenque, or Culhuacan. The same opinion may be formed respecting that of Tulhá, the ruins of which are still to be seen near the village of Ocosingo in the same district [where Toniná is located]." Juarros appears to have seen a copy or summary of Dupaix's report, and possibly Del Río's as well. His account of Palenque takes up less that a page of his 520-page book, which was originally published in Spanish in 1808. The Palenque reference drew little to no attention. An English translation was published in 1823 in London. Juarros and Bailey, *A Statistical and Commercial History of the Kingdom of Guatemala*, pp. 18–19. Several years after Dupaix's expedition, while his report still lay in a drawer in Mexico City, Alexander von Humboldt began publication in Paris of his monumental thirty-volume work covering his scientific journey through Spanish America. While in Mexico, Humboldt heard of the ruins at Palenque but never traveled to site. On his return to Europe in 1804 he learned from a German antiquary of the so-called Dresden Codex, one of four surviving bark-paper "books" filled with vividly painted Mayan hieroglyphs that had not been destroyed by the Spanish during the Conquest. In 1810, he published *View of the Cordilleras and Monuments of the Indigenous People of America*, and reproduced five pages of hieroglyphs from the codex, as well as an image of one of the stucco figures from Palenque, apparently a copy of one of Almendáriz's 1787 drawings. It was the world's first look at Mayan hieroglyphs and a figure from Palenque. However, Humboldt did not grasp what it was that he was publishing. He mistakenly identified the

bas-relief image as coming from the Mexican state of Oaxaca. And he gave no source for the hieroglyphs, although they were later mistakenly assumed to be Aztec, from the central Mexican empire that existed centuries after the collapse of the classic Maya. Humboldt partly corrects the location of the bas-relief in a note at the end of the text and places its location not at Oaxaca but near Guatemala, "according to the accounts received from Mexico" (p. 254). A. v. Humbold and H. M. Williams, *Researches, concerning the institutions & monuments of the ancient inhabitants of America: With descriptions & views of some of the most striking scenes in the Cordilleras!* (London, 1814), pp.126–34, 144–47. Actually, the first publication of a Mayan hieroglyph came in a 1796 publication showing several glyphs employed as decorative elements in a model Mexican room created for a treatise on interior decoration by Joseph Friedrich, Baron von Racknitz. Danien, Sharer, et al., *New Theories on the Ancient Maya*, p. 3.

10. The publication drew little serious notice in England but greatly intrigued the French, who had become fascinated with antiquities ever since Bonaparte invaded Egypt at the turn of the century. Del Río's account created a sensation among the French savants and in 1825 the prestigious Société de Géographie offered a gold medal worth 2,400 francs for the best eyewitness description of Palenque in particular and ancient ruins in Central America in general. The competition was on. In rapid succession, several interested parties showed up at Santo Domingo de Palenque and traveled out to the ruins. Among the most important was Lieutenant Colonel Juan Galindo. When he arrived in April 1831, he was military governor of nearby Petén and was still three years away from exploring Copán. He sent off reports on Palenque to the Société and to the *Literary Gazette,* a periodical of wide circulation in London. Because so little was known about Palenque in the general public, despite publication of Del Río's account several years earlier, many assumed after reading Galindo's report in the *Gazette* that he was the discoverer of the ruins. Galindo made no such claim. He did contend in a later article in the *Gazette,* however, that he had no knowledge of Del Río's and Dupaix's investigations at the time he arrived at Palenque. And though he never explained what had prompted him to visit the ruins, he clearly was aware of the Paris prize and clearly coveted it based on reports to the society of his later explorations, including Copán.

11. Kingsborough, Aglio, et al., *Antiquities of Mexico.*

12. P. N. Edison, "Colonial Prospecting in Independent Mexico: Abbé Baradère's Antiquités Mexicaines," *Proceedings of the Western Society for French History* 32 (2004): 195–215. Baradère, a French priest, discovered in Mexico City Dupaix's accounts of his expeditions, along with Castañeda's illustrations, and brought them back to Paris, where they became the centerpiece of a two-volume set of folios called *Antiquités Mexicaines,* which Baradère published in 1834–36.

13. Kingsborough, either as a student or later, had gained access to Mexican codices housed in Oxford's famous Bodleian Library. These were Indian "picture books," which like the Dresden Codex had survived the conquest. The manuscripts, which were created largely by the Aztecs, were illustrated not by hieroglyphs but pictographs—colorful symbols and figures sometimes described as narrative cartoons—painted on pounded bark paper, some more than twenty feet long and folded accordion-like to make them compact and portable.

Despite Spanish destruction of large numbers of these manuscripts, some were carried back to Spain and had found their way to Oxford. Kingsborough's encounter with these codices at Oxford changed his life and sent him on a quest to find and publish every document relating to pre-Columbian America that he could put his hands on. He hired an Italian artist, Augustino A. Aglio, to scour the libraries, private collections, and archives of Europe and carefully copy whatever materials relating to American antiquities he could find, including the hieroglyphic-rich Mayan codices. The result was a disorganized, richly illustrated, nine-volume set of oversize books—each volume weighing twenty to forty pounds—some with its illustrations hand colored and printed on vellum. Kingsborough initially planned for seven volumes but two additional volumes were added after his death, and a tenth was composed but never published. S. D. Whitmore, S. D. (2009). "Lord Kingsborough and his Contribution to Ancient Mesoamerican Scholarship: The Antiquities of Mexico," *PARI Journal* 9, no. 4 (2009): 8–16. The price of these so-called elephant folios was prohibitively expensive and the print runs were small. Stephens later quoted the work at four hundred dollars per copy, an enormous sum at the time, and noted that he knew of only one set in the United States. It was this fantastic sum restricting the folios to a select few that motivated Stephens to insist his books be reasonably priced to ensure their widest possible distribution. The magnificent *Antiquities of Mexico* would eventually prove to be an invaluable resource for future scholars—a massive folio collection faithfully reproducing the few surviving manuscripts of pre-Columbian America, all drawn together in one place. More than a century would pass, however, before anyone would be able to unscramble their disordered sequences and begin to make any real sense of them. The first seven volumes of *Antiquities of Mexico* were published in 1830 and 1831 and the last two in 1848. Kingsborough did not live to see the final two volumes in print. He was thrown into debtor's prison after he failed to pay the manufacturer of the high-quality, handmade paper on which Kingsborough insisted his books be printed. His father, the Earl of Kingston, died not long after his son, and if Kingsborough had lived he would have inherited his father's title and estate and been able to pay off his debts.

14. W. E. Burton, *The Gentleman's Magazine* (Philadelphia, 1837), pp. 537–38. This obituary states that Kingsborough was imprisoned because of a debt owed by his father and not due to any "extravagance" by Kingsborough himself.

15. I. Podgorny, "'Silent and Alone': How the Ruins of Palenque Were Taught to Speak the Language of Archeology," *Comparative Archaeologies*, Part 2 (2011): 527–553. Podgorny offers an interesting discussion of this issue.

16. H. Baradère, G. Dupaix, et al., *Antiquités mexicaines. Relation des trois expéditions du capitaine Dupaix, ordonnées en 1805, 1806, et 1807, pour la recherche des antiquités du pays, notamment celles de Mitla et de Palenque* (Paris, 1834). Baradère had hoped with his two volumes to win the gold medal offered by the Société de Géographie but he failed for a lack of comprehensive on-site exploration. Baradère then left France in 1835 for Mexico with ambitious plans to explore Palenque and other sites. He was last seen in Mexico in 1839, then disappeared. The speculations about the origins of this mysterious new civilization were not limited to classical and Middle Eastern cultures but included Asia

as well—Japan, China, and India.

17. Not all commentators had succumbed to the speculation that Native American civilizations must have descended from those of the Old World. Even as early as 1823 there were voices who found such speculations presumptuous. In a 1823 review in the *European Magazine* of Del Río's published account of Palenque the anonymous reviewer wrote: "Writers on such subjects have the absurd habit of selecting two distant nations, and tracing some resemblance in their ancient customs, manners, religions, and civil architecture, they draw the inference that one must have been descended from the other, forgetting that such resemblances merely prove the general analogy of our animal nature; and that man, under similar stages in the scale of civilization, will have analogous institutions, and analogous objects both of ornament and of convenience, although these may be all modified differently by various contingent circumstances." How prophetic the writer turned out to be. *European Magazine, and London Review* 83 (May 1823): 454–56.

18. M. D. Coe, *Breaking the Maya Code* (New York: Thames & Hudson, 1992), p. 80.

19. According to Waldeck's account of his life, he was already off on an expedition to South Africa at the age of fourteen. When he returned, he took up the study of art in France with the influential neoclassic painter Jacques-Louis David. He said he joined Napoleon's army as a soldier during the siege of Toulon and the Italian campaign, later following Bonaparte to Egypt. After the French defeat there, he crossed the desert deep into Africa. When he emerged, he claimed to be the only survivor of the five men who had started on the journey. Next came an expedition with pirates on the Indian Ocean. The following fifteen years of his life remain somewhat of a mystery, a period even he did not account for. He surfaced again in 1819, this time in South America, where, by his account, he joined in Lord Cochrane's naval exploits on behalf of Chile's struggle for independence from Spain. H. F. Cline, "The Apocryphal Early Career of J. F. Waldeck, Pioneer Americanist," *Acta Americana* 5 (1947): 278–300.

20. Danien, Sharer, et al., *New Theories on the Ancient Maya*, p. 13. There is also an excellent discussion citing two other pioneers in the field of Mayan hieroglyph interpretation by George Stuart at http://www.mesoweb.com/bearc/cmr/RRAMW29.pdf. It was to one of the scholars—Constantine S. Rafinesque—to whom Waldeck had written. In addition, there were others deeply interested in Palenque at the same time Waldeck was at the ruins. One was Francisco Corroy, a French doctor who lived nearby in Tabasco and had visited the ruins many times, and corresponded with Waldeck. See R. L. Brunhouse, *In Search of the Maya: The First Archaeologists* (Albuquerque: University of New Mexico Press, 1973), pp. 66–73.

21. See the Mesoweb website reference to earliest mentions of Uxmal at http://www.mesoweb.com/features/uxmal/history.html.

22. Waldeck had apparently learned of Uxmal's location from its appearance in J. S. Buchon's *Atlas of Two Americas,* published in 1825 in Paris. Brunhouse, *In Search of the Maya,* p. 74. Note also that Del Río discussed Uxmal, referring to it as "Oxmutal" in his report, which may also have prompted Waldeck's visit. In addition, Uxmal is mentioned in a history of Yucatán by the Franciscan priest Diego López Cogolludo. D. López Cogolludo, F. d. Ayeta, et al., *Historia de*

Yucathan (Madrid: Jvan Garcia Infanzen, 1688).

23. J. F. M. Waldeck, M. Mestre Ghigliazza, et al., *Viaje pintoresco y arqueológico a la provincia de Yucatán (América Central) durante los años 1834 y 1836* (Mérida, Mexico, 1930).

24. Danien, Sharer, et al., *New Theories on the Ancient Maya.* In his essay, "Quest for Decipherment: A Historical and Biographical Survey of Maya Hieroglyphic Investigation," George E. Stuart points out that Waldeck's original drawings were much more accurate than the published versions, which he may have altered to buttress his contention that Palenque was founded by people from the Old World.

25. Brunhouse, *In Search of the Maya,* p. 74.

26. See Waldeck in the "annotated bibliography" by Charles Rhyne of Reed College, as well as images from Waldeck's book, at http://academic.reed.edu/uxmal/contents.html.

27. In a remarkable coincidence, Colonel Galindo was in England at the time trying to persuade the British to cede back to Guatemala large chunks of territory that Britain claimed for Belize. Between his discussions with Lord Palmerston, he found time to attend the same Royal Geographical Society meeting. Galindo spoke to the members after Waldeck's presentation, telling them that he had "little doubt but that Palenque was built prior to the foundation of the city of Mexico in 1342." He added that he believed that Palenque and Copán had been built not by traders or conquerors from the Old World but by the ancestors of the indigenous inhabitants now living in the region. He went further. In his opinion, he said, native Indians, though now a "senile" race, had created the world's oldest civilizations. Palenque and Copán, as well as the cities later built by the Aztecs and Inca, were all "modern revivals" of a much more ancient American Indian civilization that predated even those of Japan and China. There is no account of Waldeck and Galindo engaging in conversation, though it was quite likely, and their discussion may have been heated given their personalities and their different views concerning the origin of the ancient cities. A short time later, Galindo headed back to Central America and his rendezvous with destiny, and Waldeck went on to Paris. *The Literary Gazette and Journal of the Belles Lettres, Arts, Sciences, &c.* (London: W. A. Scripps, 1835); *The Family Magazine,* no. 4 (New York: Redfield & Lindsay, 1837), p. 180.

28. Waldeck's turned out to be the more visionary assertion. Not only have archaeologists subsequently confirmed his estimate by other means—principally hieroglyphic decipherment and radiocarbon dating—but it would be another seventy years following Waldeck's declaration before tree-ring dating, the science of dendrochronology, would develop as a reliable tool for archaeological dating.

29. Since his 1838 volume was dedicated to Kingsborough, who had provided most of the money for his Yucatán venture and had recently died, Waldeck may have already agreed to or felt obligated to devote the first book to Uxmal. And perhaps more important, unlike with Palenque, no book had yet been published with images from Uxmal. Waldeck's artistic abilities are on full display in the folio. But his distortions and embellishments of Uxmal's ruins—added to his questionable accounts of his past—have clearly undermined his work on both

Uxmal and Palenque. According to one account, Waldeck had planned at some point to publish a trio of books about the Maya and his expeditions. But it would be nearly thirty years before his drawings on Palenque were published in Paris, in 1866 in conjunction with text by Charles Etienne Brasseur de Bourbourg under the title *Recherches sur les Ruines de Palenque.* Waldeck had cut a deal with the French government, which had paid him a lump sum for 188 of his drawings. A commission of six scholars, however, was set up to compare his drawings with photographs taken at Palenque by Désiré Charnay. Only fifty-six of the drawings were given a favorable report and included in the book. See Brunhouse, *In Search of the Maya,* pp. 79–80.

30. In 1952, Alberto Ruz, director of research at Palenque for Mexico's Instituto Nacional de Antropología e Historia, uncovered an elaborate tomb buried deep within the Temple of Inscriptions. The tomb contained a magnificently carved sarcophagus lid showing the great ruler of Palenque, Pakal, whose remains were found within. The discovery of the tomb, more than 1,200 years old, generated headlines around the world.

31. M. E. Miller, S. Martin, et al., *Courtly Art of the Ancient Maya* (New York: Thames & Hudson, 2004), p. 247.

32. More than 1,500 structures were mapped in the surrounding area beyond Palenque's urban core in 1998–2000, four times the estimated number located only fifteen years earlier. See E. L. Barnhart, "Palenque Mapping Project, 1998–2000 Final Report," Foundation for the Advancement of Mesoamerican Studies, 2000.

CHAPTER 14: UXMAL

1. H. H. Bancroft, *The Native Races* (New York: 1967). See footnote on p. 145 in volume 4 for earliest historic references to Uxmal.

2. Stephens was referring to the fact that the Maya had never left a history of their cities (as far as he knew). But he knew of Uxmal from Waldeck's book, published in 1838 in Paris, and an account of the site by Lorenzo de Zavala, the Mexican ambassador to France, who grew up in Yucatán and had visited the site. Zavala, "Notice sur les Monuments Antiques d'Ushmal, dans la Province de Yucatán," in Baradère, Dupaix, et al., *Antiquités mexicaines;* Waldeck, Mestre Ghigliazza, et al., *Viaje pintoresco y arqueológico a la provincia de Yucatán.*

3. The sculpture took an unusual path to the museum. It was displayed on Cruger's Island in the middle the Hudson River for nearly eighty years before being bought by the museum in 1919 with eleven other artifacts collected by Stephens.

CHAPTER 15: "MAGNIFICENT"

1. The letter from James Catherwood is mentioned in news accounts of the legal proceedings concerning his wife's affair.

2. W. Carpenter, *Peerage for the People* (London: W. Strange, 1837), pp. 734–37.

3. Newspaper coverage of the later trial.

4. Catherwood's uncle, Nathaniel Catherwood, had also been a partner.

5. New York Passenger Lists, 1820–1957 (1840; Microfilm serial: M237:_44; Line 7; List number: 808), is the manifest for the ship *Ontario,* arriving in New York

on October 23, 1840. Listed as passengers are Catherwood, his three children, and a twenty-six-year-old woman named MaryAnn Bennett, whose occupation is listed as "nurse" and who was almost certainly the children's nanny.

6. Panorama account book, New-York Historical Society

7. The book contained 34 steel-engraved plates, 29 lithographed plates, 4 wood-engraved plates, and 9 wood carvings.

8. In addition to accuracy in text and illustrations, Stephens's other major objective was to make the book as affordable as possible in order to reach the widest number of readers. He made it clear from the beginning that he did not wish to create a tome on Central American antiquities, such as Waldeck and Kingsborough had done, that was so expensive it would be available only to a privileged few. He negotiated with the Harpers to set the price at five dollars, low by the norm of the day for an illustrated two-volume set, but still a hefty sum in a country in 1841 trying to lift itself out of economic depression.

9. E. A. Poe, "Review of New Books," *Graham's Magazine* (1841): 90–96.

10. "The Antiquities of Central America," book review, *United States Democratic Review* 9, no. 38 (August 1841), http://digital.library.cornell.edu/cgi/t/text/pageviewer-idx?c=usde;cc=usde;rgn=full%20text;idno=usde0009-2;didno=usde0009-2;view=image;seq=00172;node=usde0009-2%3A1.

11. Harper & Brothers offices were destroyed years later by fire and many records of payments and printings have been lost. But contemporaries at the time estimated the sales at 12,000–20,000 copies in the first six months of publication. The book continued to sell in large numbers for decades and well into the twentieth century, and continues in print today.

12. "Incidents of Travel in Central America, Chiapas, and Yucatán," book review, *London Quarterly Review* 69 (1842): 52–91.

13. "The Antiquities of Central America," *United States Democratic Review.*

14. F. J. Cebulski, "Letter from William Hickling Prescott to John Lloyd Stephens," typescript (seminar paper), ca. 1967, 33 leaves.

15. Morison, *William Hickling Prescott, 1796–1859*, copy of handwritten letter from Stephens to Prescott dated February 2, 1841.

16. Prescott added: "The French and Spanish travelers however write with such a swell of glorification and Waldeck's designs in particular are so little like the pictures of ruins, that I had supposed there was some exaggeration in this respect. No one can be a better judge than yourself however, who are familiar with the best models in the old World, to compare them with. . . ." W. H. Prescott and R. Wolcott, *The Correspondence of William Hickling Prescott, 1833–1847* (Boston and New York: Houghton Mifflin, 1925), letter from Prescott to Stephens, March 1841.

17. Ibid., pp. 240–43, letter from Prescott to Stephens, dated August 2, 1841.

18. Lilly, L., C. S. Henry, et al., *The New-York Review*, vol. 9 (New York: George Dearborn, 1841), p. 242.

19. "The Antiquities of Central America," *United States Democratic Review.*

20. Prescott and Wolcott, *The Correspondence of William Hickling Prescott, 1833–1847*, pp. 240–42, letter from Prescott to Stephens dated August 2, 1841.

21. Although generally correct, Stephens would be found wrong on both points when further excavations and restorations were made to the ruins in Mexico and Guatemala. Columns were later found in several ruins and in one dramatic

instance the tomb of the great lord of Palenque, Pakal, was found deep in the center of one of the site's finest pyramids.

22. Juan Galindo, however, made the same claim earlier, arguing not only that the indigenous population created the ruins at Copán and Palenque but that ancient American Indians societies were the cradle of the world's civilization.

23. Some wooden lintels have proven so extraordinarily durable that they have been found at much older Classic Maya sites, such as Tikal, though most from the Classic period have rotted away, resulting in the frequently seen collapse of doorways.

24. It has been determined that Uxmal had ceased to be inhabited, except by a few Indians.

25. Prescott and Wolcott, *The Correspondence of William Hickling Prescott, 1833–1847,* p. 257, letter dated September 24, 1841.

26. Correspondence concerning the fate of the plaster casts was included by Stephens in the appendix to *Incidents of Travel in Central America, Chiapas, and Yucatan.* In the appendix he also explains the twenty thousand dollars in pledges for a national museum.

27. Catherwood would eventually join them there, where they lived most of their childhood and school years.

28. Prescott and Wolcott, *The Correspondence of William Hickling Prescott, 1833–1847,* p. 257.

CHAPTER 16: YUCATÁN

1. Cabot's mother wrote a letter to Samuel's brother Elliott in Hamburg, Germany, describing the last-minute nature of Cabot's departure. She noted that during the summer Sam had considered joining the expedition, which Prescott had apparently informed him about, but "it was understood that Stephens had given up the idea of returning, until one day Sam came out late to dinner and said he had a letter from Stephens telling him if he could bundle up his traps and come on so as to sail on Saturday (this was Thursday noon) he should be glad to have him. . . . Your father went with Sam to New York and saw Stephens and Catherwood. He was much pleased with their reception of Sam. They were in the midst of packing all sorts of things, amongst them two daguerreotypes which will be just what they want for copying the ancient monuments found in Central America. Sam thinks he shall have a chance to operate on some unlucky subject, tho' Stephens told your father it could only be fancy work if he did anything of the kind." A copy of the letter, dated October 28, 1841, is among documents in the Von Hagen papers at the New-York Historical Society, copied from the Cabot Papers at the Massachusetts Historical Society.

2. The John L. Stephens Papers, BANC MSS ZZ 116, University of California, Berkeley. Box III, Folder 200.

3. Two days after Stephens and Catherwood arrived, a Texas war schooner anchored off Sisal with an offer: for eight thousand dollars a month the Texans would provide protection along Yucatán coast against any invasion by Mexico. The offer was immediately accepted.

4. See first endnote for this chapter.

5. Catherwood describes the methods used in a short text included on his map in Stephens's *Incidents of Travel in Yucatan.*

6. Before leaving for Yucatán, Stephens wrote to William Prescott to ask if he could borrow his *Historia de Yucathan* (published in 1688 and only available in Spanish) by Franciscan missionary Diego Lopez Cogolludo, who lived in Yucatán during the mid-1600s. At the time Stephens traveled to the peninsula, there was little available about the Spanish conquest of Yucatán, let alone on its history before the Spaniards arrived. The most important work was written in 1566 by another Franciscan friar, Diego de Landa, titled "Relacion de Las Cosas Yucatán." However, Landa's manuscript remained unknown until it was discovered in Madrid by Brasseur de Bourbourg, translated, and published in Paris in 1864, more than twenty years after Stephens journeyed through Yucatán. It is unknown whether Stephens carried Prescott's copy of Cogolludo's with him to Yucatán or used it only to prepare for the trip. "Can you lend Cogolludo? (Have I spelled it right?)," Stephens asked in the letter to Prescott dated September 24, 1841, just weeks before he left New York. "If so will you send it to me immediately by Hampden's Express and please say whether I may take it with me, though probably I shall not wish to do so on account of its bulk." Prescott and Wolcott, *The Correspondence of William Hickling Prescott*, p. 257. Stephens cites Cogolludo several times in his Yucatán book.

7. An excellent account of the Spanish conquest of Yucatán can be found in D. T. Peck, *Yucatán: From Prehistoric Times to the Great Maya Revolt* ([N.p.]: Xlibris, 2005), pp. 351–53.

8. Stephens wrote that he found in Mérida one remaining fragment from Tiho's earlier Mayan occupants: an archway inside Mérida's Franciscan monastery. He explained that the "arch" was not the rounded Roman arches used by the Spanish but was constructed with a triangular apex characteristic of those he had found in all the ruins they had explored and that he identified specifically with the Maya. This singular remaining Mayan arch in Mérida and the historical record left by the Spanish conquistadors and priests describing the stepped "mounds" and temples they had found helped convince Stephens that the people who built the cities of Copán, Palenque, and Uxmal were the same race of native Indians who also built Tiho and lived in Yucatán at the time of the Conquest—and who still occupied the land.

9. Archaeologists now believe that following the rebellion during which Mayapán was overrun and destroyed by fire, political power in northern region of the peninsula was broken up and decentralized in smaller city-states like Tiho.

10. Stephens found many of the names in *Historia de Yucatán* by Diego Lopez Cogolludo, who had recorded the popular names for structures at Uxmal.

11. The first excavations were funded by the University of Pennsylvania and directed by H. E. Mercer in February 1895.

CHAPTER 17: LONDON

1. The account of what occurred at the trial is based on reports published in three London newspapers—the *Times, Morning Chronicle,* and *Examiner*. Each article corroborated the others, with only small details added or left out of some of the versions. I have combined the three to give the fullest account possible.

2. The letter is mentioned in correspondence from "PM Gaskell" and addressed to JB (Joseph Bonomi), 9 Trafalgar Place, Kentish Town (in North London) and dated Saturday the 7th. There is no indication as to month or year. The relevant

passages reads: "My dear Bonomi[,] I did not see a lengthened report of the proceedings in the unfortunate case—but in that I saw no one I think would have inferred from what passed that anything improper could have existed between Mr C & yourself. But if the counsel really succeeded in giving such an impression, as it was doubtless his dirty business to do if he could, still, as the matter stands now, excuse me if I suggest that the insertion of such a letter as that you inclose could do no good. Had it been possible *on the trial* to have cleared up any point which the jury may have mis-understood, it might of course have influenced their verdict in favour of Catherwood [. . .] I really doubt, whether it is worthwhile to send the letter—No one who knows the parties can of course suppose that there was any impropriety—and as to the public—*they* have ceased to look into the matter. And while every regard should be paid to your nice sense of honour, still I think that the Catherwoods themselves who are principally interested, would disapprove of the proceeding [...] Poor C—I heard from him just before he went to Yucatán—for the second time he seemed to feel depressed. . . ." The letter was forwarded to me in personal correspondence with author Selwyn Tillett.
3. Pendergast, *Palenque,* pp. 187–200.

CHAPTER 18: DISCOVERIES
1. Both doorjambs are on display at the American Museum of Natural History in New York, among the few artifacts that remain from Stephens and Catherwoods' expeditions.
2. There was at this time no "national museum" in Washington and Stephens may have been anticipating the opening a few years later of the Smithsonian Institution. By 1841, when the expedition left New York, the U.S. Congress had already accepted the large bequest from the estate of British scientist James Smithson that would eventually be used to establish of the Smithsonian Institution. For several years there were ongoing debates covered by the newspapers about opening a national museum with the money.
3. Traveling north to Chichén Itzá, Stephens stopped at the town of Peto, where he again met Juan Pío Pérez, who had held the post of department chief until his retirement a few years before. Since that time he had devoted himself almost entirely to the study of the Mayan language, ancient calendar, and history. He would prove a valuable resource. Pérez gave Stephens a copy of a remarkable document that he had unearthed in the government archives that would prove extremely useful later to archaeologists working to decipher the Mayan hieroglyphs. It recounted the ancient history of the Yucatec Maya. The document was a fragment from an oral history, recorded in both the Mayan and Spanish languages a short time after the Conquest. Because the Spanish had burned virtually all the bark-paper texts written with Mayan hieroglyphics, this document would prove to be among the most important accounts of Mayan history. Stephens would include it in the appendix to his book. Pérez also provided Stephens with a memorandum he had worked out explaining some of the verbal forms and the grammar of the Mayan language as well as a vocabulary comprising more than four thousand Mayan words. Stephens would later give these documents, as well as a copy of a roughly drawn 1557 map showing Indian towns that existed in Yucatán at the time of the Conquest, to the New-York Historical Society.

CHAPTER 19: CHICHÉN ITZÁ

1. P. A. Means, A. s. d. Avendano y Loyola, et al., *History of the Spanish Conquest of Yucatán and of the Itzas* (Cambridge, MA: The [Peabody] Museum, 1917), pp. 43–46

2. Sharer and Morley, *The Ancient Maya,* pp. 743–44.

3. There is evidence that groups of Indians continued to use some of the ruined sites for ceremonial purposes through the period of the Conquest.

4. The latest chronological dating of the major sites of Uxmal and Chichén Itzá indicates that they were founded between A.D. 400 (Chichén Itzá) and A.D. 500 (Uxmal). But both reached the zenith of their political power and architectural grandiosity between A.D. 750 and 1050, during periods that modern archaeologists classify as the Post- and Terminal-Classic. See A. A. Demarest, P. M. Rice, et al., *The Terminal Classic in the Maya Lowlands: Collapse, Transition, and Transformation* (Boulder: University Press of Colorado, 2004), pp. 525–43.

5. Prescott and Wolcott, *The Correspondence of William Hickling Prescott, 1833–1847;* P. E. Palmquist and T. R. Kailbourn, *Pioneer Photographers of the Far West: A Biographical Dictionary, 1840–1865* (Stanford, CA: Stanford University Press, 2000), p. 252. Stephens always gave credit to anyone he knew who had explored a site before he and Catherwood had. He did so with Chichén Itzá in his book, noting that the first non-Yucatán citizen or non-Spaniard to visit the ruins was an American by the name of John Burke, an engineer working in Valladolid who traveled to the site in 1838. Two years later, Stephens wrote, a young Austrian diplomat and botanist named Baron Emanuel von Friedrichsthal arrived at Chichén Itzá with a daguerreotype to record the ruins. A year later, in 1841, he exhibited twenty-five daguerreotype images of Chichén Itzá and several other Yucatán ruins, including Uxmal, in New York, London (at the British Museum), and Paris. Friedrichsthal died in 1842 in Vienna (apparently of pneumonia) before he was able to publish his account of his expedition. He was thirty-four years old. Though always generous in giving credit, Stephens could not resist in his book pointing out that it was he who had recommended the route through Yucatán to Friedrichsthal, who became interested in visiting Yucatán after hearing about Stephens's adventures in Chiapas and Yucatán. Prescott and Wolcott, *The Correspondence of William Hickling Prescott, 1833–1847,* pp. xxi, 691. For biographical information on Friedrichsthal see Palmquist and Kailbourn, *Pioneer Photographers of the Far West,* p. 252. Also see U. Fischer-Westhauser, "Emanuel von Friedrichsthal: The First Daguerreotypist in Yucatán," *Photoresearcher* (European Society for the History of Photography) 10 (2007).

6. Chichén's ball court would prove to be the largest in Mesoamerica.

7. At this pyramid, now called the Pyramid of Kukulkán, during the spring and autumn equinox the sun's shadow moves down the balustrade flanking the staircase and lights up what appears to be a snake's body until it reaches the serpent's head at the base.

8. When the cenote was dredged in the early twentieth century, human bones were found, along with pottery, gold trinkets, jade, and other items. Sharer and Morley, *The Ancient Maya.*

CHAPTER 20: TULOOM

1. Nelson A. Reed describes this extraordinary rebellion in vivid detail. N. A. Reed, *The Caste War of Yucatan* (Stanford, CA: Stanford University Press, 2001). Population losses, pp.141–42.
2. Tancah is today known as Tan Kah.
3. The illustration of one of the buildings, identified as Plate XLVIII in Stephens's book, *Incidents of Travel in Yucatan,* vol. 2, shows three indistinct and shadowy figures silhouetted on the steps in front of the structure. However, when Catherwood several years later produced his own book of large lithographs, *Views of Ancient Monuments,* he added to the illustration what are believed to be images of himself wearing a long brown coat with either Dr. Cabot or Stephens. The two men are holding Catherwood's measuring line as they pace off the distance in front of the building. Incredibly, Catherwood's autobiographical image is considered to be the only image of him that has ever been found.
4. Reed, *The Caste War of Yucatan.*
5. Today the Dominican Republic claims that Columbus's bones remain in Santo Domingo, and that the remains transferred to Havana and eventually to Seville were those of his son, Diego Columbus. DNA results appear to confirm, however, that at least some of the bones in Seville are those of the famous admiral and explorer.

CHAPTER 21: HOME

1. *New York Herald,* July 30, 1842, p. 2. The *Herald* ran a short follow-up article concerning the monetary loses and insurance coverage on August 1, 1842, p. 2.
2. In 1842 there was no "National Museum of Washington." Stephens was apparently referring to exhibitions and collections housed in the recently constructed United States Patent Office in Washington. In 1841, the secretary of state had assigned use of the large hall in the building to an organization called the National Institute for the Promotion of Science, a precursor to the Smithsonian Institution. Starting in 1838, Stephens had no doubt followed the intense public and congressional debates written up in the newspapers over what should be done with a half-million-dollar bequest to the United States from English scientist James Smithson. The many proposals included a National University, astronomical observatory, National Library, a scientific research institute, and a National Museum. Congress finally compromised in 1846 and created an amalgam organization, known today as the Smithsonian Institution, which incorporated many of the suggestions.
3. *New York Herald,* July 30 and August 1, 1842, both articles on p. 2.
4. Sadly, none of the daguerreotypes and Catherwood's original drawings and sketches have ever been found. In the preface to *Incidents of Travel in Yucatan,* Stephens noted some of the daguerreotypes were used as the basis for illustrations for the book.
5. W. H. Prescott and C. H. Gardiner, *Literary Memoranda* (Norman: University of Oklahoma Press, 1961), vol. 2, pp. 93–94.
6. In letters between the two men, Stephens mentions borrowing the histories of Cogolludo, Herrera, and Juarros.
7. V. W. von Hagen, *Maya Explorer: John Lloyd Stephens and the Lost Cities of Central America and Yucatán* (Norman: University of Oklahoma Press, 1947). p. 256

8. Stephens and Catherwood generally worked fast. During the writing of their first collaboration they believed John Caddy and Patrick Walker might publish their own research and illustrations of Palenque before they did. Now they learned a New Orleans bookseller named Benjamin M. Norman had traveled through the Yucatán only a month or two after they did in 1842, and took a great many notes. Originally inspired to explore the Yucatán by Stephens's first book, Norman apparently raced to publish his account and was able to get out a first edition of his book, titled *Rambles in Yucatan,* at the very end of 1842. The book describes visits to Kabah, Zayi, and Uxmal (after Stephens's visit) as well as to Chichén Itzá (several months before Stephens), and includes illustrations of the ruins and site plans made by Norman. But Stephens and Catherwood must have breathed a sigh of relief when they saw Norman's 304-page book and the meager space he devoted to the ruins. Written in a pedestrian if workmanlike style, it was no match for the 900-page book Stephens published only three months later, which included descriptions of forty-four ruined sites that they had visited, as well as the daguerreotypes and Catherwood's illustrations. Norman's illustrations were at best simple sketches that might be expected from a bookseller who was clearly not an artist—or at worst they were fanciful in the extreme. Pushed almost immediately into the shadow by *Incidents of Travel in Yucatan,* Norman's book was destined to become no more than an interesting footnote for future Mayan studies. B. Norman, C. C. Moore, et al., *Rambles in Yucatán, or, Notes of travel through the peninsula: Including a visit to the remarkable ruins of Chi-Chen, Kabah, Zayi, and Uxmal* (New York: J. & H. G. Langley; Philadelphia: Thomas, Cowperthwait; New Orleans: Norman, Steel, 1843).

9. In the original publications of *Incidents of Travel in Central America, Chiapas, and Yucatan,* the engravings were entirely devoted to the ruins. In a later edition, in 1854, Catherwood would add various scenes and landscapes unconnected to the ruins.

10. The appendix in his first work consisted of no more than six pages of correspondence concerning the failure of his plaster-of-Paris project at Palenque.

11. Included were basic items like temperature readings, a full-page table of various "statistics of the Yucatan," and population charts. Catherwood's five-page treatise with architectural diagrams was on the construction of the triangular Mayan arch. And the eight-page "memorandum for the ornithology" contributed by Cabot included a list of all the birds he observed during the expedition.

12. The historical manuscript was written from memory in the Mayan language by an unknown author who lived during the immediate post-Conquest period. Stephens provided both the original Mayan text and an English translation. Pío Pérez pointed out in his comments that this rare manuscript was the only one that had been found treating the history of the Maya. He added that the Franciscan brothers under the orders of Bishop Diego de Landa had confiscated after the conquest all the "histories, paintings and hieroglyphics" the Indians had about their history. He failed to note that Landa had all of the material, which included the Maya's hieroglyphic "books," burned.

13. Von Hagen, *Maya Explorer.*

14. Stephens was no doubt influenced concerning the possible Toltec origin of the southern architecture by Prescott, who had assembled documentary accounts of

the Toltec's history. Prescott later wrote in his famous history of the Conquest that Stephens's fieldwork helped corroborate his theory, which he claimed he had arrived at on his own: that American natives built the cities scattered through Mexico and Central America, although he only suggested it might have been the Toltecs. Prescott's research concerning the Toltecs derived from mostly oral historical accounts gathered by the Spanish in their earliest encounters with the Aztecs and other Indians. Stephens, however, as he indicated in his book published seven months before Prescott's, was not entirely convinced the Toltecs were responsible for the ruins he had explored. W. H. Prescott, *History of the Conquest of Mexico, and History of the Conquest of Peru* (New York: Modern Library, 1936), p. 688.

THE MAYA

1. This is at best a brief review of the Maya's extremely complex civilization and only begins to tell their story. For readers who would like a more comprehensive understanding there are a wealth of excellent books. The following four books, however, will provide the reader with a solid grounding in the subject: *The Ancient Maya*, by Robert J. Sharer, for a broad yet highly detailed account of the Maya civilization; *Maya Cosmos*, by David Freidel, Linda Schele, and Joy Parker, for an understanding of Maya mythology and their view of their place in the universe; Michael Coe, *Breaking the Maya Code*, for an understanding of the ancient Maya writing system told through the story of how the code was deciphered; and *Chronicle of the Maya Kings and Queens*, by Simon Martin and Nikolai Grube, for detailed accounts of the royal dynasties of eleven of the greatest Maya cities based on decipherments of their hieroglyphs. My apologies to all of the many other authors who have written superb books on the subject.

2. L. Schele and P. Mathews, *The Code of Kings: The Language of Seven Sacred Maya Temples and Tombs* (New York: Touchstone Books, 1998), pp. 133–74.

3. S. Martin and N. Grube, *Chronicle of the Maya Kings and Queens: Deciphering the Dynasties of the Ancient Maya* (London and New York: Thames & Hudson, 2000), pp. 191–225.

4. J. M. Diamond, J. M. (2003). *Guns, Germs, and Steel: The Fates of Human Societies* (New York: Norton, 2003), pp. 354–60.

5. M. D. Coe, *The Maya* (London: Thames & Hudson, 2011), p. 45.

6. A. A. Demarest, *Ancient Maya: The Rise and Fall of a Rainforest Civilization* (Cambridge and New York: Cambridge University Press, 2004), pp. 113–47.

7. Because of the suddenness of the buildup of complex Maya centers, archaeologists are still not certain whether the Mayan-speaking people had settled in the area for a long period of time or whether they had migrated to the lowland area from somewhere else.

8. http://www.newmedia.ufm.edu/gsm/index.php/Mapping_the_Mirador_Basin:_Exploration_and_New_Technology_in_the_Cradle_of_Maya_Civilization.

9. http://www.academia.edu/366565/Building_Materials_of_the_Ancient_Maya_A_Study_of_Archaeological_Plasters.

10. Coe, *The Maya*, p. 80.

11. Demarest, *Ancient Maya*, p. 83.

12. Coe, *The Maya*, p. 91.

13. Ibid., p. 231.
14. Demarest, *Ancient Maya,* p. 88.
15. D. A. Freidel, L. Schele, and J. Parker, *Maya Cosmos: Three Thousand Years on the Shaman's Path* (New York: William Morrow, 1993).
16. Ibid., p. 317.
17. Ibid., pp. 337–91
18. Sharer and Morley, *The Ancient Maya,* p. 143.
19. An untold number of these books were also gathered in great piles and burned by Spanish priests not long after the conquest of Yucatán. Three now famous accordion-like "codices," written not long before the arrival of the Spanish, have survived and are housed in European libraries and museums. They were reproduced in Kingsborough's volumes.
20. Martin and Grube, *Chronicle of the Maya Kings and Queens,* pp. 26–40.
21. Ibid., pp.190–213.
22. Demarest, Rice, et al., *The Terminal Classic in the Maya Lowlands,* p. 189.
23. Martin and Grube, *Chronicle of the Maya Kings and Queens,* pp. 101–15.
24. Ibid., pp. 203–9, 218–22.
25. Ibid., pp. 169–72, 180–84.
26. To estimate population size, archaeologists have mapped these house mounds and have included in their formula additional presumed dwellings occupied by the lowest classes who lacked house mounds but left remains such as pottery shards and other evidence of occupation.
27. Estimates have ranged wildly from 3 to 13 million.
28. G. H. Haug et al., "Climate and the Collapse of the Maya Civilization," *Science* 299 (2003): 1731–35.
29. Schele and Mathews, *The Code of Kings,* pp. 259–60.

CHAPTER 22: VIEWS OF ANCIENT MONUMENTS
1. *United States Democratic Review,* May 1843, p. 492.
2. D. W. Shaw, *The Sea Shall Embrace Them: The Tragic Story of the Steamship* Arctic (New York: Free Press, 2002).
3. Exman, *The Brothers Harper,* pp. 171–72.
4. R. Rhodes, *John James Audubon: The Making of an American* (New York: Knopf, 2004), p. 403.
5. Prescott and Wolcott, *The Correspondence of William Hickling Prescott, 1833–1847,* pp. 339-41.
6. Stephens's grand plan called for the first article from well-known Egyptologist Sir John G. Wilkinson, who, Stephens noted, would be able to compare with great authority the "supposed resemblance between American signs and symbols and those of Egypt." Wilkinson and Catherwood had known each other in Egypt. The second expert was former congressman, diplomat and U.S. Treasury secretary Albert Gallatin, who late in his life had taken up the study of Native Americans, publishing several monographs on the subject. Stephens and Gallatin, who lived in New York, were friends. The third authority was to be Alexander von Humboldt. Stephens said he was hopeful that Gallatin, who had formed an "intimate acquaintance" with Humboldt while serving as U.S. minister to France, could convince the great naturalist and explorer to contribute. And lastly, Stephens told Prescott: "The fourth and only other person to whom I

have thought of applying is yourself." He explained that by his estimate of expenses, he would only be able to compensate Prescott with a copy of the work, to be called *American Antiquities*, and $250. If Prescott agreed, Stephens said he would need an article of some twenty to thirty pages in about a year. Prescott agreed. Prescott and Wolcott, *The Correspondence of William Hickling Prescott, 1833–1847*, pp. xxi, 691, 339–41.

7. In the same exchange of letters with Stephens, Prescott also mentioned that he had been in contact with the Cabot family. The doctor had fallen ill sometime after Stephens's visit months earlier. "Your friend Dr. Cabot has had one foot in the grave, poor fellow and is still very feeble," Prescott wrote, "though I trust the great difficulty is overcome." The "great difficulty" was apparently a serious bout of appendicitis, though Stephens may have feared it was the result of something he had picked up in the Yucatán. Cabot survived and went on to become a prominent Boston physician. Prescott and Wolcott, *The Correspondence of William Hickling Prescott, 1833–1847*; Morison, *William Hickling Prescott, 1796–1859*, personal letter from Dr. Cabot son, Godfrey L. Cabot, to Von Hagen, dated February 26, 1945.

8. Only two months earlier, Catherwood had impressed society members with the range of his antiquarian knowledge when he submitted a paper to the society that illustrated his discovery eleven years earlier of the 2,500-year-old monument in Dugga, Tunisia, near the site of ancient Carthage. *Proceedings of the New-York Historical Society* (1844), p. 11.

9. The society's president, eighty-year-old Albert Gallatin, expressed his wholehearted support and noted that "the well-known character, skill and experience of the eminent artist employed on this occasion, give a complete guarantee of the scrupulous fidelity of the original drawings. Mr. Catherwood is the only artist and antiquarian who has visited and studied the most celebrated ruins of the other hemisphere and those of America." Ibid., pp. 54–57.

10. Von Hagen, *Frederick Catherwood, archt*, pp. 158–59. Von Hagen quotes the *Boston Semi-Weekly Advertiser*, May 10 and June 3, 1843.

11. During this same period Stephens was more successful on a second project, one aimed at helping Prescott. He brokered a deal between his publisher, Harper & Brothers, and Prescott to publish *Conquest of Mexico*. Stephens gained nothing financially, acting out of friendship and in Prescott's best interests. But he also knew he was adding significantly to the prestige of his publishers. *Conquest of Mexico* was published by the Harpers in late 1843 and was followed four years later by Prescott's *Conquest of Peru*. The books went through edition after edition, came to be considered masterpieces of research and narrative history, and brought Prescott fame as one of the nineteenth century's greatest historians. Prescott and Wolcott, *The Correspondence of William Hickling Prescott, 1833–1847*, p. 368.

12. Ibid., pp. 366–67.

13. Ibid., p. 381.

14. The *Times* of London reported on August 25, 1843, that when Queen Victoria went in state to close the session of Parliament, "Mr. F. Catherwood, whose talents as an artist are well-known to the public from his illustrations . . . had the honor of submitting his interesting collection of original drawings to the inspection of his royal Highness Prince Albert and their royal Highnesses, the

Prince de Joinville and the Duc d'Aunale on Tuesday."

15. Prescott and Wolcott, *The Correspondence of William Hickling Prescott, 1833–1847,* pp. 426–27.

16. "Antiquities of Central America," *Civil Engineer and Architect's Journal, Scientific and Railway Gazetter* 7 (1844): 92–94.

17. Imperial folio pages are 22 by 15 inches in size.

18. The New York edition was printed by Bartlett & Welford, also in 1844.

19. Von Hagen in his biography of Catherwood gives various numbers for the cost of the work but gives no indication of how he came by the figures.

20. Prescott and Wolcott, *The Correspondence of William Hickling Prescott, 1833–1847,* p. 466.

21. Advertisement for the sale of *View of Ancient Monuments* in the *Examiner* (London)—5.5 pounds for tinted version and 12.12 pounds for the colored and mounted version in portfolio. "Publish by F. Catherwood at No. 9 Argyll Place, Regent Street, London."

22. An article in the *Daily News* of London on March 19, 1860, titled "Baron Humboldt and Prince Albert," notes that in exchange for Humboldt presenting Prince Albert with a copy of his book *Kosmos,* Humboldt "was vexed at the prince sending him a copy of Catherwood's Views in Central America, a book," he says, "that I purchased two years ago. . . ."

23. Prescott and Wolcott, *The Correspondence of William Hickling Prescott, 1833–1847,* p. 464.

24. Ibid.

25. Ibid., p. 486.

CHAPTER 23: STEAM

1. A. C. Sutcliffe, *Robert Fulton and the "Clermont"* (New York: Century, 1909).

2. Victor von Hagen in his biography *Frederick Catherwood, Archt.* states that he did return. He cites architectural work Catherwood engaged in but gives no documentary reference for any such work. However, there was a New York exhibition of Catherwood's Central American work and a few other design items sometime in 1845. See National Academy of Design Exhibition Record, 1826–60, pp. 71–72, which gives his address at 86 Prince Street, New York. And a lithograph under Catherwood's name (and others) in June 1845 was submitted in a contest for a proposed statue in New York. See I. N. Phelps Stokes, *Iconography of Manhattan Island, 1498–1909* (New York: R. H. Dodd, 1915–28), vol. 5, p. 1792. These activities indicate that Catherwood may have been in New York, or that the materials may have been submitted by others on his behalf. There is also no record of his arriving in the United States by ship during this interval, whereas all of his other arrivals by ship had been recorded.

3. F. Catherwood, Engineers Report, British Library, p. 7.

4. A. Odlyzko, "Collective Hallucinations and Inefficient Markets: The British Railway Mania of the 1840s," University of Minnesota, 2010.

5. Catherwood, Engineers Report. All additional references in the text to Catherwood's contract and work for the Demerara Railway Company can be found in the Engineers Report, which includes a committee report to shareholders in London on April, 15, 1847, and Catherwood's full report of October 30, 1846, with appendices. Also see L. Kandasammy, "From Georgetown to Mahaica: A

Brief History of South America's First Railway," *Stabroek News,* Georgetown, Guyana, December 7, 2006.

6. M. Y. Beach, *Wealth and Pedigree of the Wealthy Citizens of New York City comprising an alphabetical arrangement of persons estimated to be worth* (New York: Sun Office, 1842), p. 22.

7. Many of the documents recording Benjamin and John Stephens's business transactions can be found among J. L. Stephens's personal papers, located at the Bancroft Library, University of California, Berkeley.

8. The buildings are gone today. Leroy Place had occupied a stretch of Bleecker Street between Mercer and Greene Streets, which is now occupied by New York University buildings.

9. A. Nevins, *The Evening Post: A Century of Journalism* (New York: Boni & Liveright, 1922), p. 191. The relation was Parke Godwin, Bryant's son-in-law and a longtime journalist at the *Post.*

10. Burrows and Wallace, *Gotham,* p. 713.

11. C. Hemstreet, *Literary New York: Its Landmarks and Associations* (New York and London: Knickerbocker Press, 1903), pp. 175–80.

12. *American Anthropologist* (1900).

13. *New York Herald,* April 25, 1846.

14. *Report of the debates and proceedings of the convention for the revision of the constitution of the state of New York, 1846* (Albany, NY: Evening Atlas, 1846). There are multiple reference to Stephens, as well as his votes, searchable online.

15. BANC MSS ZZ 116. See letter from John Dash Van Buren.

16. A. Gibson and A. Donovan, *The Abandoned Ocean: A History of United States Maritime Policy* (Columbia: University of South Carolina Press, 2000), pp. 51–52.

17. "Ocean Steam Navigation," *New York Times,* March 20, 1864.

18. J. H. Morrison, *History of American Steam Navigation* (New York: W. F. Sametz, 1903), p. 408. See also *Mechanics' Magazine,* June 26, 1847, p. 622. The cost was $120 for a first-class cabin, and $60 for second-class. Postage for a letter was 24 cents for one-half ounce or less, and 15 cents for each additional half ounce. The one sour note of the *Washington's* maiden voyage came when the seven-year-old British mail steamship *Britannia* left Boston on the same day and managed to beat the much more powerful *Washington* to England by two days, an achievement the British did not let the American forget. For a detailed history of the *Washington* and the Ocean Steam Navigation Company see the excellent account: C. Ridgely-Nevitt, *American Steamships on the Atlantic* (Newark: University of Delaware Press, 1980).

19. "The American Steam-ship 'Washington,' " http://www.theshipslist.com/1847/washington.html.

20. *Merchants' Magazine and Commercial Review* (1847), pp. 357–64.

21. *Littell's Living Age* (1847), pp. 151–53.

22. BANC MSS ZZ 116, Folder 230, Box IV.

CHAPTER 24: PANAMA

1. Obituary of William H. Aspinwall, *New York Times,* January 19, 1875.

2. H. Hall, *America's Successful Men of Affairs. An Encyclopedia of Contemporaneous*

Biography (New York: New-York Tribune, 1895), vol. 1, p. 31.

3. J. R. Spears, *Captain Nathaniel Brown Palmer, an Old-Time Sailor of the Sea* (New York: Macmillan, 1922). For information on Griffiths career see pp. 184–88.

4. A. H. Clark, *The Clipper Ship Era* (New York: Putnam, 1910), pp. 61–77.

5. R. Johnson and J. H. Brown, *The Twentieth Century Biographical Dictionary of Notable Americans* (Boston: Biographical Society, 1904).

6. A. Laing, *The Sea Witch: A narrative of the experiences of Capt. Roger Murray and others in an American clipper ship during the years 1846 to 1956* (London: Thornton Butterworth, 1933). For an excellent account of the sea trade to the Pacific coast during the Gold Rush, see J. P. Delgado, *To California by Sea: A Maritime History of the California Gold Rush* (Columbia: University of South Carolina Press, 1990). In May 2003 the trimaran *Great American II* made the Hong Kong–New York voyage in 72 days and 21 hours. The *Sea Witch* continues to hold the record for a for a monohulled sailing ship. The *Sea Witch* was later put into service by Howland & Aspinwall during the Gold Rush to carry high-valued and perishable cargo around Cape Horn from New York to San Francisco, and several times made the trip in just over one hundred days.

7. As a condition of awarding the government mail subsidies, all of the mail steamships had to be available for emergency conversion to warships if the navy needed them, and they had to be built to such specifications and pass such inspections as would permit such conversion.

8. F. N. Otis, *Isthmus of Panama: History of the Panama Railroad; and of the Pacific Mail Steamship Company* (New York: Harper & Brothers, 1867), pp. 149–55.

9. Kemble, *The Panama Route, 1848–1869,* pp. 22–23.

10. Ibid., p. 254. Kemble estimates that a minimum number of 335 traveled over the isthmus from New York to San Francisco in 1848, but he notes that official records are nonexistent and figures are difficult to accurately calculate.

11. BANC MSS ZZ 116, Box III, dated March 26, 1848.

12. Otis, *Isthmus of Panama,* p. 17.

13. W. C. Fowler, *Memorials of the Chaunceys, Including President Chauncey, His Ancestors and Descendants* (Boston: H. W. Dutton, 1858).

14. Kemble, *The Panama Route, 1848–1869,* p. 31.

15. Ibid., pp. 32–33.

16. O. C. Coy, *The Great Trek* (Los Angeles: Powell, 1931), pp. 71–74.

17. O. Lewis and J. B. Goodman, *Sea Routes to the Gold Fields: The Migration by Water to California in 1849–1852* (New York: Knopf, 1949), pp. 5–10.

18. When the SS *California* finally reached Panama on January 17, 1849, it was besieged by more than seven hundred gold seekers, most of whom had traveled down to Panama and crossed the isthmus to Panama City, where they desperately sought a way to get up to California. The *California* was built to accommodate no more than 250 passengers but left Panama for San Francisco on January 31 with just over four hundred. Kemble, *The Panama Route, 1848–1869,* pp. 34–35.

19. J. K. Polk and M. M. Quaife, *The Diary of James K. Polk During His Presidency, 1845 to 1849* (Chicago: McClurg, 1910), vol. 4, p. 235.

20. Panama Railroad Company Prospectus, 1949, New York Public Library.

21. "Congressional Summary," *American Whig Review* 9, no. 14 (1849): 208–16.

22. Polk and Quaife, *The Diary of James K. Polk,* vol. 4, entry for January 30, 1849.

23. The concession also included provisions for the railroad to revert to Granadan ownership earlier than the forty-nine years. Granada had the right, for example, to buy the railroad after twenty years for $5 million, after thirty years for $4 million, and after forty years for $2 million.

24. Aside from the three originators of the railroad, the initial directors were James Brown, Cornelius W. Lawrence, Gouverneur Kemble, Thomas W. Ludlow, David Thompson, Joseph B. Varnum, Samuel S. Howland, Prosper M. Wetmore, Edwin Bartlett, Horatio Allen, and associates. See A. Perez-Venero, *Before the Five Frontiers: Panama, from 1821–1903* (New York: AMS Press, 1978), p. 63.

25. Panama Railroad Company charter, 1849, New York Public Library.

26. The three initial partners were granted $50,000 in stock, and, perhaps more important, half ownership of 250,000 acres of additional land that had been granted by Granada as part of the concession, including mineral rights.

27. Kemble, *The Panama Route, 1848–1869,* p. 183; Perez-Venero, *Before the Five Frontiers,* p. 63.

28. "Railway Meetings," *Daily News* (London), 1849.

29. Kandasammy, "From Georgetown to Mahaica."

30. Passenger List of Vessels Arriving at Philadelphia, Pennsylvania, 1800–1882, Micropublication M425., rolls #1–71. National Archives, Washington, D.C.

31. BANC MSS ZZ 116, letter from Catherwood to Stephens, July 4, 1850.

32. Ibid., letter from Catherwood to Stephens, August 18, 1849.

33. Ibid., letter from Catherwood to Stephens, October 2, 1849

34. Ibid., letter from Catherwood to Stephens, October 19, 1849.

35. Ibid., letter from Aspinwall to Stephens, October 4, 1849.

36. Ibid., letter from Catherwood to Stephens, October 8, 1849.

37. Ibid., letter from Aspinwall to Stephens, November 15, 1849.

38. Ibid., letter from Stephens to father, December 10, 1849.

Chapter 25: Crossing the Isthmus

1. Kemble, The Panama Route, 1848–1869 pp. 146-7.

2. Oran, "Tropical Journeyings," *Harper's New Monthly Magazine* 18 (1859): 145–69, 141. Much of the narrative of the construction of the railroad is taken from this account, which was written within ten years of the events and in turn based on accounts from those involved, along with company documents and letters. Most important also was the account written by the railroad's chief engineer, George Totten, who was present throughout the construction of the railroad. See M. Eissler and G. M. Totten, "The Panama Canal," *Scientific American Supplement* 14, no. 347 (1882). Some of the information is also corroborated by handwritten accounts of various participants found in John L. Stephens's personal papers at the University of California's Bancroft library. Also see Otis, *Isthmus of Panama;* R. Tomes, *Panama in 1855: An account of the Panama rail-road, of the cities of Panama and Aspinwall, with sketches of life and character on the Isthmus* (New York: Harper & Brothers, 1855); T. Robinson, *Panama: A Personal Record of Forty-Six Years, 1861–1907* (New York: Star & Herald, 1907).

3. Oran, "Tropical Journeyings."

4. BANC MSS ZZ 116. Stephens writes his father from Panama City on December 27, 1849.

5. BANC MSS ZZ 116, Stephens writes his father from Panama City on January 22, 1850.
6. D. G. McCullough, *The Path Between the Seas: The Creation of the Panama Canal, 1870–1914* (New York: Simon & Schuster, 1977), p. 64.
7. BANC MSS ZZ 116. Stephens writes his father from Bogotá on March 17, 1850.
8. Hawks, "The Late John L. Stephens."
9. BANC MSS ZZ 116. Aspinwall writes to Stephens in Bogotá on May 13, 1950.
10. Ibid. Stephens's sister Amelia Ann writes to Stephens in Bogotá on May 1, 1850.
11. *Syracuse Daily Star*, July 10, 1850; Kemble, *The Panama Route, 1848–1869.*
12. BANC MSS ZZ 116, letters to Stephens from President of Granada dated April 29, 1850, and from Victoriano de Diego Paredes to Benjamin Stephens, May 31, 1855.
13. Hawks, "The Late John L. Stephens."
14. Eissler and Totten, "The Panama Canal."
15. BANC MSS ZZ 116. Catherwood writes from Panama City to Stephens at Bogotá on June 6, 1850.
16. Ibid. Catherwood writes to Stephens at Navy Bay on July 4, 1850.
17. Oran, "Tropical Journeyings."
18. Eissler and Totten, "The Panama Canal." This contains G. M. Totten's own account of the building of the railroad, published in 1882.
19. Tomes, *Panama in 1855,* pp. 112–14.
20. BANC MSS ZZ 116. Catherwood writes from Panama City to Stephens in Navy Bay on July 4, 1850.
21. Ibid. Catherwood writes from San Francisco to Stephens in New York on August 28, 1850.
22. Ibid. Catherwood writes from Benicia, California, to Stephens in New York on October 20, 1850.
23. Ibid. Catherwood writes from San Francisco to Stephens in New York on January 1851.
24. Ibid. Nephew Pratt Stephens writes from San Francisco to J. Stephens at Bogotá on April 1, 1850.
25. Ibid. Catherwood writes from Benicia, California, to Stephens in New York on October 20, 1850.
26. W. Nelson, *Five Years at Panama: The Trans-Isthmian Canal* (New York: Belford, 1889), p. 147.
27. Robinson, *Panama,* p. 15.
28. Eissler and Totten, "The Panama Canal."
29. Estimates in many thousands were also likely exaggerations put out by rival transport companies in Nicaragua and Mexico hoping to scare off tradesmen and laborers (and passengers) from traveling to Panama. And it worked. Newspapers in New York and other cities frequently described the lethal unhealthiness of the isthmus and repeated the high number of deaths among the workers, which eventually made recruiting all but impossible, at least in the United States.
30. United States Board of Consulting Engineers on Panama Canal, J. F. Wallace, et al., *Report of the Board of Consulting Engineers for the Panama Canal* (Washington, DC: U.S. Government Printing Office, 1906), p. 18.
31. J. B. Bishop, *The Panama Gateway* (New York: Scribner's, 1913), p. 48. Totten states that 835 out of 6,000 died. *Report of the Board of Consulting Engineers for the Panama Canal*, p. 18.

32. BANC MSS ZZ 116, letter to Stephens at Navy Bay from George W. Matthews dated March 18, 1851.
33. Ibid. Aspinwall writes from New York to Stephens at Navy Bay on April 10, 1851.
34. According to the manifest of the steamer *Empire City,* Stephens arrived in New York on July 7, 1851.
35. BANC MSS ZZ 116. Stephens writes his father from Navy Bay on January 27, 1852.
36. Eissler and Totten, "The Panama Canal."
37. The name was changed later to Colón by the New Granadan government.
38. "City of Aspinwall," *Daily Alta California* (San Francisco), 1852. See also Totten's account in "The Panama Canal."
39. This account is given in Von Hagen's *Maya Explorer,* for which no reference is given. No other such account could be found, and the opposite evaluation of Stephen's health appeared in Hawk's obituary in *Harper's Magazine.*
40. See letter Francis M. Preston, July 24, 1851.
41. According to the manifest for the steamer *Georgia,* Stephens arrived on April 21, 1852.
42. Hawks, "The Late John L. Stephens."
43. BANC MSS ZZ 116. Stephens writes his father from Navy Bay on January 27, 1852.
44. BANC MSS ZZ 116. A copy of his hotel bill for the dates April 20 through May 6.
45. BANC MSS ZZ 116. Stephens writes his father from Navy Bay on January 27, 1852.
46. *New York Evening Express,* May 21, 1852; *New-York Tribune,* May 21, 1852.

CHAPTER 26: TOGETHER AGAIN

1. "No. 297 Site of One of the First Discoveries of Quartz Gold in California," California State Historical Landmarks in Nevada County, California Environmental Resources Evaluation System.
2. BANC MSS ZZ 116. Catherwood writes Stephens from San Francisco on June 11, 1851.
3. A. Delano and I. McKee, *Alonzo Delano's California Correspondence: Being Letters Hitherto Uncollected from the Ottawa (Illinois) Free Trader and the New Orleans True Delta, 1849–1952* (Sacramento, CA: Sacramento Book Collectors Club, 1952).
4. *Sacramento Transcript,*1851; *Sacramento Daily Union,* 1853.
5. BANC MSS ZZ 116. Catherwood writes from San Francisco to Stephens on June 11, 1851.
6. Ibid. Catherwood writes from San Francisco to Stephens January 1851.
7. "Banking Institute," *Daily News* (London), 1852.
8. The site has never been identified and no ruins of an ancient civilization like the Maya are known to exist in California.
9. BANC MSS ZZ 116. Catherwood writes from London to Stephens in Navy Bay on April 28, 1852.
10. Catherwood had once chided Stephens that he should destroy the letters that he sent to Stephens, "knowing how lax you are about your letters." Ibid., Catherwood to Stephens, August 28, 1850. Whether this amounted to a policy on

Catherwood's part also to destroy letters he received, we do not know. Regardless, without Stephens's letters a major part of their relationship has been lost. Stephens ignored Catherwood's entreaty, fortunately, and saved at least some of his correspondence.

11. Ibid. Catherwood writes from London to Stephens in New York on June 25, 1852.
12. Ibid. Aspinwall in New York writes Stephens in Hempstead, New York, on July 13, 1852.
13. Ibid. Spies in New York writes to Stephens in Hempstead, New York, on August 18, 1852.
14. Ibid. Various letter from Spies to Stephens describe the arrival of steamers with news from the isthmus.
15. U. S. Grant, *Memoirs and Selected Letters: Personal Memoirs of U.S. Grant, Selected Letters 1839–1865* (New York: Library of America, 1990); U. S. Grant and J. M. McPherson, *Personal Memoirs of U.S. Grant* (New York: Penguin Books, 1999), p. 235.
16. BANC MSS ZZ 116. Spies in note to Stephens on "Wednesday" but undated.
17. *New York Herald*, September 21, 1852; *New York Daily News*, 1852; *Brooklyn Daily Eagle*, September 22, 1852.
18. Stephens, *Incidents of Travel in Greece, Turkey, Russia, and Poland*, p. 33.
19. Catherwood's "biographical notice" in the 1854 British edition of *Incidents of Travel in Central America, Chiapas, and Yucatan* states that he and Stephens met a second time nearly two years following their time together in Panama. Catherwood's September 20, 1852, arrival on the SS *Pacific* with his son appears in the ship's manifest for the "District of New York – Port of New York." Passenger Lists of Vessels Arriving at New York, New York, 1820–1897. The National Archives.
20. BANC MSS ZZ 116. Catherwood writes from Panama to Benjamin Stephens in New York on April 23, 1850.
21. Various dates have been given for the day Stephens died. October 10, 1852, was engraved on a silver plate on his casket. See death notice in Stephens's Bancroft papers. His death certificate states October 14. His biographer Von Hagen gives the date as October 5 and 13 in his book *Maya Explorer*. But the consensus of the newspaper obituaries was that he died on a Tuesday evening, which would have been October 12. There is no dispute that he was interred in New York City's Marble Cemetery on Friday, October 15. Stephens's death certificate, issued by the New York State Department of Health, stated that the cause of death was hepatitis. John Lloyd Stephens Collection, 1946–47, New-York Historical Society, Von Hagen Papers.
22. BANC MSS ZZ 116. The details of Stephens's funeral are contained in wtwo unidentified death notices found among his papers at the Bancroft Library.
23. New York City Marble Cemetery, a national historic landmark, is generally closed to the public, but can be visited by appointment or on certain days of the year when it is open to the public. It is located at 52–74 East Second Street between First and Second Avenues in the East Village. Stephens's crypt is one of the most prominent, centered directly opposite the gate as you enter. Nearly a century after Stephens's interment, a ceremony was held in his honor on October 9, 1947, during which a plaque and a cartouche of a Mayan glyph designed by Catherwood were place above the entrance to the vault.

CHAPTER 27: MISSING

1. "West Mariposa Gold Quartz Mine Company," *Times* (London), December 15, 1852. p. 9.
2. *Daily Alta California* (San Francisco), August 30, 1852.
3. "Gold Hill Mining," *Sacramento Daily Union*, 1853.
4. W. H. Chamberlain and H. L. Wells, *History of Yuba County, California with illustrations descriptive of its scenery, residences, public buildings, fine blocks and manufactories* (Oakland, CA: Thompson & West, 1879), ch. 38. The railroad project was dropped the next year and resumed after four years in 1857 with new survey.
5. W. J. Lewis, F. Catherwood, et al., *Report of the Engineers on the Survey of the Marysville and Benicia National Rail Road* (Marysville, CA: California Express, 1853).
6. *Times* (London), March 22, 1854, p. 13; Stephens and Catherwood, *Incidents of Travel in Central America, Chiapas, and Yucatan*.
7. It could be argued that Catherwood, who seemed perennially short of funds, had decided to cash in on Stephens's book. With Stephens gone and at that time no international copyright law, he clearly would have been able to make his own publishing arrangement in England. While that could have been a motivation, the book—and their arduous exploration itself—had been a joint venture to some degree, and while Stephens was alive he reaped most if not all of the book's monetary benefits, which proved to be substantial. It is conceivable also that he and Stephens had discussed and Stephens has approved such an edition before he died.
8. Stephens and Catherwood, *Incidents of Travel in Central America, Chiapas, and Yucatan*. All following references are from the 1854 revised English edition.
9. The Collins line was formally called the New York & Liverpool United States Mail Steamship Company.
10. Shaw, *The Sea Shall Embrace Them*. Shaw's excellently researched book is a riveting account of the SS *Arctic*'s final voyage. Information here about the ship's background and its final voyage and sinking have been taken from Shaw's book, as well as eyewitness newspaper accounts. See, specifically, "The Loss of the Arctic," *New-York Daily Tribune*, October 13, 1854, p. 1; "Loss of the United State Steamer Arctic," *Times* (London), October 13, 1854, p. 13.
11. "Letter of Credit #7185," *Daily Alta California* (San Francisco), April, 15, 1855.

EPILOGUE

1. Based on the priest's account and reports from nearby Indian villagers, Stephens believed the city might still be occupied. "If he is right," Stephens wrote, "a place is left where Indians and an Indian city exist as Cortez and Alvarado found them; there are living men who can solve the mystery that hangs over the ruined cities of America; perhaps who can go to Copán and read the inscriptions on its monuments." Tikal had been abandoned, however, like all the Classic-era Mayan cities, a thousand years earlier.
2. Pendergast, *Palenque*. Pendergast quotes from a March 18, 1840, dispatch sent from Frederick Chatfield to Belize superintendent MacDonald: "Mr. Stephens & the Yankified English artist who accompanies him, are gone to Quesaltenango, intending to get to Palenque across the Mexican border" (p. 143).

3. I. Bernal, *A History of Mexican Archaeology: The Vanished Civilizations of Middle America* (London and New York: Thames & Hudson, 1980), p. 132.

4. Aguirre, *Informal Empire*. Digging through a number of foreign office dispatches, Aguirre devotes a fascinating chapter (ch. 3) to the problems of British colonial administration, using the Central American antiquities debacle as a prime example.

5. This would have been a moment of sweet vindication for Stephens. Chatfield had belittled Stephen's expedition to Central America in a dispatch to Colonel MacDonald ten years earlier: "I have no intelligence of the Travellers. Stephens is flying about the country to get materials for his Book." But, of course, Stephens had no way of knowing about either dispatch.

6. Finally, in 1854, frustrated British Museum trustees commissioned two foreigners who were traveling through Central America, German explorer Moritz Wagner and Austrian naturalist Karl Ritter von Scherzer, to go to the ruins and investigate the practicalities of removing the sculptures. However, the two men were unwilling to risk their lives going to Copán while a war was under way between Honduras and Guatemala. They settled on investigating Quiriguá instead. Scherzer produced a report on the ruins there for the museum. But in the end the entire project was dropped and it would be decades before the British obtained any significant Mayan sculptures.

7. J. Peréz de Lara, "A Brief History of the Rediscovery of Tikal and Archaeological Work at the Site," http://www.mesoweb.com/tikal/features/history/history.html.

8. I. Graham, *Alfred Maudslay and the Maya: A Biography* (Norman: University of Oklahoma Press, 2002). Graham provides a fascinating and affectionate account of Maudslay's life.

9. Although Teobert Maler was Austrian, some of his work was sponsored by the Peabody Museum at Harvard University.

10. Graham, *Alfred Maudslay and the Maya*.

11. Coe, *Breaking the Maya Code*. Coe gives a masterful account of the long and arduous work involved in the decipherment of the Maya's hieroglyphs. In addition, he covers the history of Maya research through the twentieth century with interesting biographical snapshots of many of the characters involved.

12. Eissler and Totten, "The Panama Canal."

13. http://www.czbrats.com/Articles/prropen.htm.

14. Robinson, *Panama,* p. 21.

15. McCullough, *The Path Between the Seas*.

16. http://www.panarail.com/en/history/index-03.ht.

Index

Pages in *italics* contain illustrations.